THE TEMA

Recreation, Resources,

in the Northern Ontario Wilderness

The Temagami Forest Reserve was once designated by the Ontario government as a region to be managed primarily in the interests of sustained yield forestry. Today the district supports many activities: local forestry and several mineral operations exist alongside tourism and other forms of recreational land use, and much of the area is subject to a major aboriginal land claim launched in the 1970s by the Temagami Ojibwa.

Bruce W. Hodgins and Jamie Benidickson provide a historical account of the evolution of the district and the succession of efforts to implement administrative arrangements for the management of natural resources and the reconciliation of conflicting land uses. Drawing on original archival material dating from the mid-nineteenth century, they describe developments in the forest and mining industries, native occupation, and recreation and settlement. They examine these developments in the context of broader influences – Ontario politics, federal-provincial relations, and the North American conservation and environmental movements – to provide an insightful analysis of the complex relationships that have shaped the Temagami region of today.

BRUCE W. HODGINS is Professor of History and Director of the Frost Centre for Canadian Heritage and Development Studies, Trent University. He is also the director of Camp Wanapitei on Sandy Inlet, Lake Temagami. He has written about John Sandfield Macdonald, and is co-author, with Margaret Hobbs, of *Nastawgan: The Canadian North by Canoe and Snowshoe.*

JAMIE BENIDICKSON is an independent policy analyst and legal historian living in Ottawa.

THE TEMAGAMI EXPERIENCE

Recreation, Resources, and Aboriginal Rights in the Northern Ontario Wilderness

---

Bruce W. Hodgins and

Jamie Benidickson

UNIVERSITY OF TORONTO PRESS

Toronto Buffalo London

Toronto Buffalo London
Printed in Canada
Reprinted 1990

ISBN 0-8020-5800-0 (cloth)
ISBN 0-8020-6713-1 (paper)

Printed on acid-free paper

Canadian Cataloguing in Publication Data

Hodgins, Bruce W., 1931–
The Temagami experience

Includes index.
ISBN 0-8020-5800-0 (bound) ISBN 0-8020-6713-1 (pbk.)

1. Land use – Ontario – Temagami, Lake, Region – History. 2. Temagami Forest Reserve (Ont.) – History. 3. Natural resources – Ontario – Temagami, Lake, Region – History. 4. Indians of North America – Ontario – Temagami, Lake, Region – Claims. 5. Indians of North America – Ontario – Temagami, Lake, Region – Land tenure. 6. Algonquian Indians – Claims. 7. Algonquian Indians – Land tenure. I. Benidickson, Jamie. II. Title.

HD319.05H63 1989 333.3′09713′147 C89-093136-4

This book has been published with the help of a grant from the Social Science Federation of Canada, using funds provided by the Social Sciences and Humanities Research Council of Canada. Publication has also been assisted by the Canada Council and the Ontario Arts Council under their block grant programs.

Contents

Preface

The authors' essential relationship with the Temagami country – a relationship from which this book originates – is that of recreational paddlers to a much-favoured landscape. Indeed, one of us for nearly twenty years has been director of a wilderness camp on the shores of Lake Temagami and has frequented the area as summer resident, canoeist, and winter camper for more than three decades, serving youth camp and cottagers' associations in several executive positions. The other's less-extended and less-extensive familiarity with the Temagami area is also based on the recreational attractions it offers. By disposition, then, we both incline to a vision of Temagami in which appreciative uses rank equally with extractive ones.

Despite the personal dimensions of our initial interest in the particular historical subject of this volume, we hope that the Temagami story presented here will be of interest to anyone concerned with this part of the northern Ontario wilderness, and to all those concerned with the not-uncommon challenges of resource development, recreational land use, and aboriginal rights in other parts of Canada.

During the course of our research we have become deeply indebted to a host of friends and associates who gave assistance and advice. Ruth Snider, Isabel St Martin, Tom Roach, Larry Turner, and Pamela Glenn helped with specific research tasks. Carol Cochrane, Larry Hodgins, Tim Gooderham, Bill Gooderham, Bella White, and Peter Gillis provided information and suggested research sources that might otherwise not have been located. Several of the above along with Elaine

Mitchell, Donald Smith, Jim Morison, and Joseph de Pencier read parts of the manuscript and offered valuable criticism and insight. Anonymous reviewers who reported to the University of Toronto Press and the Social Science Federation of Canada made particularly helpful suggestions. Thanks are also due to Steve Gardiner for his assistance with maps, to Jamie Allum for indexing, and to Bill Gooderham and Larry Turner for advice about illustrations. The co-operation of archivists at the several Canadian record depositories detailed in the notes is gratefully acknowledged. At various stages of the research Trent University and the Social Sciences and Humanities Research Council of Canada provided financial support for which the authors were and are most appreciative.

Special thanks are due to Gerry Hallowell of the University of Toronto Press for his guidance and encouragement.

The Temagami forest

Logging, Temagami, by Frank Panabaker

A campsite on Lake Temagami, 1898: Father Charles Paradis seated beside tent

Preparing a shore dinner

OPPOSITE

top The Lady Evelyn Hotel, Lake Temagami, 1908

bottom Sir William Mulock, Dan O'Connor, and other early investors in the Temagami Inn, about 1905

The steamer *Belle of Temagami* at Wabikon Camp dock

Winter supplies and equipment
destined for Gowganda silver camp,
about 1909

OPPOSITE

The Lodge, Camp Chimo

An Indian guide and his family, Temagami District, about 1909

Cochrane's Camp Temagami, about 1910

Mrs W. Petrant, Granny Turner,
the operator of Lakeview House,
and Mrs Faith Newcomb, wife of the founding president
of the Temagami Association, Robert B. Newcomb,
on Bear Island in the early 1920s

The Hudson's Bay Company post at Bear Island about 1919

Chief Frank White Bear (left) of the Teme-augama Anishnabai
and Second Chief Aleck Paul, 1913

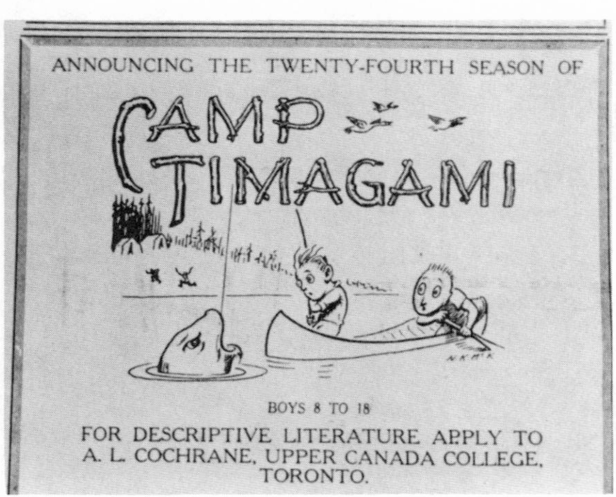

Camp Timagami advertising, mid-1920s

OPPOSITE

Regatta day on Bear Island

Shore supper, Camp Chimo

The passenger office and dock, Temagami Boat Company

The Temagami waterfront and the Ronnoco Hotel about 1930; the Temiskaming and Northern Ontario Railway is in the foreground.

The Milne Lumber Company, 1954

The Temagami waterfront in the mid-1950s

OPPOSITE

top The Red Squirrel Road blockade against lumber road development,
1 June 1988: Michael Paul (standing at left)
leads prayer at a tobacco-burning ceremony;
Chief Gary Potts lights the fire.

bottom Temagami stand-off:
police confront demonstrators marching to protest delays
in construction of road access to timber supplies,
September 1988.

Chief Gary Potts and Second Chief Rita O'Sullivan
of the Teme-augama Anishnabai
meet Attorney-General Ian Scott on Bear Island
in September 1986 to discuss land claims.

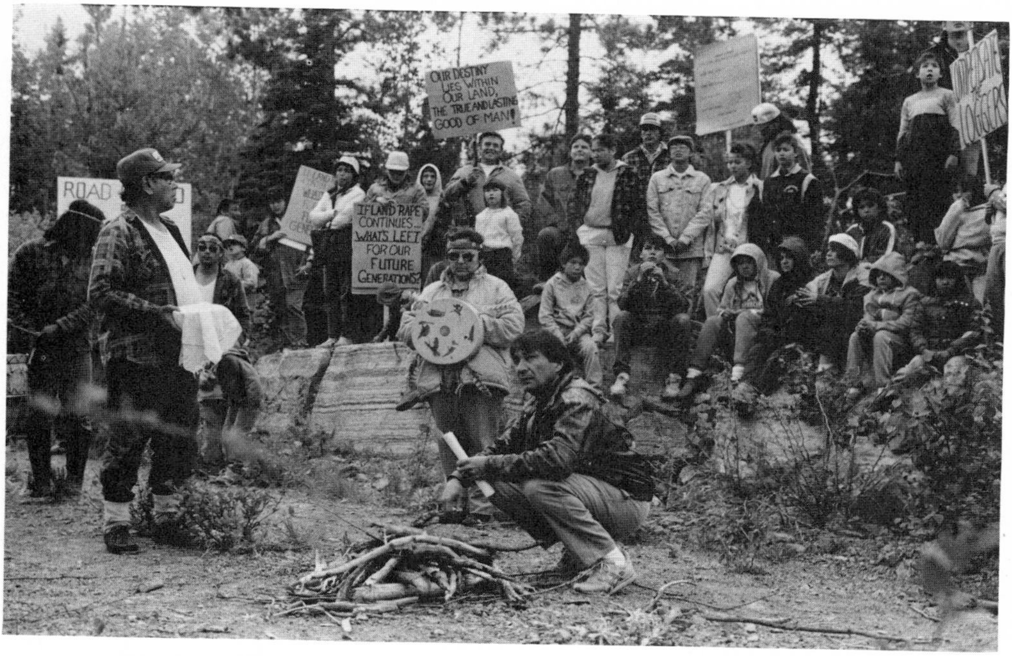
OUR DESTINY LIES WITHIN OUR LAND, THE TRUE AND LASTING GOOD OF MAN!
IF LAND RAPE CONTINUES... WHAT'S LEFT FOR OUR FUTURE GENERATIONS?

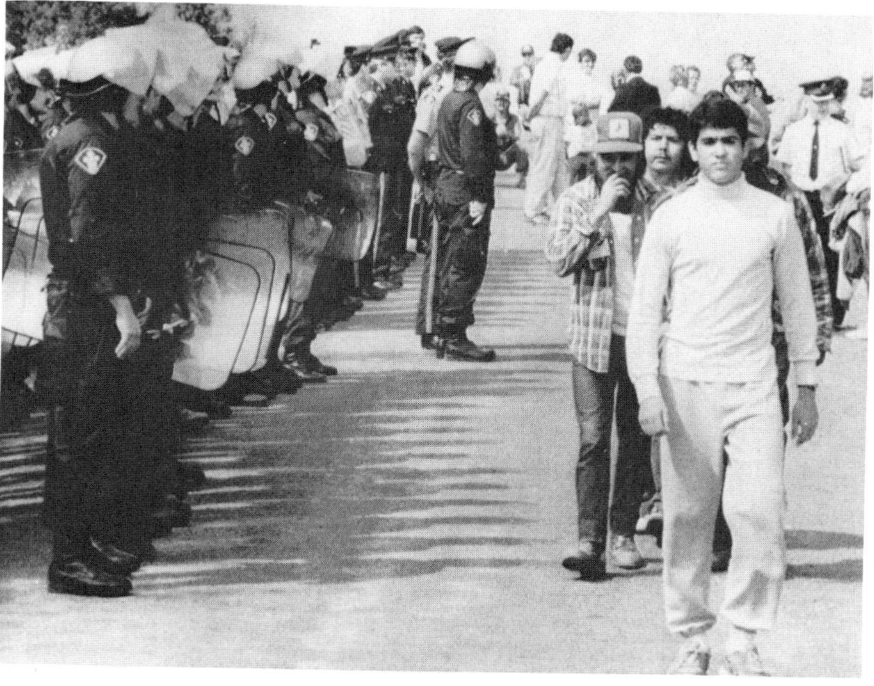

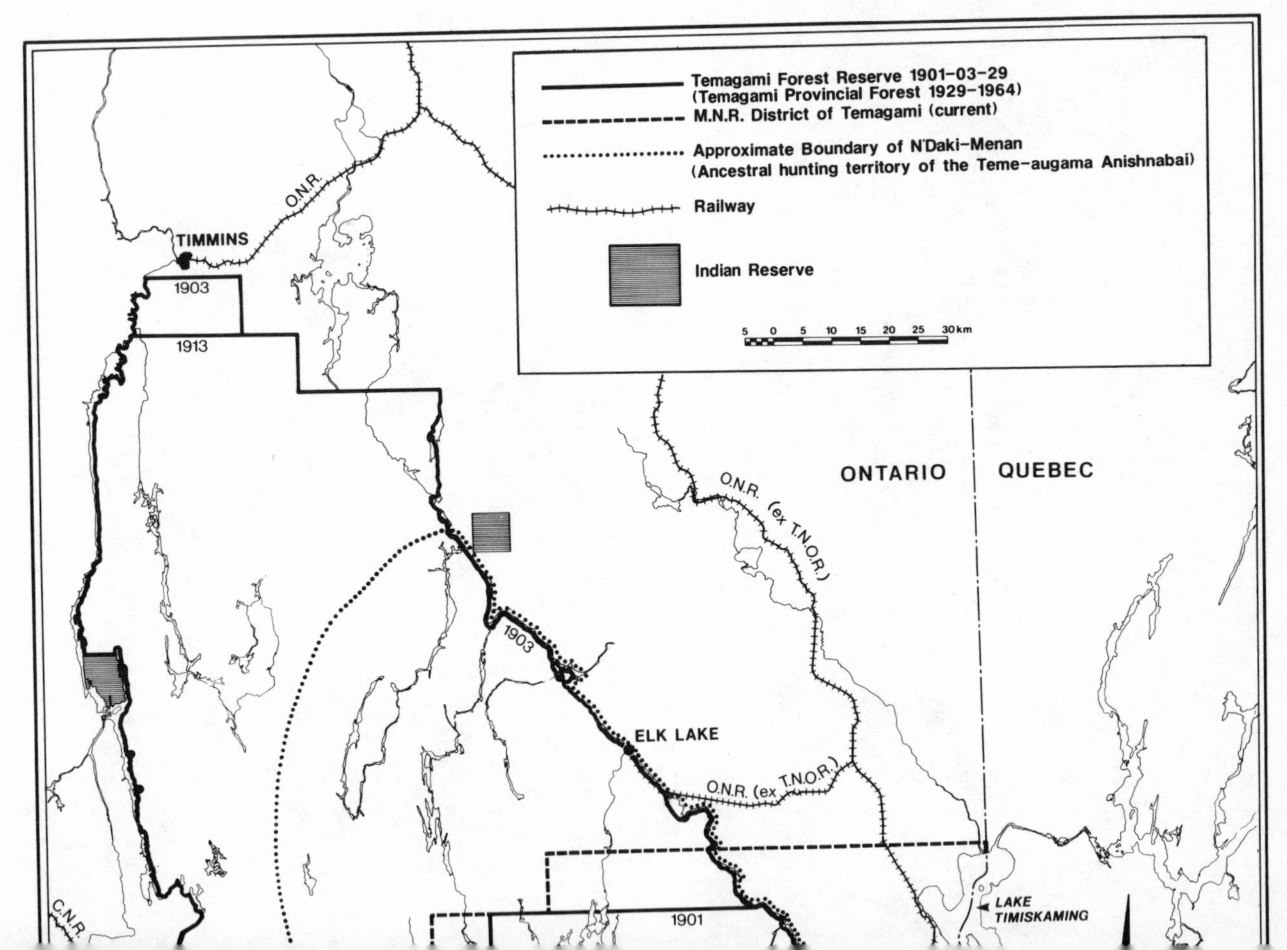
Temagami Forest Reserve 1901-03-29
(Temagami Provincial Forest 1929-1964)
M.N.R. District of Temagami (current)
Approximate Boundary of N'Daki-Menan
(Ancestral hunting territory of the Teme-augama Anishnabai)
Railway
Indian Reserve
5 0 5 10 15 20 25 30 km
TIMMINS
O.N.R.
1903
1913
ONTARIO
QUEBEC
O.N.R. (ex T.N.O.R.)
1903
ELK LAKE
O.N.R. (ex T.N.O.R.)
1901
LAKE TIMISKAMING
C.N.R.

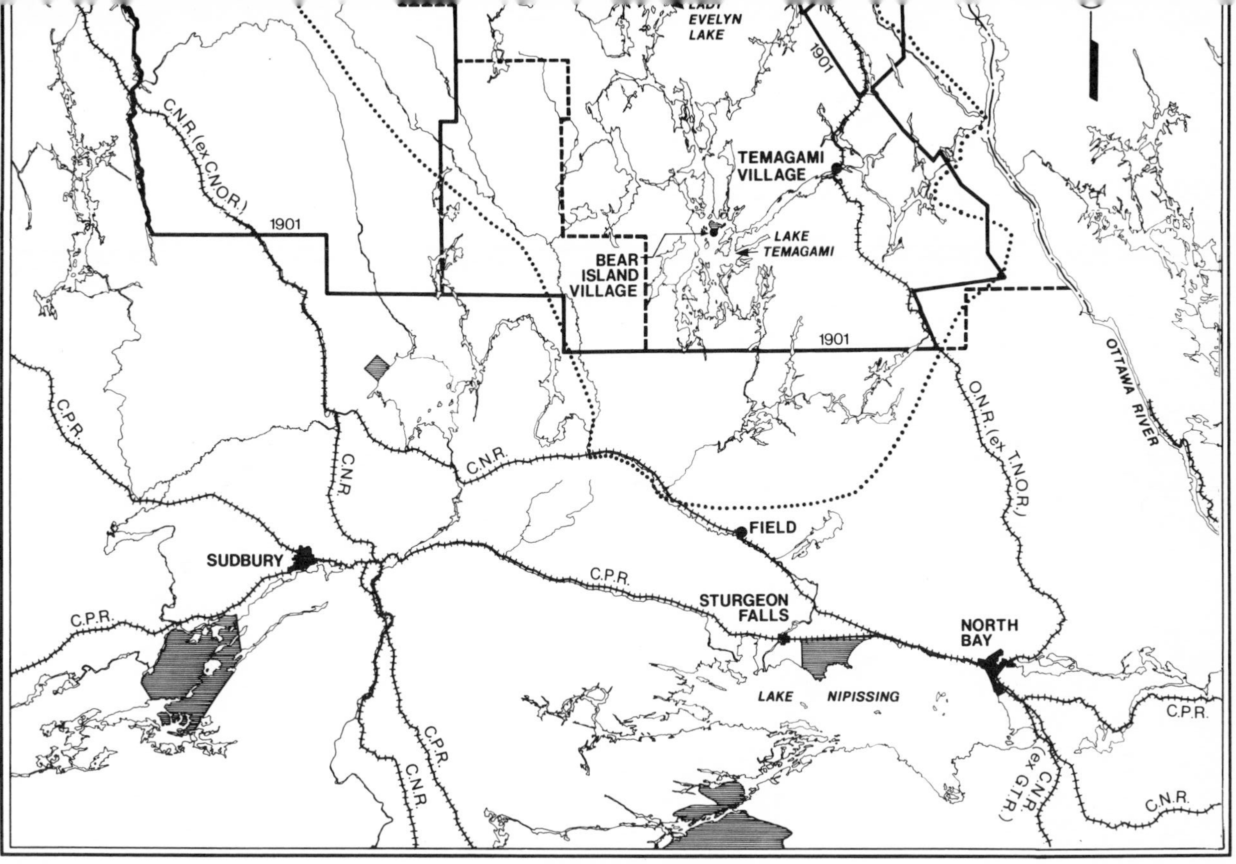

1 The Temagami country

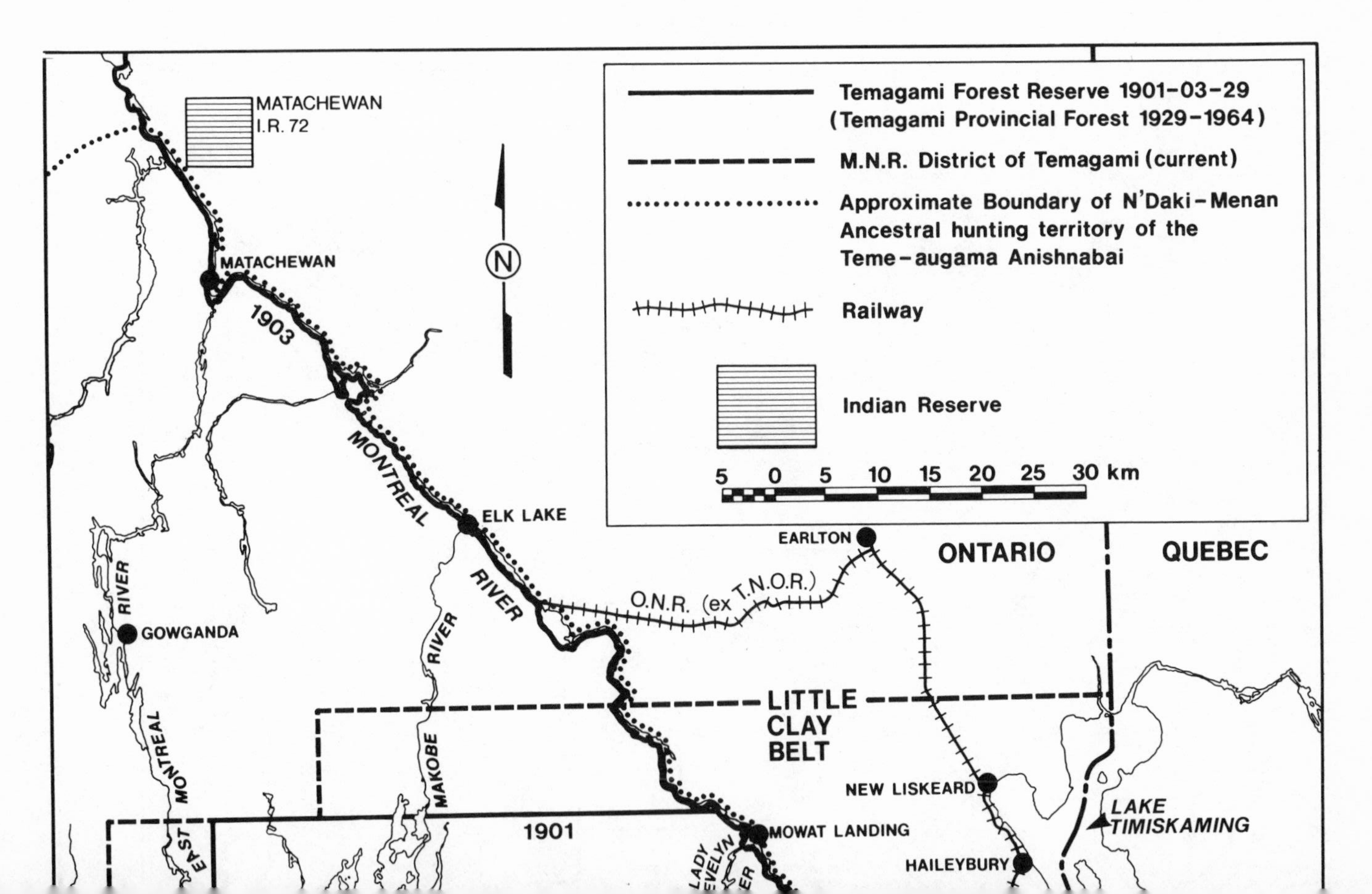

MATACHEWAN
I.R. 72
MATACHEWAN
1903
MONTREAL
ELK LAKE
RIVER
RIVER
GOWGANDA
RIVER
MONTREAL
EAST
MAKOBE
RIVER
O.N.R. (ex T.N.O.R.)
EARLTON
ONTARIO
QUEBEC
LITTLE
CLAY
BELT
NEW LISKEARD
MOWAT LANDING
HAILEYBURY
LAKE
TIMISKAMING
1901
LADY
EVELYN
Temagami Forest Reserve 1901-03-29
(Temagami Provincial Forest 1929-1964)
M.N.R. District of Temagami (current)
Approximate Boundary of N'Daki-Menan
Ancestral hunting territory of the
Teme-augama Anishnabai
Railway
Indian Reserve
5 0 5 10 15 20 25 30 km
N

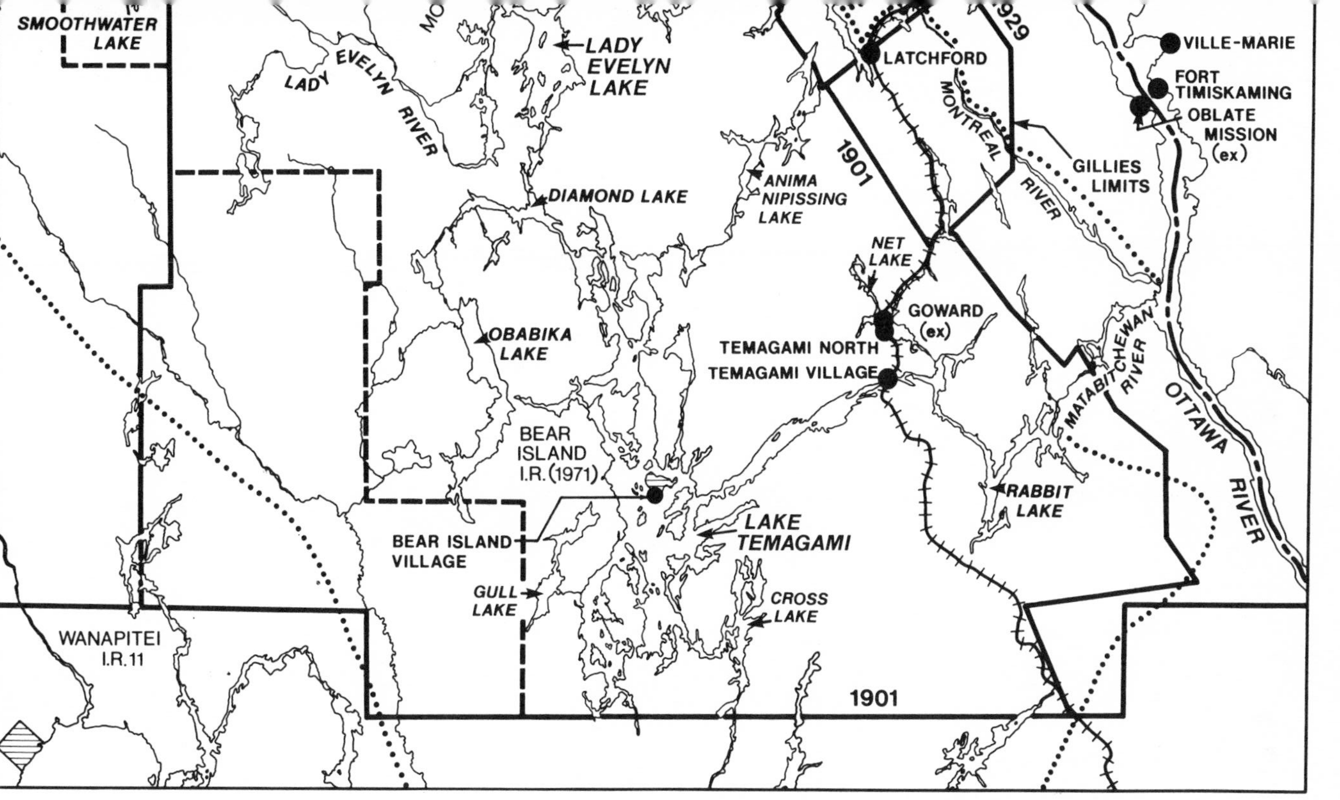

2 The heart of the Temagami country

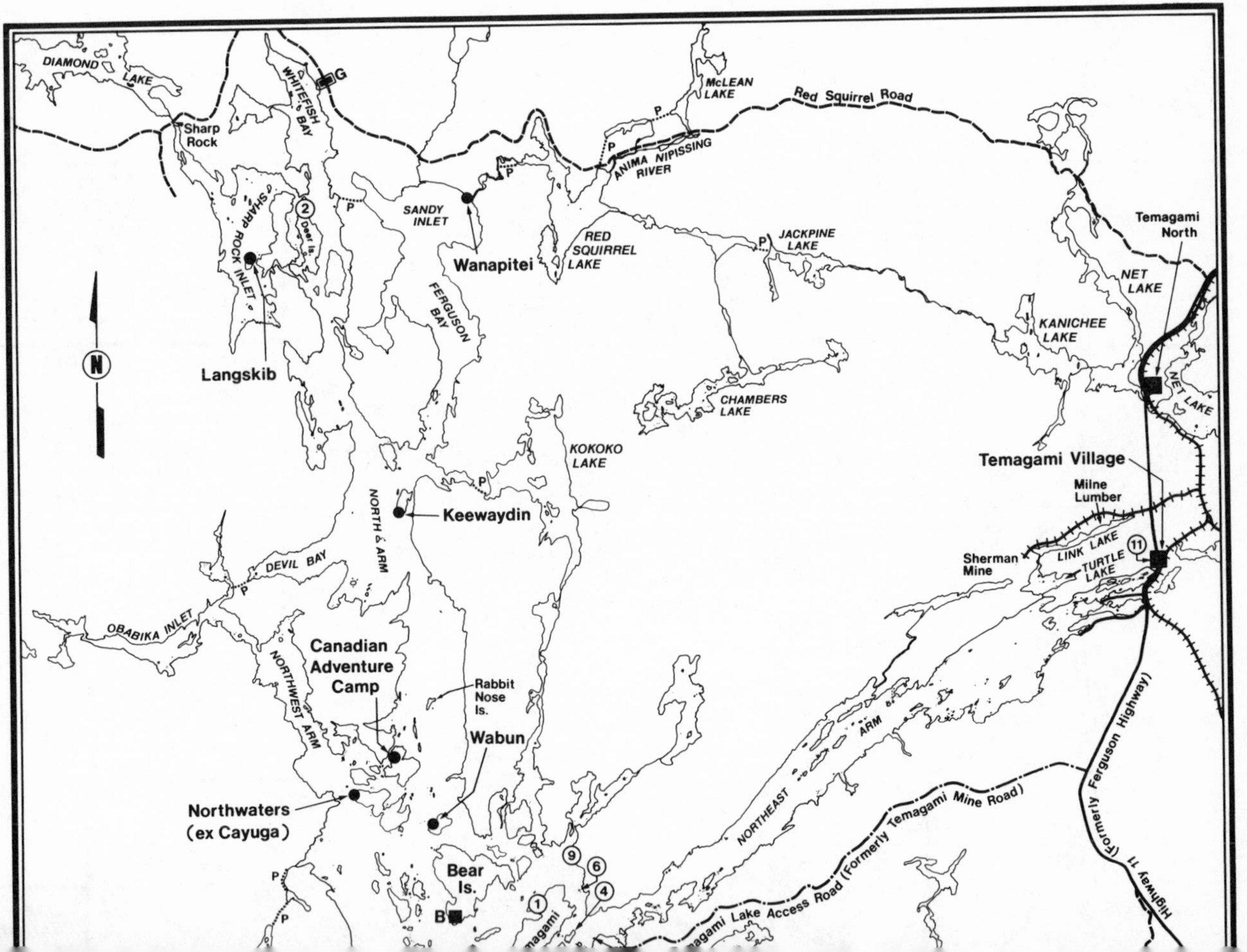

DIAMOND LAKE
Sharp Rock
WHITEFISH BAY
G
McLEAN LAKE
Red Squirrel Road
ANIMA NIPISSING RIVER
SHARP ROCK INLET
Deer Is.
SANDY INLET
Wanapitei
RED SQUIRREL LAKE
JACKPINE LAKE
Temagami North
NET LAKE
KANICHEE LAKE
FERGUSON BAY
Langskib
CHAMBERS LAKE
KOKOKO LAKE
Temagami Village
Milne Lumber
Keewaydin
NORTH ARM
DEVIL BAY
Sherman Mine
LINK LAKE
TURTLE LAKE
OBABIKA INLET
NORTHWEST ARM
Canadian Adventure Camp
Rabbit Nose Is.
Wabun
Northwaters (ex Cayuga)
NORTHEAST ARM
Highway 11 (Formerly Ferguson Highway)
Lake Access Road (Formerly Temagami Mine Road)
Bear Is.
B
P
N

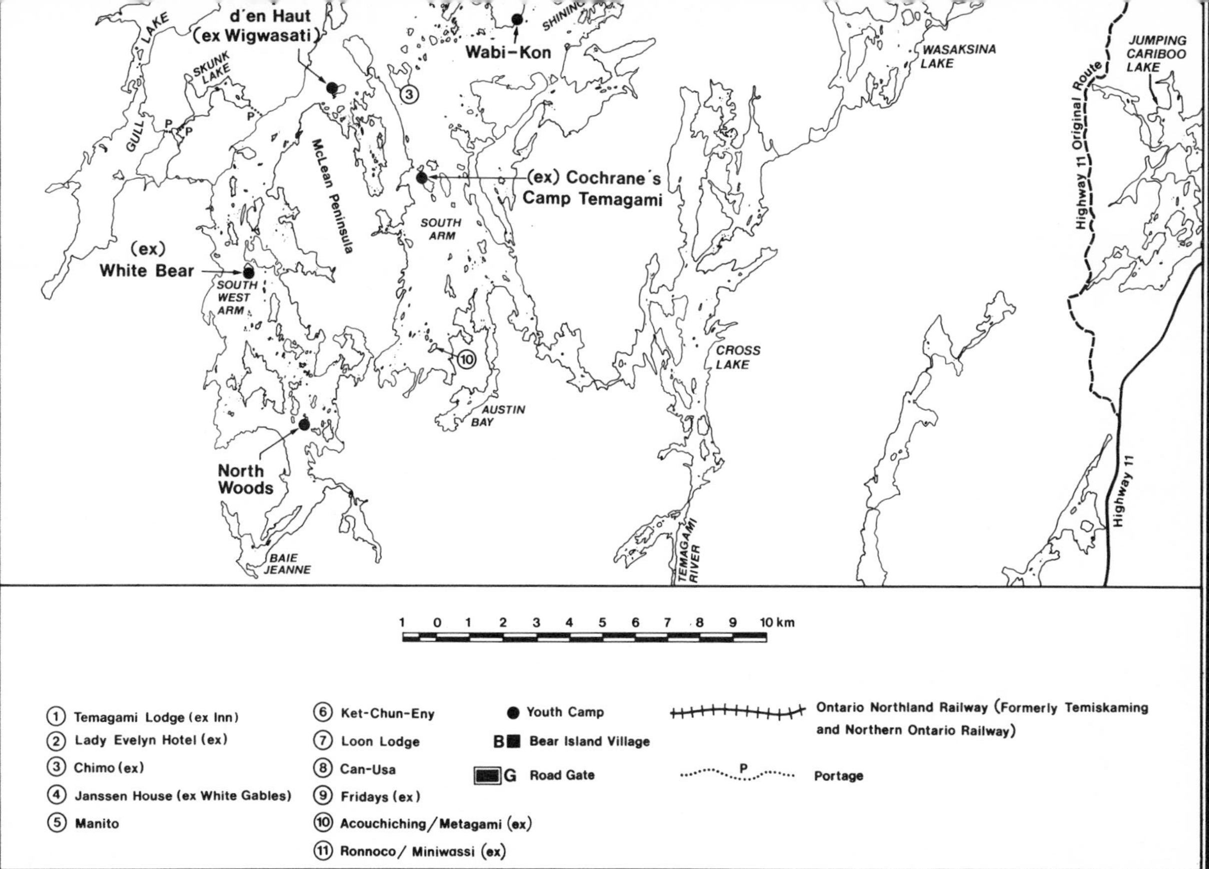

3 Lake Temagami

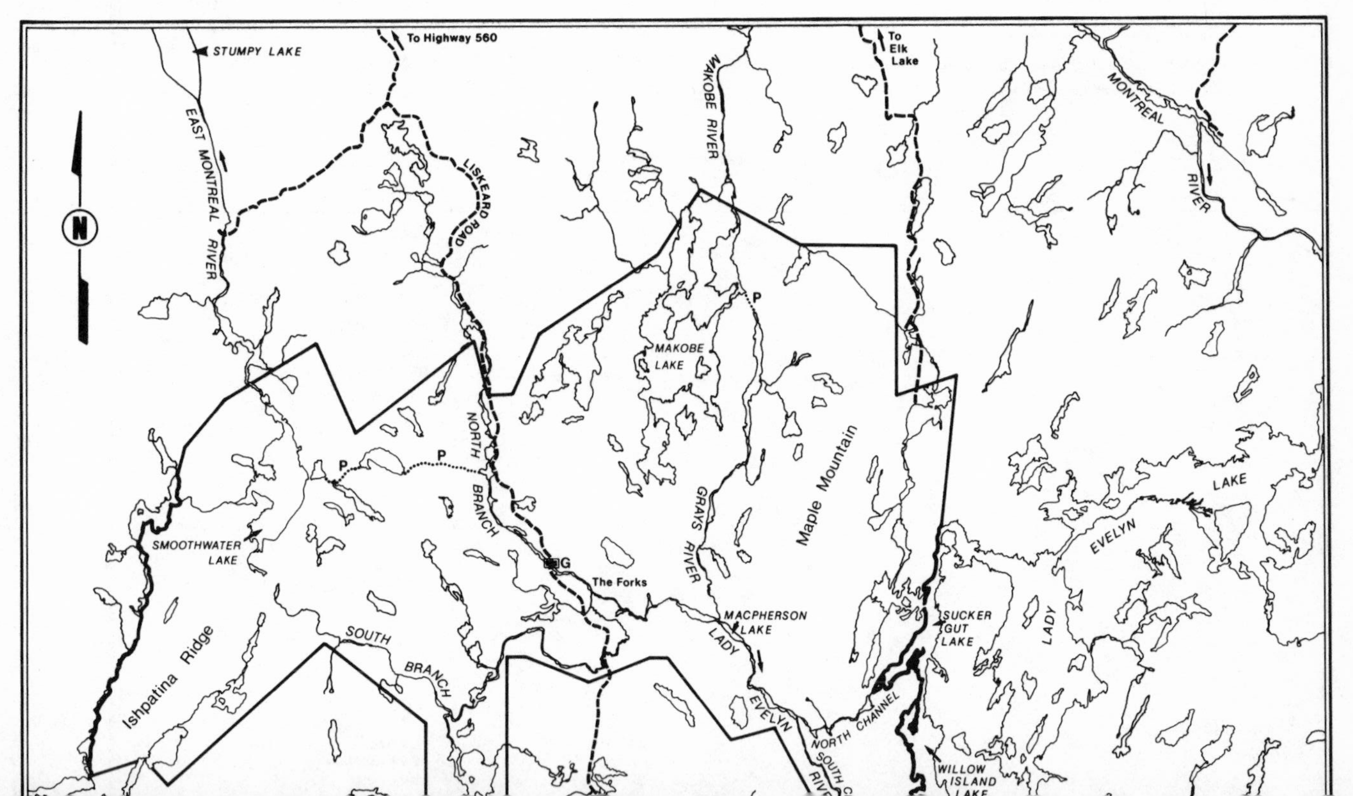

STUMPY LAKE
To Highway 560
MAKOBE RIVER
To Elk Lake
MONTREAL RIVER
EAST MONTREAL RIVER
N
LISKEARD ROAD
MAKOBE LAKE
P
P
P
NORTH BRANCH
Maple Mountain
LAKE
EVELYN
GRAYS RIVER
SMOOTHWATER LAKE
G
The Forks
MACPHERSON LAKE
SUCKER GUT LAKE
LADY
Ishpatina Ridge
SOUTH BRANCH
LADY EVELYN
NORTH CHANNEL
SOUTH C
RIV
WILLOW ISLAND LAKE

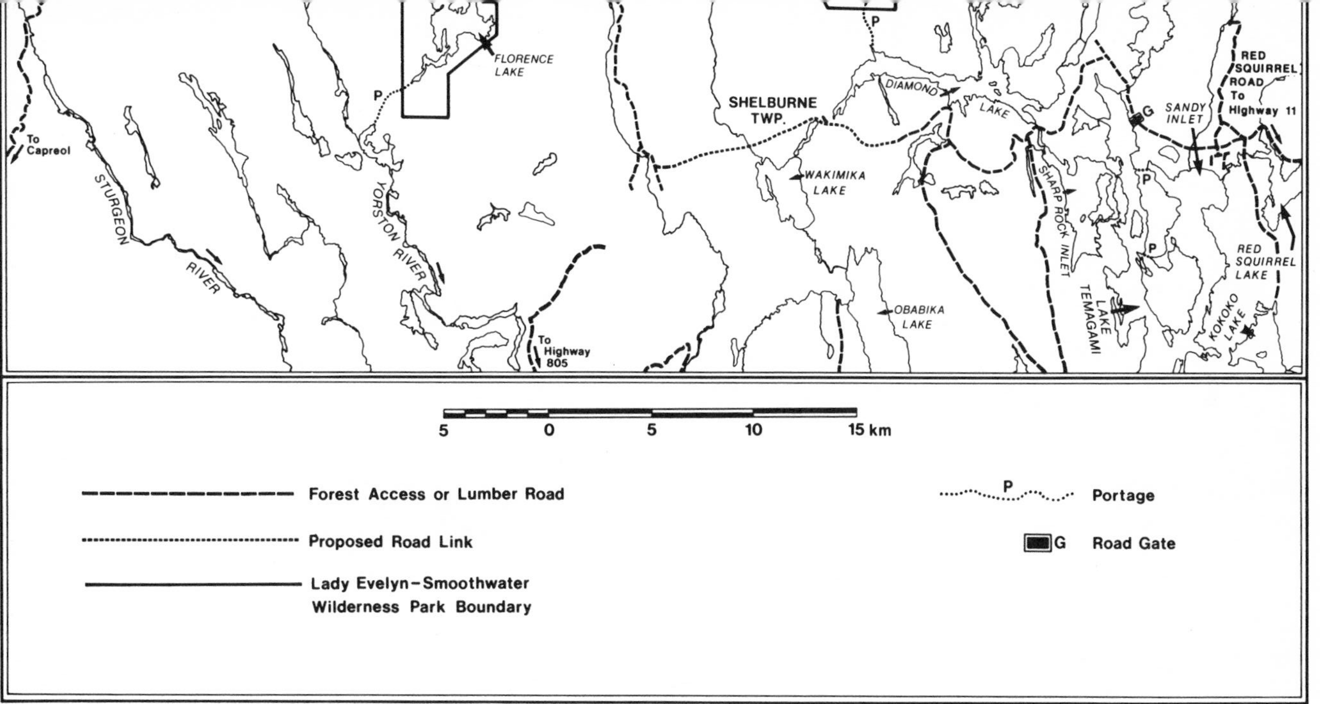

4 Lady Evelyn–Smoothwater Wilderness Park

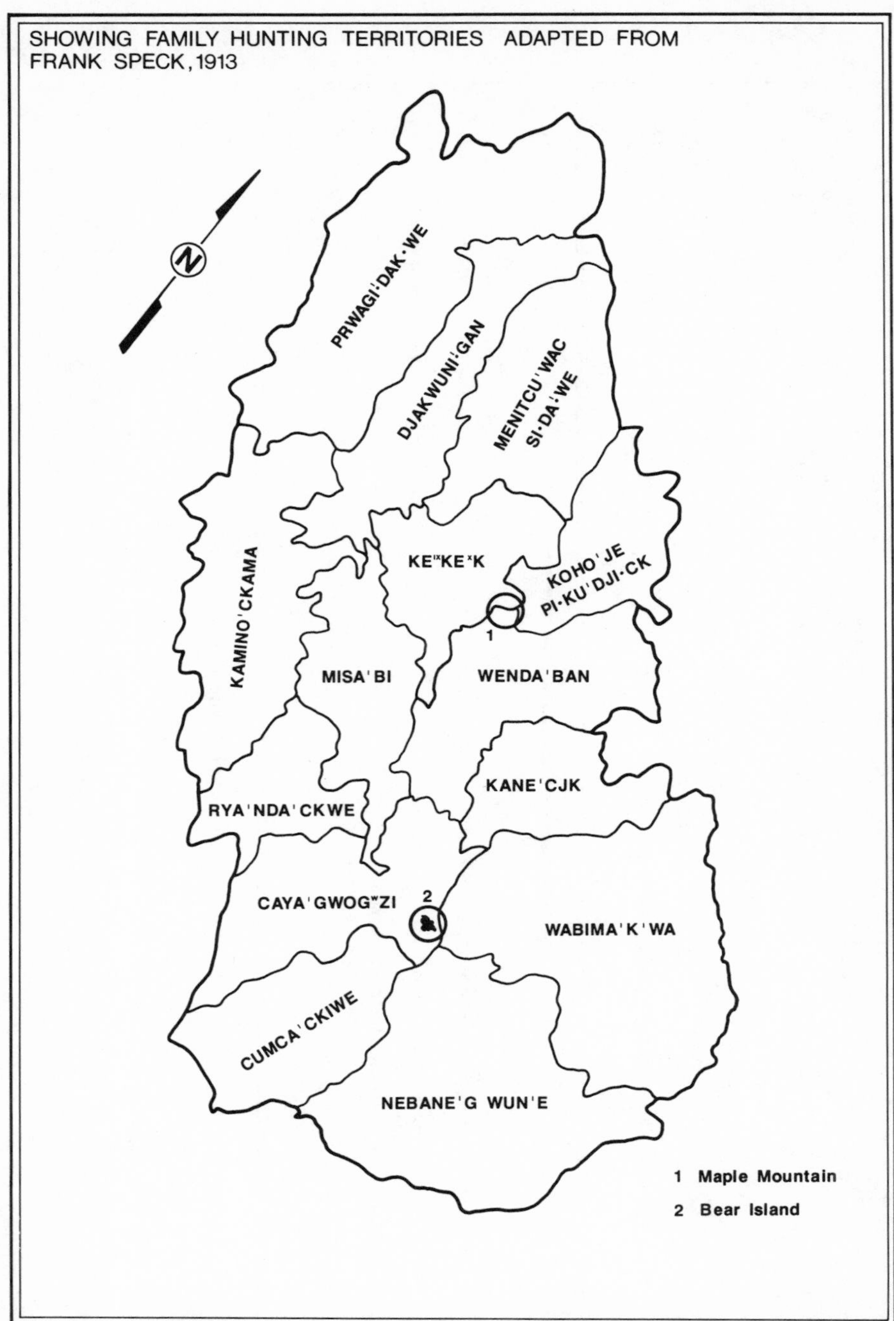

5 N'Daki Menan

The Temagami Experience

Introduction

The extent of the district to which we refer as the Temagami country (see map 1) is neither precise nor constant. As the distinguished Australian historian Sir Keith Hancock wrote of the landscape that was his subject in *Discovering Monaro: A Study of Man's Impact on His Environment* (Cambridge 1972), 'the name is enchanting, but the entity is elusive.' Ontario has never maintained a geographical district that corresponds exactly with our understanding of the Temagami country. The area certainly includes much more than the heartland immediately adjacent to Lake Temagami itself and to what is now the Lady Evelyn–Smoothwater Wilderness Park (maps 2 and 4). It is somewhat larger than the boundaries of the original Temagami Forest Reserve established in 1901 with the stated intention that sustained-yield pine forest management might be implemented there. The area we discuss is also larger than the administrative unit currently known to the Ontario Ministry of Natural Resources as the District of Temagami. Both the original Temagami Forest Reserve and today's administrative district exclude the communities of Elk Lake and Gowganda to the north and the Temagami River in the south. But MNR's District of Temagami includes the Tritowns – Cobalt, Haileybury, and New Liskeard – which are outside though often closely associated with the history of the Temagami country as we present it here. The boundaries of the Temagami Forest Reserve as extended in 1903 approximate our definition, but encompass territory beyond the Arctic watershed close to Timmins, where somewhat different influences and priorities prevailed. The boundaries of the Temagami country are also close to the N'Daki Menan, the aboriginal homeland of the Teme-augama Anishnabai (maps 1, 5), although our focus extends farther westward into the valley of the Upper Wanapitei River and northeast into the upper Grassy and Opikinimika. However, we have not attempted to integrate all the outlying areas into our story and analysis in a comprehensive manner. Gowganda, for example, enters as a frontier mining town, disappears, and then as a recreational centre returns to our discussion of land use and management in the area overall. This is true as well for several other communities whose local stories – whatever their general interest – are not consistently linked to the central themes of this inquiry into the evolution of land-use conflict in the broader Temagami country.

Two cultures, one Algonkian and the other Euro-Canadian, have occupied the Temagami country, each in its own way. Each has interacted with the landscape and, increasingly, with the other. For the aboriginal inhabitants, the Temagami country has been homeland, the centre of their identity and their existence as a community. They have named the topography, the trails and waterways, to mark them with their experience. Nomenclature continues to evolve as one aspect of the process of aboriginal cultural renewal. Temagami's significance for those of European ancestry has been more varied and, indeed, marked by internal conflict. For most, the district was an outpost beyond the limits of their civilization. For some, Temagami is the site of their permanent residence and the focus of their social and economic lives; for others, the district is perhaps a cherished retreat, a wilderness refuge from the occupational pressures of lives centred elsewhere.

Environment and history have compelled coexistence between the peoples of Temagami and their surroundings. The same forces have influenced the uncertain coexistence between the two cultures – aboriginal and European. On the environmental side, Temagami's relative isolation and ruggedness restricted access and thereby limited the impact of human activity. Thus, raiding bands of Iroquois, rival fur trade ventures, and railway promoters have all been constrained in their attempts to gain control of the district and its prized resources – furs, minerals, timber, and natural vistas. Viewed historically, the varied and often conflicting objectives of those interested in the landscape and resources of the district have preserved or been forced to preserve a balance, at least until recent times.

Resource interests, recreational users, provincial officials, and the Teme-augama Anishnabai each influenced the development of the Temagami area from the last half of the nineteenth century to the 1980s.

Each has been responsible for introducing or controlling change in different parts of the Temagami Forest. To preserve a valuable heritage, recreational users focused their attention on Lake Temagami itself and on the well-travelled canoe routes of the interior. The Indians emphasized their distinctive position as original owners with a claim to a large reserve or, more recently, to a substantial land base and a continuing role in long-range management. Resource interests – generally short-lived – extracted the forest and mineral wealth from those portions of the district that were accessible by water from commercial corridors around the Temagami periphery. While firmly asserting jurisdictional authority, the province of Ontario monitored the initiatives of others only loosely after its own plans to manage the forest of the Temagami country for sustained yield collapsed early in the century.

Neither the ownership of the Temagami country nor the manner in which its future is to be determined are completely clear today. The explanation for the present uncertainty lies in the historical experience of the two cultures and the multiple purposes they have sought to achieve in occupying the landscape.

CHAPTER ONE

The Homeland and Its People

Human beings arrived on the shores of Teme-augaming, 'the place of deep water,' long before the dawn of European history. From 'time immemorial' – at least five thousand years ago – aboriginal inhabitants made the Temagami country their N'Daki Menan or homeland. The homeland of the Teme-augama Anishnabai, 'the people of the deep water,' extended beyond the immediate environs of Lake Temagami, encompassing generally an area of some 4,000 square miles. Development of that area over the past century or more is the subject of this book, but the recent history of the Temagami country cannot be understood in isolation from the aboriginal and environmental past. Indeed, the story of Temagami involves a complex and continuing interaction between the broader political and economic forces that have influenced development throughout Ontario and distinctive local circumstances, both cultural and geographic.

The original inhabitants maintained 'nastawgan,' a network of trails and waterways providing access to the hunting territories that evolved as social organization developed within the area. The principal routes also channelled communication between the Temagami country and the outside. Later visitors entering the N'Daki Menan travelled through a landscape that remains rich in meaning and in memory for the Teme-augama Anishnabai today. To the west the homeland encompassed Shuonjawgaming, 'the place of the smoothwater.' Lady Evelyn Lake, so named in the late nineteenth century, had long been known as Moozkananing, 'the haunt of the moose.' Majamaygos, 'the speckled trout stream,' or Lady Evelyn River, flowed into Moozkananing and later into the Kawassidjewan, which in translation means 'tumbling water seen at a distance' and is now called the Montreal River. By means of the Teme-augaming Zeebi, 'the river flowing from the deep water,' most of the waters of Lake Temagami reached Nahmay Zeebi, the Sturgeon River en route south to Lake Nipissing and Georgian Bay.[1]

The names given to landmarks in the district symbolize the spiritual significance of the environment for the aboriginal inhabitants, although the evolution of nomenclature again attests to the overlap of cultures here. Through translation, Devil's Mountain along the intricate shoreline of the main lake retains some continuity with Manidoo-nasaybee Puckwudina, 'the devil coming down.' But few now recognize the congruence of Maple Mountain with Cheebayjing, 'the place where the spirit goes.' No doubt for centuries, as now, men and women gazed under moonlight through the forest on the waters of Teme-augaming and contemplated their own mortality.

Yet human life on the N'Daki Menan is but a blink of an eye to the eons of geological time. The Precambrian topography of the Temagami country evolved over the last three and a half billion years following the first emergence of rock above the ocean's surface.[2] Huge mountains were forced upward only to be largely worn down again. Another mountain-building process began one and three-quarter billion years ago, creating great pink granite igneous peaks, worn down in their turn by glaciation and storms.

Vast quantities of sediments washed down from the mountain tops settled on the igneous and metamorphic rocks. Pressed by their own weight, frequently under water, these sediments were transformed into solid rock, often thousands of feet thick. The oldest sedimentaries are those interspersed among the Keewatin volcanics. Other sedimentaries include the Cobalt conglomerates and slate and the Lorrain arckose and quartzite. More recently, geologically speaking, strips of Nipissing diabase intruded through cracks in the sedimentaries. The presence of valuable mineral deposits in these formations provided the foundations for a silver mining boom at the beginning of the present century.

The Nipissing diabase intrusions created numerous rugged and sharp ridges. On Lake Temagami itself, these ridges include Ferguson and Devil's mountains in the North Arm, the former stretching more than 1,600 feet above sea level, with a cliff face of several hundred feet. Eroded remnants of conglomerate also have left great hills but, like Caribou Mountain just southeast of Lake Temagami's Northeast Arm, they are slightly more rounded. Higher than all these, to the west stands both Ishpatina Ridge peaking at 2,275 feet (the highest point in Ontario) and Maple Mountain at over 2,075 feet. Throughout, the landscape and water courses exhibit the strike or line of regional geological shearing, usually but not always along a northwest-southeast axis.

At least four times, glacial ice reached northern Ontario, including what was to become the Temagami country. The ice from the most recent glaciation, the Wisconsin period, began to retreat from the area about eleven thousand years ago. This was about a thousand years after the Nipissing area had cleared and opened a huge water outlet from 'Lake Algonquin,' an enlarged version of the Upper Great Lakes, draining to the Atlantic Ocean through the Ottawa valley.[3] About ten thousand years ago, the ice was gone. But as the glacier retreated northward over the Arctic watershed, the melt and rain waters were trapped between the surviving ice-field and the divide, creating the large Lake Barlow-Ojibway. With drainage blocked from reaching Hudson Bay to the north, Barlow-Ojibway rose and grew until it spilled southward into the Ottawa. Its southern extremities included what would remain Lake Timiskaming and reached the southwest side of the present Montreal River, where shorelines and great beaches can still be observed. Later, when the waters north of the divide could flow into the emerging James Bay, the southern waters of Barlow-Ojibway slowly dried up, leaving the remnant Lake Timiskaming and the Little Clay Belt, its soil created from the runoff into the lake from mighty post-glacial rivers. To the north, on the floor of the main body of Lake Barlow-Ojibway, there was left behind the Great Clay Belt and the remnant Lake Abitibi.

After the ice receded, a subarctic climate persisted until about six thousand years ago, when warmer temperatures and the current climate became established. In time flora and fauna spread north. The present forest species became fully established only about five thousand years ago, about the same time as the earliest evidence of human habitation. The Temagami country that emerged was in a border zone between the great boreal forests, dominated by spruce and balsam fir, and the Great Lakes–St Lawrence hardwood and pine forests to the south. Most of the Temagami country was within the northern reaches of the once-extensive white and red pine belt. Pine remained the predominant species because the 'normal' ecological system included moderate forest fires that facilitated regeneration.[4] Pine and fire were at the core of the complex ecological system of the Temagami country, within which human beings played an integral role for millennia. Pine was eventually recognized as a major economic and aesthetic resource surrounding the place of deep water.

From archaeological and anthropological inquiry we now know something about the early inhabitants of Temagami and about their relationship with the local environment. During the past twenty years, archaeologists working in the N'Daki Menan have uncovered extensive remains from certain periods of occupation. There is some possibility that the tools, bones, and personal effects found in various digs in the Temagami area were discarded by people from whom some of the present Teme-augama Anishnabai are descended.[5] When research focuses on the time of initial contact with Europeans and it is possible to supplement the evidence of artifactual materials with oral tradition, cultural knowledge, and traditional skills, indications of continuity become clearer. The results of archaeological and anthropological research on the Temagami area have recently been put under public scrutiny in judicial consideration of aboriginal land claims covering much of the Temagami country, for the legitimacy and effectiveness of provincial efforts to manage the resources of Temagami are inescapably tied to questions about the status and origin of contemporary aboriginal residents.[6]

The earliest evidence of human habitation in the Temagami country originated in the middle of the Archaic period, about 3000 BC. Finds from the era indicate that flint from local or regional sources was utilized in a variety of ways by occupants of the sites uncovered. The finds also demonstrate that seasonal mobility took place along the waterways of the area and between various hunting grounds where fowl and game could be procured. In the Temagami country the transition from the Archaic to the Laurel Woodland period (400 BC–AD 800) is marked by the introduction of decorated pottery, the use of seine nets for fishing shallow waters, and the manufacture of birch-bark canoes.[7] The inhabitants penetrated even the most remote waterways of N'Daki Menan,[8] although their number probably never exceeded one hundred and fifty.[9]

Life-styles and cultural details are much clearer for the people who lived during the Late Woodland period (AD 800–AD 1600) particularly during the century or so before 'contact' with Europeans in the first half of the seventeenth century. Before this contact, inhabitants of the N'Daki Menan seem to have emerged as a distinct, Algonkian-speaking people. Although fur traders were to call them nomadic, the description is not entirely accurate. They had a relatively extensive homeland, which sustained their hunting, fishing, and gathering through regular cycles of seasonal migration. They congregated periodically, especially in the early summer, and they had some consciousness of being a community. A 'band' is what the English would later call such a community. Because of their distinctive position at the juncture of several large Algonkian-speaking groupings, such as Ojibwa, Cree, and Algonquin, the contemporary Teme-augama Anishnabai prefer the word 'tribe' when describing themselves both in the past and in the present.

The homeland of the 'Temagamis' around the time of early contact with Europeans encompassed a large territory covering, according to current tribal leaders, about 3,823 square miles. It is headwaters country, as the preceding geological description shows. Lake Temagami, in the south-central portion of the homeland, has a surface area of 50,000 acres with a water volume of four billion cubic metres and a surface elevation of 965 feet above sea level. The lake has more than 1,200 islands and 570 miles of shoreline including 200 miles of island shoreline. The wider homeland extended from the confluence of the Temagami and Sturgeon rivers in the southwest to the height of land by the big bend in the West Montreal River on the northeast. It also extended from the height of land between the East Montreal and the north-flowing Grassy in the northwest to a very short coastline along Lake Timiskaming between the mouths of the Matabitchuan and the Montreal rivers in the southeast. It thus included all the watersheds of the Lady Evelyn and the upper Sturgeon. But, though it included Elk Lake, it excluded Matachewan and the lands of the Little Clay Belt draining into the Montreal River and Lake Timiskaming from the northeast. It also excluded both the Mattagami watershed to the north and the upper Wanapitei and Chiniguchi watersheds flowing to the southeast.

As occupants of a transitional vegetation zone, the Temagamis had sufficient advantages in the form of access to a variety of plant and animal species. It is claimed, for example, that the Tomiko River was known as 'canoe-building river' because stands of birch trees supplied bark of the proper size and thickness for canoe making. Friday Lake provided ironwood, a strong but flexible wood for use on sleigh runners and as axe handles. Norris Lake was known as 'the basswood bark place,' the bark being transformed into rope for use in making nets. Upper Bass Lake was designated as 'Burl Lake' because of a type of growth on the sides of trees that was made into bowls and other wares. Small groves of maple trees used to produce syrup were once located on Temagami Island in central Lake Temagami, on the South Arm of the lake and around Kokoko, Rib, Sugar, Diamond, and Smoothwater lakes. Blueberries were another extensive food resource whose growth was sometimes encouraged by ground fires.[10] The Temagamis, like other Algonkian-speaking people of the Late Woodland culture, were deep-water fishermen who used gill nets and gathered annually at summer lakeside locations. They naturally hunted available game including woodland caribou, moose, white-tailed deer, rabbits, and partridge. Their keen knowledge of the techniques of forest manipulation and the locations of fall fisheries, bear snaring points, marten trapping creeks, fisher runs, caribou runs, wintering areas and crossing points, moose yarding areas, and winter and summer access and exit routes was the means by which they supported themselves from the resources of the land. Periods of regionally isolated deprivation, apparently a consequence of natural periodic and seasonal fluctuations in resource availability, were incorporated into the myths and legends of the Temagami people.[11] A contrasting explanation attributes major fluctuations in resource availability to depletion caused by fur trade pressures in the Temagami area. Specifically, it is alleged that the original native inhabitants, referred to as the 'Outimagami,' disappeared between 1620 and 1660 when the demands of the fur trade depleted local animal populations, and that on two subsequent occasions similar occurrences drove any remaining descendants of the original community from the territory.[12]

Like other Late Woodland Algonkian people, the Temagamis believed that every life form was composed of a body, a soul and a spirit. When death occurred, the body returned to the earth, the soul travelled to a heaven, and the spirit stayed in the homeland watching over subsequent generations. Maple Mountain was venerated as Cheebayjing, 'the place where the spirit goes,' the sacred resting ground of the ancestors' spirits. Animals were consecrated. After a beaver, bear, or otter was killed, the Temagamis would hang the head in a tree, leaving offerings to appease the creature's spirit. Special cords were made to drag the body of an animal back from the hunting ground, as a manifestation of respect for the spirit that allowed the creature to be taken. Certain locations became associated with particular rituals. Ames Lake was called Negig-ajodjen or 'hanging otter place.' Lady Dufferin Lake was known as Negigwaning, 'the place of the otter heads.' Another sacred location near Lady Evelyn Lake was Amick-tigwan-ago-ji-gonay-neyasing, 'the place of hanging beaver heads.' Underlying the rituals was the notion that, if the spirits of animals were kept happy, they would replenish their kindred on earth. Superfluous killing would anger the spirits, who would no longer reproduce, leaving the country barren. The fur traders of the seventeenth to the late nineteenth centuries encountered great difficulty in convincing Indian trappers to kill more than they considered sufficient, and this is partially attributable to the religiously inspired conservation of the native community.[13]

In the areas of lakes Temagami, Nipissing, Timiskaming, and Abitibi, inhabited by Algonkian-speaking people, the existence of tribal homelands was recognized by their inhabitants and by members of adjacent groups. Nevertheless, some fluidity existed in regard to borders. Thus, Temagami Indians engaged in resource extraction from sites outside their homeland, including Mattagami Lake and Lake Abitibi.[14] It is also likely that the Temagamis sometimes congregated with other bands for brief periods in the summer while participating in intertribal ceremonies, such as 'the feast of the dead.'[15]

Well before contact with Europeans, the Temagamis practised exogamy, the introduction of marriage partners from outside the tribal boundaries.[16] Biologically it was not safe for Algonkian communities, which usually – as in the Temagami case – numbered fewer than two hundred, to practise endogamy continually; five hundred was the smallest safe number for a system of 'marriage isolate.'[17] The Temagami pattern of 'migration by inter-marriage' spread outward through one, two, and three neighbouring bands, resulting in marriage relationships 'all the way around the points of the compass.'[18] Of course, internal marriage – that is, endogamy – continued to exist, but only if marriage partners were from a different clan.

The purpose of the clan system was to regulate marriage, for children whose fathers were of the same clan were considered unsuitable marriage partners. For marriage purposes women moved more often than men, but when a man moved into the Temagami homeland, married, and had children, the children bore the totem or clan affiliation symbol of the father. Thus it is assumed that the clan identities of the Temagamis developed as a result of exogamy. For instance, 'Old' Dan Misabi introduced the beaver clan to Temagami when, sometime after 1850, he migrated from the Shawanaga band on Georgian Bay.[19] Although clan affiliation is a nebulous and inconclusive means of determining band origins ('Totems within a group could ebb and flow as lines die out and new marriage partners come in'), the rattlesnake clan has been traced back to 1700; it was established prior to the period of detailed records.[20] The processes of migration into the headwaters country around Temagami are important to the identity of this community, for while the Temagamis had much in common with other Algonkian people, they are distinguished by the cultural mix that resulted as new members entered from neighbouring areas while others departed.[21]

The basic political structure of the Temagamis evolved before contact with Europeans or soon thereafter. The head personage was the 'ogima' or chief. A second chief, 'anike ogima' – that is, 'next to the chief' – often delivered the messages of the chief and called councils. A third official was known as 'mizinawe,' the 'man who collects' provisions for traditional feasts and councils. The chief's executive powers were limited; he could do little without the consent of the subordinate chief and men of the tribe. Although there were no established laws to regulate behaviour in this egalitarian and classless society, a violation of the common welfare required a general meeting. Here the men would discuss the matter and determine an appropriate reprimand. A new chief, who had to be a born member of the tribe, was empowered either by the appointment of his predecessor or by a general election.[22]

By the fifteenth century, the Temagamis had established significant trading relations with people far from the homeland. Old Huron and other Iroquoian clay pottery and pipes have turned up in digs close to and within the N'Daki Menan, including Smoothwater Lake, Duncan Lake, and Sand Point on Lake Temagami itself. Indeed, the various Algonkian-speaking peoples north of Nipissing and all the way to the James Bay lowlands were trading their excess meat and skins for corn and cornmeal from the Huronian area around the south shore of Georgian Bay. This was often through the auspices of Nipissing middlemen who might winter with the Hurons. Thus, before contact with Europeans, the Temagamis had indirect trade routes with people living quite far away. Residing immediately south and southwest of the Temagamis, the Nipissings fulfilled the prehistoric middleman role so that 'the French trade was built on the back of the Huron-Nipissing trade.'[23] The Temagamis were thus involved with influences emanating from well outside their homeland.

Despite the evidence of external contacts and trade, the Temagamis lived rather close to the subsistence level and within the ecological limits of their environment. Thus, like neighbouring populations, they reacted to early fur trade contacts in a way that puzzled the Europeans. Trade items 'supplemented rather than supplanted' Algonkian tools, weapons, and wares. In the early days, guns became a major trade item, but for some time they did not replace the traditional bow and arrow. The Temagamis rarely visited a trading post more than once a year, and between these trips, guns were often in need of repair and gunpowder or shot ran out.[24] Furthermore, throughout the fur trade era, there are numerous occasions, recorded in various trading-post journals by frustrated traders, of Indians deciding not to trap for a season. If big game or hare was abundant, the hunters could be found 'frittering away their time feasting on venison' instead of trapping, while harvesting only enough beaver for food and clothing.[25] Conversely, when game was scarce, the Indians were preoccupied with feeding their families, and again trapped only enough beaver for meat and clothing. The 'subsistence need predominated over fur hunting';[26] although this is a reference to James Bay Crees, it also fits the experience of the Temagamis. Their relative self-sufficiency even meant that, in initial contacts, the Algonkian peoples seemed to have had the advantage. They lived off the land and its waters and often kept the trader alive with 'country provisions.' 'In the early days,' according to the distinguished ethnologist Edward Rogers, 'the trader was probably more dependent upon the Indian for survival than was the Indian upon the trader.'[27]

It was in 1620, twelve years after Samuel de Champlain had established Quebec and five years after he had passed through Lake Nipissing, that Europeans first heard of the Temagamis. In 1615, Champlain had noted the Rivière d'Estarjon (Sturgeon), flowing into Lake Nipissing, which the local native people ascended to trade with the people there, 'who live by the chase and by fishing. It is stocked with great abundance of both animals, birds and fish.'[28] Jean Nicolet, a French trader and interpreter of Algonkian and Iroquoian languages, wintered with the Nipissings in 1620 and reported on the 'Outimagami' and other eastern people. Nicolet's experiences were recorded twenty years later by the missionary to the Algonkians, Father LeJeune, in the 1640 section of the *Jesuit Relations*: 'Leaving the River des Prairies [the Ottawa] when it turns directly to the North, that we may go to the Southwest, we come to Lake Nipisin, where the Nipisiniens are found. These have upon their North the Timiscimi, the Outimagami, the Ouachegami, the Mitchitamou, the Outurbi, the Kristinon, who live on the shores of the North sea whither the Nipisiniens go to trade.'[29] The 'Outimagami' and 'Lac Timagaming' appear on maps by the French cartographer De l'Isle, dated 1700 and 1705, although their location north of Nipissing and around Lake Timiskaming is rather notional.[30]

Meanwhile, for twenty or so years after 1640, the *Relations* contain several references to Nipissings trading French goods far to the north among diverse Algonkian tribes in return for furs. Often these northern peoples were all subsumed under the name 'Nipissings'. Until the destruction of Huronia by the Iroquois in 1648–9, most of the northern furs passed through Huron hands before reaching the French; French-

Temagami contact was not direct.[31] Thus European diseases, like the smallpox that ravaged Huronia, may have had only minor effects to the north.[32] Then suddenly the Nipissings, and indirectly the Temagamis, became enmeshed in acute imperial rivalry originating in far-off centres of metropolitan power. Such a pattern of competing external influences would repeat itself down to the present.

The Iroquois or Five Nations Confederacy, with a complex political organization centred in what is now upstate New York, were clearly imperialistic. Out of notions of prestige or vengeance, or driven by population pressures or food shortages, they moved first in 1642 to drive out the Allumette Algonquins on the Ottawa and to cut that line of trade. Then they attacked Huronia, almost totally destroying the village-based Huron nation. The Iroquois were clearly their own masters, although they were encouraged and partially armed by their Dutch allies at New Amsterdam.[33]

Raiding parties of the Nadoways, as the Nipissings and Temagamis called the Iroquois, penetrated deep into the tribal lands of the Algonkian peoples. In 1650 they raided the Nipissings and perhaps the Temagamis; in 1660 they raided the Abitibis. Sealing the Ottawa route, for a time they cut off all trade links with the French. By 1665, after an inconclusive peace in the mid-fifties, the Iroquois had reached the east coast of James Bay, where they spread fear and wreaked havoc well into the mid–1670s, although an uneasy Iroquois-French peace was established in 1667.[34] While the main Iroquois routes tended to be to the southeast from Lake Timiskaming and due west from present-day southern Ontario, in the mid-sixties they were again in the Lake Nipissing area and penetrating northward apparently through the homeland of the Temagamis. Father Claude Allouez, in 1667, found many Nipissings far to the west by Lake Nipigon where they had fled for safety, probably along inland routes and probably helped by their Cree trading partners.[35]

While no written record survives of Iroquois raids on Temagami, the oral tradition of the Teme-augama Anishnabai supports the likelihood that such attacks occurred. Four distinct raids have been identified.[36] One tale recounts an ambush by Temagamis of a party of about three big canoes of Nadoways paddling up the Temagami River toward Cross Lake. Using a floating lynx skin as a decoy, the Temagamis lured the invaders into a swift current, pounced upon them, and killed all but one. In another encounter a large party of Nadoways was camped at Matawapika, where the Lady Evelyn empties into the Montreal; on spying some Temagami canoes, three Nadoway canoes took off in pursuit all the way into the southern part of Lake Temagami where a large party of Temagamis were encamped. The local inhabitants hid in partly dug pits; the Nadoways camped nearby. At night, a Temagami man swam to the site and set the Iroquois canoes afloat. The trapped enemy were killed in the water or on shore. Perhaps the most popular tale concerns a Temagami attack on Nadoways camped on what is now Rabbit Lake. At night the Temagamis carefully slit the bark of the enemy's canoes. 'At dawn, the Temagamis attacked the Nadoways who tried to flee quickly in their canoes. As they paddled out into the water, the slit canoes sank, and the local Indians clubbed the hated enemy to death in the water.' There are also stories of a bloody encounter on the small 'Stinking Islands' at the beginning of the North Arm, but details are vague; decaying bodies gave the islands their names.

During several of the dark years of hostility with the Iroquois, the Temagamis may have withdrawn temporarily from the main lakes and watercourses of the N'Daki Menan. They may even, briefly, have retreated a short distance to the west of their homeland. But they returned.[37]

For a short time the tiny French colony of Canada, clinging to a narrow belt on the banks of the St Lawrence, had itself been fighting for its very existence against the Iroquois. In 1664 New Amsterdam had become New York, and the English replaced the Dutch as Iroquois allies, although the Iroquois were subservient to no one. After the peace of 1667, with the Iroquois in full control of what is now most of southern Ontario, life for the French, the Nipissings and their upland trading neighbours slowly returned to 'normal.' For the Nipissings this included renewed trade contacts via the Ottawa with the French. In 1671 the Jesuits reported that the 'Nipisiniens' were back at their old positions on their own lake.[38]

Far to the north, the Hudson's Bay Company, in 1670 (the year of its foundation) established Charles Fort at the mouth of the Rupert River. This outpost became a permanent base two years later. The next year, 1673, the company established Moose Fort at the mouth of the Moose, and in 1679 Fort Albany at the mouth of the Albany. Moose Fort soon became headquarters for the HBC operations, and a powerful new English presence was established in the north.

More secure during the 1670s, French mercantilism and French missionaries moved to meet the English challenge. The French reached Chicoutimi by 1670; in 1672 Father Albanel crossed overland to take a look at Charles Fort, and as a result a headwaters post at Mistassini was established. But when Louis Joliet crossed overland in 1679 to James Bay he returned to sound the alarm that, without drastic action by the French, the English would persuade most interior Indians to trade with them on James Bay.

The Temagamis and the neighbouring Nipissings were now surrounded on three sides by great imperial forces: the Iroquois to the south (and the English beyond them), the French down the Ottawa valley and east in the interior, and the English sitting enticingly on the salt-water bay. This pattern of competing external influences would long remain a feature of life in the district. The Temagamis continued as subsistence hunters and gatherers who traded furs southeast whenever possible; they were now also making a few lengthy voyages northward – via Matachewan, what later became known as the Frederick House River, and the lower Abitibi and Moose rivers – to the English at Moose Fort. The Temagamis survived, or so it seems, and they remained independent.[39]

Until the late 1670s, the French expected Nipissing and other Algonkian middlemen to transport furs from the interior to the St Lawrence. For a time French authorities encouraged exploration and missions while discouraging *coureurs de bois* and other internal French traders. Indeed, the Canadian *coureurs de bois* were usually acting illegally. The French believed in conserving their very limited resources. But the Nipissings were on the exposed flank, and more and more Algonkian-speaking people were trading north with the English. So in 1673 the French established a temporary fort on Lac Piscoutagamy (now Night Hawk on the Frederick House River) to try to induce such Indians not to travel farther toward James Bay.[40]

Then in 1679 or immediately thereafter, the French established another small fur post on the west shore of Lake Timiskaming, at the easily accessible core of a very rich fur country. Located on a low island (now gone) by the mouths of two rivers, the Montreal and the Matabitchuan or Meydabeejewan ('the place where two rivers come together'), the post, under the auspices of what in 1682 would become the Compagnie du Nord, was intended to provide a direct challenge to the ascendancy of the Hudson's Bay Company. In 1683, on behalf of this concern, Sieur d'Argenteuil received a charter to cover the Timiskaming trade. In a grand sense he was charged with doing all he could to persuade peoples 'from the farthest north' to stop trading with the English at Hudson Bay.[41] The Timiskaming trade was to acquire the bountiful pelts trapped by various Algonkian peoples in the vicinity, including those of the Temagamis, pelts that had formerly been collected by the Nipissings and were now at risk of being traded to the

English.[42] The French now had a post close to the frontier of the N'Daki Menan and on the Temagamis' main eastward route. Although the French usually called all the Indians who came down the two rivers to the post 'Temiscamingues,' they almost certainly contained a preponderance of Temagamis.[43]

In 1686, with a small military force, Pierre Chevalier de Troyes visited the post at Timiskaming for La Compagnie du Nord, proceeded over the height of land, and erected a post on the east shore of Lake Abitibi, before canoeing to James Bay to capture all three English posts of Moose, Albany, and Charles.[44] Although the English successfully recaptured Albany in 1693, de Troyes destroyed Moose and the post at the Rupert when the English evacuated in 1686.

In 1688–9, the Iroquois struck at the French heartland around Lachine and Montreal and also raided Timiskaming, destroying the post and its inhabitants. It is even possible that the Nadoways again raided into the Temagami country.[45] Gradually, however, the French and their Algonkian allies gained the upper hand. The Algonkian 'Ojibway' drove any remaining Nadoway totally out of the north. By 1695 Algonkian-speaking 'Mississaugas' and other Ojibwa had driven the Nadoways and other Iroquoian people out of most of what became southern Ontario, back into the heartland of the Five Nations Confederacy (in what became upstate New York). The victorious 'Ojibwa' warriors came mainly from Manitoulin Island, the north shores of Lake Huron and Georgian Bay, and communities farther north. Among other goals they were interested in circumventing the Iroquois and making direct trading contact with the Anglo-Americans far to the southeast. With England and France briefly not fighting following the 1697 Treaty of Ryswick, peace was established in 1701 between the French and the Algonkian nations on the one hand and the Iroquois on the other.[46] At the peace ceremony there was 'a Temiskaming Indian at the head of a party of his nation,' which, by inference, included the Temagamis.[47]

During the great War of the Spanish Succession from 1702 to 1713, the English did not have the advantage of the Iroquois alliance. The latter remained a powerful but neutral force. Nevertheless, when world-wide geopolitical considerations were taken into account at the signing of the Treaty of Utrecht in 1713, James Bay was restored to the English. Though the Hudson's Bay Company and the French would contest the boundaries of their respective spheres of influence until the Conquest, military conflict was more or less gone from the northland. The Temagamis could trade either way.

A few fleeting and unlicensed earlier attempts notwithstanding, the

French were not persuaded to re-establish a permanent post in the Lake Timiskaming-Abitibi area until 1720. A French map of 1699 identified 'Isle Metebetchouen' and noted there 'un magazin d'entrepos.'[48] Little posts 'chez les Tahitibis' (Abitibis) and on the 'Metebeschouan' are mentioned in a 1701 account. But a 1707 report admitted that most 'Temiskamings' and most 'Abitibis' were trading their furs, which were of high quality, 'aux anglais établis dans le fond de la Baye d'Hudson.'[49]

Fundamental changes had occurred with regard to French imperial policy in North America. In France by the late 1690s, every man, woman, and child who could possibly afford one had a beaver hat. There was a heavy glut of beaver pelts; the quantity 'far exceeded what the market could absorb.' For a time French policy tried to control supply, partly by again trying to insist that the Algonkian canoeists themselves take their skins to the St Lawrence. For the most part, however, the more distant tribes, including the Temagamis, simply refused. In the north, they just canoed to English posts on James Bay. In the southwest, they visited English-American traders over the Appalachians or traded with the Iroquois.

For metropolitan political and military reasons, French policy in North America transcended market forces. Under an aging Louis XIV, France was concerned that English dominance in America would significantly alter the balance of power in Europe and undermine the French hegemony. Only by nurturing and supporting the economic health and independent status of Indian nations in the interior could France contain the English, both along the American seaboard and in Hudson Bay. These Indian nations included those to the southwest, ultimately down to what became New Orleans, as well as the Algonkian peoples to the northwest, almost to the shores of James Bay. For France, beginning in 1701 and continuing through the eighteenth century until the Conquest, 'the fur trade was mainly an economic weapon in Anglo-French imperial rivalry.' This strategy held even though the beaver glut ended about 1730. Without the fur trade, military and diplomatic alliances were impossible. The Algonkian trappers of the Timiskaming-Temagami-Abitibi area had to be dissuaded from canoeing north to James Bay, and their lands and independence had to be guaranteed. The Timiskamings and other Algonkians thus 'dictated the terms of the trade to both the English and the French.' It was competitive trading, eighteenth century style.[50] The Temagamis prospered.

For France, for Canada, and ultimately for Temagami, the French policy required a high commitment and a firm hand in Paris, because the English, including the Americans, outnumbered the French, including the Canadiens, by more than ten to one. The habitants were concentrated in the few seigneuries along the St Lawrence, while land-hungry Americans would soon be streaming westward over the Appalachians. For almost sixty years the policy seemed to work, though ultimately it would fail. Canada would become English, and the Temagamis would lose the French alliance.

Meanwhile, in 1720, Governor Vaudreuil issued a *congé* or licence for the Timiskaming trade to Paul Guillet. Officially, the trading territory covered almost the entire *petit nord*; it stretched from Nipigon on the west to Abitibi on the east, specifically including 'Lac Timagamingue.' Guillet established a major post about 1724 on Lake Timiskaming, this time on its east side, at the Narrows midway up the shoreline. This he did a few years after he had re-established the post on Lake Abitibi. These two posts were supplemented by a series of trading 'huts' or temporary posts, perhaps briefly including one on Lake Temagami. By 1727 the Timiskaming trade had become the third most valuable fur lease in the French Empire after that of Green Bay and the area west of Superior. With wide fluctuations, it continued to grow well into the 1750s.[51]

In an attempt to compete with the French, the Hudson's Bay Company re-established Moose Fort in 1730 and soon made it the company's southern headquarters.[52] Circumstantial evidence suggests that the Temagamis were major traders at the Poste de Temiscamingue, although they were usually subsumed under the general designation 'Temiscamingues' (variously spelled). Later the Temiscamings were more carefully identified interchangeably with the 'Algonquins' around the head of the lake. Sometimes in this period all the Indians around the general Lake Timiskaming area were called *gens de terre*, inland people, sometimes *tête de boule*, sometimes Moosonis *gens de terre*, if they came from the northwest and had previously traded with the English on the Moose; sometimes these terms only referred to Algonkian peoples on the east, that is the present-day Quebec side of the Timiskaming-Ottawa water system. But as Professor W.J. Eccles has argued, the regional population simply had to include Algonkian trappers living in and around lakes Temagami and Smoothwater and trading with the French at Timiskaming. 'Temagami is right in the centre of the trading area ... They were not ghosts. They are not a myth, they are there ... The animals didn't come and skin themselves. Indians had to go out and harvest them and to get the yield of furs they would obviously be getting, you would need a considerable number of Indian hunters.'[53] The use of generic terms did not imply absorption of one tribe by another.[54]

Or, as Edward Rogers argues, if the French had first arrived in the middle, that is around Lake Temagami, people there would have received clear identification and all the others 'would have been funny speakers.'[55]

In the complex controversy relating to the legal nature of aboriginal claims in the Temagami district today, discontinuity in the pattern of occupation is one ingredient in the analysis of those who seek to refute the existence of aboriginal title. The suggestion that the Temagami country was unoccupied for significant parts of the eighteenth century is associated with the proposition that game in the area was exhausted after the Timiskaming post was re-established and that, as a consequence, all or most of the population moved elsewhere or starved. This conclusion is supported partly on the basis of the scarcity of records from the Timiskaming post. In Eccles' view, this analysis rests on 'no evidence at all,' and the reverse may well be true. He explains the scarcity of records from the fact that the French military were the ones who kept the better records. As the local Indians were independent allies, the Timiskaming post did not have to be armed, and there was no potential military threat. Lack of records cannot be equated with lack of trade or lack of a people with whom to trade.[56]

The affirmative case for continuing occupation is supported by the fact that some Temagamis were recorded as continuing to trade occasionally at Fort Albany and at Moose Fort when the latter was re-established. The English identified them as Soushoagamy, 'Smoothwater People,' coming from Shoonswewagamingue or Smoothwater Lake in the N'Daki Menan. The journey followed a direct route down the East Montreal, over an easy portage, and down the Frederick House and Moose rivers to James Bay.[57] But by the 1740s, the Soushoagamy had ceased travelling to James Bay. In part this was due to the fact that the French posts offered better terms for their furs, by treating the smaller marten pelts as equivalent in value to one beaver; it was also due to the French custom of carrying goods from the main stations right to the Indians.[58] 'This mobility gave them an enormous advantage over their English rivals on the Bay, who were content to remain where they were and wait for the Indians to come down to them.'[59]

The final struggle between France and England for ascendancy in eastern North America came during the Seven Years' War, which lasted from 1756 to 1763. Conflict had actually begun in the Ohio valley in 1755, one year before war had been officially declared in Europe. For North America, the struggle ended in 1760 with the capitulation of Montreal, one year after the fall of Quebec. French policy still called for

French control, through Indian allies, of the Ohio-Mississippi corridor. The Iroquois had thought that the Ohio was within their imperial domain, while the restless American colonists regarded it as territory available for their own expansion. But for the time being the Americans, the Iroquois, and the English worked together to frustrate the French and their vast array of Indian allies.

The French, the Canadiens, and their Indian allies, including the various Algonkian-speaking nations, fought valiantly. The allied Indians were a 'tremendous military force.' The French supplied them with military support and their families with food, thus freeing the Indians 'so they could apply their time to hunting English; from hunting deer.'[60] Frequent references exist to those who fought alongside the French, the Nipissings, *gens de terre,* and Indians from the Pays d'en haut.[61] Non-participation by the Temagamis would have been quite anomalous. Then in 1760 the St Lawrence fell to the English, and in 1763, at the Peace of Paris, Canada and the interior were permanently ceded to Britain. And what of the independent Algonkian allies? What about the Temagamis and their N'Daki Menan?

The warriors among the *gens de terre* returned to their families and homelands in the northland. More than two thousand from north of the Great Lakes, from the *petit nord,* had been involved, and it would be 'astonishing' if the number had not included any from the Temagami country.[62] But the French traders had forever left their *postes* at Timiskaming and Abitibi, and to trade the Temagamis now had to cross the height of land to visit the English at Moose Fort.

Far to the southwest, beyond Detroit in the Illinois and the Ohio country, the situation was quite different. There the Indian nations felt particularly deserted and isolated, while they continued to want European goods, including arms. English Americans seemed to be enveloping them – potential colonists, land speculators, traders. These Americans did not seem to like Indians. The British soldiers, in the few places where they existed, were sometimes sympathetic, sometimes not; they seemed condescending and rarely helpful. In this frustrating situation, many of the aboriginal nations rallied, rose, and fought under their great leader Pontiac. For some time they were astonishingly successful. Many forts that the British had just taken over from the French fell. Ultimately, however, the Indian nations' shortage of arms proved decisive, and the English broke the back of the Pontiac alliance. For the British it had been an expensive episode. Increasingly, London authorities perceived the real problem to be their unruly land-hungry American subjects, not the Indians. Something had to be done. The obvious answer was to adopt the former French policy: guarantee the interior Indians their autonomy and their homelands, not only in the southwest but in the north as well.

The result, on 7 October 1763, was the Royal Proclamation of King George III. Part four of the proclamation was specifically designed to halt the 'Great Frauds and Abuses' committed, presumably by Americans, against 'the several Nations or Tribes of Indians, with whom we are connected, or who live under our Protection.' (Recently the Constitution Act, 1982, explicitly preserved any rights or freedoms recognized by the proclamation.) By the same proclamation, 'Canada' became 'Quebec' with boundaries strictly confined to what is now southern Quebec and a narrowing wedge up the Ottawa River and westward to the southern tip of Lake Nipissing. The Temagami country was thus clearly not within 'Canada,' which was now to be called 'Quebec.' Rather, it was protected as Indian land.

Part four of the Royal Proclamation identified British-claimed lands outside the various colonies and outside the jurisdiction of the Hudson's Bay Company as being 'Our Territories.' In these 'Countries' the Indian nations were 'not to be molested or disturbed in the Possession of' their lands, which 'not having been ceded to or purchased by Us are reserved to them or any of them, as their Hunting Grounds.' Persons who had already 'seated themselves upon any Lands within the Countries above described' were to 'remove themselves' forthwith. Everywhere, even within the defined boundaries of the various colonies, now about eighteen in number, Indian lands could be ceded only through public negotiations and only directly to the Crown. The proclamation implied that land outside the colonies would not, in fact, be ceded in the foreseeable future. The point was that neither American settlers nor English soldiers were to molest the autonomous Indian peoples who lived under royal British protection, including the inhabitants of Temagami.

In the face of an almost irresistible tide of American settlers streaming over the mountains, the British policy quickly proved ineffectual southwest of the Great Lakes. In fact, the American Revolution began twelve years after the Royal Proclamation was issued. In contrast, with some exceptions the policy seemed to prevail for a long time in the northwest where settlers and lumbermen were still distant.

With the Royal Proclamation the homeland of the Temagamis, whatever its actual bounds at the time, was within the extended confines of the British Empire. Nevertheless, the Temagami people remained more or less sovereign. N'Daki Menan, previously recognized and protected by the French, was now guaranteed by the British. British authorities wished this guarantee and pledge to be interpreted generously and liberally. That was the policy's self-interested purpose. It certainly was not meant to be restrictive on the Indian or to freeze tribal boundaries forever. Even if the bulk of the ancestors or the current Teme-augami Anishnabai moved into the Temagami country after 1763 (which seems most unlikely), their 'Hunting Grounds' would still have been protected by the proclamation.[63]

Although the Hudson's Bay Company factor at Moose Fort reported in 1761 that English-speaking traders from Montreal were already 'as thick as Muskettos' in the interior, Fort Timiskaming on the site of the old French *poste* appears not to have been permanently established until the mid-1770s.[64] Rather quickly, however, various Montreal 'Pedlars,' the future Nor'Westers, immigrants from Scotland, New England, and upstate New York, were taking over and expanding the fur trade once managed by the French. Soon they were using French Canadian and Métis voyageurs to paddle their great freight canoes. The HBC monopoly was very short-lived. Again rival metropolitan forces would impinge upon the Temagami country.[65]

In 1774, as the Americans to the south became increasingly restless, the British greatly extended the Quebec colonial boundary so as to include the Ohio valley and, it seemed, all of present-day Ontario south of the height of land. Then, in 1791, this 'Quebec' was divided into the provinces of Upper Canada west of the Ottawa and Lower Canada to the east. Unceded and still 'protected,' N'Daki Menan now seemed to be included within the boundaries of a British colony, one in whose southern lands Loyalists and British and American immigrants were settling in significant numbers.

Soon the 'Canadian trade' was again getting the better of the James Bay trade. Inland Indians in the Abitibi-Timiskaming area and beyond generally traded their best furs for the lighter goods, such as cloth, handled by the Pedlars; they traded inferior summer pelts for the guns and shot and Brazilian tobacco handled only on James Bay. Sometimes the Pedlars themselves persuaded Indians to travel to James Bay and buy heavy goods to resell to the locals. The Pedlars also dispersed very generous amounts of 'debt,' that is commodity advances to the Indians to tie them to the Canadian trade. This proved more effective than the red captain's uniforms sometimes given by the HBC to prominent inland Indians, including, apparently, some 'Soushoagamys' from Smoothwater.

To meet the competition HBC traders reversed the century-old policy against interior posts. In 1774 Cumberland House on the Saskatchewan River in the far northwest became the HBC's first inland house. South of James Bay the company established Wapiscogamy or Brunswick House, near the Upper Missinaibi, tentatively in 1777 and as a fully operational post from 1781 to 1791. New Brunswick House began operations in 1788 on Micabanish or 'Brunswick Lake' just west of the Upper Missinaibi to compete with Pedlars around Michipicoten. In 1785, the company opened Frederick House, just a few miles north of the height of land from the N'Daki Menan, on what had been called the Piscoutagamy on the Temagamis' main route to James Bay.[66]

At first the various Pedlars in the Timiskaming-Abitibi area were only loosely allied; sometimes they were even in competition one with another. For a time Donald McKay and his brother operated a little post on Lake Mistinikon on the West Montreal upstream from Matachewan. This place, often called Langue de Terre, had probably been a subpost for a time during the French regime. It was actually within the confines of the N'Daki Menan. In 1789 William Grant and his partner, Richard Dobie, bought out the interests of former Montreal firms that had been in the Timiskaming trade, and in 1790 purchased the supplies of a remaining competitor from Abitibi. In 1792 the Grant-Dobie interests opened a subpost on an island right beside Frederick House. Two years later the Hudson's Bay Company opened two small new houses, one on Lake Abitibi and one on the west side of Kenogamissi Lake on the Upper Mattagami. This location was selected to replace the unprofitable Frederick House and to compete with Langue de Terre for the western Temagami and neighbouring trade. The same year, 1794, the Timiskaming interests countered by having Donald McKay establish, about thirty miles to the south, what was to become the important post of Matawagamingue on Lake Mattagami, slightly northeast of present day Gogama. Although many of the Pedlars in 1787 had organized themselves into the North West Company, it was 1795 before the Nor'Westers, apparently greatly assisted by Alexander Mackenzie, reached a final merger agreement with the Grant-Dobie-Cameron interests and were ready again to take on the Hudson's Bay Company in earnest, both in the *petit nord* and in the far northwest.[67]

In the next few years, this second wave of intense fur trade competition reached its peak. In 1797 the Hudson's Bay Company established a house right under the noses of the Nor'Westers at Michipicoten, and in 1800 the latter established two sites, one called the Flying Post at the source of the Groundhog, a tributary of the Mattagami, and one at Hayes Island on the Moose River itself, just upstream from Factory Island. By 1806 each side had pulled back from this overextension. With the commercial rivalry of the HBC and the North West Company, the Temagamis and other inland Algonkians began 'playing off one company or concern against the other.'[68] During this period the Temagamis traded with the HBC at Frederick House and Kenogamissi House and with the Nor'Westers at Matawagamingue and Fort Timiskaming.[69]

By 1813 the HBC had abandoned all but one of its southern posts, including Frederick House, retaining Kenogamissi, from which, the next year, it established an outpost 'within range of a glass of Matawagamingue.'[70] The rivals literally chased prospective Indian trappers to entice them to do business.[71] Although it seemed throughout the interior of 'British' North America that the Nor'Westers had the slight advantage, both trading networks became overextended; finally, in 1821, the Nor'Westers merged with the Hudson's Bay Company under the latter's ascendancy. This was to be a bitter blow for Algonkian Indians. Monopoly was not good news, and they knew it. Ties with the north would become tenuous, even though the political situation had changed drastically since the Royal Proclamation.

Although centred on Lake Temagami, the wider homeland of the Temagami Indians included lands draining north to James Bay, south to Lake Nipissing and Georgian Bay, and east via Lake Timiskaming and the Ottawa to the St Lawrence. Thus geography, while exposing the N'Daki Menan to a variety of cultural and commercial contacts, simultaneously reduced the likelihood of sustained dominance by any one source of external influence. Not surprisingly, the history of the Temagami country has involved a continuous process of adaptation and reversion as a succession of economic, cultural, and political interests have entered the area and been forced in their turn to accommodate to the evolving local dynamic.

CHAPTER TWO

Just beyond the Canadian Periphery: The Temagami Indians in the Nineteenth Century

'Of all the places I have been since I came to Hudson's Bay, this is the most wretched of all.'

James Hackland, Temagami Island post, 1857

The fur monopoly established by the merger of the Hudson's Bay and North West companies in 1821 presented new problems for the Temagami Indians. But the unchallenged ascendancy of the HBC would be imperfect and short-lived as a number of small-scale competitors penetrated the area from the south and southwest. Furthermore, the increased commercial incursions from both the HBC and its local rivals were only one of several types of contact experienced by the Temagamis over the sixty or so years following the merger of the two fur trade empires. Taken together, the effects of the different incursions were at once economic, social, and political. The community and its ecological base survived potential crises of disease, fire, and commercial conflict. Yet slowly, the Temagami district would be brought closer to the orbit of Canadian influences. Although this area was ignored – probably because of oversight or neglect – when in 1850 Canadian officials treatied with the aboriginal residents of lands along the shores of Georgian Bay, the North Channel of Lake Huron, and Lake Superior, the Canadian influence around Temagami increased. In the 1870s, following Confederation and Canadian acquisition of the vast Northwest from the Hudson's Bay Company, the Temagamis, now geographically within Ontario, sought unsuccessfully to be included in the evolving treaty system designed for aboriginal peoples.

The earliest nineteenth-century fur traders actually stationed in the Temagami country were apparently agents of the American Fur Company who operated out of Sault Ste Marie and established a short-lived post on Lake Temagami in the fall of 1821. Chief Factor Joseph Beioley of the Hudson's Bay Company who was touring Timiskaming in June 1822 learned from an informant that 'the American Company have established a Post this Season at a large Lake where they get abundance of Fish – and which he considered to be between Lake Nipissing and Lake Timiskaming in a S.W. direction – about 3 days walk in the Spring of the Year and about 4 days paddling from the latter Place.' Beioley's source, Angus Cameron, had served in the district for twenty years at Matawagamingue post. The new post, Cameron advised his visitor, was already interfering with HBC operations.[1] Cameron's limited knowledge of Lake Temagami is evidence of both Temagami's isolation and the previous absence of active trading there.

Throughout the 1820s and 1830s transient independent traders moving up the French River to Lake Nipissing and beyond threatened to disrupt the HBC monopoly in the *petit nord*. The company was trying to keep prices at Timiskaming the same as those at Moose Fort, and its traders were trying to limit credit. The arrival of free traders made the Indians appear 'disloyal' to the HBC when in fact they were merely engaging in competitive marketing. In 1825 Cameron reported that 'Petrimeaux and a band of vagabonds from Timagaming came in with a few skins' and that 'runaways from here to Lake Huron and Nipesangue are at Timagaming at present.' Chief Trader John McBean at La Cloche on the north shore of Georgian Bay informed Fort Timiskaming that 'Tebendeau,' another Temagami Indian, had 'gone over' to the 'opposition' on Lake Nipissing, taking many others with him and returning with a strong invitation to urge 'your Indians to come and trade Blankets and cloth at 1 La [large] Beaver each.'[2] The free traders secured financing from merchants at Newmarket, Sandwich, and especially Penetanguishene. For the Temagamis this marked the introduction of 'the Georgian Bay interests.' This new Upper Canadian influence would soon be linked financially to York (called Toronto after 1834) and would thereafter be a continuing factor in the evolution of the Temagami district.

Governor George Simpson, who took over the HBC's Northern Department in 1821, and both the Southern and Montreal departments by 1826, was the crucial and dynamic figure in the company during these years and until 1860. Governor Simpson clearly believed that the prolongation of the company's fur trade in the *petit nord*, especially the Timiskaming-Abitibi districts, depended upon isolating the nearby Algonkians from significant contact with Canadians. In 1827 and 1830 he transferred Abitibi and then Timiskaming to the company's Southern Department from the Montreal Department. As much as possible these posts were to be outfitted from James Bay, and Indians were thoroughly discouraged from canoeing southeast down the Ottawa River. Nevertheless most food provisioning and liquor still came up from Montreal. In 1834 Simpson even transferred the Nipissing trade from the Lake Huron District (La Cloche), where it had been since the North West Company era, to the Timiskaming District, in a further effort to cut contacts with 'Canada.'[3]

The Temagami country was an important part of the rich Timiskaming trade. In 1830 Simpson argued that no part of the country had surpassed the returns from Timiskaming and that it had been the generous credit and trade policies of the Pedlars that had attracted Indians to Montreal. This had to be reversed. The Lake Huron areas, however, were doomed, he admitted; agents there should urge Indians to hunt their lands out, before petty and ruthless fur trade competition and the encroachment of lumbermen and settlers destroyed the trade anyway.[4]

Governor Simpson's policy of 'stabilization' could not work permanently.[5] Even HBC supplies for Timiskaming and hence Temagami increasingly came up the less costly Ottawa route. By 1839 regular winter sleigh transport extended as far north as Mattawa. Furthermore, Nipissing and Temagami Indians welcomed the competition supplied by Georgian Bay interests. In 1833 Samuel Peck and Charles Harris, two free traders working from Penetanguishene who had been regularly trading on Nipissing, moved up to Lake Temagami and wintered over there into 1834 'with a large outfit.'[6] Unless agents of the American Fur Company stayed over in 1821–2, Peck and Harris were probably the first Europeans to winter on Lake Temagami.

Chief Trader Angus Cameron at Fort Timiskaming moved quickly to have Harris bought off and enlisted into the service of the HBC. He sent Chief Trader Richard Hardisty to Nipissing to check the entire Georgian Bay advance. He dispatched Harris himself back to Temagami in September 1834 to open an official outpost. The 'Temagamingue' post was thus established on the south side of Katay-Teme-augama, 'Old Temagami Island,' just beyond the ancient Wabikon, the summer

'Flower' settlement of the Temagamis. After the winter of 1834–5, the harassed Peck left Temagami for good.[7]

In 1836 Governor Simpson justified to the HBC's London Committee the establishment of the Temagami post on the grounds that it would collect the furs trapped in the area by what he called the Lake Nipissing Indians, 'who, without it were in danger of falling into the hands of the opposition on Lake Nipisingue.'[8] Simpson used the term 'Nipissing Indians' to refer to Temagami Indians who had previously, he assumed, traded down by the mouth of the Sturgeon River at the HBC's Sturgeon Hall. But it is true, according to the Temagamingue Debt Book for 1838–40, that Indians from south of the N'Daki Menan were also trading at the outpost.[9] Generally speaking, though, the Temagami outpost was supplied from Timiskaming and open only from autumn to spring, with three or four hands hired to transport the outfit, to tend the potato garden, and to make the fall fishery.

Indians from Temagami continued to trade at neighbouring HBC posts, including Fort Timiskaming, Nipissing and Matawagamingue. They also dealt with opposition traders, such as Cawayass, a Nipissing Indian who had worked at the Temagami outpost until 1840 when he went into opposition, and Roderick McKenzie out of Mattawa, also a former HBC employee who collected the furs of Temagami Chief Nebanegwune when the outpost was closed. The Temagamis traded wherever they thought they could get the best deal. Simpson was able to inform the HBC's London Committee in 1836 that the trade was slowly increasing and that the overall Timiskaming and Abitibi hunting grounds were as rich in furs as at any time in living memory.[10]

The Temagami post remained a subsidiary of the Timiskaming district throughout the nineteeth century – although district headquarters was shifted from Fort Timiskaming to Mattawa around 1883–4. The post's fluctuating fortunes of expansion and abandonment continued to be closely tied to the activities of the HBC's opposition. Although there was no urgent need to maintain the Temagami post on a continuous basis, the HBC faced recurring incursions from independent traders. So until 1857 the HBC operated the Temagami post only intermittently. In 1846 illness – probably tuberculosis – and manpower shortages resulting from attractive alternative employment in the south closed the post until 1848 when a new recruit was found to fill the vacancy. Thus, from about 1836, a semi-permanent European presence existed on Lake Temagami and, despite temporary periods of inactivity, that outside influence would never really be removed.

Military rather than commercial considerations brought one early visitor to Temagami in the late summer of 1837. David Taylor of Kingston – a lieutenant in the Royal Engineers – stopped briefly at the HBC's post on the east side of Temagami Island in the course of a survey for the Upper Canadian Legislature to determine 'the practicability of making a navigable communication between the Ottawa and Lake Huron.' Taylor's exploratory journey was one of three undertaken for the same purpose at a time when the security of Upper Canada's communications network along the Great Lakes route was considered vulnerable to the United States.[11]

In Toronto, where he arrived under orders with 'six barrels of pork, and nine of biscuits, one tent etc.,' Taylor reported for final instructions from the colonial government. Proceeding via Yonge Street to Holland Landing, Taylor completed arrangements for provisions and equipment in nearby Newmarket and secured the services of a canoeman, Louis Tupas, 'at three pounds fifteen shillings per month, with the promise, if he behaved well, and exerted himself, something was to be added when our exploring should cease.' All three survey parties set off on the Holland River on 27 July, headed for Lake Simcoe and on to Penetanguishene where they separated to begin exploration.

Taylor's route took him along the shore of Georgian Bay and up the French River to the HBC post on Lake Nipissing. From here, the party proceeded up the Sturgeon River to the 'Forks' at the mouth of the Temagami River where the community of River Valley is now situated. Taylor found that the waters of the Temagami River were shallow in late August. On 1 September, he entered 'Lake Tamagamingue' and concluded that as a means of communication between the Ottawa River and Lake Huron his route was unpromising. The land, he reported, was 'craggy and broken,' 'principally granite.' Pine and white cedar forests along with 'ash, beach, birch and larch, of an inferior growth' covered a terrain ill-suited to agricultural use (agricultural potential appeared to be Taylor's definition of 'good land'). The accounts of local Indians led him to believe that to the north and northwest the land was even 'worse.' But the Temagami Lake waters were 'deep and beautifully clear,' abounding in fish. After two nights at the HBC post on Temagami Island, Taylor pressed on up the Northeast Arm en route to Timiskaming. Taylor clearly did not regard his route through Temagami as a propitious one. Indeed, from 1837 until the mid-fifties, the district seems to have been forgotten by government officials from Canada.

By the end of the forties, however, mineral exploration and preliminary extraction along the north shores of lakes Superior and Huron, including Georgian Bay, aroused interest in the area just to the south of Temagami.[12] Indians had not surrendered their lands, and aboriginal title was unclear. In 1846, Chief Shinwauk (or Shinguakouse) of the Garden River community along Lake Huron's North Channel complained to George Ironside, Indian agent on Manitoulin Island, that mining was widespread on Indian land. Indeed, the Montreal Mining Company had obtained rights to a very large tract. Although Indian affairs technically remained a British responsibility until 1860, Canadian authorities in the new and 'responsible' Lafontaine-Baldwin Reform ministry agreed with the governor-general, Lord Elgin, in 1849 that it would be highly desirable to obtain unimpaired title. T.G. Anderson, superintendent of Indian affairs for Canada West, and a provincial land surveyor named Alexander Vidal were dispatched to visit Indian coastal communities in preparation for a treaty. They travelled west to Fort William by steamer and most of the way back to southern Georgian Bay by open canoe in rough and cold late-autumn weather, but they did not travel inland to consult non-coastal communities. Anderson, who subsequently expressed the view that he had arranged for the Indians to cede land 'from Pentanguishene along Lake Huron and Lake Superior and back to Nippegon,' was somewhat offended not to be asked to participate in the formal treaty ceremony that followed his expedition.[13]

In November, before the Vidal-Anderson report was submitted, Chiefs Shinwauk and Nubenaigooching and up to a hundred Indians and Métis clashed with officials of the Quebec and Lake Superior Mining Company at Mica Bay on Lake Superior; fortunately no lives were lost. A rival mining promoter, Allan Macdonell, had evidently encouraged the Indian resistance. The government dispatched a force of a hundred rifles to the area. The chiefs, Macdonell, and others were arrested and transported to Toronto. Elgin and the Executive Council in January 1850 appointed the experienced William Benjamin Robinson, brother of Chief Justice John Beverley Robinson and of Peter Robinson, and thus a member of the most prominent Tory family in Toronto, to treat with the Indians. He visited various coastal communities in the spring and summer of 1850 and invited the Indians to attend grand councils at Sault Ste Marie in early September. Lord Elgin himself made a state visit in late August.[14]

Negotiations on the surrender of aboriginal land rights proceeded in two separate councils and resulted in the two Robinson treaties, one covering the lands fronting on Lake Superior and the other the lands fronting on Lake Huron, including northern and eastern Georgian Bay.[15]

The assembled chiefs and headmen were assured that only small portions of the lands in question were suitable for European-style agriculture, that mining and, in the future, forestry were of much greater concern. Most of the land would remain Crown land. The Robinson-Huron treaty guaranteed 'the said chiefs and their tribes the full and free privilege to hunt over the territory now ceded by them and to fish in the waters as they have heretofore been in the habit of doing,' except those portions sold or leased to individuals or companies. The treaty thus seemed to give greater recognition to the continuation of traditional life-styles than had previous treaties recently concluded with respect to more southerly lands.

Whether the Indian residents of the Temagami district who occupied territory on either side of the James Bay watershed were represented in some way at the signing of the Robinson-Huron treaty to surrender their ancestral lands has become a subject of intense controversy. There is no evidence to suggest that the Temagami Indians were invited to the councils at Sault Ste Marie. Perhaps their existence was not even mentioned to Robinson as he was preparing for the negotiations. Neither Chief Nebanegwune nor any other person from Lake Temagami or the entire N'Daki Menan attended or signed the Robinson-Huron treaty, in which neither the Temagami Indians nor Lake Temagami itself were mentioned.

Later, however, government authorities generally assumed that the land cession covered by the Robinson-Huron treaty extended northward to the James Bay divide, then the boundary between the Province of Canada and the HBC territory of Rupert's Land. Although the agreement states that the treaty was between the Crown and 'Ojibway Indians, inhabiting and claiming the eastern and northern shores of Lake Huron ... and inland to the height of land,' the government's interest in the north was then largely restricted to coastal areas along the Great Lakes. Indeed, even the description of the alleged northeasterly limits of the land involved is open to at least two interpretations. The treaty designated twenty-one Indian reservations for the seventeen identified bands and provided for the immediate distribution of £2,160 among these communities and a perpetual annuity of £600 cash subject to possible future adjustments based on population or resource yield.

Inland 'Indians inhabiting French River and Nipissing' – that is, two specifically identified bands led by chiefs Dokis and Shabokishick – were added in a separate paragraph to the original fifteen bands, almost as an appendage, hence the £160 addition to the original £2,000 grant. Authorities seemed rather vague about the designation of 'a band' or indeed a tribe, but under the Royal Proclamation of 1763 British negotiators did recognize that groups of Indians and their chiefs could not surrender land that was not part of their hunting grounds.

Chief Tagawinini, who did sign the treaty, led a small community of Indians concentrated around Lake Wanapitei ('Wanabitibing' in the treaty). That lake empties south via the Wanapitei River into the French. Tagawinini and his 'band' received a small reserve, two miles square, near the southwest corner of Lake Wanapitei. In legal proceedings regarding land claims around Lake Temagami, the Ontario government recently argued that the Lake Wanapitei reserve was also intended to serve the Temagami people whose leader, Nebanegwune, had allegedly been a mere headman of such limited status that he did not merit an invitation to the treaty ceremony.[16] Yet the Temagamis' social and commercial relations at the time were primarily south to Lake Nipissing, east to Lake Timiskaming, and north over the divide, not to the southwest. In fact, a wedge of the Nipissings' hunting territory actually lay between the N'Daki Menan and Lake Wanapitei in the complex Chinaguchi area.

The first record of the Temagamis' involvement with officials regarding land claims was in 1849. Twenty-two Temagamis ('Tawnawgawming' in the documents) had travelled to Manitowaning that year and, along with other Indian groups, had 'taken presents' from George Ironside, the Indian superintendent. These traditional ceremonies of gift exchange were something quite separate from annuities under treaty and of course predated the Robinson-Huron agreement. In August 1850, Chief Nebanegwune himself and fifteen other Temagamis again participated in the ceremonies at Manitowaning. The British authorities decided to end such 'costly' presentations in Canada in 1851; they gradually curtailed the value of the gifts until 1858 when the practice ceased. In 1851 twenty-one Temagamis led by Kakaka canoed to Manitowaning for the gifts, and in 1852, thirty-five Temagamis, including Kakaka and perhaps Nebanegwune made the voyage for what may have been the last time. On these two occasions (and perhaps in 1850, although the visit of that year appears to precede the formal signing of the Robinson treaties), several Temagamis seem casually to have accepted treaty money as well. Nebanegwune may even have requested treaty money for a last time in 1855.[17] However, the Temagamis received no reserve, recognized no political link with Tagawinini and his band from Lake Wanapitei, and repeatedly claimed that they had not been a party to the Robinson treaties.[18] The resolution of these issues has occupied Canadian and provincial officials for more than a century and has profoundly affected the relationship between the Temagami Indians and other later arrivals to a district that became a highly valued part of the provincial landscape. Yet at the time of the Robinson-Huron treaty, the interests of hopeful resource developers centred on the Great Lakes area: the Temagami district remained largely unknown and ignored.

'Of all the places I have been since I came to Hudson's Bay this is the most wretched of all,' wrote James Hackland upon arrival at the Temagami Island post in October 1857.[19] Two months later, when the chimney of the post manager's house blew down, Hackland pronounced the dwelling to be 'the most confounded place I have ever been exposed to since I came in the service.'[20] In response, the new manager – whose commitment to improvement may have been strengthened by the presence of his wife – initiated a period of sustained development on the site and expansion of facilities, establishing the foundation on which the post operations rested for nearly two decades.

In the new year, 'White Bear' (Wabimakwa), 'White Bear's son,' and his grandson, Tonené, were employed squaring logs for a new dwelling house, one of several new buildings at the post. These men, who first appear here and in the records of history as humble employees of a vast and foreign commercial empire, later became leaders of the Temagami people. In 1864, seven years after his arrival on Lake Temagami, Hackland was comfortable enough to have commenced sawing posts for a new porch.[21] At the time of his departure to assist ailing Chief Trader J.W. Simpson at Timiskaming, Hackland had secured the foundations of the HBC's Temagami operations and had established more or less regular trade relations with the Teme-augama Anishnabai. Cana Chintz, White Bear, Sayaguasay, Wendaban, and their families came frequently to the Temagami Island post, leaving furs and acquiring, as the HBC account books indicate, a wide range of material goods. But the most significant era of the Temagami trade, a period of intense competition with a succession of independent traders, still lay ahead.

Continuous efforts to monitor the movements of opposition traders were vital to the success of the HBC in areas where competitors were common. Close surveillance was standard practice between Timiskaming and Temagami where the post manager was expected to 'keep a good lookout in your quarter for strange gentry. We are determined to protect the trade as far as we can.'[22] In the fall of 1865 an Indian from the Nipissing district provided advance warning that opposition traders approaching from the south should be expected in the area. Three weeks later Sayaguasay confirmed that an opposition party was on its way. This news sent the post's new manager, John Stockland, into action on the lookout for the rivals and raised his suspicions about which of the local Indians were loyal and which were helping the competition.[23]

Twenty-five bags of flour found in the bush on a small island were Stockland's first real indication that the opposition had entered the Temagami country. The arrival of Dokis (appearing in the records as Duggas, Dukis, Duchas, and Michel L'Aigle) produced for Stockland and his assistants a more active winter than they might otherwise have experienced. Additional trade goods and even a small lodge on Lake Capenmeckapmack, about half a day's travel to the southeast, were needed to respond to the opposition. Another party of opposition traders was less closely covered. Stockland, who had been in bad health from the time of his arrival at Temagami, found constant monitoring of the rival traders a difficult burden: 'self for my d——d shanty to see after our neighbours.' But he expressed confidence that the opposition was not doing well and that the Indians by and large were deterred from active trading: 'the Indians would give them furs,' he wrote, 'but they are afraid and what they do give them is done very quietly.'[24] The Temagami post manager was satisfied with the results of the first serious season of competition from Dokis when the opposition left for Lake Nipissing in mid-May with 'very little furs as far as I can learn.'[25]

Dokis returned to Temagami the next fall and succeeded in doubling his previous season's total to ten packs of furs, despite the strenuous efforts of Stockland's crew. To prevent furs from falling into opposition hands, the HBC traders were even forced to collect them from Indian camps. Stockland knew this was a 'bad habit,' but he concluded that there were 'plenty traders not far distant that will gladly do it.' Opposition traders also frequently introduced liquor, sometimes in generous quantities, to the Temagami fur trade. In the mid-1870s George Lennon, master of the Temagami post, expressed particular alarm over the influence of liquor traders, including Dokis, on Temagami Indians.[26]

Lennon believed that the Dokis operation – despite its persistence – was sufficiently vulnerable that 'if the Company can by almost any hazard prevent him from getting the furs he will not be able to meet his liabilities and must eventually give away' and 'have to sink.' Lennon urged a concerted effort against him and other opposition traders active between Temagami and Matachewan. To Colin Rankin, his immediate superior at Timiskaming, Lennon proposed a new strategy for the development of the Temagami post, a strategy again founded clearly on the assumption that Temagami's contribution to the HBC lay as much in its ability to shelter the interior trade from competition as in its own fur-producing potential. He recommended a new post between Temagami and Matachewan in order to reduce the expense of winter voyaging in the area and to strengthen the role of the two existing posts.[27] Rankin received a similar message one year later from another Temagami post manager, advocating a small post at Round Lake.[28] But the initiative passed again to Dokis, who planned to strike directly at the centre of the HBC's operations on Lake Temagami itself.

By the mid-1870s the pressure of fur trade competition in the Temagami district had taken its toll on the facilities of the old Temagami Island post. At the start of the 1874 outfit George Lennon found the house 'in a miserable condition ... pretty old and shakey' and very much in need of repair.[29] His immediate successor, Arthur Ryder, thought the post was on its last legs and in 1875, for strategic reasons, recommended relocating to Bear Island at the centre of the lake:

> Duckas intends, I believe to build near here next summer. He has chosen the best site on the lake – viz – just where all the roads to this post, except one, meet. As it would be impossible to compete with him successfully while this post remains in its present position, I would urge its removal to the same place as Duckas intends to build. The dwelling house must be rebuilt soon, and it is as easy to put up a new one there as here. It is certainly for the company's interest that the move be made, and I therefore hope it will meet with your approval.[30]

Beginning work almost immediately, the HBC cleared and occupied the site Dokis had intended to use, thereby forcing him to locate on an adjacent but less desirable property. By the fall of 1876, construction of four buildings was completed – a dwelling house (thirty-two by twenty-two feet), a store (thirty-one by thirteen feet), a provision store (eighteen by fourteen feet), and a kitchen (nineteen by twelve feet). Dokis was a mere twenty yards away.[31]

The small HBC contingent at Temagami was constantly on the move during the 1875–6 season, responding to active competition from both Dokis and a trader named Ninnywish. 'Both the Oppositions are walking now in every direction and I must keep the men constantly on the move.' Dokis' decision to locate within twenty yards of the new Bear Island post permitted Arthur Ryder and his assistants to keep track of Indian trading with the opposition. This may have been a contributing factor to the post's success in the 1876 outfit when trade at Temagami surpassed previous years' totals in mid-March. By comparison, Dokis and Ninnywish fared very poorly. Yet both returned to Temagami in the fall of 1877 with more goods than ever. The Dokis operation grew still more the following season, with both Dokis and his associates active in the district around Matachewan. Ninnywish established a trading point on the Sturgeon River late in the season and then began to build another near Matawagamingue. Though Ryder was unable to monitor this additional opposition outpost, he was confident that Dokis would keep a close watch and that the two would end 'cutting one another's throats.' During the late 1870s Ninnywish also traded around Ryder's subpost on Diamond Lake, Fort Destruction, which was largely maintained, despite its cost, to check the competition.[32]

In addition to surveillance of the opposition, timely visits to Indian camp grounds, and even the intermittent operation of outposts such as Lake Capenmeckapmack or Fort Destruction, HBC efforts against competitors involved the careful maintenance of the trade relationship with the individual residents of the Temagami country. Post managers, operating within tariff guidelines established for the Timiskaming district and very much aware of the seasonal patterns of life in the region, were responsible for the debt accounts of the Indians. The debt relationship was a significant economic instrument of the fur trade. It was also a most direct source of strain between post managers and the Temagami people: 'But once those indolent d——ls get a bag of flour at there back it don't cost them a thought where the next one is to come from.'[33]

Along with competition in the district, the Indians' preferences and occasional lack of interest greatly affected the HBC's trade in furs at the Temagami post. In 1857, for example, James Hackland accounted for the limited success of the local trade with the argument that the Temagami Indians go where they can get the trade goods they desire. A year later the post manager recorded that the White Bear family produced little fur for Temagami: 'I suppose they are afraid if they came here they would not get so much as at Témiscamingue.'[34] But at Timiskaming Simpson insisted that fur prices were the same at both trading posts and urged Hackland to ignore White Bear's complaint about the local tariff.

'I wish very much,' Arthur Ryder complained bitterly to Colin Rankin of the 1875–6 cash tariff, 'that whoever made it had to try to get fur at those prices on Temag-gue lake just one year!' Dokis and Ninnywish were paying prices above the HBC tariff, as Ryder himself proposed to do 'rather than lose furs unless you forbid it when you write.' Somewhat more calmly Ryder wrote again at the start of the next outfit to ascertain the highest price he might pay for fur and to express a strong preference for Dokis's practice – 'pay a nominally good price for the Fur and charge high for the goods.' An attempt was soon made to apply this precise strategy. When Ninnywish's high fur prices forced the Temagami post traders to increase their own payments, John Turner, an assistant at the post, initiated an agreement with Ninnywish to raise the price of flour from $10.00 to $12.50.[35] Temagami traders looked forward, however, to occasional brief periods of comfortable monopoly in the local trade. When Dokis left the district temporarily in the early spring of 1879, John Cummins, who had taken over Ryder's responsibilities as post manager, contemplated with satisfaction the prospect that 'I can do what I like now.'[36]

The Temagami post managers anxiously monitored the debt relationship of the Temagami band members. When Cana Chintz traded a good part of his furs elsewhere and was unable to pay his debt to the HBC, Stockland 'told him he had done wrong.' The post manager assumed he had offended Cana Chintz but had little recourse when told simply that the debt would be paid the following year.[37] Other post managers evidenced greater determination to recover balances they believed were owed to the company. Commenting on a credit of three dollars that Jenejuce had obtained at Timiskaming, Arthur Ryder described the Indian as 'an infernal scamp and he ought not to have got anything.' When Jenejuce then asked for debt at Temagami, Ryder took a bear skin from him, 'to pay what he owes the Co. and gave him nothing more.' This form of collection was apparently considered acceptable in this situation, for it was believed that Jenejuce was quite prepared to withhold furs and refuse to repay his debts.[38]

In utilizing debt arrangements, other Temagami Indians appeared to have been adept in taking advantage of the opportunities provided by the existence of competition – including competition between HBC posts. 'Equna,' having been denied an advance by Arthur Ryder, got forty dollars of debt from Dokis. On the other hand, the knowledge that the opposition was about to visit Masenekegick's camp prompted Ryder to extend debt to the latter even though Masenekegick already owed debt to Timiskaming. This was the best means of obtaining his furs later in the season. When HBC traders from the Nipissing post, which was in some difficulty and threatened with closure, came north in 1879 to collect furs from Wendaban to cover his debt there, their Temagami counterpart was astonished that they announced low prices: 'They must be fools to report such low prices when they are after furs on a/c. If they tell Wendaban he is sure not to give them half his furs.'[39]

Wendaban was evidently quite capable of taking advantage of rival trade arrangements of any kind, for only a few months later he began to receive supplies from a new HBC post on Lake Wahnapitaeping. John Cummins expressed his intense frustration to Colin Rankin: 'What is the good of us trying to keep the Matachewan Indians from trading with the traders if the company's people from La Cloche send Indian traders to intice them out among the traders. It is to [sic] bad that, the company's people should oppose each other so.'[40] On New Year's Day 1879, John Cummins also reported a speech by Chief Tonené on the importance of paying debts: 'he told them that they ought to pay everybody, but especially the HBCo. as a man that was known to be honest always when he was in want of anything could go to the stores and get it. In speaking of those that did not try to pay, he told them to try themselves and see how long one of them would give another debt if he thought he would not pay.'[41] Yet the tariff structure and the debt network represented only one aspect of the competitive framework of the fur trade in the Temagami district.

On New Year's Day 1879, following an all night dance on Bear Island, Cummins provided a feast for the population and carefully recorded the provisions consumed during the event: '90 lbs flour 30 lbs pork 2 lbs tea 7 lbs sugar 6 lbs raisins 4 lbs butter 2 lbs tobacco.' Anxious not to be outdone, Dokis fed the Indians three times a couple of days later, serving 'all sorts of cakes that he brought up from Toronto on purpose for their feast,' which the attentive HBC official estimated 'must have cost him every cent of sixty dollars.'[42]

Apart from furs, Temagami was also known, even at the time of Joseph Beioley's early inquiries in 1822, as 'a large Lake where they get an abundance of fish.' Over the course of the nineteenth century, Temagami and nearby lakes continued to supply trout and whitefish to the local population and often to the residents of Fort Timiskaming. Temagami's fish production supplemented the fur traders' diet and reduced the costs and inconvenience of transporting pork to the relatively remote post. The fall and spring fishing seasons, particularly the former, became an important part of the annual cycle of activity for Hudson's Bay Company personnel at Temagami and for some of the Indians of the district.

In early October, often immediately upon arrival at the start of a new outfit, the post manager and his assistants set their nets around the lake. The trout were expected first, followed by whitefish later in the month.

After very modest catches of one or two fish per day in October of 1857, James Hackland's daily catch increased to ten or twelve for much of November. When ice formation forced him to curtail use of the nets in early December, Hackland estimated a catch of some 263 fish, concluding that 'the fall fishing was but poor.' He attributed the disappointing results to the limited participation of Indians in fishing and to a shortage of reliable nets. Nets left from the previous season were 'entirely useless,' and only the three nets brought in with the current outfit had been effective; old nets were sent to Timiskaming to keep chickens out of the garden. Hackland estimated in a Christmas Day letter to Chief Trader John W. Simpson at Timiskaming that Temagami needed twelve new nets, '4 of large and 8 of small mesh.'[43]

John Simpson must have been disappointed in the outcome, for he had earlier appealed to Hackland for 'all the fish that can be spared – 8 kegs at least.' The Timiskaming fort regularly requested Temagami fish, which were duly forwarded when available. Even in a poor year, such as 1875, when only five kegs of fish were caught from twenty-four nets, the Temagami post managers might use the fishery to further their relationship with Timiskaming officials. Thus, Arthur Ryder refused to provide a trout requested by the Timiskaming Oblate missionaries, but in late October 1875 sent his superior, Colin Rankin, '2 fresh Trout as a trial.' And, as requested by Mrs Rankin, Ryder instructed that the salt trout be cut as large as possible.[44]

The Oblates, at least on occasion, obtained their own supplies of fish from Temagami, for John Stockland reported one fall that 'the little Priest from Tems_que [sic]' had arrived on a combined mission and fishing expedition. While Stockland supplied Indians with goods in the shop, the priest was 'hard at them in the shed.' Stockland attributed the departure of Wendaban and his wife in the middle of the night to their lack of enthusiasm for the priest. The post manager himself was pleased to see the priest on his way with six kegs of fish, 'having finished his mission.'[45]

Fishing production levels fluctuated from year to year and for a variety of reasons. The number of usable nets naturally influenced the total catch, as did the skill, experience, and enterprise of the post manager and his assistants. It appears that Hackland's suggestion that twelve nets could be used at the Temagami post underestimated the general practice that later developed. In October 1865, an exceptionally good year, Stockland's journal entries indicate that he took forty-five trout on the fifth, seventy trout from eighteen nets on the seventh, sixty trout from twenty-two nets on the nineteenth, and two full kegs of fish on the twenty-third. The post managers sometimes associated low water levels with good fishing and high levels with poor, but there are too few references to present a consistent picture.[46]

Poor fishing results were recorded in 1857, 1859, 1866 (when the difficulties of a very limited trout catch were compounded by inadequate salting, which required overhauling the already packaged kegs late in November), 1874, and 1875.[47] In 1875 the Temagami post manager commented extensively on the difficulties and disappointments of the operation, noting that 'Our fishing has been almost a total failure, although we have done our best' and that 'constant gales disarranged and broke the nets, and the fish were very scarce.'[48]

The involvement of the Temagami Indians was often a key element in the success of the fishery. Sayaguasay took advances from the Temagami post against the fall fishing return in October 1857, and in so doing may have been one of the lake's earliest commercial fishermen. He and his family brought fish to the post several times during the season, and he is probably the Indian fisherman of whom Hackland said in a Christmas Day report for 1857, he 'did pretty well.'[49] Only three Indian fishermen had been involved to any degree in the fall fishery, much to the distress of Hackland. Chief Trader Simpson urged Hackland the following year to 'encourage the Indians to persevere. Let them have 6 Martins for a keg of good fish.'[50] The initiative was reasonably successful in the short term, for nine or ten of the twenty-eight kegs caught in 1858 were attributed to Indian fishermen. Generally though, native fishermen appear infrequently in the Temagami post journals. Hackland found them less interested in the 1860 season, while a successor lamented in 1874, 'I am afraid that I cannot get anyone to commence the fishing and it is time. I can't even hire an Indian. They are all anxious to be off to there [sic] hunting grounds.' He was eager to acquire an assistant who understood fishing. Ryder, beginning his term as Temagami manager in 1875, hired an unidentified Indian to show him the best fishing sites, but the Indians seem to have had no further involvement.[51]

Apart from the fall fishery, which was the most intensive fishing activity of the year, Temagami HBC employees sometimes spent mid-winter days repairing and making nets. Occasional attempts were made to fish under the ice, but the spring fishery was ordinarily not underway before break-up in mid-May. John Cummins reported in 1879 his discovery of a small lake with plenty of fish. Ambitiously, he anticipated having fresh trout all winter long.[52]

Rudimentary forms of agriculture played a role in the life of the

Temagami post from mid-century and also engaged the efforts of the native population to some degree. The potato harvest was an important fall activity for HBC personnel both before and after the move to Bear Island. After planting six kegs, James Hackland gathered only ten in 1857 but – despite a few poor harvests – production remained substantially above this level and reached a mid-century high of sixty-nine kegs in 1865. These results were apparently achieved without any attention to the field between planting in May and the return of company personnel in the fall, for the post was generally abandoned during the summer growing season. In 1879, after Malcolm McLean had been left in charge for the summer, the potato field yielded eighty-five kegs.[53] Arthur Ryder sought to diversify the range of crops available and in October 1875 requested a few packages of cabbage, turnip, and other seeds. 'They would be very nice for whoever is here next fall, above all things they would *save the Pork*.'[54] After the move to Bear Island, Ryder expressed his desire for agricultural improvements and a horse. 'I do not *by any means* wish to appear discontented,' he wrote to Colin Rankin: 'But I know that we could raise more potatoes and all kinds of vegetables at a very small cost. Then there is any amount of hay to be had near here, so I don't think it would be hard to keep a couple of cows, or, better still, sheep. A couple of the latter would be very welcome when our fish runs short in the spring.'[55] Yet there is little indication that livestock became a regular feature of the Temagami post operations, or that the district in general was ever regarded as promising terrain for the expansion of agriculture in Ontario.

References to Indians in agriculture are rare, but the HBC turned to White Bear in 1858 for seed potatoes to complete planting of newly broken ground.[56] Twenty years later Tonené had twenty-five kegs of seed potatoes on hand and proposed to work for the Timiskaming post during the summer in order to pay for an assistant who would do his planting. In the late 1870s Tonené sought guidance from HBC employees on the purchase of a horse and was later responsible himself for what must have been an astonishing sight on the lake: 'Tanne Got His Cattle up hear and never hurt the canow'.[57]

Despite Temagami's rugged geography and the harsh winter climate of the district, agriculture appeared increasingly to be a part of the Temagami Indians' future in the 1880s. John Cummins reported a remarkable speech by Tonené to members of the Temagami band on New Year's Day 1879. The chief had requested flour, axes, a plough, and other supplies from the government to start a small farm, 'for the white men were coming closer and closer every year and the deer and furs were becoming scarcer and scarcer as each year passed so that in a few years more Indians could not live by hunting alone.' Tonené advised the Temagami Indians to clear land wherever they liked and assured them they would not be disturbed.[58]

The Temagami band's tentative adoption of agricultural practices and use of provisions from the HBC and other traders were by no means an indication that traditional country foods were being abandoned. Indeed, throughout the nineteenth century the Temagami Indians relied on game, notably moose and deer. In 1875–6 and 1876–7, which were hard winters with deep snow, large game was rare, and HBC records indicate that the Temagami post sold more provisions than usual. In contrast, when hunting was good it was the favoured activity of Temagami residents.[59]

The prominence of Bear Island as a focal point for social activity and trade on the lake and the modest interest shown by some of the Temagami Indians in agricultural prospects were important background elements in the emergence of the aboriginal land claims issue during the 1870s, and the associated issue of a possible reserve for the Temagami Indians. Canadian Confederation had taken place in 1867. Geographically it had involved only Quebec and Ontario north to the height of land, and Nova Scotia and New Brunswick. In 1870, after protracted negotiations, the HBC surrendered its territorial rights in the huge Rupert's Land of the Northwest to the Crown, which transferred them to the new Canadian Dominion. The HBC secured provisions for receiving back as private property certain lands both for future real estate development and around its numerous posts. The HBC was also careful to ensure that it would not be responsible for claims arising where Indians asserted that they had not yet surrendered ancestral hunting grounds.[60] Bear Island was, of course, technically in the Canada of 1867 and not in Rupert's Land, as Moose Fort and Mattagami clearly were. But psychologically, Temagami was only slowly being incorporated into the Canadian scheme of things. As a result, the questions of the status and ownership by the HBC of its property on Bear Island became a matter of considerable significance and complexity for the Temagami Indians. At Confederation 'Indians and land reserved for the Indians' were recognized as a federal or Canadian governmental responsibility, while 'crown land' and natural resources passed into provincial jurisdiction. This division of authority compelled the participation of both orders of government in the administration of contentious matters in the Temagami district.

In 1877 Second Chief Tonené and two other Temagami Indians met

Charles Skene, the federal Indian agent from Parry Sound, who was visiting the Nipissing band for the annual distribution of treaty money. This was the first of several discussions with Skene during which the Temagami people patiently explained that they came from a community 'living north of Lake Nipissing,' far up the Sturgeon River, and that they wished to receive money and presents similar to the gifts that their former chief, Kakaka, and others had once received from the Manitoulin agent. A delegation from Temagami repeated the story the following year, and in 1879 Tonené – by this time principal chief – told Skene, 'We never ceded our lands and know nothing about the Treaty.' They said Manitoulin was too far away and urged Skene to sort out the situation with his Manitoulin colleague J.C. Phipps and with officials of the department in Ottawa.[61] For much of the next decade Tonené pursued extended but fruitless negotiations with government officials.

Although the Manitoulin agent did not link Tonené's group with the earlier visits of Indians from what the records describe as 'Taw-naw-gaw-ming,' he noted that there were bands living near the height of land who had not made treaty. Phipps added that the eastern end of the north line of the Robinson treaty was indeed 'rather vague' but might 'be made to stretch a good way ... and include the Lands in question.' He argued that if the Temagami Indians were brought in, they should be administered from Parry Sound. Skene, echoing Tonené's 1879 New Year's warning, believed that it would be very 'hard' if lands were to be taken away, as lumbering and other forces from the outside pressed in upon them, without an adequate reserve 'being marked off for them.' He wondered if perhaps the Whitefish Lake band had ceded the tract of the Temagami Indians without understanding the implications. Clearly, in 1880, both the Parry Sound and Manitoulin agents regarded 'Temagamingue Indians' as a band. They also seem to have thought that the Robinson-Huron treaty was somehow supposed to have extended north to the height of land, the northern boundary of Ontario as far as the federal government was concerned.[62]

The Temagami situation had by this time been drawn to the attention of Indian Affairs officials in Ottawa. In 1880 Deputy Superintendent Laurence Vankoughnet checked with Colin Rankin of the HBC at Fort Timiskaming and discovered that a small amount of money that Rankin had given the Temagami Indians was Ontario money from the Surplus Distribution Fund, presumably a tiny welfare dole, and that the band had not shared in the Timiskaming 'flour' grant. Skene denied that Tonené had occasionally received some of the Nipissing money, certainly not since his arrival; he also doubted that Chief Dokis had received funds on behalf of the Temagami band as Tonené had once reported. For his part, Rankin, who was now a means of communication between Skene and Tonené, was certain that Tonené's band had never officially received any payment from Indian Affairs. He believed this was grossly unfair in the face of encroachment from the south. Vankoughnet himself was becoming increasingly concerned. He asked Skene to find out what Tonené claimed 'as the hunting ground for this tribe' and on request sent along the latest and quite inadequate regional Ontario map. The Ontario map, 'Plan of the Nipissing District North of the French River,' taken from the *New Topographical Atlas of the Province of Ontario* (1879), included a few basic features around a huge 'Lake Tamagamingue,' but did not extend even as far as the lake's northern end. Politely, Skene said thanks for next to nothing and set off for Nipissing.

At Nipissing, Tonené stuck to his story about a grant from Chief Dokis, claiming that a young Dokis verified it, though Skene was sure that it had to be an isolated, insignificant incident. Tonené wisely did not think much of the Ontario map and with help made his own sketch, indicating the band's hunting grounds. The rough sketch map clearly showed Temagami, Wappoose (Rabbit), Anima Nipissing, and Cross lakes, as well as the Montreal and Sturgeon rivers, but it did not mark outer limits. These grounds were verified by Gilbert Dawis, Skene's Shawanaga guide who had been up the Sturgeon with Dokis, and by several Nipissing Indians. Tonené claimed that most of his band resided 'on a small island in Lake Temagaming,' but that they would want the reserve elsewhere. White men, Tonené reminded Skene, were already taking timber from along the Montreal River within the northern portion of their ancestral grounds.[63]

Vankoughnet concluded that the land claimed by the Temagami people – which he estimated at about 2,770 square miles – 'does not appear to have been surrendered' and that Ontario – now owner of the territory – would have to be approached on the matter. He sought advice from Prime Minister Sir John A. Macdonald who was also the superintendent-general for Indian affairs, but Macdonald, possibly feeling that the current federal-provincial agenda was rancorous enough, requested further information and deferred the matter. Continued pressure from the Temagami Indians relayed through the dedicated and conscientious Skene led in 1883 to the introduction of an annual financial grant similar to that provided to other bands under the Robinson treaty. But again, the Indian reserve issue was left unresolved, although a federal land survey was prepared.[64]

The situation was unsatisfactory from all perspectives. Skene chided his superiors, remarking simply that the Temagami band members 'will want to know what they are to do.' Tonené continued to press Indian Affairs officials – Thomas Walton was now (1884) Indian agent at Parry Sound – for a reserve suitable for farming. John Turner of the Hudson's Bay post at Bear Island reported that game was becoming scarce, adding that 'as this Band lives almost entirely by hunting, trapping and fishing, something must be done or serious destitution will prevail.'[65]

G.B. Abrey, the official surveyor sent to Temagami at federal expense, visited the lake in 1884, but did not report until the following year. Abrey's report, completed in February 1885, complained that when he had got to the 'Tamagamingue Indian Village' in September 1884, after a hard trip from Manitoulin via Lake 'Wahnapataeping,' he found that 'the chiefs and head men were all absent.' Upon the return of Nebanegwune's son Mathias, the second chief, Abrey learned that, before Tonené set off for his winter trapping territory, the Indians had gathered in council and decided on a site for their reserve. This Abrey outlined on an accompanying blueprint map. It included all the southern part of the lake, with the northern boundary centred on the point between what is now called the South Arm and Austin Bay and stretching east of Cross Lake, with the southern line roughly at the very south of Lake Temagami; it contained about one hundred square miles of land and water. Abrey thought it better to restrict the allocation and to have the southern shoreline generally as the northern boundary. His reserve would have had the same southern line (but shorter), including all the McLean Peninsula and the South Arm, the south shore of Cross Bay, and the west shore of Cross Lake. Abrey acknowledged that the land of the Temagami district was unsuitable for the Indians' projected agricultural pursuits, yet he offered the conclusion that 'the quantity asked for would be very much in excess of the requirements of these people.' Abrey estimated the Indian population at about one hundred, in nineteen families.[66] Abrey, incidentally, contacted Harry Piper, managing director of the Zoological Gardens in Toronto, concerning 'an Indian boy ... some 16 years old, 30 inches high, a dwarf, a pure blooded Ojibwa ...' Piper subsequently wrote to the HBC postmaster at Temagami to say that 'If a favourable arrangement could be made he might be an addition to our collection at the Zoological Gardens.'[67]

Federal officials politely tried to get Ontario authorities to act on the Abrey proposal for a reserve, arguing that 'these Indians are and always were a distinct Band whose home when not hunting was at Lake Temagamingue and having a Chief or Chiefs over them and their claims to share in the annuities of the Ojibwas of Lake Huron have been recognized.' Walton, whose department left him in ignorance of the Abrey plan until October 1885, independently urged his minister to press Ontario for the creation of a reserve as outlined by Tonené – a reserve covering much of the Temagami territory that David Taylor had considered so unpromising fifty years earlier. Not knowing of the Abrey blueprint, Walton forwarded to Ottawa a rough map of the proposition prepared by Tonené himself, adding that the chief's sketch was 'perfectly intelligible to anyone who, like myself, has been once or twice over the route.'[68]

Walton recognized – as did other federal officials – that no progress was possible without provincial agreement and that such agreement was threatened by the presence of valuable natural resources. Already, lumbermen were approaching the fringes of the region, and in 1887 the *Nipissing Times* reported that gold had been discovered by P.A. Ferguson of Mattawa and John Caverhill of Montreal on the 'shore of Lake Temagaming'; mining operations were expected to begin the next year. To Walton fell the task of persuading Tonené to accept the Abrey proposal restricting the extent of the proposed reserve in comparison with Tonené's hopes. And while the chief reluctantly acquiesced in this curtailed claim, Oliver Mowat, Ontario's attorney-general and premier, agreed merely to give the Temagami matter 'due consideration' when he felt better.[69]

Rugged, isolated, perhaps desolate, as some early fur traders had perceived it, Temagami in the late nineteenth century was a small but already notable source of conflict in federal-provincial relations and in aboriginal affairs. Competition between rival fur trade companies was being replaced by intergovernmental disagreements and, as the economic potential of the pine forest and other resources became better understood, would soon be supplemented by conflict between rival commercial interests centred in the Ottawa valley and in Toronto.

CHAPTER THREE

Southern Forces in the Temagami Country

'Some people up there who have travelled around a good deal assure me that we will realize quite as much from the timber in that part of the Province as we have realized for all that we have sold since Confederation. So mote it be.'

J.M. Gibson to E.H. Bronson, 23 June 1899

Following the early struggle of rival fur trading empires and the continuing clashes involving 'independents,' in the late nineteenth century several new groups began to show interest in the headwaters country of Temagami. Lumbermen, missionaries, prospectors, railway promoters, pioneering sportsmen, and recreational canoeists entered the district as new rail lines from southern centres to Mattawa, Témiscaming, North Bay, and Sturgeon Falls dramatically lessened the complexity of reaching the Temagami periphery. From these small railway centres, travellers then followed the Sturgeon and Temagami rivers or Lake Timiskaming and the Montreal River into the Temagami heartland. Government surveyors who explored the Temagami area documenting the landscape, highlighting the resources, and laying the foundations for much broader interest were among the first agents of this new form of southern penetration.

The Geological Survey of Canada (GSC) was interested in far more than geology. Survey officials provided detailed descriptions of their routes for the benefit of other travellers, and they recorded climatic information and often carefully noted flora, fauna, topography, and evidence of settlement or economic activity, both native and non-native. In 1855, for example, when Alexander Murray explored the shores of Lake Nipissing and parts of the Sturgeon River, he recorded discussions with the HBC post manager on the Sturgeon. Spring floods were an obstacle to potato cultivation near the post, as the water sometimes rose above the lower sill of the house. Local Indians sold furs and birch-bark canoes to Lake Huron traders. They also sold cranberries for about five dollars a barrel (a family could pick as much as four or five barrels in a good day). Murray's impression of the Sturgeon River itself was imprecise. 'It is said to proceed from Lake Temagamang, about half a degree of latitude due north from the post, and to be very rapid and difficult to navigate.' In the following year, Murray did ascend the Sturgeon, although he did not venture over to Lake Temagami itself but crossed instead to Wanapitei waters. After examining Lake Wanapitei, he travelled down the river to the French.[1]

The next significant exploratory work, which also circumvented Lake Temagami, was carried out by the Canadian Pacific Railway (CPR) in a series of route surveys during the 1870s. A CPR crew consisting of W.A. Austin and two associates surveyed from Mattawa via the Ottawa and Montreal rivers to a point about halfway between the Montreal and an unspecified branch of the Moose in the 1871–2 season. A few years later, Marcus Smith examined the eastern portion of Lake Nipissing and part of the Veuve River. Then, at the end of the decade, W.A. Austin reported to Sandford Fleming, the railway's chief engineer.

Austin, instructed by Fleming to keep the rail line twenty feet above Lake Nipissing 'in the event of the Ottawa and Lake Huron Canal being built,' and advised by the 'Chief of the Nipissing Indians' that 'the Indians were unwilling that any road or railway should traverse their Reserve,' had some difficulty locating a suitable route. He did, however, re-examine the Sturgeon valley and concluded – among other things – that 'a bridge of two bays of 60 feet' would be needed to cross the Temagami River. Of the Sturgeon itself, Austin stated that the river 'from its source to Lake Nipissing, is about 130 miles long, rapid in many places, but yet fine reaches of smooth water exist. Its course is south-east, through a generally rough country, and yet offering facilities on its banks for the site of a railway.' A year before Austin's survey, Miles and Co., in *The New Topographical Atlas of the Province of Ontario*, projected the Nipissing route of the CPR as running alongside the Sturgeon. The Canadian Pacific eventually adopted a more southerly course, however, and the Sturgeon valley was not used for railway building for several decades.[2]

The CPR surveyors of the 1870s were not alone in the Temagami country, for the GSC began an extended period of intensive exploration with the journey of Dr Robert Bell in 1875. During the next thirty years, Dr Bell and other officials of the GSC, especially A.E. Barlow, continued to examine the Nipissing and Timiskaming districts with some interruptions arising from 'the more pressing nature of the work in connection with the Sudbury mining district.'[3]

In his 'first exploration inland,' Bell proceeded up the Whitefish River from the north shore of Lake Huron. After portaging to the Wanapitei system, he crossed to the Sturgeon, continuing upstream well beyond the point Alexander Murray had reached in 1856. Bell passed through Paul Lake to Stull Creek and over to Smoothwater Lake – then known as White Beaver – on the East Montreal. This section of the expedition involved the crossing of the Great Lakes – Ottawa River divide, an important commercial watershed that later significantly influenced the development of the forest industry of Temagami.

Bell's descriptions of the territory through which he travelled show a particular concern for detail and a desire to define with some certainty the boundary between the Huronian and Laurentian formations of the Canadian Shield, a line that Murray had earlier observed near and along the shores of Lake Huron. Between the Sturgeon and Smoothwater Lake Bell noted the great ridge 'composed of massive crystalline green diarite.' This was Ishpatina Ridge, the highest location in Ontario. About fifteen miles below Smoothwater Lake, the East Montreal River enters what Bell described as 'a very beautiful-shaped expansion, about three miles long, which I named Lady Dufferin Lake' in honour of the governor-general's wife. Downstream from there, some ten and a half miles before the forks of the Montreal, Bell observed quartz veins and found considerable evidence of copper and iron deposits.[4]

A dozen years passed before Bell, who became one of the GSC's assistant directors in 1877, was again active in Temagami exploration. With the assistance of A.E. Barlow, Bell examined the Temagami region, including Lake Temagami itself, in great detail in 1887 and 1888. The explorations of these years were intended – at least in part – 'to ascertain more precisely the northern extensions and the distribution of the great mineral bearing belt of Huronian rocks which commences on the Georgian Bay of Lake Huron and crosses the Canadian Pacific Railway at and in the vicinity of Sudbury.' In 1887, Bell ascended the Montreal River, crossed the height of land to the Frederick House River, and, after some work there, recrossed the divide to follow the Montreal down to what he called its 'junction with the northern outlet of Temagami Lake' at Matawapika Falls. Bell then entered Moozkananing, 'the haunt of the moose,' which, consistant with imperial custom, he renamed Lady Evelyn Lake in honour of the sister of the former governor-general, the Marquis of Lorne. Traditions of empire thus began to compete with traditions of nature in the Temagami country.

Meanwhile, in July 1887 Barlow entered Lake Temagami via the Matabitchewan River, to explore its shores and islands. He left Temagami in mid-September by way of White Bear and Rabbit lakes and the Matabitchuan back to Lake Timiskaming, carefully surveying his return route. Barlow found that his work was impeded by 'smoke caused by the unusually large number of bush fires' and by the scarcity of available canoemen.

In 1888, Bell concentrated his attention on the area lying just west of Lake Temagami. He especially hoped to discover evidence of 'copper, nickel, argentiferous galena, iron ores, gold-bearing quartz veins' in the Huronian rocks northeast of Sudbury. He ascended the Wanapitei for twenty miles above the lake and after returning to the lake, crossed over to the Sturgeon River, as in 1875. He then carefully surveyed the Sturgeon above the part examined by himself in 1875, so that its entire course was now covered. Passing through Lake Temagami to Lady Evelyn Lake, Bell 'track surveyed' the latter in detail. He stayed at the cabin of the Indian Wendaban on the Northwest Arm and noted a mountain rising 1,100 feet above the surrounding level. This he named Maple Mountain. From the summit he viewed the 'rough triangulation of the region to the west of it, which had hitherto been a blank on all maps.' He noted the Trout Streams, now called the Lady Evelyn River, entering Wendaban's bay from the southwest, and he explored two routes between that bay and 'Nonwakaming' or Diamond Lake, all in preparation for new GSC maps.[5]

For his part, Barlow in 1888 explored more of Lake Temagami, Cross Lake, the Temagami River, and part of the Sturgeon. He was accompanied by A.M. Campbell whose field notes record the pattern of daily life on the survey. Campbell mentioned a wide variety of wildlife, especially birds. In mid-July on the Sturgeon near 'J.R. Booth's farm' he saw kingfisher, hawks, owls, ducks, and sandpipers, while a great horned owl was observed much later in the summer. Bass fishing was good in the Temagami River, and at Tetapaga Creek, where Campbell took note of 'a dozen of the largest bass I have seen.' Barlow's guide, Peter Commanda, had little difficulty supplying the party with partridge. Private interests in the area that summer included a couple of prospectors working around Cross Lake, while Walton of Indian Affairs visited Bear Island at the same time as the surveyors.[6] Bell's and Barlow's explorations finally culminated in 1899 with the publication of the latter's *Report on the Geology and Natural Resources of the Area Included by the Nipissing and Temiskaming Map-Sheets*. The report detailed the results of previous work by government surveyors and by the various CPR route surveys.

On the Ontario side of the region, only the portions south of Lake Temagami had been divided into townships. Concessions and alternate lot lines had been cut, the customary prelude to inventory and disposal. However, in the general district around Lake Temagami, soil suitable for agriculture existed only in the Little Clay Belt around the north end of Lake Timiskaming, in the Sturgeon valley south of its confluence with the Temagami River, and along the shoreline of the Montreal River above Bay Lake. Most of the district, Barlow's report confirmed, was unsuitable for agriculture. Around Lake Temagami itself only small tracts could be farmed. Barlow raved about the white pine, noting extensive cutting in the southern and eastern areas of his survey, that is, outside the Temagami country. Here, he confirmed Bell's earlier impression that the district included sections of 'incalculably valuable timber.' Apart from the timber resource and possibly mining, 'by far the greater portion of the region will only be valuable as a health and recreation ground for tourists and sportsmen. The great tracts of forest as yet untouched by the axe, the vast number of picturesque lakes, both great and small, with fish and game in abundance seem to render the district especially attractive for such purposes.'

Moose and red deer, the latter having moved into the area only during the previous twelve or so years, were prominent in Barlow's account of wildlife. Both species were gradually extending their territories. The wolf was also now much more common than before. In contrast, the woodland caribou were disappearing, except around Kipawa, and the black bear was being depleted by over-hunting. The otter and the beaver were 'fast becoming extinct in this region,' though in remotest areas they might still be seen. But the fisher, marten, muskrat, skunk, porcupine, and red squirrel were common. The economic potential of both lake trout and whitefish was significant. Both species 'attain their largest dimensions in the clear depths of Lake Temagami.' The coveted brook trout were only found in certain streams, and by far 'the largest and finest specimen of this fish in the whole region may be procured in the streams entering Willow Island Lake at the west of Lady Evelyn Lake.' This was Wendaban's country, and the Trout Streams were soon to become immensely popular among vacationing anglers. Above all, the black bass were numerous and large, especially in Temagami, Lady Evelyn, Red Cedar, Anima Nipissing, White Bear, Net, and Rabbit lakes. But potentially the most valuable fish, after trout and whitefish, were the pickerel.[7]

The 1899 GSC report also reviewed possibilities for gold, silver, nickel, copper, iron and other valuable minerals. Concerning gold and silver Barlow noted a major quartz vein by '"Mattawapika" as the last stretch of Lady Evelyn Lake is called.' He also mentioned the 'Cockburn location' on small islands just inside Cross Lake from Lake Temagami and three 'locations' on Lake Temagami itself owned by P.A. Ferguson of Mattawa. Location A was on the east side of Sandy Inlet; B was on the north shore of the Northeast Arm of Temagami 'about two miles east of the portage into Caribou Lake'; C was on Ferguson Island, southwest of B. Also on Lake Temagami, at Denedus Island near Muddy Water Bay was a location owned by James Holditch of Sturgeon Falls. Assaying for gold and silver from a spot on the east side of Temagami Island produced negative results, but considerable iron and copper pyrites were present nearby. Mathias Island, two miles north of the Bear Island HBC post, also had a good quartz vein. In the Temagami area, iron ore was most evident on the Louis Islands near the east shore three miles from the end of the Southwest Arm and near the west end of Turtle Lake, north of the Northeast Arm. 'The compass was much affected.'

Archibald Blue, director of the Ontario Bureau of Mines, toured the area between lakes Timiskaming and Temagami in 1900. He noted some similarity between copper and nickel claims in the region and those of the Sudbury district. Indeed, the Canadian Copper Company, which was then active in the Sudbury fields, also had a camp on the west shore of Net Lake, only slightly north of Temagami's Northeast Arm.[8] The existence of these and other mineral prospects scattered throughout a valuable pine forest where Indian claims remained largely unrecognized and certainly unresolved greatly influenced the subsequent evolution of the area.

Around and within the Temagami district, forces and events of the last quarter of the nineteenth century were accelerating the transformation of this once-isolated land, apparently integrating its destiny more closely with the social and economic evolution of the developing province of Ontario. The publication of Barlow's report by the GSC confirmed and circulated more widely the favourable views about the mineral prospects of northeastern Ontario that had been fostered a decade earlier by private assessments put forward in evidence to the Royal Commission on the Mineral Resources of Ontario.[9] To the south and west of Lake Temagami communities were emerging in the Sturgeon valley and in the rapidly expanding mining district centred on Sudbury. The forest resources of this district had also begun to attract attention shortly after mid-century. By 1866, J.R. Booth, for example, had cutting rights in Field, Badgerow, and Crerar townships in the southern fringes of the district. Settlement in the vicinity of the old HBC post of Sturgeon Hall got underway in the late 1870s, while the community upstream at Field originated as one of Booth's lumber depots. The population of this area rose markedly after 1881 when railway connections were completed between Sturgeon Falls and North Bay. By the time of incorporation in 1885, Sturgeon Falls had 1,500 residents and was linked by Lake Nipissing steamer to North Bay and Callander.[10]

With the exhaustion of readily accessible pine towards the end of the 1880s, Sturgeon Falls experienced a brief period of decline. After the arrival of pulpwood processing, however, the fortunes of the community – always heavily tied to the forest industries – soon temporarily revived. In 1894, Paget, Heat and Company of Huntsville obtained water-power rights on the river and established the first pulp mill in the area. This operation was sold in 1896 to the Sturgeon Falls Pulp Company. With some assistance from the municipal council, this company erected a mill before English investors arranged to purchase the enterprise from its local organizers. The new venture obtained an extensive pulp limit by agreement with the provincial government in 1898 and continued to operate as the Sturgeon Falls Pulp Company. In exchange for running the pulp mill at a capacity of 5,000 tons per annum and undertaking to construct 'with all convenient dispatch' a paper mill producing 30,000 tons per annum, as well as following certain stipulations as to investment, the company received the right to 'select and delimit or set out 75 square miles of unoccupied and unlicensed public land from and in said territory,' on an annual basis. This vaguely defined territory extended five miles on both sides of the shores of the Sturgeon River and its tributaries, with the exception that 'no cutting shall take place on the west shore of Lake Temagaming nor on streams flowing into Lake Temagaming north of the intersection of the shore of said lake by the said straight line' running east-west immediately south of Bear Island, nor on the islands of Lake Temagami. This was the first of many island and shoreline protection measures over the years. The agreement covered spruce, poplar, tamarack, jack pine, and hardwood six inches or more in diameter. However cutting of these species was prohibited 'in or on the immediate proximity of territory covered with green merchantable pine available for lumbering purposes or which may be considered by the Government to be pine-bearing lands.' Ontario explicitly reserved the right to dispose separately of pine.[11] It has been said that the Sturgeon Falls agreement 'resulted in a mill that processed one million spruce logs a year, created employment for six hundred men in the bush, and gave rise to a town of Sturgeon Falls, population 3,000.' Liberal Premier George W. Ross certainly defended the arrangements in these terms.[12] On the other hand, the Sturgeon and a number of other early pulp concessions were sharply criticized by the Conservative opposition in the provincial Legislature for secrecy and absence of competitive bidding in their formulation.[13]

Economic development in the Sudbury basin began later than in the Sturgeon valley, but resulted in a more dramatic and lasting impact on northeastern Ontario. Promising mineral discoveries of 1883 became the basis of 'highly favourable' prospects for the Sudbury mining camp by the end of the decade. The enormous success of Sudbury did much to arouse interest in the surrounding territory. Prospecting activity, in particular, increased with the realization that valuable mineral deposits could be found in the vast northern Shield area of Ontario.[14]

A substantially different pattern of social and economic development was unfolding in the Timiskaming area to the east of Temagami during this same period. Here, Ottawa valley lumbermen had been active from at least mid-century. In addition, the Oblate order completed a permanent mission in 1863 on the Upper Canadian side of the Narrows. The presence of these Catholic missionaries encouraged the influx of French Canadian settlers, an important part of Quebec's widespread colonization movement, which was so active during the late nineteenth century. Father Charles Alfred Paradis, a young Oblate who would soon become one of Temagami's more colourful residents, established a model farm north of the mission on the Quebec side in what became Baie des Pères and lobbied enthusiastically on behalf of the area in the early 1880s. More comprehensive efforts were carried on by the 'Société de Colonisation de Lac Témiscamingue,' efforts that achieved some modest success. By the end of 1885, thirty-seven families were in the district, and their numbers continued to grow. In 1886 the Oblates transferred their mission from the Narrows to a site beside Paradis's farm, thus establishing Ville Marie.[15]

Transportation and communications problems around Lake Timiskaming continued to restrict the pace of development, although some advances were made during the decade. Three portages on the Ottawa River below Lake Timiskaming were eliminated in 1885 when a fifteen-mile road was constructed on the Ontario side between Mattawa and Seven League Lake. Tramways were completed on the Quebec side in 1887; about the same time the Railway Company of Timiskaming was formed to provide a rail link from Mattawa to the foot of Lake Timiskaming. This line was not completed until 1894, however, after the railway had sold its interest to the CPR. Meanwhile, steamer transportation continued up the lake. *The Mattawa*, Lake Timiskaming's first steamer, was introduced by a Quebec lumberman in 1882.[16]

Most of the early interest in the settlement prospects around Lake Timiskaming originated in Quebec. Ontario's concern for the area developed more slowly, not reaching full intensity until after 1900. One early promoter, though, was Charles Cobbald Farr who emigrated to Canada from England in 1870 and subsequently worked for the Hudson's Bay Company at Hunter's Point and at Fort Timiskaming. In 1885, Farr purchased thirty acres of land on the western shore of the lake, naming the property Haileybury in honour of the English public school he had attended as a boy. From Haileybury, Farr urged Oliver Mowat's Ontario government to support and promote colonization in the northeastern portion of the province and encouraged railway construction of the proposed Nipissing and James Bay Railway as a means of facilitating access to the area.[17] The provincial Department of Crown Lands surveyed this area in 1887, dividing it into townships, eight of which were opened for sale in 1891 at fifty cents per acre. North of Haileybury, the rival community of New Liskeard (the second of what eventually became 'the Tritowns') soon came into existence.[18]

Farr remained an advocate of agricultural settlement throughout the 1890s, producing a pamphlet on *The Lake Temiskamingue District*, in 1893 and lecturing in England during the winter of 1895–6. The practical results of his efforts to promote settlement in 'New Ontario' remained limited, but there was at least a growing belief that favourable agricultural prospects were to be found in the fertile clay belt districts to the north of Timiskaming.[19]

Within the Temagami area itself, prospects for agriculture on a substantial scale were never considered very promising. The views of Edward Haycock given to the Royal Commission on the Mineral Resources of Ontario were quite typical in this respect. 'The land around the lake is not good for farming; there are a few spots that would make good farms, but only a few; it is nearly all rock – I am speaking of the country just around the lake.' In the vicinity of the HBC post, potatoes were being cultivated, and an Ontario surveyor who was in the area in

1900 reported the Indians' statement that the growing season was long enough for all ordinary vegetables to become fully mature if they were planted at the proper time. The Indians' tendency, though, was to 'leave all agricultural matters in abeyance until the finish of the spring hunt late in June.' James Mowat, an Orkneyman who retired after service with the HBC on James Bay and at Fort Matachewan, settled on the Montreal River and was reported in 1900 to be 'growing a flourishing crop of oats and potatoes.' '[H]e has a comfortable cabin, a very substantial barn, several head of cattle and quite a large clearing.'[20]

The most ambitious attempt at Temagami farming was Charles Paradis's scheme to establish at Sandy Inlet, at the north end of the lake, the headquarters of a colonization program to repatriate French Canadians from Michigan and New England and have them settle in northeastern Ontario.[21] In 1891 Paradis obtained permission from Bishop R.A. O'Connor of the huge diocese of Peterborough to undertake independent colonization and mission work. Paradis realized almost immediately that the first area to be seriously settled would have to be just north of the CPR line, west of Sturgeon Falls near the recently estabished community of Verner. Ontario had opened to settlement sixty-eight townships near the line, granting land at fifty cents an acre. In 1893, Paradis issued a pamphlet, 'Mission du Sacré-Coeur, Lac Timagami,' explaining the opportunities and advertising his grand design.

Paradis lived on Lake Temagami at various times, at Sandy Inlet, on Bear Island, and perhaps briefly at a site in the Southwest Arm. He also interested himself in the Verner area, and was otherwise occupied with promotional trips to Montreal and the French-Canadian community of Michigan. By the end of 1892, two missionaries were helping him on Lake Temagami, and more than a dozen workers were preparing the land north of the CPR. Two miles west and slightly north of Verner, along the railway, Paradis constructed a tiny chapel and residence called Domrémy in memory of Jeanne d'Arc, whom he increasingly venerated. The Sturgeon River was about eight miles north of Domrémy, and Paradis travelled back and forth by canoe in summer to Sandy Inlet via the Sturgeon and Temagami rivers. He and his men also cut a twenty-six-mile winter road from Domrémy north following the township boundaries to Baie Jeanne at the southern tip of Lake Temagami's Southwest Arm. Paradis also began construction of a chapel on the northeast side of Bear Island, away from the mistrusted HBC post.

In the spring of 1895, Paradis's first large body of settlers arrived in the

Domrémy-Sturgeon area. They came mainly from around Lake Linden, Michigan. Backed by Quebec's Société Générale de Colonisation et de Rapatriement, the project initially involved well over 2,000 people. In Toronto, where he briefly saw Liberal Premier Sir Oliver Mowat, Paradis had tried to secure formal assistance from the Ontario Department of Crown Lands. He wanted four dollars a head, a commitment that whole townships would be set aside for the settlers, and a road construction program prior to their arrival. The department would only agree to sell land to actual settlers and to employ some of them in building a limited number of roads.

Paradis had better luck in Ottawa with T.M. Daly, the Conservative minister of the interior, whose department was responsible for immigration. Daly provided $400 to help cover Paradis's Michigan expenses and $1,000 via the Quebec Colonization Society to help the settlers get established. There was also support to transport a small group of Swedish immigrants to the area. The *colons* from Michigan eventually arrived, but there were fewer than originally planned, and the only preparatory work accomplished was that done by Paradis's own lay colleagues. A dissatisfied minority of the new settlers became allied with Father Desaulniers of Verner whose criticisms and complaints led to a full public hearing by the Quebec Colonization Society into Paradis's conduct.

Although Paradis was completely vindicated in the eyes of the Department of the Interior, the bishop of Peterborough was less convinced. In the summer of 1895, Bishop O'Connor sent his trusted vicar-general, Father D. Laurent, on a fact-finding mission throughout the Nipissing district. Laurent interviewed Paradis for three hours and found him a most 'dangerous man,' a 'disturber.' 'Cunning, untruthfulness and violent of speech are the words I am compelled to use, harsh as they may sound,' he wrote. 'This whole scheme at Tamagaming is a fake and if the locality were not so far back no sane man would pay any attention to him.' Although Laurent did not have time to go to Sandy Inlet, he reported that only forty or fifty acres had so far been cleared at the retreat, and that only two log cabins had been constructed.

In the south, Laurent claimed that Paradis was trying to focus development at Domrémy, in order to help himself, his adherents, and his own projected road to Temagami and 'to destroy Verner and Warren villages.' 'That is not colonization but a conspiracy to defraud.' The hoped-for northern road was 'a hoax' that Paradis used to keep his followers in line; the province had no intention of settling the back country, Lake Temagami, in Laurent's view, not being 'an object point of any value.' O'Connor revoked all Paradis's rights and facilities throughout the diocese, except on Lake Temagami if he chose to reside there.

Bishop O'Connor evidently believed that missionary work primarily meant ministering to the Temagami Indians at Bear Island rather than promoting colonization. In the following year, 1896, O'Connor agreed with a suggestion from Bishop Lorrain of Pontiac to have Bear Island temporarily serviced from the Oblate mission on Lake Timiskaming.

Paradis nevertheless persisted with his independent colonization efforts. When Wilfrid Laurier and the Liberals won the Canadian general election of 1896, Paradis immediately petitioned for public funds to purchase machinery for a rolling mill in the Domrémy area, to pay for $900 worth of seed grain from Manitoba that had proved very successful, and to finish a much-needed grist mill. Private capitalists, he claimed, declined to invest in struggling settlements. He pointed out that he had worked for Canada for 'twenty years.' 'I am poor and crippled, with debts contracted for no other end than to serve my country,' he wrote, 'and still I want to stick to that career until the last.' To promote repatriation he asked for a salary of $150 a month. An expanding Department of the Interior was impressed with his dedication and put Paradis on the Quebec Colonization Society's payroll, at $50 a month.

Paradis's plans for settlement north of Domrémy then received great encouragement in August 1896. Accompanied by L.O. Armstrong, chief colonization officer of the CPR, who arranged the trip, a reporter who signed himself 'Henri' visited the new French Canadian settlements from Mattawa to Sault Ste Marie. He deprecated Verner and held out his greatest praise for the large, beautiful area being developed by Father Paradis, stretching mainly north from the 'village' of Domrémy. Though Precambrian rock protruded here and there, 'Henri' reported – in contrast to the prevailing view – that the soil was basically excellent; a mica mine discovered by one of the three orphans living with Paradis would soon be in production. 'Henri' referred to Paradis's 'happy and contented' settlers. 'Henri's' only complaint concerned the slow pace at which the Ontario authorities built back roads.[22]

Paradis, Armstrong, and several entrepreneurs with interests in the Sturgeon Falls area were associated in an ultimately fruitless venture known initially as the Timagami Railway Company and subsequently as the Ontario Northern and Timagami. The Timagami Railway Company received a federal charter in 1898 to build from the CPR line between Sturgeon Falls and Verner to a point on the south end of Lake Temagami. The plans called for an electric railway using hydro power from falls along the Temagami River. In their petitions for subsidies and time extensions, the railway's promoters stressed the agricultural and settlement prospects of the lands between Sturgeon Falls and Lake Temagami, as well as the potential for minerals and forest products. The new pulp mill at Sturgeon Falls was presented as a convenient market for settlers' timber. 'The road will also form a means of communication for bringing in supplies for the lumbermen, in cutting and marketing the timber in the large sections of the country contributory to Lake Timagami and Lady Evelyn Lake.'[23] For Paradis, the Timagami Railway was really another important step leading from Domrémy to the north end of Lake Temagami. But the plan was not without opposition.

Bishop O'Connor and other Paradis critics effectively lobbied the federal government against him. In late February 1899, while Paradis was in Ottawa hoping to obtain a four-month advance from Clifford Sifton to enable him to remain in the Temagami district – and presumably to advance the railway – Department of the Interior officials announced his dismissal from the service, effective at the end of March.

Paradis retained his beloved Mission du Sacré-Coeur at Sandy Inlet. There his life remained centred until a disastrous fire on the site in 1924. But the full vision was never realized, and other resources of Temagami district ultimately proved to be of greater significance than the limited agricultural potential upon which the hopeful priest had intended to rely. Ironically, Paradis's enthusiasm for railway access and agricultural settlement may have strengthened the case for protection and management of Temagami timber.

Temagami pine, whose importance had been recognized previously by Bell and Barlow, attracted commercial interests at least by the early 1890s. In 1893, the Nipissing and James Bay Railway used the services of Ontario Forest Ranger John C. Kennedy and of D.W. St Eloi of North Bay to evaluate and report upon the potential forest cut. St Eloi estimated that 309 million feet, board measure (Mfbm), of pine existed in the tract between the north of Gladman Township and the south end of Rabbit Lake in a band extending four miles east of the proposed and surveyed rail line. Along the east side of Rabbit Lake and extending eight miles to the east, he thought there might be 105 million feet, while 140 million feet was estimated to lie between the Temagami River and Hang Stone Lake. North of this area, up to Muddy Lake and the south shore of the Northeast Arm, and as far west as Rabbit Lake, St Eloi found a further 310 million feet. More good pine existed to the west of Lake Temagami and north of the Northeast Arm.

Kennedy's estimates were more conservative, possibly reflecting his decision to consider only timber capable of making a twelve-inch log. Still, Kennedy informed the railway company's directors that 'on the west side of Rabbit River there are 6,000,000 or 7,000,000 feet more of pine to the south end of White Bear Lake.' He found 20 million feet of pine along the northeast side of Rabbit Lake northerly to White Bear Lake, while an equivalent amount of pine was located along the shores of White Bear and Net lakes. Within two miles of the Northeast Arm, Kennedy considered that 100 million feet of good pine could be located. Without providing any estimates, he also considered the islands of Lake Temagami to be significant potential sources of additional timber.[24] The Nipissing and James Bay Railway made good use of these reports in preparing its promotional materials. Similarly promising assessments then became increasingly common and signalled a major transition in public perceptions of Temagami's future.

Temagami's pine became the subject of official provincial interest not only because of its great extent but for its location as well. The major watersheds were again crucial determinants of opportunities for lumbermen as they had been for fur traders in previous decades. J.M. Gibson, the provincial commissioner of Crown lands, examined the Temagami forest personally in 1899 and reported his findings and conclusions to E.H. Bronson, a prominent Ottawa valley lumberman who had recently retired from the Ontario cabinet. Gibson wrote, 'There is plenty of white pine all around that section of the country,' a situation he found still more attractive in light of the available water transport routes. There were three serious possibilities: the Sturgeon route, the northern outlet through Diamond and Lady Evelyn lakes to the Montreal River, and a chain from the Northeast Arm into White Bear Lake and the Matabitchuan. 'As to this last outlet,' Gibson observed, 'some artificial work would probably have to be done, but it is easily feasible, and the general result is that for all the pine timber in that section we shall have competition between Ottawa and Georgian Bay lumbermen. Some people up there who have travelled around a good deal assure me that we will realize quite as much from the timber in that part of the Province as we have realized for all that we have sold since Confederation. So mote it be.'[25]

Despite the prospects for water transport, railway promoters continued to press the view that railway construction should precede the disposal of the pine limits on the grounds that a railway would be the most economical means of transport.[26] But however valuable it was as a source for lumber production, and by whatever means this might be transported to mill and market, the pine of Temagami was also gaining recognition as an aesthetic attraction. Competition between agriculture and forestry had long been anticipated, but now the forest itself was the subject of potentially conflicting use for extractive and recreational purposes.

The Nipissing and James Bay Railway promoters were among the first to recognize the enormous commercial potential of recreation in Ontario's northern wilderness. In 1884, an early prospectus referred to the 'pleasant and healthy' climate of the area and predicted an influx of tourists and vacationers. 'Hundreds of people from all parts of Canada and the United States,' the railway suggested, 'will gather here every summer to enjoy the scenery, to renew their health and strength in its invigorating atmosphere.' A year later the scenery of the Temagami country was described as 'beautiful, resembling that of the Thousand Islands of the St. Lawrence.' *Our Northern Districts*, the Ontario government's principal early promotional effort, described Temagami's 'clear crystal waters' as 'a very elysium for sportsmen,' and later suggested that Temagami was regarded as, 'from a picturesque point of view, the finest lake in America.' 'Altogether with its elevation, bracing air and romantic scenery,' the government concluded, 'it appears to have the makings of an ideal summer resort in it.'[27]

Canoe trip reports from this early period are rare, but W.R. Wadsworth and a few friends paddled through Temagami in the early 1890s, later recounting the experience in the *Canadian Magazine. Forest and Stream* in an early 1894 issue began a series entitled 'Away Up North,' describing for recreational canoeists a number of Temagami routes travelled by a survey crew during the previous summer. A.E. Barlow, in his *Report on ... the Nipissing and Temiscaming Map-Sheets*, wrote that 'Nonwakaming and Lady Evelyn lakes ... have of late years become rather well-known topographical features, as they form a considerable portion of a favourite canoe-route between Lakes Temiscaming and Temagami, commencing at the long portage which runs from Haileybury post-office to Sharp Lake.'[28]

Vacationers who travelled through the 'rather well-known topographical features' of the Temagami country included Ernest Voorhis, who eventually became a cottager on Lake Temagami, and the young poet Archibald Lampman. Lampman's poem 'Temagami' contributed to the early image of Temagami as a fabled and romantic region in the rugged northern forest. Duncan Campbell Scott, another literary figure and an official with the federal Indian Affairs administration, attributed Lampman's heart trouble and early death to exertion during an 1896 canoe trip that began on Lake Nipissing and passed through Lake

Temagami en route to the Matabitchuan and the Ottawa. 'His physicians traced the trouble to his heart and then were recalled by his companions the feats he had performed in the wilds of Temagami, his labours at the portage and the camping place, and their fruitless endeavours to restrain him from doing an undue share of the work.'[29]

L.O. Armstrong, the CPR's chief colonization officer was another pre–1900 Temagami visitor who contributed to the growing popularity of the area. In addition to his railway responsibilities, Armstrong was a wilderness writer and lecturer who became an active contributor to *Rod and Gun in Canada*, where the full account of his August 1898 canoe trips eventually appeared. Armstrong praised Lake Temagami as an 'ideal lake' that was 'shaped like a chrysanthemum, whose pistil is Bear Island, and whose petals, extending in every directon, enable us (on a lake which is not over fifty miles across in any direction) to travel several hundreds of miles without visiting the same spot twice'.[30]

Armstrong actually made three trips to the Temagami area in 1898. In the winter – as part of a doomed promotional effort on behalf of the Timagami Railway – Paradis had persuaded him and one or two others to snowshoe from a point near Verner on the CPR line to the south end of Lake Temagami. Armstrong confessed that this trip was 'the hardest walk of my life,' but he nevertheless eulogized Temagami: 'In winter the lake becomes a great white expanse, the islands look like green leaves scattered in profusion over its bosom, and it is still lovely.' Then in May, presumably following the Matabichewan route to Net Lake, Armstrong crossed over to Anima Nipissing. He then paddled down Anima Nipissing Lake, through Red Squirrel, to visit Paradis at his Sandy Inlet retreat, leaving the Temagami country via Cross Lake, the Temagami River, and Sturgeon Falls.

Besides Paradis and Armstrong, the canoeing party in August included the presidents of two American fishing clubs, a senior Montreal newspaperman (most likely 'Henri'), a senior railway official, and a professional photographer. The group rallied in Mattawa to connect with the new CPR spur line to the Quebec village of Témiscaming. From there, Armstrong and his associates took a Lake Timiskaming steamer to Haileybury where they were met by eight Indian guides – probably from Temagami – with four birch-bark canoes. They paddled and portaged to the Montreal River, proceeded upstream to Matawapika Falls, crossed into Lady Evelyn Lake, and then Diamond, where they camped. From Diamond Lake the group portaged over the Sharp Rock portage onto Lake Temagami at its then northern outlet. Finding the portage from Whitefish Bay to Sandy Inlet too overgrown to use, they paddled to Devil's Bay and northwards again to Paradis's farm, where the party stayed overnight. The next day Armstrong's group camped on Devil's Island and climbed Devil's Mountain. On the following day at High Rock Island the party posed for a widely circulated promotional photograph. Often during a short evening fish, the group caught as many bass as the sixteen of them could eat, and they instituted a 'heavy penalty' on anyone who killed more than could be consumed.[31]

In the course of his 1887 exploration of the Lake Temagami area, Robert Bell recorded that a good hunter could obtain $400 worth of furs. 'With thrift and ordinary foresight,' he continued, 'these Indians could lead a most comfortable life & save money more than our average farmers.' Barlow ten years later observed that only Temagami, Bay Lake, and Long Point on 'Quinze Lake' were still receiving 'any great quantity of furs' during the 1890s, although at Mattawa and Baie des Pères (Ville Marie) 'a considerable number of skins come in casually.' The Sturgeon River HBC post had been affected by the railway and was abandoned in 1890. Fort Timiskaming was abandoned as a regular trading post but not finally closed until 1902–3. Bay Lake and Matachewan were closed by the winter of 1898–9. Temagami, a small but important post, continued to operate although the local fur trade was in decline: 'the gradual opening up of considerable areas in this district to settlement, and the diminution in point of number both of the fur-bearing animals and the Indians who are chiefly engaged in their capture, is already having a marked effect, showing a gradual, or in some cases a rapid decrease in the number of skins annually brought to market.' HBC annual reports on the fortunes of the Temagami district noted interference from lumbering operations in the early 1890s. In 1896–7 Temagami's losses were the highest in the Timiskaming district. As the decade closed, the profit picture had improved, but by 1910 Temagami was part of the HBC's new Lake Huron district, and management's attention began to shift to meet the needs of 'tourists, sportsmen and pleasure-seekers.'[32]

The growth of southern commercial interest in the Temagami district rendered the position of the Temagami Indians increasingly precarious. The 1887 census recorded ninety-three Indians in the Temagami band; ten years later that figure was down to seventy-five. Barlow concluded that the population was 'Slowly but surely decreasing.'[33] With evidence of mounting pressure for access to the resources of the area, the Indians' need for security and assistance grew. Some observers had previously remarked on the unfairness of the situation in which this ever-more-vulnerable community remained without compensation for the loss of its ancestral lands. But awareness of the possible uses for Temagami resources seemed to make the Ontario government even more unresponsive to the repeated claims made by the Indians and on their behalf by federal Indian Affairs officials.

In the spring of 1887 Indian Agent Walton renewed his appeal to Sir John A. Macdonald for greater efforts. Walton noted the recent Ferguson gold discovery on the 'shore of Lake Temagaming' and reminded Macdonald that such discoveries would 'not facilitate' a grant from Ontario. Walton himself experienced awkward questions from John Turner of the HBC post. What could the Indians possibly do? Turner asked; they hardly wanted to clear land that Ontario had not agreed to transfer. The federal government was also publicly confronted by the Temagami question when the Muskoka–Parry Sound MP, who was under pressure from the Parry Sound band, introduced a motion in the House urging action.[34]

When Walton visited Bear Island in 1889, Tonené requested farm implements, seed, and harness for some of his people who were prepared to begin clearing. Tonené wrote again for more seed supplies – oats, peas, corn, and timothy – in February 1890. He also reported that eighteen and a half acres had been cleared. Only four of the cleared acres were on land within the south end reserve that had been proposed; the other clearings were around the lake where heads of families believed it best to settle in light of the continuing uncertainty about the reserve. Nevertheless, Walton obtained approval to satisfy Tonené's request for supplies. As the Temagami Indians waited patiently during the early nineties for positive action on the question of their reserve, they continued to request and to receive nails and tools from federal authorities for building in the Austin Bay portion of the south end of the lake.[35]

In a further effort to induce a favourable response from Ontario, Indian Affairs enlisted the aid of the federal Department of Justice. A formal minute-of-council was also passed reviewing the entire story and requesting Ontario's co-operation in the transfer of land for an Indian reserve.[36] Nothing happened. Reluctantly, and in some desperation, federal authorities sent the Temagami matter to the Canada-Ontario Board of Arbitrators, established to resolve a range of long-standing intergovernmental disputes. Here, too, Canada's request was stymied when Aemelius Irving, the provincial counsel, persuaded his federal counterpart, W.D. Hogg, that the matter exceeded the board's terms of reference and that the preferable procedure remained direct Canada-Ontario negotiations. Substantively, however, Hogg still held that the Temagami Indians had not been present at the signing of the Robinson-Huron treaty, and that their land rights had not been 'extinguished.'[37]

Vankoughnet's successor as deputy superintendent at Indian Affairs, Haytor Reed, as well as his secretary, Duncan Campbell Scott, urged Aubrey White of Ontario's Department of Crown Lands to agree to a conference to settle the matter, emphasizing Abrey's survey for a reserve of one hundred square miles. Aubrey White agreed only to raise the matter with his political masters. Even Clifford Sifton, federal minister of the interior responsible for Indian affairs in the Laurier government, sought in vain the co-operation of his fellow Liberal, Ontario's commissoner of Crown lands, J.M. Gibson.[38]

Thus, in 1898, when W.B. McLean, the new Indian agent in Parry Sound, travelled to Temagami, he heard a 'strong appeal' from the community, 'a bright and intelligent body of Indians.' Again, through Ontario's intransigence, there were no results. In fact, the question was not resurrected in Ottawa until 1905. By then, seven years later, the world of the Temagami Indians had changed forever, as the Ontario government took active steps to respond to Temagami's now widely recognized mineral, forest, and tourist potential.

CHAPTER FOUR

Establishing the Temagami Forest Reserve, 1897–1906

'Posterity has no political influence and the easy course of using the public resources for the needs of the passing hour would seem the most attractive from the standpoint of personal and political convenience.'

The *Globe*, 20 February 1900

At the turn of the century, long-established Indians continued to trade in furs while contemplating an agricultural future in the Temagami district. Pulp cutting had been introduced to the Sturgeon valley, and E.H. Bronson, J.R. Booth, Gillies Brothers, and others were already cutting pine just to the east near Lake Timiskaming. Recreational canoeists had discovered the beauties and the fish of the Temagami lakes. Ontarians in general and the entrepreneurs of Toronto and Ottawa in particular were looking for commercial opportunities in New Ontario. Farm communities had penetrated the lower Sturgeon and Veuve River valleys; early settlers had reached the Little Clay Belt near the new communities of New Liskeard and Haileybury. Railway talk was everywhere. Copper and nickel developments at Sudbury continued to excite the imagination, and survey parties provided enticing reports of new mineral prospects. Thus, Temagami with its varied natural resources stood face to face with the expanding Ontario frontier.

Temagami was perceived as the best pinery in central Canada and soon became the centrepiece of Ontario's new forest-management system with the creation of the Temagami Forest Reserve in 1901. This was a part of the province's fleeting commitment to an elaborate system of land classification and managed development, and for Ontario a crucial event in the history of the North American conservation movement. To ensure the efficient exploitation of natural resources for ordered economic growth, the forest reserve system would keep marginal agriculture and other harmfully competitive uses out of prime pine forests, curtail fires, and permit scientific resource management. But in light of the variety of resources and opportunities, a policy that accorded paramountcy to the measured development of the pine forest industry would not go unchallenged.

A meeting of the second congress of the American Forestry Association at Montreal in 1882 marked the arrival of the timber conservation movement in Canada.[1] All the eminent Canadians there, including scientists, politicians, interested laymen, and lumbermen like E.H. Bronson, agreed with the general resolutions of the congress, which declared that forest fires, wasteful cutting practices, poor wood utilization, and improper land clearing were combining to deplete the forests of North America. Led by representatives of the lumber industry, the meeting called for more extensive co-operation between governments and timber operators to maintain parts of the public domain as perpetual forest lands.

A flurry of legislative activity emphasizing the control and suppression of the forest fire menace followed the Montreal congress. Fire not only destroyed much merchantable timber, but also, in the somewhat erroneous belief of the age, made it much more difficult for white pine to reproduce naturally. Indeed, it was a dictum of the era that if natural reproduction were to be achieved on forest lands the danger of fire must be eliminated. In 1885 Ontario followed a Quebec initiative for fire protection with its own fire ranger system on accessible Crown land, licensed and unlicensed. On licensed land the system provided for cost sharing between the provincial government and the licensees. The large, more progressive lumber companies from the Ottawa valley vigorously supported these measures. Their commitment may be explained by self-interest in protecting standing timber, but it is also true that they fervently believed that 'the suppression of forest fires ... is the only way by which future timber supplies ... can be secured; that done and the question of reproduction will very likely largely look after itself.'[2]

The administrative arrangements intended to provide a forest management program for the Temagami district were largely formulated under the Ontario Forest Reserves Act of 1898. The evolving background to this act during the previous few years is itself a central episode in the Ontario forestry story. As Ontario moved to establish a system of forest reserves in the late nineteenth century, the most serious threat to the future of the forest industry and therefore to the provincial treasury was still seen to lie in questionable agrarian expansion onto marginal land. At the same time the conservationist techniques of scientific pine forest management and the idea of economic development through perpetual use and permanent harvesting were gaining recognition.

Flowing from the enthusiasm of the 1882 Montreal congress, in 1883 the federal Conservative administration of Sir John A. Macdonald had appointed J.H. Morgan federal commissioner of forestry, charged with investigating the forest lands of most of western Canada and examining the need for tree planting.[3] After publishing a number of reports, Morgan was released from his position in 1885. Nonetheless, in 1885 Macdonald secured the establishment of Canada's first national park, at Banff Springs in the Rocky Mountains. Commercial and private recreation for prosperous vacationers was a principal objective of this initiative, but the park was also in part a forest reserve; supervised lumbering would be permitted. The federal initiative therefore stressed 'usefulness' through adaptation and development rather than strict environmental preservation.[4]

In eastern Canada, natural resources, including lands and forests, were provincial rather than federal responsibilities. And, in contrast to American practice, lumbering took place primarily under licence on Crown land, not private land. As far as forestry was concerned, provincial parks and forest reserves would thus have a differing purpose from those in the United States. In 1883 Ontario established the office of Clerk of Forestry, a position with primarily educational functions, within the provincial Department of Agriculture. Robert W. Phipps, the first clerk, issued reports on problems arising from the settlement of lands unfit for agriculture, on reforestation, and on the value of forest reserves, but his attention focused largely on tree planting and forestry in settled areas of southern Ontario.[5]

Ontario's next initiative followed the *Report of the Royal Commission on Forest Reservation and a National Park* when in 1893 the province established Algonquin Park as a 'public park and forest reservation, fish and game reserve, health resort and pleasure ground.' The primary purpose of the 1,733-square-mile park was watershed protection, to preserve year-round water flow for downstream lumbering and power developments. Much of the park was already under pine licence, often cut over, and lumbering of mature pine trees under government supervision would continue; only agriculture would be banned. From the beginning Algonquin Park was seen as a multiple-use area.[6]

Although popular writers often associated Algonquin Park with the later system of forest reserves and even viewed Algonquin as the first provincial forest reserve, experienced observers generally distinguished between the two concepts: parks such as Algonquin emphasized watershed management, game preservation, and recreation alongside lumbering, while forest reserves were primarily expected to ensure the perpetual use by the forest industry of successive crops of pine timber.[7]

After Thomas Southworth became Clerk of Forestry in 1895 the office was relocated to the Department of Crown Lands. In 1898 it was upgraded to a bureau with Southworth as director. Southworth was a vigorous and effective advocate of forest reserves. In northern Ontario, he saw 'a section of heavily wooded country, differing in many respects from the fertile region of southern Ontario.' Large parts of this area were unsuitable for agriculture but 'excellently suited for the production of successive growths of timber,' a process that could be facilitated if the principles of natural regeneration were properly understood and applied. Like the lumbermen, he regarded fire as the major cause of the failure of pine reproduction, but Southworth went further and blamed careless lumber operators for causing many such blazes. His primary argument, however, was that 'certain areas not adapted to cultivation should be reserved from settlement.'[8]

The efforts of a provincial royal commission appointed in June 1897 to investigate means of 'restoring and preserving the growth of white pine and other timber trees upon lands in the province which are not adapted for agricultural purposes or settlement'[9] also contributed to the passage of Ontario's Forest Reserves Act in January 1898, even before the commission submitted its final report. The Forest Reserves Act authorized the lieutenant-governor-in-council 'to set apart from time to time such portions of the public domain as may be deemed advisable for the purpose of future timber supplies.' The legislation prohibited agricultural settlement within the boundaries of forest reserves. Hunting, fishing, trapping, and the possession and use of firearms and explosives were also initially banned, but, after amendment in 1900, the statute provided that these activities, along with non-agricultural use and occupation of the lands, including prospecting and mining, might eventually be permitted under regulation. Forestry enthusiasts welcomed the act as 'the initial step in preparing for a rational system of forestry' intended to ensure proper harvesting of existing stands of timber and to provide a perpetual source of income to the province. The Bureau of Forestry hailed the act as 'the inauguration of a scientific forestry system in Ontario.'[10]

In April 1899 and February 1900, the Eastern Forest Reserve, comprising 80,000 acres in Frontenac and Addington, and the 45,000-acre Sibley Reserve north of Lake Superior were established. Both districts had been lumbered and subsequently burnt over before the emergence of a new growth of young pine.[11] Because so much of Ontario's pine lands were already under licence to lumbermen, provincial officials were anxious to incorporate Temagami into the system of forest reserves before private interests became established in the area. Though lumber and pulp limits bordered the Temagami country, it was still possible to identify 'many million feet of white and red pine among which the axe of the lumberman has not yet been heard.' The creation of a large forest reserve would also help to control the movement of casual summer visitors, whose presence, if unregulated, would naturally lead to pressure on the land for a variety of other uses.[12]

The decision to focus on the Temagami country was based on an extensive accumulation of evidence. Exploration surveys by Bell and Barlow for the Geological Survey of Canada, the work of provincial line surveyors, and reports by railway surveyors had consistently emphasized the promise of the region for development, especially for forestry. In the spring of 1899, Southworth and his two superiors, Liberal cabinet minister and Commissioner of Crown Lands J.M. Gibson and Assistant Commissioner Aubrey White, canoed through the Lady Evelyn and Temagami lakes to familiarize themselves with the district.[13] Gibson wrote personally to his friend and former colleague E.H. Bronson, who had never visited Temagami, to extol the canoe trip, 'one of the most enjoyable I ever took part in. You should certainly have been with us.' The white pine, he said, was most plentiful, and it could be floated out from one of Temagami's three outlets. The result of the alternative routes would be healthy competition between Ottawa and Georgian Bay lumbermen for the pine timber of the region. 'In any case,' Gibson concluded, the Temagami area should be made into a forest reserve or park, thus following 'the suggestion you made some time ago.'[14] Bronson subsequently sent his approval of the full forest reserve idea to E.J. Davis who succeeded Gibson as Crown lands commissioner.[15]

Rod and Gun in Canada reported that 'one result' of the high-powered canoe trip would probably 'be the creation of a special forest reserve in the "Lake Temagaming" area.' The sports magazine assessed the plan favourably, but added that, while the potential for reforestation was important, the preservation of grounds for game was even more significant.[16] The Toronto Liberal organ the *Globe* also enthusiastically endorsed the concept of a forest reserve around the Lady Evelyn and Temagami lakes.

> This is one of the finest timber districts of the Province, having an abundance of white and red pine in virgin forest. The regard thus shown for the future supply of timber in Ontario shows a broad view of public duty. Posterity has no political influence and the easy course of using the public resources for the needs of the passing hour would seem the most attractive from the standpoint of personal and political convenience. But Ontario enjoys the unique distinction of having consideration for the needs of the future, before the exhaustion of the present timber supply.[17]

The core objective of a pine forest reserve operated on a sustained-yield basis in the long-term interest of the province was understood and accepted by the influential Toronto paper as well as by the forestry officials and lumbermen who initially promoted the project.

As an important aspect of its broadening efforts to encourage economic development in New Ontario, the Liberal government of George W. Ross in 1900 launched a general exploration and survey of northern Ontario. Ten survey parties, each including several specialists, were established to carry out the work. They were instructed by Commissioner of Crown Lands E.J. Davis, who was responsible for the administration of the project, to report on promising localities across the north, 'to show the advantages afforded by nature for their economic development,' and 'to indicate the most favourable ways in which they may be opened up for occupation by roads, railways or waterways.' Thus, at the same time that it contemplated a forest reserve at Temagami in the interests of sustained yield, the provincial government set in motion an inquiry into the general resource potential of the region. To the extent that the survey was successful in identifying or confirming other valuable development possibilities, it threatened to undermine the policy to accord paramount status to the pine industry.[18]

Accompanied by two experienced surveyors and a geologist, George R. Gray of Toronto led Survey Party No. 3 in the Temagami district. Between late June and mid-November the survey crew travelled hundreds of miles through Lake Temagami and Lady Evelyn Lake and along the Sturgeon and Montreal rivers and their tributaries, as well as the Spanish and the Mattagami. By splitting up and carefully planning its reprovisioning, Survey Party No. 3 was able to examine at first hand a great deal of the Temagami country before reporting on prospects for agriculture, timber harvesting, mineral development, and recreation.

'The districts explored by us,' Gray began 'proved to be in all respects, much more valuable than we had expected to find. On this side, or south of the Hudson Bay watershed, the timber and minerals are the most valuable assets of the province, although we find localities containing large areas of good agricultural lands.' Gray was especially interested in the white and red pine, noting that pine grew in belts and was scarce in the far north. He speculated that a century earlier the area had been ravaged by terrible fires. 'The territory lying east of Lake Temagami and south as far as the surveyed townships, with the exception of small portions that have been burned, is all pine forest.' But areas north and west of Net Lake and down the Matabitchuan as far as the licensed areas near Timiskaming had suffered from fire. West of Lake Temagami there was also good pine, but it was somewhat more scattered and did not stretch as far as to the Sturgeon. Between the Sturgeon and the Wanapitei rivers were, however, great stands. Around Lady Evelyn Lake, there was a 'sprinkle of pine,' but 'eastward we found that it had been burned,' and was now covered with the usual second growth of jack pine, birch, and poplar. Gray estimated 1,650 square miles of pine stands. He was also impressed with the potential for harvesting spruce pulpwood, especially north of the height of land, and jack pine, especially south of it. He estimated 4,500 square miles of valuable pulpwood or probably 5,436,000 cords.

Potential hydro sites attracted specific comment from several members of the exploration party, no doubt in part because of current popular interest in power projects at Niagara and elsewhere in Ontario. The surveyors, De Morest and Silvester, identified the seventy-five-foot drop of the Sturgeon River at Kettle Falls as 'an important water power.' Other locations on the river had already drawn the attention of developers. On the upper Lady Evelyn River, 'the only power of any importance' was at Helen's Falls and rapids, where an estimated one-hundred-foot drop occurred. The geologist who accompanied Gray's party was impressed by the forty-foot drop at Matachewan Falls near the Montreal River's great northern bend. Gray himself enthusiastically praised the potential of water-power sites throughout the district to support 'extensive manufacturing enterprises.' He singled out the four big falls north of the surveyed townships on the Sturgeon, the two main Montreal River sites above Bay Lake, Kenogamisse on the Mattagami, and Nonwakawan Falls and the almost continuous swift descent on the lower Grassy.

From an agricultural perspective, the lands examined offered isolated potential. Gray concluded that the northern parts of the area he surveyed could be used for agriculture, although he saw them covered in pulpwood. This was the Little Clay Belt, soon the subject of an active advertising campaign and short-lived enthusiasm among agricultural promoters.

The 1900 survey echoed earlier observations about the very significant attractions of the landscape and resources for summer vacationers. In the main report, Gray predicted that the Temagami area would 'prove a paradise for the followers of the rod and gun and a resort for all lovers of the picturesque in natural scenery.' This assessment applied to the entire territory covered by Survey Party No. 3 and supported Gray's prediction that 'when the country is known to the sportsman, it will be invaded by them "en masse," and districts hitherto untrodden by the foot of man will become the haunts of the pleasure seeking Nimrod.' Gray and his colleagues were enthusiastic about sport fish, especially speckled trout along the Lady Evelyn River, often called the Trout Streams (a translation of its Indian designation), and along its tributary, named after Gray himself. Hunters would find large game, notably moose and caribou, in abundance along the Sturgeon and Obabika rivers. 'Beaver and otter are very scarce,' Gray noted. Mink, marten, and fisher, he surmised, had been over-trapped.

Gray and his associates added little to existing knowledge of the mineral prospects of the district. The 1900 survey, however, confirmed the existence of some promising locations where work was already under way and thus indirectly encouraged further prospecting. Just up the Lady Evelyn from Mattawapika Falls, for example, Klock of Klock's Mills had found some evidence of copper. The party's geologist found a quartz vein with a trace of gold at the northern narrows of Lady Evelyn. On a large island called Terry's Location, two miles northeast of Bear Island on Lake Temagami, a test pit had revealed gold, silver, and copper. An assay on the east side of Emerald Lake showed considerable gold and silver. On the northeast shore of 'Lake Wannapitae' considerable gold and traces of nickel and silver had been found.[19]

From the perspective of the Temagami district, the overall result of the provincial survey of 1900 was to consolidate existing knowledge and thereby to focus attention on the varied commercial potential of the area. That potential included not only the pine timber in which Ontario was then largely interested, but other and possibly inconsistent economic activities, not to mention the resident native population. Survey Party No. 3 had inventoried resources, but it did not speculate on the problems of management that the juxtaposition of resources might produce.

In November Southworth advised his superiors about the situation around Lake Temagami. The Temagami area, 'a territory of virgin timber,' was already attracting a growing tourist trade that would soon lead to a demand for land for truck farming, summer residences, and speculation. These activities and mining, which was also anticipated, 'would greatly increase the danger from fire' so that 'there would arise the necessity of disposing of the standing timber sooner than would perhaps be otherwise desirable.' The creation of a forest reserve here would permit the commissioner of Crown lands to control the area more effectively, although the property interests of the Hudson's Bay Company and the Sturgeon Falls Pulp Company's pulp-cutting rights to up to seventy-five square miles would have to be respected. Southworth admitted that 'a small band of Indians' existed within the proposed forest reserve, but said that they had no reservation and no 'proprietary rights' that he was aware of; besides, the existence of the forest reserve would increase their employment as guides.[20]

A few weeks later, Assistant Commissioner Aubrey White prepared a memorandum of his own for the Crown lands commissioner to consider. 'It may be said,' White argued, 'that the largest body of pine timber in Ontario still in the hands of the Crown is to be found in this region.' He reviewed the claims of mining interests, pulp operators, railways, the Hudson's Bay Company, and the Indians in the area, but concluded with the recommendation that the Temagami district should be set aside as a forest reserve. White was anxious, however, to do more than merely set aside a forest reserve and advocated a more comprehensive management program than had previously been contemplated. Some Temagami pine was apparently nearly ready for disposal to the lumber industry, and White hoped to regulate the manner in which it would be cut. Management regulations were to be supervised by a ranger, 'clothed with magisterial and other powers,' and access to the district should be controlled by permits.[21]

In accordance with White's recommendations, an order-in-council dated 7 January 1901 set aside 1.4 million acres or 2,240 square miles, an area significantly larger than that set aside for Algonquin Park in 1893. The designated area, believed to contain three to five billion feet of pine timber, was to be called the Temagami Forest Reserve.[22] 'In all probability if this region had been dealt with in the ordinary way followed where pine-covered land is presumed to be available for settlement, the presence of squatters and others following upon the opening up of the country would have been followed by devastating fires. The attractive character of the locality to tourists and sportsmen, who resort thither in increasing numbers, rendered it all the more advisable to place it under strict regulations, so as to avoid this danger.'[23] Creation of the Temagami Forest Reserve, then, was regarded as an important initiative in the provincial management of conflicting resource uses.

The Temagami Forest as originally delimited in 1901 was geographically centred on Lake Temagami (see map 1). It comprised the upper Temagami River watershed (that is, north of Red Cedar Lake), the entire Lady Evelyn watershed, the headwaters of the Macobe watershed, plus the upper Sturgeon, apart from its extreme northwestern headwaters. The East Montreal River was outside the Temagami Forest, as was the Wanapitei. The northeast boundary was along the Montreal River opposite Mowat's Farm, cutting back southwest from the bank to avoid the licensed Gillies Limit and Bay Lake. The southeast boundary was just downstream from Rabbit Lake on the Matabitchuan River. It thus straddled the divide between the Ottawa River system and the Great Lakes. In addition, the new forest reserve covered about two-thirds of the historic aboriginal hunting grounds (see maps 1, 5).[24]

Forest protection, especially fire prevention, was crucial to the success of the forest reserves program, and a small staff of rangers served in Temagami during the summer of 1901. Regulations introduced in 1902 represented a more comprehensive attempt to control competing activities within the forest reserves and to safeguard the timber resources. Access and travel within reserves became subject to the supervision and control of rangers, while strict guidelines regarding the use of fire were set. Prospectors were brought under a new fee permit system, and mining operations were subject to approval by the commissioner of Crown lands. The roasting of sulphurous ores and other industrial processes potentially harmful to young pine were prohibited within the reserve. This measure doubtless represented a reaction to the unhappy experience of ore processing around Sudbury, where the practice of heap roasting had had a devastating impact on the landscape. The presence of a Canadian Copper Company camp at Net Lake inside the Temagami Forest may have sharpened the concern. Regulations governing railway smokestack and furnace screens were also brought into effect.[25] Allegedly because of the rangers, 'no material damage' from fire took place in the Temagami Forest during 1900, 1901, and 1902; the rangers prevented 'serious loss in timber' by efficiently putting out two serious lightning fires and another fire 'started from an unextinguished camp fire of some tourists from Pittsburg, Pa.'[26]

The more serious questions about forest management had not yet been confronted. The obviously central issue of cutting procedures was not squarely addressed in the original Forest Reserves Act of 1898, nor in the 1902 regulations. The importance of 'future timber supplies' was acknowledged, and officials anticipated 'perpetual use,' but the means to this end was not spelled out, although J.M. Gibson had expressed approval of careful government supervision of cutting in 1899.[27] Aubrey White noted in 1901 that some Temagami pine was already mature and suggested restrictive cutting practices that would amount to 'some new departure.'

> If we could go further and provide for a close supervision of the cutting, a system of disposal by which we shall be able to prevent the cutting of trees below a certain diameter and some provision for the disposal of the debris left after the cutting of the timber which will lessen the danger from fire, we may make this region perhaps the most valuable asset of the Province and a permanent perennial source of revenue.[28]

The deputy minister's proposals were ultimately made in vain.

When Southworth successfully pressed for a major expansion of the boundaries of the Temagami Forest in December 1903, cutting regulations had still not been implemented. Southworth's thrust was directed against competing resource activities, as new pressures from mining and prospecting were evident and the increasing popularity of fishing, hunting, and canoeing in northern Ontario also threatened the pine forests. If the Temagami Forest Reserve was expanded, he believed that the prospectors' behaviour could then be satisfactorily regulated through the existing licensing system, while canoeists travelling up the Montreal River to Smoothwater Lake, to the territory west of the original boundary, could be brought under the supervision of rangers. 'Whether they go because of the excellent fishing and small game and shooting, or to get beyond the territory patrolled by the rangers in order to indulge in the shooting of big game out of season, is a question.'[29]

Southworth argued that the purpose of forest reserves was to set prime pine lands aside from agricultural settlement and for the 'perpetual use' of furnishing 'timber supplies and public revenue.' An expansion to prevent fires, ensure 'proper supervision,' and control development was clearly in the public interest. There was some urgency, for it was the practice of the department to name townships as they were opened for settlement, and this had happened before 1901 in the Sturgeon valley just south of the 1901 Temagami Forest boundaries. Now it was happening in the Little Clay Belt, on the northeast side of the Montreal River. Three new townships – James, Barker, and Auld, straddling the Montreal – were thus opened for settlement. No one had yet received a patent but, by extending the Temagami Forest boundary upstream, at least the southwestern halves of these two townships could be closed to settlement. The director of forestry's recommendation for a significant northward and westward extension of the TFR was supported by Aubrey White. Thus, with the approval of the lieutenant-governor-in-council, a further 3,700 square miles were added to the Temagami Forest in December 1903 (see map 1). The enlarged Temagami Forest covered 5,900 square miles or 3,776,000 acres. When the second edition of James Elliott Defebaugh's *History of the Lumber Industry of America* appeared in 1906, Temagami was shown to be nearly 1 million acres larger than the next largest forest reserve in Canada, the 2,880,000-acre Rocky Mountains Park. In fact, the Nipigon Reserve, established in June 1905 and extended in November of the same year, exceeded the Temagami Forest by nearly a million acres. But because Nipigon was essentially a pulpwood reserve, Temagami remained the principal pinery in the Ontario system.

The Temagami Forest now stretched northwest into the Arctic watershed to include the Grassy River and the eastern side of the headwaters of the Mattagami. The extreme northern border enclosed what is now the southern portions of the city of Timmins, although this protrusion was well beyond the pine-tree line. More logically, the extension of 1903 incorporated the west or right bank of the Montreal, upstream past Fort Matachewan, and then all the headwaters of the West and East Montreal branches, including Lake Gowganda. In the west the border followed the old fur trade canoe route from the Wanapitei headwaters to the Mattagami and contained almost the full upper Wanapitei valley (but not Lake Wanapitei); in the extreme southwest, the Temagami Forest now took in the upper Vermilion River, an important tributary of the Spanish.

Aubrey White recognized that some of the pine in the new addition 'has attained its full growth, and the question will soon have to be considered of what disposition shall be made of it, and under what regulations or system.' The basic management decision had still not been taken. More seriously, 1,850 square miles of the new addition were covered by existing pulpwood agreements. Imperial Paper Mills of Sturgeon Falls had rights to cut pulpwood to a width of 5 miles on either side of the Sturgeon River for a total of 350 square miles. Spanish River Pulp and Paper had similar rights on the Vermilion for 200 square miles.

The Montreal River Pulp Company (to be taken over in 1905 by J.R. Booth) had the same rights on much of the upper Montreal and the Macobe and two other of the Montreal's tributaries, for 1,300 square miles. The extension of the Temagami Forest Reserve did not affect their rights. Perhaps even more serious in terms of potential conflict with the pine industry were railway land-grant provisions – 5,000 acres per mile constructed for the James Bay Railway, chartered to build from Capreol, just northeast of Sudbury, to Lac Abitibi; this endangered up to 600 square miles. Fortunately, White reported, no mining locations had been patented or leased in the added territory; all but a very few of thirty-seven previously surveyed locations had been abandoned, though around Mount Sinclair, west of Fort Matachewan, there were rumours about an asbestos mine. Absolutely no pine cutting had been licensed in the entire area.[30]

The Ottawa valley lumber barons, who in 1900 had formed the Canadian Forestry Association, welcomed the original creation of the forest reserve system, and Temagami's designation in particular. E.H. Bronson wrote to Premier Ross to express his enthusiasm and, at the time of the 1903 extension, even suggested that the Temagami Forest be extended farther eastward to the central portion of the Lake Timiskaming shore, even though this would include lands then under licence. 'Utterly valueless for settlement,' the Shield country thus included would be kept free of fires and saved for proper lumbering, all to the financial benefit of the Crown.[31] Premier Ross approved of the sentiment, but the boundaries were not further extended.

Rod and Gun, which between 1901 and 1904 was the official organ of the Canadian Forestry Association, also welcomed the creation of the Temagami Forest because it was free of pine licences. This would provide the government with 'an opportunity of dealing with the timber as may seem to it wise without being hampered by any vested or other interests.' Although acceptable alternative management programs were not easily identified, *Rod and Gun* argued that, 'The timber cannot be allowed to remain useless and be left to die of old age. Such a policy of masterly inactivity would be more utterly unprogressive than any system of license could be.' *Rod and Gun* proposed a careful forest survey followed by government-supervised cutting and urged the Canadian Forestry Association and the general public to accept this proposal, whose success 'would have an important bearing on the whole future of forest administration in Canada.'[32] No clear harvesting policy emerged, although E.J. Davis, the commissioner of Crown lands, reported that the cutting policy being formulated in 1904 would be based on the assessment of experienced government officials who would designate trees for cutting so as to reduce the threat of fire and permit the continued growth of underdeveloped wood. When a new reserve was created in the Mississagi area, Davis hinted at reasonably close government regulation of the cut. 'These are areas,' he indicated, 'that will not be used for settlement, and can be worked as permanent reserves, disposing annually of the timber that is ripe, and allowing that which is not fully developed to remain until it is at the proper stage for cutting to the best advantage.'[33] Yet in 1906, the nature of Ontario's cutting regulations for the forest reserves was still unresolved, and speculation continued. Perhaps the German model would be adopted, in which only one-twentieth of a company's timber limit could be cut each year and an equal proportion replanted. With perpetual leases, some thought that the timber licensees might agree to such an approach on condition that the settlers would be excluded.[34] Although the policy objective was clear enough, the means to achieve it had yet to be determined.

Nevertheless, the Temagami Forest became the keystone in a belt of forest reserves established across northern Ontario – Mississagi, a pine area of 3,000 square miles west of Temagami, set up in 1903 and enlarged by 2,000 square miles in 1913; Nipigon, a pulpwood area of 7,300 square miles created in 1905; and the Quetico boundary reserve of 1,795 square miles in northwestern Ontario created in 1909.[35]

In the Temagami Forest, the chief threat to the paramountcy of pine came from the dynamic northward push of Ontario's economic frontier amid widespread enthusiasm to develop 'New Ontario.' Railway talk was the widespread symptom, railway building a not-uncommon reality.[36] It was all part of the reaction to the Sudbury copper-nickel developments that followed the construction of the CPR. Soon to be a part of the Grand Trunk network, the Canadian Northern line from Toronto had reached the CPR at Nipissing Junction in 1886. Furthermore, popular knowledge of the existence of the Clay Belts briefly reinvigorated Ontario's old agrarian tradition; the pioneer-oriented sons and daughters of southern Ontario's farm population would not all need to head west to obtain land. The CPR spur line north from Mattawa had reached Témiscaming by 1894. By the turn of the century the Ross government was promoting agricultural settlement, at fifty cents per acre, northwest of New Liskeard, the village it favoured over Haileybury, despite the vigorous propagandizing of C.C. Farr, the founder of Haileybury. The Nipissing and James Bay Railway had been chartered back in 1884 to run from the CPR at North Bay to Lake Timiskaming and beyond, via the eastern tip of Lake Temagami. For financial reasons and because of internal disunity, the line had not been built; control passed to the Grand Trunk and from it to the William Mackenzie and Donald Mann interests. These two men were more interested in their own chartered line, the James Bay Railway, soon to be called the Canadian Northern Ontario Railway, that was to run north from Capreol.[37]

By 1900 it was clear from all this promotion that the reasonable economic prospects of New Ontario involved far more than northern pine. In the face of the repeated failure of private capital to undertake the construction of a rail line to Timiskaming, the Ross government eventually decided to proceed with a railway into the northern region as a provincial enterprise. Commissioner of Public Works F.R. Latchford explicitly presented the likelihood of mineral discoveries as a reason for pursuing the building program, and on the basis of widely available information there can be little doubt that northeastern Ontario's promising resources were well known to the cabinet. Lake Temagami had not been overlooked in the railway's planning; its tourist prospects and 'very promising' mineral indications were well known to the engineering staff.[38]

The Timiskaming and Northern Ontario Railway (TNOR) was chartered as a Crown corporation in 1902. Latchford, an Ottawa valley MLA, and the Ottawa lumber barons would have preferred the line to move north from Mattawa. But the Ottawa valley's influence was already in decline. Toronto-based politicians and the Toronto Board of Trade ensured that the railway would go north from North Bay. It would be Toronto's development road, not Ottawa's or Montreal's. Ross appointed A.E. Ames, head of an expanding Toronto brokerage firm, the chairman of the commission for the TNOR. Ames's father-in-law was George Cox, president of the Bank of Commerce and of the Central Canada Loan and Savings Company.

In 1903 construction began in earnest. For a time there had been talk that the line would pass east of Rabbit and White Bear lakes, not touching Lake Temagami. In the end, partly through the urging of Dan O'Connor, the former mayor of Sudbury who was now interested in tourist and mineral development on Lake Temagami, the line passed by the end of the Northeast Arm of Lake Temagami. As explained by the TNOR, the decision to direct the line westward to the lake was influenced by 'the very great prospects' of expanding tourism and the desirability of 'bringing a large area of territory in touch with the railway.'[39]

In early 1903, at Mile 103, well north of Lake Temagami, construction workers 'noticed traces of cobalt bloom.' After mid-1904, with the founding of Cobalt – the third of the Tritowns – word of the mineral possibilities (especially silver) spread rapidly, and by 1905 the great northern boom was on. The Temagami Forest Reserve would soon experience the consequences. In late 1904 a few service trains pushed through the 'heavy green forest composed of white and red pine, spruce, black and yellow birch, cedar, hemlock, balsam and maple.'[40] Official service began in January 1905, and a major stop for the 'Cobalt Flyer' was at the new Temagami Station at the tip of the lake's Northeast Arm. By then Ames had resigned the chairmanship of the commission. Robert Jaffrey, like Cox a senior director of Central Canada Loan and president of Globe Printing, which owned the Toronto *Globe*, replaced Ames as chairman.

Rail construction resulted in increased pressure to harvest pine. Obviously, a broad right of way had to be cleared. In August 1905, the government provided $10,000 for clearing in that year along the TNOR line in the Temagami Forest. In requesting this special allocation, Frank Cochrane, the new minister, noted that Temagami contained 'the largest body of white pine timber in the hands of the Crown in any one locality in the province. It would be a public calamity if this timber should be destroyed by forest fires.' But the previous policy of stationing fire rangers along the rail line had failed to prevent the outbreak of several fires, and occasionally hazardous conditions occurred. The clearing policy was thus designed in order 'that the danger might be materially lessened if not altogether averted.' Cochrane further recommended that the necessary steps be taken to obtain the merchantable value of all wood removed during the clearing process.[41] The government did not prepare an advance estimate of the cost of clearing along the TNOR right of way within the Temagami Forest. A subsequent calculation revealed that by 1908 net costs of the clearing exercise had reached $74,551.52. This figure represented a total outlay of $120,123.35 less timber sales of $45,571.83.[42] William Milne and Sons Lumber Company of Trout Lake near North Bay was one of the early beneficiaries of cutting along the rail line and would become a well-established operator in the district. At Latchford, where the TNOR crossed the Montreal, the Empire Lumber Company established a large sawmill, bought forty-seven lots from the railway, and secured a contract to transport logs and lumber.[43]

These railway lots were part of the Crown lands transferred or to be transferred to the TNOR adjacent to stations along the railway line.[44] The TNOR thus acquired ownership of lots around Temagami Station; it sold none of them until 1909. Nevertheless, the Crown's position as exclusive landowner (apart from the unresolved aboriginal claim) in the Temagami Forest had been breached. Furthermore, Mackenzie and Mann were proceeding with their own plans to build the James Bay-Canadian Northern Ontario Railway through the western reaches of the Temagami Forest – once they completed their line from Toronto to Capreol, which they did in 1908. The CNOR would carry with it the 5,000-acres-per-mile land-grant provision. Mackenzie and Mann in 1904 had also secured a charter to build a major rail line from Ottawa to Capreol via North Bay. Although this plan proceeded very slowly, it involved a second projected railway just south of the Temagami Forest, one that would angle to the northwest part way up the lower Sturgeon valley and then south of Lake Wanapitei.

Father Charles Paradis was still trying to link his francophone settlements by the Sturgeon and Veuve rivers with Lake Temagami and his Sandy Inlet retreat by means of his proposed Timagami Railway.[45] But even after Paradis reorganized the company and obtained greater backing in 1906 by shifting the planned southern terminus to Sturgeon Falls, the project was never completed.[46]

Railway promotion and development were only one source of potential conflict with a policy intended to recognize the primacy of Temagami pine. The provisions relating to logging for pulpwood in the three limits existing within the Temagami Forest continued. Pulpwood operations clearly had to be taken into account in any plan for the management of the pinery. Although the three existing concessions had been granted before the extension of the Temagami Forest, actual cutting had begun only in the Sturgeon Falls Limit. After its corporate reorganization of 1898, the Sturgeon Falls Pulp Company obtained an extensive pulp limit covering parts of what would become the Temagami Forest Reserve. As part of its existing pine policy, however, the provincial government prohibited pulp cutting 'in or in the immediate proximity of territory covered with green merchantable pine available for lumbering purposes or which may be considered by the Government to be pine-bearing lands.'[47]

In 1900, the Sturgeon Falls Pulp Company transferred its rights and privileges to Edward Lloyd Limited, a large British paper manufacturer that had been seeking an opportunity to invest in Canada. Yet the new owners soon discovered reasons to regret their investment, for former management had made limited progress on construction and the work done was questionable. Edward Lloyd Limited was unsuccessful in legal proceedings against the Sturgeon Falls Pulp Company, and because of the stigma attached to the former name, Lloyd transferred its rights to

Imperial Paper Mills of Canada. In October 1903, the modern paper mill, producing forty-five tons of newsprint per day, and the groundwood mill, producing fifty tons of pulp per day, began operations.[48]

In 1905, Northern Sulphite Mills of Canada Limited was formed to build a sulphite plant at Smoky Falls, upstream from Sturgeon Falls. John Craig, managing director of Imperial Paper Mills, was among the incorporators. The mill was expected to open in 1906, and Imperial Paper Mills was to take the lease for $7,500 for thirty years, plus $2 per ton on sulphite pulp used by the Sturgeon Falls mill. As Imperial Paper faced continuing financial difficulties, the pulp mills were eventually taken over by receivers and operated at a profit. The paper mill remained idle and, together with the Smoky Falls sulphite mill, was put up for sale. When conditions improved in 1907 the paper mill went into operation again, but it appears that the sulphite mill at Smoky Falls was never reopened.[49]

It is difficult to say exactly when the company started cutting to permit the opening of the mill in 1903, but employment in the woods operations was estimated at three hundred men. Though the agreement specified the necessity to choose and get approval for the seventy-five square miles on which to operate, no departmental records seem to exist covering this procedure. Indeed, like other pulp companies, the Sturgeon Falls operation regarded the entire watershed as its property. Although it was impossible to identify pulp-cutting locations within the Sturgeon Falls Limit, presumably cutting began in the proximity of the mill and of the main waterways, and moved back as resources were depleted.[50]

The Montreal River Pulp Concession, covering 1,300 square miles in the northern half of the TFR, was comparable to the Sturgeon Falls Limit. An agreement signed on 3 March 1902 by the Montreal River Pulp Company stipulated the spending of $100,000 in eighteen months. Problems in negotiations with the Ontario and Quebec governments for water-power rights on the Ottawa River led to one eighteen-month extension. By 1905, the company was at last apparently ready to proceed when F.H. Clergue's developments at Sault Ste Marie experienced severe financial difficulty. This again impeded progress on the Montreal River limits because there was an overlap of financiers, and a general disinclination to invest in pulp. Late in 1905, J.R. Booth of Ottawa bought out rights to the concessions.[51]

To the southwest, only 200 of the 2,833 square miles of the massive Spanish River Pulp Concession lay within the Temagami Forest. This limit had been one of the areas granted to the Spanish River Pulp and

Paper Company in 1899. Whereas the first agreement covered a term of only two years, once compliance with the conditions was shown, the agreement was renewed for a period of twenty-one years, adding to the company's privileges the right to cut jack pine and tamarack by board measure for use other than in the manufacture of pulp or paper, and the right to cut railway ties for five cents per tie.[52] Thus, shortly after the creation and subsequent extension of the TFR, officials contemplating a management plan faced major potential complications arising from pulpwood operations within the pine preserve. Dependent communities were becoming established and would emerge as sources of pressure for continuous development of provincial resources.

Another potential source of serious conflict over the paramountcy of pine was the still-unsettled matter of Indian claims. Between 1897 and 1905 the world of the Temagami Indians changed dramatically. With the establishment of the Temagami Forest, they seemed almost to become squatters on their own land, severely restricted and controlled in their life-style by a provincial regime that hardly recognized them and barely tolerated their presence, except as short-term casual employees. When in 1905 R.J. Watson, the local MP, pressed new Deputy Superintendent-General of Indian Affairs Frank Pedley for results, Pedley assured him that Canada would not consent to Ontario's disposal either of islands within the proposed hundred-square-mile Indian reserve or of Bear Island. Pedley received other warnings about the implications of the TFR and the encroachment of the Sturgeon Falls Pulp Company, which had been 'cutting and removing timber for the last three years' close to or within the southern part of the proposed Indian reserve. Pedley also learned that a 'good many cottages are going to be built next summer' and that timber would be cut 'everywhere especially on Bear Island. The federal interest had to be protected.'[53] Clearly, early land-use conflict in Temagami was not just between pine and other competing uses, but among these other uses as well.

'With further reference to my letter to you of 15th May 1896 regarding the Indian Reserve surveyed,' Pedley somewhat caustically began a letter to Aubrey White in 1905. Pedley asserted, in a direct challenge to Ontario's forest-management ambitions, that until the Indian reserve was confirmed, 'it will be necessary that no timber be disposed of within the area located as a reserve, or on Bear Island where it is understood the Indians are living.'[54] Perhaps Aubrey White's delay in replying to the federal government had something to do with the views on the position of the Temagami Indians expressed in his memorandum of January 1901 on the subject of the TFR. White had then candidly advised the commissioner of Crown lands that the Indians were 'in an unfortunate position.' He continued:

> They came within the scope of the Robinson Treaty of 1850, but by oversight or neglect they were not notified of the holding of the treaty and consequently were not represented, and there being no body to bring their claims forward no reservation was laid out for them, which would certainly have been done had there been anybody to press their claim ...
>
> When this matter came up, as this Department was aware of the great quantities of pine which existed in the territory and that the area asked for was entirely out of keeping with the number of the Indian population and it was further considered that we were not legally bound to give a reserve, no action was taken and the matter rested in that position. Although this is not an actual ownership it is an interest which I consider should be brought before you.[55]

Treaty developments elsewhere in Ontario had implications for the Temagami situation. Treaty No. 9, or the Ontario James Bay Treaty, was negotiated in 1905 between Canada and most of the Crees and Ojibwa living north of the lands covered by the Robinson treaties. The new treaty had been pending for some time. Canada had originally considered the height of land as the northern boundary of Ontario, but in 1884 the province won a long judicial battle with Canada and Manitoba for control of the Kenora–Thunder Bay area, and in 1889 imperial legislation had the northern boundary of Ontario declared to be the Albany River and southern James Bay. Around the turn of the century, prolonged legal controversies over Ontario's responsibilities in northwestern Ontario relative to Treaty No. 3 convinced Prime Minister Laurier that it would be best to secure prior agreement with Ontario before entering into surrender treaties with Indians living in what was now the northern part of the province. This took several years. The province agreed to pay over to Canada the amount needed to cover the annual treaty money. Ontario also agreed to set aside Indian reserves for each band 'not greater than one square mile for each family of five' and not to include valuable hydro sites. The southern boundary of Treaty No. 9 was defined vaguely and ambiguously as 'the height of land and the northern boundaries of the territory ceded by the Robinson' treaties.

Federal authorities then made the somewhat embarrassing discovery that untreatied Indians – 102 of them – resided during the summer around the Hudson's Bay Company post at Matachewan. This was well known in the district and had been noted in the report of Ontario's 1900 survey and exploration. The Matachewan post was located just north of the Forks of the Montreal River, on the northeast side of the West Montreal branch. It was near but clearly south of the height of land. The ancestral hunting grounds of the Indian people summering there, while primarily north of the divide, actually straddled it. The lands claimed by the Temagami band stretched beyond the Forks, but only on the southwest, thus excluding the Matachewan post. The river was also the boundary, as extended in 1903, of the Temagami Forest. Ontario agreed that the Matachewan Indians should be dealt with by treaty. This was done on 20 June 1906, when the band was incorporated into Treaty No. 9. They secured an Indian reserve of sixteen square miles due north of the post, but still south of the divide.[56] This episode made the position of the Temagami Indians even more anomalous and their claims for attention even more commanding.

The Mattagami band of Crees, on the northwestern edge of the Temagami Forest but over the divide, was also 'treatied' in 1906. Duncan Campbell Scott, the federal negotiator, showed his usual intellectual dichotomy on his 1906 trip, much of it by canoe. The expedition led to several new poems, 'Spring on Mattagami,' 'The Height-of-Land,' and 'The Fragment of a Letter.' Scott viewed the Indians and their environment dramatically and sympathetically. Yet he was condescending toward them and their belief system and pessimistic about the future of native culture. More poetic than most, Scott was in attitude not atypical. This was part of the problem. Scott appointed as temporary secretary Pelham Edgar, a poet in his own right and later head of the Department of English at Victoria College. The expedition also included a Dr A.G. Meindl, two policemen, two Métis guides, and a young assistant. The group had reached Matachewan by paddling upstream from the train at Latchford. They returned via Lady Evelyn Lake and Lake Temagami to the station, stopping off at Bear Island en route.[57]

By the time of the Mattagami treaty – indeed, by February 1905 – a great political change had taken place. The thirty-four years of Liberal rule in Ontario had ended with the victory of James Whitney and his Conservatives over the beleaguered forces of Premier George Ross. This change would dramatically affect the fate of the conservation movement, of northern Ontario generally, and of the Temagami Forest in particular. The Ottawa valley lumbermen, with their great interest in northeastern Ontario, now clearly lacked the influence they had had in the old regime.[58] In fact Ross himself had already curtailed their power. The allegedly deleterious role of the Ottawa lumber barons and other 'monopolists' had been one of the chief issues dividing the two political parties. The Conservatives were champions of progressive, democratic reform and liberal capitalism. Their electoral power base was in Toronto, in the larger towns of southern Ontario, and in the far north of the province. For the new government, conservation had more to do with accessibility and popular control over natural resources than with long-range forest management and sustained-yield forestry measures. The new government pushed ahead aggressively with northern development, focusing on railways, mining, and the increased extraction of resources generally. Northerners, represented by Frank Cochrane, a Sudbury mineral speculator who became minister of the reorganized Department of Lands, Forests and Mines, secured considerable influence in the Whitney government.[59]

Thomas Southworth observed shortly after the election that such progress as Ontario had achieved towards a rational system of forest management had 'not come as the result of pressure upon our legislators by a well informed public opinion.' Much further effort was required, he argued, to examine and map existing forest reserves, to apply scientific forestry principles to their management, and to extend the reserve system to all the non-agricultural lands remaining in the hands of the Crown.[60] The political transition offered little to indicate that these developments could be expected. Lumbering interests were still awaiting a general Temagami cutting policy when the Ross government fell, and the new regime had different priorities. While foresters looked on with some frustration, the northern mineral boom would not wait. The new railways would transport prospectors north past Temagami and move the ore south past Temagami. Mining financiers and executives would stop to relax on the lake, using Indian guides. Silver would be found, west up the Montreal River valley, at Elk Lake, Gowganda, and beyond. Land-use conflict intensified, further undermining the paramountcy of pine, while the strains on the Temagami wilderness and its inhabitants increased.

CHAPTER FIVE

Mining and Lumbering in the Forest Reserve, 1905–1914

The Temagami Forest Reserve had been set aside to provide Ontario with a sustained yield of its pine timber. Yet in the years between the arrival of the Temiskaming and Northern Ontario Railway on the shore of Lake Temagami and the outbreak of the First World War, the pine lumbermen remained frustrated by the unwillingness of Premier Whitney's Conservative government to establish a long-range management policy. Only short-range, ad hoc decisions involving relatively minor harvesting were made with regard to pine, while cutting expanded. The northern Ontario silver boom reached its peak in this period, challenging the original concept of forest reserves and undermining the integrity of the Temagami Forest in particular: to the Whitney government, mining was at least temporarily more important than forestry. The conservation ethic faltered; it was not as important to the democratically minded small businessmen who backed the new provincial regime as it had been to the Toronto financiers and Ottawa lumber barons who had supported the discredited Liberals. Even Thomas Southworth in the Bureau of Forestry was obliged to devote his attention to southern wood lots and reforestation rather than to the management of the great pine forests of northern Ontario.

Some pine lumbering took place under special circumstances shortly after the expansion of the TFR boundaries. In 1905, a comprehensive wood clearing program was instituted along the line of the TNOR where it passed through the Temagami Forest to reduce the likelihood that railway fires could consume extensive tracts of the valuable pinery. In

1908, Minister of Lands, Forests and Mines Frank Cochrane introduced legislation to authorize the sale of pine-cutting rights within forest reserves for mature and fire-damaged trees; however, consistent regulations for application and enforcement were not forthcoming.[1] Between 1908 and 1916 the department let a series of limits in the Temagami Forest, ostensibly because of wind or fire damage. In response to the demands of locally entrenched operators, the licences were repeatedly renewed – generally for areas much larger than that originally damaged. The largest early limit, granted in 1912, covered 4½ million board feet of jack pine along the Grassy River.[2] This was a far cry from the vision of 1900 that had involved a full inventory of forest resources and careful long-term management under the direction of trained professionals.

Land-use competition from mining was a large part of the problem. By the summer of 1905 the excitement accompanying the silver boom in nearby Cobalt was overwhelming. Between 1901 and 1911, the official census figures showed a population increase in the District of Temiskaming from 3,778 to 37,076.[3] All this activity around Temagami had profound implications for forestry.

On 14 August 1905, the Whitney government announced the withdrawal from further mineral exploration and development of the area known as the Gillies Timber Limit. This was an unusually shaped unit of about one hundred square miles just outside the Temagami Forest Reserve about fifteen miles north of Temagami Station and straddling the Montreal River and, in part, the TNOR. The northeast tip of the Gillies Limit almost reached the outskirts of Cobalt. The provincial decision allowed the Gillies Brothers Lumber Company (of Braeside, on the Ottawa River near Arnprior) time to cut the remaining stands of pine before threatening prospectors burned it down and eliminated both company profits and Crown timber revenues.

The next year, 1906, saw the establishment of the Hydro-Electric Power Commission of Ontario, designed initially to transport cheap hydro electricity to municipally owned power commissions. In the midst of popular enthusiasm for an interventionist role, Premier Whitney made ambiguous statements implying plans for a publicly owned mining operation in the Gillies Limit. After the timber was removed, he said, the limit would be kept 'and we will use it for the benefit of the people and the Province of Ontario.'[4] Favourable public response to the announcement astonished Whitney and even pleased Southworth. The Ontario government thus backed awkwardly into the mining business on the fringes of the TFR.[5]

The government's exclusion of prospectors from the Gillies Limit and subsequent plans to develop the tract itself set the excited rumour mills of the Cobalt camp in motion; rumours of mineral wealth in the limit spread rapidly. Faced with the problem of finding a mine and determined to kill rampant speculation, the government offered a bonus of $150 per inch for the discovery of a silver vein carrying more than 500 ounces of the mineral. In this way the government hoped to find a potential site for a silver mine. The use of fire to clear land was banned despite the presence of heavy overburden. Three or four miles of trenches were dug, but those who claimed that they knew of large silver payloads were unable to produce significant discoveries. The real winners were mining students Thor Brown and G.R. McLaren, who received $1,050 for finding a seven-inch silver vein on 19 July 1906.[6]

On 1 October 1906, when the Gillies Brothers Lumber Company relinquished its cutting rights in the area, the Ontario government proceeded with plans to develop the site that Brown and McLaren had found.[7] Professor Willet G. Miller assumed the unusual responsibility of bringing a mine into production. Following a series of delays and disappointments involving labour difficulties, equipment delivery, and proximity to the TNOR's spur line to Kerr Lake, drilling eventually failed to reveal a rich or persistent silver deposit. After considering whether to invest more public funds or to sell the property to private interests who would then assume the potential risks and rewards, the department decided to sell.

> It was one thing to work a rich deposit of ascertained value, and quite another thing to adventure the funds of the Province, with results which might be satisfactory or might be unsatisfactory – even such chances as a private company risking its own capital might deem itself in every way justified in taking. In short, while quite willing to work the mine for the benefit of the Treasury, if it had turned out to be a bonanza similar to some of the well-known Cobalt mines farther north, the Department did not deem it desirable to speculate with the Province's funds, notwithstanding the fact that the Legislature had placed them at its disposal.[8]

The failure of this experiment may have injured the cause of increased public involvement in the development of natural resources in Ontario, although this venture was, from the outset, highly unusual.

The mine and other properties in the Gillies Limit were sold by public tender in 1909. In four sales held in June, July, September, and November, eighty-one parcels containing 1,671.71 acres were sold for

$711,458.30. According to the conditions of sale, purchasers were required to spend annually $20 per acre for seven years in stripping or opening up mines, sinking shafts, or other actual mining operations. The Crown also reserved a royalty of 10 per cent on the gross proceeds (less freight and smelter charges) of all ores, metals, and minerals taken from the land. If workable deposits were found, the government expected that 'a reasonable share of the profits will be obtained for the public benefit.'[9] The provincial government was thus able to recover some of the costs incurred in the operation of the provincial mine, but no clear or consistent approach to the Gillies Limit emerged. Premier Whitney commented that his government had 'no settled policy, whatever,' and would 'endeavour to be guided by developments or results just in the same way as a businessman would conduct any enterprise.'[10]

A crowd of claim stakers and their assistants occupied the Gillies Limit with their lanterns until midnight on 19 August awaiting the opening of a further portion of the area to staking the next day. Despite the presence of many guns and the fierce competition to establish claims quickly, reasonable order prevailed in the staking process. However, The *Engineering and Mining Journal* reported that the rush to the claim recorder's office was a good deal less orderly. Eager claim stakers returned to the recording office in Haileybury on special trains, automobiles, bicycles, fast power launches, and horses. It was impossible to maintain discipline in the line-up as several people tried to register the same claim. The mining journal expected 'much litigation' to result.[11] Nevertheless the Gillies Limit produced no lucrative mine.

The first major silver finds actually within the boundaries of the Temagami Forest Reserve were made in August 1906 on what came to be known as the White and Darby properties near Maple Mountain. Although interest soon shifted northward, experts in 1909 were still of the opinion that 'surface showings' and accessibility should have indicated a bright future. Early access for prospectors to the Maple Mountain district was by steamer up the Montreal River to Mowat's Landing near the Mattawapika, then to the northwest corner of Lady Evelyn Lake and around Sucker Gut to the portage to Hobart Lake, and then via small lakes and a creek to Anvil Lake. Native silver was found in a narrow belt on Nipissing diabase running northward on the eastern side of Maple Mountain. The formation extended along a chain of lakes from the western shore of Anvil Lake to Stull Lake.[12]

The only producing mine in the Maple Mountain area was on the site discovered by the White brothers in 1906. Although the results were modest in comparison with other mines in northeastern Ontario, the operations encouraged road construction and thus opened another corner of the Temagami Forest – at least temporarily – to commercial activity. A short wagon road from Lady Evelyn Lake to the Maple Mountain mining camp was cut through the bush, while a thirty-mile winter road linked Haileybury to the Maple Mountain camp via Mowat's Landing.[13]

The most important silver rushes in the Temagami Forest occurred at various sites along the Montreal River system. Restless prospectors like Tom Saville considered the Cobalt field staked out and stagnant. In the fall of 1906, Saville found silver at Elk Lake, a widening of the Montreal, fifty miles upstream from the TNOR crossing at Latchford. A late spring and unusually wet summer in 1907 hindered development, as staking spread west twenty-five miles over the craggy ridges, swamps, and lakes toward Lake Gowganda on the East Montreal.[14] In the summer of 1907, thirty-five huts or cabins were located in the Temagami Forest at Elk Lake and eighteen on the opposite bank. One hundred and thirty prospectors and miners attended a four-day Ontario Bureau of Mines school at the camp. Elk Lake, the following year, was a proper village of two hundred inhabitants, really two villages: Elk City (east side) and Smyth or James (west side), with hotels, stores, a claim recorder's office, and a post office.

Major silver finds were made in 1908 about eighteen miles to the west, near Miller Lake, and the rush intensified. An overflow reached Gowganda Lake a little farther west, where further discoveries sent another rush to the west side of that lake. After rich Gowganda claims were recorded at the Elk Lake office in September 1908, the excitement became extreme. Within two weeks prospectors travelling by canoe had staked most of the land around Gowganda, and that winter W.H. Collins of the Geological Survey reported that, 'Thousands of prospectors, regardless of deep snow and severe cold, are entering the country.' By the late spring of 1909 prospectors had staked thousands of claims. Claims on which no work had been done changed hands at exorbitant figures. The Bureau of Mines expressed severe concern at the wild speculation but, before 1909 ended, 7,000 claims around Gowganda and 2,000 more in the outlying area had been staked in less than two years.[15]

Mining and prospecting activity after 1908 combined with existing pulp-cutting operations to produce heavy volumes of traffic along the Montreal River. The winter rush to Elk Lake in 1907–8 assumed proportions that one source described as 'unprecedented in the history of Ontario.' By then the TNOR line had been extended well beyond New

Liskeard, and a short six-mile spur had been built from Englehart to the new agricultural village of Charlton. From there, 850 'teams' (loads) of freight and passengers were carried in sleighs over the twenty odd miles of winter road across the Little Clay Belt to Elk Lake. Early in the winter the rate was $2.50 per hundredweight, but with increased demand this rose to $4.50 by late winter. That summer the roads were firm enough to accommodate stages, which met north- and south-bound trains at Earlton for the ride to Elk Lake. But for heavy gear and freight, river travel was preferable.

From Latchford, where commercial water transport was introduced after the crossing of the railway in 1905, steamers operating between three small obstructions in the Montreal provided ready summer access to Elk Lake. Beginning in 1907, J.R. Booth operated two steamers to transport men and supplies to his pulpwood camps. More importantly, by 1908 the Montreal River Navigation Company had three steamers on the three reaches of the river. One would leave Latchford after the train departed and take passengers to Pork Rapids where a horse-drawn tramway carried freight and baggage over the short portage. A second steamer carried passengers and freight some thirty miles to Mountain Chutes (in the first years there was also a short lift at Flat Rapids), where another tramway handled the short carry to a third steamer to complete the journey to Elk Lake. The entire route could be completed 'by supper time.' The Upper Ontario Steamboat Company of New Liskeard had seven steamers on the river and in one day could take passengers well above Elk Lake, to the mouth of Stoney Creek. Four new scows were planned. Meanwhile, the Richardson Navigation Company was projecting a fleet of large motorboats to compete with the steamers.[16]

The real problem for prospectors in this section of northeastern Ontario was getting beyond Elk Lake to Gowganda and points west. Elk Lake is on the frontier between the Clay Belt and a particularly rugged part of the Canadian Shield. Indeed, the East Montreal River flows north from Gowganda Lake for more than twenty miles over numerous rapids before reaching the Forks near Matachewan, from where the main branch runs southeast to Elk Lake and Latchford. To begin with, in 1907 and 1908, summer prospectors travelled by canoe upstream from Elk Lake to Stoney (now Sydney) Creek, up it, and through ponds and streams back to the river just below (but north of) Gowganda, thus bypassing the Forks. In the winter of 1908–9, the provincial government constructed an overland sleigh road west from Elk Lake and running north of Long Point Lake and then southwest over a chain of lakes, including Miller, to Gowganda.[17] (It cost between $30 and $50 per ton to ship ore to the TNOR over the winter roads.) This route was too muddy and rough for summer use, however. By the late winter of 1910, the sleigh road had been slightly rerouted off the lakes and was said to be usable year round, but it still proved unsatisfactory that summer. Even after rebuilding in 1911 the summer route remained shockingly rough and unsatisfactory for freight. In January 1910, the Timiskaming and Gowganda Transport Company was advertising daily service from the train at Charlton, in 'comfortable, covered sleighs with foot-warmers and modern conveniences,' three and three-quarter hours in the afternoon to Elk Lake and another five hours in the morning for the twenty-seven miles to Gowganda. On the return journey, a hardy traveller could leave Gowganda at 7:30 AM and be in Toronto twenty-four hours later. Even by 1908, Gowganda was well serviced by hotels, banks, and small shops.[18]

Most miners despaired that transportation east could ever be made satisfactory, especially for the ore. A few canoed up the Wanapitei River from the CPR, via Dougherty Lake to the upper Sturgeon, and across to the Montreal system at Smoothwater Lake. Biscotasing was only seventy miles to the west, and here the transcontinental line of the CPR crossed the Spanish River. The CPR vigorously promoted the historic fur trade canoe route from Biscotasing east via Fort Mattagami and the upper Grassy. In June 1909, *Rod and Gun* still believed this to be the best route for prospectors and workers, though hardly for ore. Small launches and wagons were appearing on some of the laps, and lumbermen Booth and Shannon established a complex transport system by letting contracts for various portions of the route.[19]

The main hope for prospectors in terms of reliable access to the new mineral districts lay with Mackenzie and Mann and the James Bay Railway, which became the Canadian Northern Ontario Railway (CNOR). Construction of 271 miles of track from Toronto to Capreol was completed in 1908, but not before the CPR itself built a Sudbury-Toronto line. Mackenzie and Mann immediately pushed farther north up the Vermilion River valley, along a route that passed through the southwest corner of the Temagami Forest toward the headwaters of the upper Wanapitei River. But by late 1908, the CNOR had reached only as far as a place it called Sellwood (now Moose Mountain) near the Vermilion, still south of the TFR. A trail or winter road already ran north from here to 'Burwash Camp' on Burwash Lake. This route was extended to Welcome Lake on a short tributary of the upper Wanapitei. From Welcome in the summer of 1909 hardy prospectors and merchants could canoe and portage across to the Sturgeon, up Stull Creek, over to

Smoothwater Lake, and thus eventually to Gowganda. In winter prospectors could snowshoe a more direct route, less than forty miles in length, and thus potentially much faster than the more obvious but circuitous TNOR–Elk Lake route.[20]

Early in 1910, the CNOR, which had been scheduled to build to Burwash, was rerouted somewhat to the northwest, close to Oshawong Lake at Gowganda Junction (a spot near where the line crossed the upper reaches of the Wanapitei). From here the Geological Survey reported that a forty-five-mile all-weather road was to be built to Gowganda. But only a winter road was actually cut and used.[21] Nevertheless, this opened up a better canoe route, certainly to West Shining Tree Lake and perhaps to Gowganda, than the one from the south-flowing rivers around Sellwood. Canoes now travelled via Meteor Lake, then downstream on the north-flowing Opikinimika River, over two short portages in and out of Allen Lake, into West Shining Tree, and thus eventually on to the West Montreal.

The Shining Tree area soon became the primary destination for prospectors because Gowganda was already in decline. In 1896, a geologist reported traces of gold and iron around the north end of Shining Tree Lake. This lake was about twenty miles southwest of Gowganda on a tiny tributary of the West Montreal. No significant developments occurred until 1909 when Tom Saville discovered silver by the lake. Other claims and actual development work followed, but no great amounts of silver were recovered.[22]

Meanwhile, in 1909, gold had been discovered on the Porcupine just beyond the far northwest corner of the Temagami Forest. Two years later a TNOR spur line reached South Porcupine from Porquis, stimulating the great gold rush. The gold fields lay north of the Shield and the pine forest. To clarify beyond any doubt its priorities in the event of any actual conflict between mining and the future of the Temagami Forest Reserve, however, the Ontario government removed the two northernmost townships in 1912 – those next to Porcupine – from the Temagami Forest. But in 1911 Messrs Gosselin, Speed, and Frith had discovered gold inside the Temagami Forest on West Shining Tree Lake some ten miles west of the original Shining Tree Lake and sixty-five miles south of the Porcupine. (The present village of Shining Tree, at first called Tungsten, is on West Shining Tree Lake; the West Montreal River runs between the two Shining Trees.) The new Shining Tree rush almost emptied the Gowganda fields. By the autumn of 1912, several gold discoveries, including one by Saville, had been made and considerable work accomplished.[23]

The previous year (1911) the CNOR had pushed northwest another fifteen miles to Deschenes and Duchaban lakes. From there (by what became Westree), eighty miles north of Sudbury, a nineteen mile winter road was built to West Shining Tree and soon extended six miles to Wasapika. In summer travellers and freight could either be taken by a short corduroy road from Ruel Station (ten miles down the line from Westree) onto the Opikinimika River or else use Deschenes Creek onto the same river. That summer, assisted by two small control dams, enterprising rivermen were transporting freight and passengers by motorized pointers on the Opikinimika to within two miles of West Shining Tree Lake.[24] In 1913, Ontario Commissioner of Roads J.F. Whitson urged that the winter road be upgraded for summer use, at least past Wasapika. This would have required a 325-foot bridge over the Opikinimika narrows. Such a road, Whitson argued, would greatly facilitate the development of timber resources.[25] While a hotel, a store, and a post office existed in Tungsten (Shining Tree), the road east of the Opikinimika was only slowly upgraded. Still deplorable in the summer of 1918, it was really only completed to Wasapika in 1920. From there to Gowganda, twenty odd miles away, was even then only a winter track.

Despite a few rich surface deposits, the Shining Tree gold camp soon developed a bad reputation. Heavy forest cover, a deep glacial overburden, and poor transportation made prospecting difficult. Speculation had been rampant, but by 1914 it was evident that the area would not yield massive quantities of either gold or silver. War forced the most marginal operations to close. As a later commentator argued, 'Early development was retarded by the indisposition of prospectors to work their claims sufficiently to expose their possibilities to the engineer and at the same time prices were put on the prospects which would hardly have been warranted for fully developed mines.'[26]

Throughout the Gowganda–Shining Tree rushes, the CNOR had presented the Conservative government of Ontario with a problem. Mackenzie and Mann were, at least until 1911, prominent Toronto Liberals associated with the Bank of Commerce. The Whitney regime certainly favoured Toronto, but the CNOR route along the west of the Temagami Forest bordering the precious mineral boom was a serious challenge to the profitability of the TNOR, the government line running along the eastern side of the TFR. No matter that the CNOR was now heading north and west to Winnipeg, rather than northeast to Lake Abitibi along the route earlier projected for its predecessor the James Bay Railway. The private railway also had a federal charter to build from Ottawa to Capreol. That line, completed in 1914, skirted the southern edge of the Temagami Forest in the lower Sturgeon valley and ran west just south of Lake Wanapitei. The provincial government was therefore in no great haste to complete road transport from the CNOR to Gowganda. TNOR officials deliberated for two years over the question of alternate routes to the Elk Lake and Gowganda district before settling on a twenty-eight-mile link from Earlton. Three other possibilities were thereby eliminated, or at least deferred: a Sudbury-Gowganda link, a line south and west from Porcupine, and an extension of the existing Englehart-Charlton branch. Two of the routes surveyed would have introduced major arteries through the TFR, greatly increasing fire hazard in the forest and facilitating access to the woodlands. When the TNOR eventually completed a branch line west from Earlton over the Clay Belt to Elk Lake in early 1913, prospectors' enthusiasm for Gowganda was already in decline.

The main effect of the new TNOR spur line was to destroy the steamboat business on the Montreal River, upstream from Latchford. All five boats of the Upper Ontario line were laid up. A big dam built in Latchford in 1910 partly to even out the river by Pork Rapids only served that transportation purpose for two years. The Latchford boom collapsed permanently, but the village survived as a small lumbering centre that continued to look to the Temagami Reserve for resources. When a delegation from Elk Lake, Gowganda, and Sudbury waited on Minister of Lands, Forests and Mines W.H. Hearst in April 1914 to urge that the TNOR spur be extended to Gowganda, the minister firmly rejected the request. The TNOR continued to study but never completed the Gowganda link.[27]

In the period preceding the First World War, mining activity in the Temagami Forest also occurred around the end of the Northeast Arm of Lake Temagami itself and on nearby Net Lake. The Barnet family of Renfrew sought to secure interests it had dating from 1890 on Temagami Island and at one point had claims covering more than four hundred acres. Beginning in 1898, Dan O'Connor seemed to be prospecting everywhere, around the long-known iron ranges north of the Northeast Arm and among the mispickle and copper concentration near Net and White Bear lakes. In 1903 A.E. Barlow credited O'Connor with promoting interest in the iron ranges of Temagami; his 'earnest and persistent advocacy of their economic importance has been one of the most powerful factors in directing public attention to them.' O'Connor persuaded the Ontario Bureau of Mines to have Professor A.P. Coleman visit the sites in 1899 and to have Professor Willet G. Miller study the ore bodies in 1901.[28] Despite Miller's favourable reaction and

O'Connor's promotional efforts, the Temagami iron range did not immediately experience development for two reasons. First, without railway services, the cost of initial development work would be high; and second, lands within the Temagami Forest were initially closed to prospecting. In 1902, however, regulations were passed allowing prospecting within the TFR. Dan O'Connor sold some of his holdings in the iron formation nearest to the Northeast Arm about 1903. He also endeavoured to interest other parties in the region, including T.B. Caldwell. H.W. and W.J. Fleury gained control of some of the claims, while the Caldwell-Mulock group acquired others.[29]

The Caldwell-Mulock group represented a strong combination in the field of mine exploration. Sir William Mulock was the Liberal representative in Parliament for North York, a cabinet minister in Sir Wilfrid Laurier's federal government, and the vice-chancellor of the University of Toronto. Thomas Boyd Caldwell (1856–1932), the son of Boyd Caldwell, carried on Boyd Caldwell and Company, the family milling, sawmilling, and merchandising business in Lanark. T.B. Caldwell's first cousin William Clyde Caldwell (1848–1905), also a miller, was Liberal member of the Ontario Legislature for most of the time since 1872; he too had interests in the Temagami area. During a canoe trip to Temagami in the summer of 1903, W.C. Caldwell commented that an American visitor from Duluth would probably want to see his iron mine.[30] It is likely, therefore, that W.C. Caldwell was involved in the Temagami iron property with his cousin T.B., who was also on the trip.

The iron potential of those ranges attracted a good deal of interest in the years before the First World War, although actual production never got underway. The Caldwell-Mulock group undertook diamond-drill work in exploration of their property east of Turtle Lake in the summer of 1904 and again the following year. Conditions were difficult, however, and drilling results were disappointing. The drilling equipment, provided by the Ontario Bureau of Mines as part of an exploration support program operated by the government between 1894 and 1909, included a 35 per cent subsidy of the drilling costs. M.H. Newman, a representative of the United States Steel Corporation conducted an intensive examination of the Temagami iron ranges in 1903. His findings confirmed that the iron-bearing material of Temagami would require beneficiation, and samples were accordingly submitted in 1903 and again in 1907 to the Ontario Bureau of Mines for concentration tests. Encouraging results achieved in 1908 attracted German investors, who obtained an option in 1913. This group also sank diamond-drill test holes, but they were forced by the outbreak of the war to abandon their plans. The difficult Temagami iron formation then lay dormant awaiting technological advances and the exhaustion of richer, more easily worked ore bodies elsewhere.[31] Iron mining was thus a latent source of complication for forest management.

O'Connor sold his 'Big Dan' gold mispickle and iron pyrites property south of Net Lake to the Temagami Mining and Milling Company, which ceased operations in 1908 after producing small quantities of ore. The Little Dan Mine, to the west of the main rail line, by Arsenic Lake, went to R.G. Leckie of Sudbury and was subsequently resold; by 1910 it had produced considerable mispickle ore for arsenic and some gold. The most consistent actual producer in the area was five miles north of the Big Dan at James Lake. Discovered in 1903, this became Leckie's iron pyrite mine; the ore was processed in the south to obtain sulphuric acid, not iron. Here between 1907 and 1909 the Northland Mining Company employed some thirty-five men in development work, but by 1910 operations ceased.[32]

The other major pyrite zone that saw some development was also an O'Connor property. Located on the south side of Sulphur Bay almost directly east of Ferguson Island in the Northeast Arm of Lake Temagami, the deposit had been identified by 1900. Willet G. Miller reported an assay chart for the site in his study on iron formations in the Temagami area. Miller assayed a sample weighing thirty-three ounces, with sulphur content at 26.20 per cent, copper 0.48 per cent, nickel 0.27 per cent, with a gold value of $1.40 per ton, and no traces of silver. Some limited production occurred in the early years of the First World War.[33]

Gold 'occurrences' were reported on the shores of Emerald Lake as early as 1897, and prospects on Emerald and neighbouring Manitou Lake were commented upon favourably by the 1900 Northern Ontario Survey. In 1901 Willet Miller explored this area carefully, after his examination of the Temagami iron ranges; he noted recent blastings but found 'no signs of the precious metal.' Surveyors noted that Emerald was near the edge of a particularly valuable pine belt stretching northwest from Cross Lake (Temagami's Southwest Arm) and up to nearby Wawiagama Lake. A.P. Coleman described an iron range quite similar in extent. Various claims were staked and a small amount of work undertaken on both Emerald and Manitou. In 1909 the Golden Rose Mining Company of Toronto was incorporated, but serious work was not undertaken until 1915; in 1919 Golden Rose went into liquidation.[34]

Meanwhile, the Ontario Department of Lands, Forests and Mines attempted to manage the pine lands of the Temagami Forest and preserve them from fire and other threats. Ranger L. Loughren, reporting directly to Aubrey White, initially assumed responsibility for a small staff of forest rangers. Loughren was succeeded in the summer of 1906 by S.C. MacDonald, who served his first season as superintending ranger at a salary of four dollars a day. More permanent arrangements were evidently desirable, however, in light of mounting problems for the pine lands arising from mineral prospecting, poaching, and illegal timber cutting of the valuable pine and pulpwood resources. Once again, necessity rather than a consistent program for forest management provoked action on the part of the provincial administration. MacDonald thus assumed the position of chief ranger at Temagami in January 1907.

As chief ranger, MacDonald supervised the work of between forty and fifty summer forest rangers who patrolled the Temagami Forest from seasonal headquarters at a new forestry building on Bear Island. A year-round residence for the chief ranger was erected on Forestry Island in the bay opposite Temagami Station, a more convenient location for transport and communication links with other representatives of Ontario's growing forest-administration service. MacDonald left Temagami in 1909 to become Crown timber agent in New Liskeard. His successor, G. Clarence Hindson, had no forestry training and was allegedly offered the office of chief ranger at Temagami as 'a reward' for political service. Hindson had gone north at the start of the Cobalt silver rush and in 1908 had managed a successful provincial election campaign for R.T. Shillington, Conservative candidate in the provincial riding of Timiskaming. Despite his lack of qualifications, Hindson was a conscientious public servant, a man of high integrity who commanded great respect.[35]

As Ontario's summer forest-ranger staff expanded dramatically before the First World War, Temagami obtained a disproportionately large share. In 1902, 15 rangers out of a provincial total of 105 served on Ontario forest reserves and Crown lands, Temagami receiving the largest number of the 15. In 1904 rangers helped extinguish two potentially serious fires, one near Net Lake and one on Horse Island. In 1905, 59 rangers patrolled construction work along the TNOR alone. By 1906 the total provincial summer-ranger staff was 623, 109 of whom served in the forest reserves at a cost of $41,885; again Temagami was favoured. Another slight increase came in 1907. The Temagami contingent included 70 rangers in 1908 when a serious fire broke out as a result of prospecting in the Gowganda area. Aubrey White defended the large size of the crew at Temagami, arguing that hordes of prospectors and tourists 'using fire for cooking, for warmth, smudges for flies and smoking' made such a force of rangers necessary. 'Considering how careless the average man is in the use of fire it is not to be wondered at that we had fires in this immense reserve during last summer, which was the driest and most prolific of forest fires we have had for years.' By 1910, 288 rangers served in Ontario's forest reserves. Over 130 of these worked in Temagami. White later noted in further defence of the forest rangers' effort at Temagami, 'If we had not had very efficient fire ranging in that reserve since the mining excitement began, the large quantity of pine timber growing there would, in all probability, have gone up in smoke.'[36] The Temagami contingent rose to a peak of 137 in 1912 and 1913 compared with 20 in the extensive but more remote Nipigon Forest. Wet weather and 'close supervision' eliminated the fire threat in 1912. Despite the rangers, two serious fires occurred in 1914 within the TFR, 'damaging 1,000,000 board feet measure of red and white pine and some 4,000 railway ties' and necessitating the selling of two fairly extensive timber berths.[37]

The rangers usually patrolled the forest by canoe. They cleared and maintained portages for the purpose of fire patrol as well as for the use of recreational paddlers. Ideally, rangers were good canoeists, good woodsmen, and good navigators, as well as good fire fighters. Problems could arise if they were less able canoeists than the tourists or prospectors whom they encountered in the TFR. Occasionally the rangers themselves were careless. John Harman Patterson, a prospector, came upon several lost young rangers and wondered why 'inexperienced boys' were sent on such important work: 'They know absolutely nothing about the forest or forest fires and though however anxious to do their duty they may be, their lack of knowledge prevents them from succeeding.' An American visitor to the district in 1906 recorded the story of an all-night paddle from the upper Sturgeon River to Bear Island to catch the steamer en route to the North Bay train with a ranger who had shot himself in the leg with a revolver. The most uncomplimentary remarks, however, were made by a Camp Keewaydin canoeist who found the hind feet of a deer on the Sturgeon River at Goose Falls: 'Fire Rangers must have passed this way. Being Game Wardens they are the only persons who can safely kill deer out of season.' White admitted that skilled 'bushmen with the necessary education and judgement' were the best rangers, but timber drives and early fall logging competed with the forest service for experienced woodsmen. Recruits, therefore, were often obtained from the Toronto School of Practical Science, active men with some education who generally gave, with experience, 'fairly good service.'[38]

The timber situation in the Gowganda mining area was particularly troublesome for forest management. The provincial response again demonstrated that resource-management decisions for Temagami were often guided by local economic pressures rather than the long-term goals articulated when the reserve was set aside. Eager developers established a badly needed sawmill to produce building supplies and began to cut pine without formal authorization. Two blocks of pine timber were later put up for sale by public auction, thus imposing some order on the behaviour of the irrepressible mining community.[39]

Pulpwood cutting continued during this period, despite concern for the pine. After the change of government in 1905, Frank Cochrane cancelled five pulp agreements, including the Montreal River agreement, for alleged non-performance of conditions. The same month in which the agreements were cancelled, they were re-offered for sale by public competition. The Conservatives thus implemented one procedural change that had been central to their criticism of 'secret' deals during the Liberal regime. The investors' indifference and the unfavourable market conditions were obvious when only two concessions were sold.[40] The Montreal River Pulp Concession, an area of 1,700 square miles, was sold to J.R. Booth for a bonus of $300,000 upon the collateral of a nearly completed Ottawa mill valued at $1.5 million. Booth obtained the right to cut spruce, poplar, whitewood, and jack pine, eight inches and up in diameter, by cordwood measure but not within or close to 'pine-bearing lands.' From 1907 to 1914, Booth operated in the townships of Barber and James, while from 1915 to 1923 the company cut in Banks, Wallis, and Roadhouse, maintaining a depot at Elk Lake. Between 1907 and 1923, pulpwood taken from the concession was floated via the Montreal River to Lake Timiskaming and from there transported under the auspices of the Upper Ottawa Improvement Company to the mills in Ottawa. This could take up to four years. To this extent, at least, Ottawa-based commercial operations retained their interest in the Temagami district after northern railway construction had reoriented the flow of developing commerce to Toronto.[41]

At Sturgeon Falls to the south of the Temagami Forest both the pulp mill and the paper mill were in trouble between 1906 and 1912; operations were frequently shut down because of market conditions and recurring financial difficulties. Creditors seeking to recover from Imperial Paper pressed the company and attempted on occasion to seize its assets. In 1912, a provincial order-in-council approved the assignment of the Sturgeon Falls pulp limit by Imperial Paper Mills of Canada

Limited to the Ontario Pulp and Paper Company Limited. In surrendering the right to cut hardwood, the company gained the additional right to cut balsam, while the length of the agreement was changed to twenty-one years dated from 1 April 1911. Because a shortage of water power limited the output of the paper mill, the capacity clause was changed to 15,000 tons of paper and 150 hands.[42] The Ontario Pulp and Paper Company, organized specifically to run the Sturgeon Falls mill, was financed by a syndicate represented by the Dominion Bond Company, which was also interested in the mill at Espanola. Following reorganization of several northern Ontario pulpwood operations in the years immediately preceding the First World War, the Spanish River Pulp and Paper Company assumed control of 550 square miles of territory in the Temagami Forest.[43]

In the first decade of the century, while the lumber industry enjoyed good conditions, pulp and paper development was generally disappointing. Financial resources, supplies of wood and water, reliable markets, and cheap transportation were not yet favourably united. Indeed, despite Ontario's 'manufacturing condition,' 'official policy confined itself to waiting for the United States to deplete its remaining pulpwood stands and turn to Canada's.'[44] In the next decade however, progress was evident, so that by 1920 when the Riddell-Latchford Timber Commission was established, the commission had more than enough material to assess the pulp as well as pine policies and practices of the province.

It was clear to the timber commissioners that provincial authorities had frequently not been able to discriminate between pine and pulpwood areas. An important statement by Mr Gibson, counsel for the Spanish River companies operating on the Sturgeon, defined the extent of the problem as the pulpwood operators in northeastern Ontario perceived it: 'Do you know that there were no townships in this area [Sturgeon limit] that did not contain more or less merchantable pine? ... So that from the very moment we began to cut we were faced with the difficulty of having no townships upon which there was no pine?'[45] From the perspective of pine-forest management within a reserve, of course, the existence of pulpwood cutting raised concerns about the consistency of the policy under which the Temagami Forest had initially been established. It would be some time, however, before Ontario attempted to introduce comprehensive measures to manage the relationship between the lumber and pulp industries.

Challenges from mine owners, pulp cutters, rival transportation empires, tourists, and the Indians were not the only problems facing the Temagami Forest and the resource-management ideals on which it rested. Well before 1914, the conservationist ethic within the Ontario government that had made the forest reserve system possible in the first place, was in eclipse. Writing shortly after the transition from Liberal to Conservative rule in Ontario, Thomas Southworth anticipated that the province's forest reserve system might eventually cover from 40 to 50 million acres. By 1914 however, even with the recent addition of the 2,000-square-mile Mississagi Forest Reserve and an extension of 811 square miles to Algonquin Park, Ontario's park and forest reserve land totalled only about 14.5 million acres or 22,574 square miles. Nor, despite legislation authorizing the purchase of timber rights from licensees within forest reserves, was there much pressure for expansion from within the provincial administration. On the other hand, federal officials from the Commission of Conservation continued to emphasize the goal of a continuous forest reserve belt linking the existing Temagami and Nipigon reserves. Indeed, the Commission of Conservation urged a westward extension of the system to incorporate the Lake of the Woods watershed, primarily as a means to protect the flowage of the Winnipeg River and the power it provided to western Canadian communities. Yet it was acknowledged to be unlikely that Ontario would act: 'the area is so large and the immediate possibilities for revenue so limited that it seems doubtful whether reservation would be considered justified at the present time by the provincial authorities in view of the very large expense involved.'[46]

The conservation ethic was, however, still alive among a small but growing body of professional foresters, mainly at the University of Toronto's forestry school, and among some leaders in the forest industries. These professionals criticized and gradually shifted into a position of opposition toward the government's woodland policies. Judson Clark, the only professional forester within the Bureau of Forestry, resigned in 1906 after disagreements over forest-management procedures and was not replaced for six years. Bernard Fernow, dean of the forestry school at the University of Toronto from 1907 to 1919, moved from extolling the reserve system to open criticism of provincial policy. He was a proponent of state-run, German-style forestry and had enthusiastically promoted the idea of a contiguous belt of northern forest reserves. Fernow became convinced, however, that since the Conservatives had come to power forest management on the reserves had 'failed to gain headway' and that demand for timber revenues alone determined policy. He predicted that, at existing rates of cutting, the supply of pine would be exhausted within twenty-five years and other merchantable species badly affected. 'The scant supply of forest products with the exception of pulpwood is evident,' and even the bulk of that he noted was north of the divide into the Arctic watershed and thus relatively inaccessible.[47]

There were ample reasons for such pessimism. Through departmental reorganization in 1905 the Conservatives had once again removed the director of forestry to the Department of Agriculture and given him responsibility only for reforestation of southern woodlots and the prevention of fires along rail lines. In 1912, following further reorganization, E.J. Zavitz became provincial forester in the Department of Lands, Forests and Mines. Though Zavitz was professionally trained, his mandate remained fairly restricted. Even after 1917, when he was placed in charge of all forest fire-fighting services for the province, Zavitz was not responsible for general forestry policy. Still it was true to claim, as a Whitney pamphlet did in 1913, that with 'nine billion feet of pine on these reserves ... worth an average of $8 per thousand, which represents an asset of say seventy millions of dollars,' the establishing of the forest reserves had virtually eliminated 'the danger of destruction by fire,' because 'no settlement or squatting is allowed' and 'great precautions are taken by fire ranging to prevent the start or spread of forest fires.' It was also true, however, that the government planned no other action.[48]

When the war clouds burst over Europe in August 1914, the Temagami country was in its usual summer splendour. The clean headwater rivers flowed to Nipissing, Timiskaming, and far off James Bay. Though smoke-belching locomotives travelled around much of the forest perimeter, most of the pine remained uncut, nor had it suffered serious fire damage in living memory. Southern forces, especially Toronto interests and the Ontario government had further penetrated northern sections of the province. The TNOR had carried ambitious prospectors to the northland and much ore to the south. The railway also carried southward some of the disappointed and faint-hearted who turned out to have been mere sojourners of the boom. That summer in the Temagami Forest most of the mines were shut. On Lake Temagami itself, as the world was shaking, little steamboats plied its myriad arms carrying happy vacationers. Up in the headwaters dedicated canoeists continued to explore wilderness waterways. The cumulative result of this varied activity, combined with the persistent presence of the Temagami Indians and the failure of the Ontario government to pursue development of a forest inventory and long-term operational plan for the Temagami Forest Reserve, was that land dedicated in 1901 as a pine reserve had, by 1914, virtually become a multiple-use territory. The problems of managing the forest in light of the serious potential for conflict had not been seriously examined. Nor would this change for some decades to come.

CHAPTER SIX

This Is Ontario's Heritage

As those responsible for the selection of the route had anticipated, private and commercial recreation expanded rapidly following the arrival of the Timiskaming and Northern Ontario Railway on the tip of Lake Temagami's Northeast Arm.[1] Holidaying canoeists soon shared Temagami waters with cottagers, summer youth campers, and the vacationing guests of newly established lodges and lakeside hotels. Summer vacationers greatly appreciated the relative isolation of the Temagami district, which provided unlimited opportunities for wilderness canoe travel or for rustic outdoor life at remote cottage sites. Yet much if not all of this 'appreciative' activity was potentially in conflict with the production-oriented objectives that underlay the creation of the Ontario system of forest reserves.

Careless recreational travellers certainly represented an immediate threat in terms of increased fire risk around Temagami. If the government had not originally sought to exclude recreational visitors, officials had clearly hoped to bring them under supervision in order to minimize their impact on the pinery. Nevertheless, as tourists arrived in moderate but increasing numbers in the years before and after the First World War, Ontario gradually began to recognize potential economic advantages in recreational activity. Indeed, the reorientation of provincial policy was such that government publications came to advertise Temagami as a prominent holiday destination, while the provincially owned TNOR vigorously promoted Temagami's recreational attractions. As provincial policy regarding recreational land use evolved slowly in response to particular circumstances at various locations across Ontario, provincial officials may not have recognized the potential of the tourist community to become an articulate source of criticism of the forest resource industries' performance in the Temagami district. Early controversies over water-level management on and around Lake Temagami suggested the existence of environmental concern, although it would be some time before the full implications of tensions between the resource industries and environmentalists emerged clearly.

The North American 'summering movement' of the late nineteenth and early twentieth centuries, in which Temagami played an important role, resulted from the combination of several factors, including accelerating urbanization and improved transportation. A supportive ideology – a wilderness ethic, perhaps – was also widely articulated and served to promote a renewed interest in the natural environment and outdoor travel. Urban residents of the great American and Canadian cities were attracted to Temagami and other wilderness spaces as refuges from occupational pressures. 'Here the brain-fagged, nerve-racked denizens of our great cities may find rest, real rest, from the clash and clang, the hurry and the worry of the ten months' grind in the treadmill of business life.' Real life, distinguished from mere physical existence, was to be found in the good air, 'where the eye can look unobstructed on God's dome and sweep the circle of the sky, where there is a breadth of vision forbidden to the man of the crowded centres.'[2] L.O. Armstrong, a few years after his lengthy Temagami canoe trip with Charles Paradis, speculated on Canada's vast potential for wilderness recreation: 'Canada has room enough in her illimitable stretches of forest, with lakes, streams, and mountains, extending practically from ocean to ocean, for all who may come. In addition to her other attractions, Canada can give space enough to make playgrounds for the world.'[3]

According to the *North Bay Times*, a wilderness camping vacation was 'typically Canadian. No other civilized country has a great northwoods combined with lakes and rivers, where the lover of nature can study her unadorned loveliness in all its grandeur.' The appeal of Temagami was sometimes specifically directed to a Canadian audience: 'To us Canadian born, it is a glorious heritage, one that we all should be intimately acquainted with, not only for our own personal pleasure and recreation, but for first-hand information of the natural resources and beauties of our own Canada.'[4]

A major impetus for the expansion of Temagami tourism came from transportation interests seeking the benefits of increased traffic into remote holiday districts. In 1899 the Canadian Pacific issued the first edition of its pamphlet *Timagaming: A Glimpse of the Algonquin Paradise*, which projected a popular image of Temagami as a region of clear cool air with enchanting scenery and superb fishing and hunting. The railway's brochure describes a fishing expedition where the 'silent waters' of Lady Evelyn Lake 'are but a setting for islands that seem to float on its molten surface.' Entering Temagami from Sharp Rock portage, one sees the only disappointing view of the lake. But after a mile, this 'fabled heaven of the Algonquins begins to assume the witchery of form and colour which must haunt any mortal who has fallen under its spell until he dies.' The Grand Trunk Railway information offices in Chicago, New York, Boston, and Pittsburgh also offered details on Temagami holidays to potential American visitors.[5]

Armstrong, the CPR's chief colonization agent, claimed that 'the prettiest way to visit Temagami is to go by way of Timiskaming – to Timiskaming station on the Canadian Pacific Railway.' Travellers were advised that they could reach the district with only 'moderate expenditure.' When the TNOR became the only railway to reach Lake Temagami itself, the government line responded to the heavy volume of tourist traffic by scheduling direct connections with Grand Trunk and Canadian Pacific trains at North Bay. Thus, in the 1906 season, published travel times showed Temagami to be relatively accessible to major urban centres. From Toronto, rail service to Temagami took ten hours. The trip from New York or Chicago took twenty-four hours, though Detroit and Buffalo were only fifteen hours away, and a through Pullman service was available from the latter centre throughout the tourist season. In addition to offering convenient connections, the TNOR catered to the particular needs of the tourist industry with a specially designed 'artistic modern station' and restaurant where northbound and southbound trains stopped for twenty minutes.[6]

A diversified array of services appeared on the lake itself to meet the needs of summer visitors who came as campers, canoeists, and fishermen, cottagers or youth campers, or to enjoy the facilities of the new lodges and resorts. Fraser Raney, writing on 'Canoe Trips in Temagami,' suggested three forms of camping in the district. Many visited the north for its fresh air and scenery 'having no wider outlook than that obtained from a permanent camp – sleeping under canvas or in a log cabin.' American tourists were said to favour camping with guides, and '[t]o the stranger who is a tenderfoot, a guide seems absolutely essential.' Raney reserved 'the third and highest degree in the order of campers' for those who set out 'with nothing but a good map and a compass' and 'a light safe canoe.'[7]

Canoeing parties continued to lead summer vacationers in using and popularizing Temagami's recreational potential, often following routes detailed in James Edmund Jones's innovative guidebook and manual *Camping and Canoeing*, or in the pages of the leading sportsmen's magazines. As casual entry to the TFR was not subject to scrutiny or control, no reliable estimate of the numbers and distribution of summer paddlers is possible, but Canadian and American sportsmen frequented the area. The majority of Canadian visitors appear to have come from Toronto, while a surprising number of the American travellers – at least those whose records survive – were from the Cleveland area.[8]

Fishing was a particular attraction. From Smoothwater Lake it was reported: 'By trolling with from two hundred and fifty to three hundred feet of wire line we had no trouble in catching lake trout at any time we cared to fish.' In one day at Mattawabika Falls nine men using grasshoppers for bait handily landed seventy bass, ranging between two and five pounds. The veracity of this account is attested to by the presence in the fishing party of a local judge! Hunting, too, drew sportsmen to this area, especially when rail service increased the convenience of transporting game.[9]

Ontario's game laws at the time the TFR was established were the result of evolutionary process, recently accelerated by an alarming public inquiry. In 1892, the Royal Commission on Fish and Game described a pattern of 'merciless, ruthless and remorseless slaughter' that posed an immediate threat to several species. 'The clearing of land,' Commissioner G.A. MacCallum wrote, and 'the cutting down of the forests, the introduction of railways, the ravages of wolves and the indiscriminate hunting of the human assassin and the use of dynamite and nets have all contributed to the general decrease of game and fish of this land.' Settlers, Indians, boys, and pot-hunters were singled out as notable abusers of the closed seasons across the province. Strengthened game and fisheries legislation soon provided for Ontario's first permanent game wardens and numerous deputy wardens in a concerted effort to enforce protection measures more effectively. Algonquin and Rondeau parks, when established in 1893 and 1894 respectively, were designated as wildlife reserves.[10]

Whether as an extension of existing game-protection measures or more likely as a means to preserve the exclusivity of the forest reserve system the Forest Reserves Act of 1898 explicitly provided that 'no person shall ... hunt, fish, shoot, trap or spear or carry or use firearms or explosives within or upon such reserves.' Within two years, this prohibition was modified and made subject to regulations established by order-in-council. Hunting subsequently took place in Temagami and other forest reserves, while the province endeavoured to reinforce the operation of game laws within the reserves. A regulation of 1906 prohibited firearms 'having a barrel of greater length than four inches' in the Temagami, Nipigon, and Mississagi Reserves during the closed season for moose, reindeer, and caribou.

The policy shift of 1900 and the succession of technical adjustments intended to implement effective game practices within Temagami and other forest reserves by no means concludes this episode in Ontario's awkward and uncertain recognition of non-timber interests in forest management. When re-enacted in 1910 the Forest Reserves Act restated without change the 1900 statutory prohibition against hunting and fishing except under regulations. By September 1911 Aubrey White felt compelled to advise his minister frankly that, 'No regulations have been made under this Act and as a result no hunting or fishing can take place in a forest Reserve.' With game season about to begin, the harried administrator reported numerous letters from the general public confirming a popular expectation that hunting and fishing ought to be permitted. Finally, in October 1911, hunting and fishing by sportsmen were authorized in the forest reserves on the same basis as elsewhere in the province.[11]

Comparisons with increasingly populated and less remote resort districts such as the Kawartha or Muskoka regions of southern Ontario enhanced the lure of Temagami for wilderness travellers. In the 1907 edition, Karl Baedeker advised readers of his *Dominion of Canada*: 'The scenery resembles that of the Muskoka Region but is on a bolder and more striking scale, while the cottages with which the Muskoka Lakes are lined are almost wholly lacking.' In the view of another Temagami traveller, 'The scenery as a whole is more satisfactory than the Muskoka, Georgian Bay or Algonquin Park districts, as there are no extensive "burns," or bare rocky ridges outcropping towards the sky, to mar the landscape ...'[12]

The search for physical isolation also drew to the Temagami area pioneers of the youth camping movement. Two private youth camps for boys were established on Lake Temagami in the early 1900s. The American one, Camp Keewaydin, and its Canadian counterpart, Camp Temagami, were soon recognized leaders in the youth camping field and contributed, each in its own way, to the further development of the Temagami area as a diversified summer recreation centre. Both operations flourished, accounting jointly for several hundred summer visitors each year in the prewar period.

In 1902, A.S. Gregg Clarke, a Harvard graduate and founder of

Keewaydin's forerunner, the Kamp Kahkou canoe-tripping camps in northern Maine, entered northern Ontario in search of a more rugged and remote setting in which to relocate. Finding Temagami well-suited to his needs (Keewaydin later advertised 'A summer of real camping in real woods. Not at a make-believe "camp," on the shore of some crowded New England lake or pond'), Clarke set up operations on Lake Temagami and established a permanent base camp in 1904 on Devil's Island on the lake's North Arm. That season the group totalled 66. Keewaydin's fees for the youth program ranged from $95 for one month at the Devil's Island camp up to $225 for the two-month James Bay canoe trip planned for 1908. Clarke informed his stockholders in 1914 that the camp had accommodated 226 campers, guides, and staff that year, up slightly from the previous season despite a slight decline in adult guests that Clarke attributed to the war and competition from other operations. Clarke was also anxious to maintain an adult visitors' operation, the 'Keewaydin Club', which had proven to be very profitable under the direction of his associate George Creelman.

The Keewaydin program emphasized wilderness canoe-tripping as a means of furthering the physical and moral development of American boys. 'It is a rough, healthy life in the home of nature; an out and out camp life, full of exercise and healthful, invigorating sport.' The canoe-trip experience was central to a Keewaydin summer, and with François Le Clair of Mattawa as head guide in the early years at Temagami, the camp experimented with local routes and more remote expeditions. In 1903 some campers followed the Mississagi to Huron Lodge at Desbarats where they could attend a performance of L.O. Armstrong's play *Hiawatha*. Successful trips were run north to Lake Abitibi in the same season and in 1904. Keewaydin's first trips to James Bay took place in 1911, three years after they were originally proposed.[13] Through Keewaydin, for some American boys, the end of the frontier announced by Frederick Jackson Turner in 1893 may have been deferred.

Camp Temagami appeared to at least one observer as a far more 'happy-go-lucky' enterprise. A.L. Cochrane was a drill instructor at Toronto's Upper Canada College when, in 1900, he began to organize canoe trips in the Muskoka district for boys from the school. By 1903, finding Muskoka no longer satisfying, he selected a cluster of islands in Temagami's South Arm as a base for his popular summer outings. Cochrane's camp was described as 'a rendezvous where boys may meet during the summer, and, under capable supervision, spend their holiday in instructive recreation and pleasure.' Canoe trips naturally continued to hold a central place in the camp's range of activities. Trips varying in length from a few days to several weeks provided experience in portaging, tent pitching, and outdoor cookery. Each boy would 'take turn at similar duties for his own instruction and the general good of the party.' 'Nothing,' the camp brochure claimed, 'is so fascinating to the adventurous spirit of a boy as a trip of this nature.' The in-camp program emphasized the development of skills oriented towards water safety and life-saving proficiency, an approach consistent with Cochrane's position as Canadian representative for the Royal Life Saving Society. Testimonials indicate that the program was highly regarded. George R. Parkin, an active popularizer of imperial federation who became acquainted with Cochrane while serving as headmaster of UCC from 1895 to 1902, highly recommended the experience at Camp Temagami to interested inquirers and provided an endorsement for the brochure.[14]

The youth camps were dedicated to character building through vigorous outdoor living and wilderness appreciation. As an English magazine commented of the Keewaydin program: 'Self-reliance, resource, and independence are brought out as much as possible, so that the boy may become a true white Indian.' In the ethos of the era, these qualities were valued as much for their reapplication to urban life as for their immediate utility on the trail: 'the young fellow who has learned to take care of himself in the wilderness has a better chance to succeed in any walk of life to which his lot may call him.'[15]

It is difficult to situate clearly the philosophy of these youth camps in their formative years in the continuum of early-twentieth-century youth organizations ranging from the natural to the militaristic.[16] Ernest Thompson Seton's Woodcraft Indians represented one dimension of the spectrum, while the Boy Scout movement was demonstrably oriented towards the opposite extreme. The Temagami camps fell somewhere in between, and participated, for a mixture of reasons, in both traditions. A.L. Cochrane's sentiments and experience certainly tended towards the Boy Scout model, yet the camp's informality and the collegial character of the relationships it fostered through the years confirm the lack of organizational rigidity and discipline. Keewaydin, like Temagami, served a somewhat exclusive clientele of those likely to assume positions of leadership in their communities. Corporate ownership and the existence of separate camping organizations in the network also contributed to the carefully structured program that continues to characterize Keewaydin's approach to the wilderness. Indian and Métis guides, though, represented a clear link to the natural or pragmatic tradition and an affirmation of experience alongside technique and routine in learning and development.

Organized youth camping for girls was also contemplated soon after Keewaydin and Camp Temagami were established. In 1907, T.M. Nelson of the Chambersburg Trust Company in Pennsylvania acquired Island No. 661 with the intention of establishing a camping place for young women from Penn Hall, a preparatory school associated with Wilson College. The project was apparently unsuccessful, and it was several years before a youth camp for girls was introduced to the Temagami area.[17]

The enthusiasm of canoeists was paralleled by the awakening interest of urban Canadian and American vacationers in potential cottage sites where 'the formalism and restraint of the city can be laid aside to the benefit of mind and body.' Lake Temagami's aesthetic appeal had been discussed as early as the 1880s, and a government brochure, entitled *Our Northern Districts*, proclaimed in 1894 that 'with its elevation, bracing air and romantic scenery,' Lake Temagami 'appears to have the makings of an ideal summer resort in it.' A decade later, *Smiley's Canadian Summer Resort Guide* announced that the Temagami islands were being surveyed and would soon go on sale.[18]

The statement regarding island sales proved to be premature, but in 1904 surveyors were sent to examine the islands of Lake Temagami in the recently established TFR. Under instructions issued in March 1904, Ontario Land Surveyor T.B. Speight was urged to 'proceed with as little delay as possible' to examine and report upon the Lake Temagami islands. He was to number the islands and to assess each in order to 'ascertain its suitability for a summer resort.' Speight's report provided detailed descriptions of each of the islands his survey crew examined, along with general advice regarding policy for the islands. He recommended, for example, that islands greater than five acres in size should be divided into two or more parcels. Several of the larger pine-covered islands Speight considered to be 'too valuable to be disposed of for summer residences before the timber asset has been realized upon.' Temagami Island, near the centre of the lake, had several million feet of good red and white pine. Speight attempted to change the name of Muddy Water Bay to Sunnywater: 'Muddy Water Bay is a misleading title, and arises from the fact that the extreme east end of that arm has a muddy landing at the portage.'[19]

As Speight was unable to complete the islands survey before leaving to fulfil other engagements at spring break-up, Aubrey White recruited Alexander Niven to continue the examination and assessment. '[I]t is all important that a very accurate survey should be made as probably a plan or a reduction thereof will be published and used for the sale or lease of these islands.' White, of course, was familiar with the ongoing but then relatively quiet controversy surrounding Indian land claims at Temagami when he speculated here about island sales. The Niven party carried forward the investigation and appraisal of the islands' suitability for cottages.

Then during the summer of 1904, before the Ontario government settled on a general disposal policy for Temagami islands, a party of vacationing canoeists from Cleveland actually attempted to claim several islands.[20] A long association between Cleveland residents and the Temagami district grew from this initial contact; and indeed one of these early visitors eventually became the founding president of the cottagers' association on Lake Temagami. Such links between one American urban centre and a particular recreational locale in Ontario were not uncommon in the province's history.

Public discussion concerning policy for the Temagami islands was formally introduced to the Ontario Legislature during the 1904 budget debate. Liberal Crown Lands Commissioner E.J. Davis considered these islands to be an important new field for summer tourism and recognized that many suitable cottage sites similar to those in the Muskoka, Lake Simcoe, and Peterborough districts were being made accessible by the construction of the Timiskaming and Northern Ontario Railway. Serious consideration would need to be given to the question of allocating the islands to summer resort purposes, including cottages; letters received by the government indicated that substantial public interest already existed. One month later, debate resumed on a motion by opposition spokesman Dr Beatty Nesbitt, who urged that, because of the great risk of speculation, the Lake Temagami islands be leased on a one-per-person basis and not sold. In reply Davis explained that reports on the summer resort and timber potential of the islands had not yet been received from the surveyors and asked that the department's hands not be tied prematurely. He gave his assurance that the government intended to formulate policy to preserve the beauty of the islands and would not act in haste to dispose of them. Procedural wrangling cut short the day's debate before any possible conflict with Indian claims was raised for discussion.[21]

Outside the legislature, discussion of summer resort lands was taken up by *Rod and Gun*. In a lead editorial, it was argued that such lands were in demand, 'but from want of a fixed policy the sale has been slow.' A proper policy, *Rod and Gun* suggested, would provide income for the provincial government, whose squandering of timber areas had damaged revenue prospects from timber lands. Quebec's practice of leasing preserves was rejected, for 'they keep away people who would spend money, they give very little revenue to the province, and are a source of annoyance and bad feeling amongst the people.' Before the Temagami islands issue was officially settled, a provincial election resulted in the replacement of the Ross Liberals by the Whitney Conservatives. The responsibility for resolving the island lease question now rested with a new commissioner of Crown lands, Frank Cochrane.[22]

The Temagami islands leasing policy finally appeared in August 1905. It was intended to be a comprehensive response to a specific local situation involving very desirable recreational properties within an area presumably set aside for forest management. Lake Temagami islands became available for leasing, one per person, for a period of twenty-one years, with an option to renew the lease for an equal period. Rent, payable yearly in advance, was set at twenty dollars for the first half-acre or less and three dollars for every additional acre or part-acre. 'No dwelling house would be erected of a less value than three hundred dollars, unless a plan and description of same have been approved by the Minister.' Frank Cochrane recommended that islands of more than five acres in size should be retained by the Crown, 'both because of the large quantities of timber upon some of them, and also in order that the general public who may not obtain leases of individual islands may have some place which they may use as camping grounds.' The concept of public campgrounds in the north was thus introduced in Ontario apparently in advance of widespread popular demand. But Cochrane's recommendation reflected no appreciation of potential conflict between recreational visitors and the forest industry.

In most respects localized pressure for the allocation of land for recreational purposes in various districts across Ontario, rather than a preconceived approach or philosophy, governed the provincial response. Practice dominated policy as provincial authorities gradually developed an overall perspective on this comparatively new form of land use. Indeed, there were exceptions to the general rule of reserving the larger Temagami islands, and some larger sites were leased for commercial purposes to camps and hotels. From 1905 until 1942, however, a lease rather than a grant-in-fee simply remained the basis of tenure for cottages and resort operators alike.

In 1906, the first year in which the official policy was in effect, thirty-four leases were prepared, including twenty held by Americans. Pre-1906 claimants (not all of whom regularized their positions under the official leasing policy) included the early Clevelanders. H.C. Woods, the local manager of the HBC post at Bear Island, and two more senior company officials, C.C. Chipman and E.O. Taylor, also occupied or claimed attractive islands before the implementation of the leasing policy. Most of the early cottagers were people of some means, though a large number were far from wealthy. Lawyers, doctors, journalists, stockbrokers, educators, and academics were represented in the cottaging community. Mining prospectors or promoters who had met with some considerable success were also to be found. A few cottagers were very prosperous businessmen or prominent politicians.

Among the Canadians to lease islands in the early years were several individuals active in the development of northeastern Ontario's resources. Lumberman J.A. Gillies of Braeside leased Island 664, but later voluntarily forfeited it. John Trethewey, one of the very successful principals in mining undertakings around Sasaginaga Lake, leased a small island opposite the HBC post in 1908. He had previously constructed Lake Temagami's first boathouse with a slipway on the site, and the Ontario government's modest annual rent of twenty-three dollars was doubtless a small price to pay for more secure tenure. Printer, publisher, and sometime prospector Frank Herbert Newton leased Island 977, southwest of the HBC post, but retained his interest in the property for only a few years. A few residents of Haileybury, South Porcupine, Cobalt, and, of course, Temagami Station were also among the early cottagers, though most of the Canadians who claimed Lake Temagami islands before the First World War gave Toronto as their permanent address.

The largest contingent of early American cottagers originated in Cleveland and other Ohio cities. New York, Buffalo, Philadelphia, Pittsburgh, and Detroit also appear on the records. One entry in the lease books from Chattanooga, Tennessee, and one from London, England, represent the extremes of distance. Some of the Americans – like Robert B. Newcomb and Frank Cobb, who were both Cleveland attorneys – appear to have begun their cottaging days at Temagami. Others retreated to the northern Ontario wilderness after experience in less remote and more populated recreational districts. Frank Anderson from Ohio, for example, took the train north from Toronto in 1910 in hopes of finding a fishing retreat more isolated than his current location in the Adirondacks. He took over Island 977 from Frank Herbert Newton and was soon joined by his brother, who obtained neighbouring Island 974. Samuel F. Haserot, the owner of a large cannery in Ohio and plantations in Hawaii, journeyed north from his cottage near Powassan and selected Island 1128 in Temagami's Northwest Arm in 1908.[23] At the request of Lieutenant-Governor J.M. Gibson, who as the commissioner of Crown lands had been instrumental in the establishment of the Temagami

Forest Reserve, an exception was made to the leasehold procedures for island residents. In 1909, cabinet agreed to an outright sale of Island 99, which Gibson had occupied as a lessee since 1906.[24]

The initial enthusiasm for Temagami islands resulted in about fifty leases by the time war began. New leases were rare in the war years, although the numbers increased again sharply in the 1920s. A dozen new leases, including one to Ernest Voorhis, a public servant and a Temagami canoeist of the 1890s, were signed in 1920. There were seven additional leases in 1921 and 1922 and ten in 1923, the year in which George W. Lee, chairman of the TNOR, leased Island 210. Only nine new leases were arranged in the following year, but this level more than doubled when, in each of 1925 and 1926, twenty-two leases were signed for Temagami islands.[25]

Revived interest in Ontario resort lands following the war was not confined to Temagami. In fact, the deputy minister of lands and forests regarded the phenomenon as sufficiently widespread that some standard approach should be taken to the cottage lands of Lake of the Woods, Rainy Lake, Lake Huron, Georgian Bay, and other attractive locations where summer residency was rapidly becoming well established. 'There is a large number of persons who seek seclusion while spending the summer or fall and in order to do so they desire to acquire land many miles beyond civilization and beyond the districts where the land is regularly open for sale and, in fact, beyond surveyed territory.' This group, in the deputy minister's view, was 'on the increase,' and he recommended leasing until the land was surveyed or opened for sale. At the same time it was argued that 'it would not be in the public interest to dispose of prime points of land or outstanding islands of beauty at the regular prices but they should be specially valued and sold at such prices as may be considered fair and reasonable.'[26]

In 1904, the Temagami Steamboat and Hotel Company began operations under the managerial direction of Dan O'Connor, the former mayor of Sudbury, whose detailed knowledge of the Temagami area came from his personal experience as a prospector. O'Connor had been one of the first to recognize Temagami's potential for commercial recreation and had lobbied actively for a railway route that would help to bring this about. Financial backing for the initial venture was provided by W.G. Gooderham and Alex and David Fasken. This group immediately established the Ronnoco Hotel, little more than a hundred yards from the TNOR station in the new lakeshore village of Temagami. The Temagami Inn, on Temagami Island, in the centre of the lake, and the Lady Evelyn Hotel on the North Arm were soon added.

The Ronnoco catered essentially to stopover traffic and, through O'Connor's Temagami Canoe Company, provided outfitting and guiding services. Facilities at the Temagami Inn and the Lady Evelyn Hotel were more luxurious. These Temagami hotels, *Smiley's Canadian Summer Resort Guide for 1906* declared, 'are not the result of a slow gradual growth, but prepared for the best class of guests, with every regard for their comfort and convenience. There is an excellent menu, and the best brands of liquors and cigars are kept.' Matthew Parkinson, writing in the *Canadian Magazine*, informed his readers that 'Temagami combines the comfort of home with the freedom of the absolute wilderness.' The three hotels of the Temagami Steamboat and Hotel Company could accommodate up to 550 guests at daily rates of $2.50 to $3.50 per person, among the highest in the province during this period. Weekly rates of $16 to $21 were available for the residential or resort-oriented vacations in which the two island hotels specialized. At full occupancy in the height of the season, these three hotels brought in approximately $10,000 per week, but the Lady Evelyn Hotel with its 108 beds was destroyed by fire early in the 1912 season and never replaced.[27]

A typical day's activity at the hotels included guided fishing expeditions on Lake Temagami or nearby lakes, where boats were left for use by guests. As a break from fishing, steamer and launch tours could be arranged around other camps and resorts or perhaps to the abandoned HBC post on Temagami Island. Keewaydin's adult program made use of 'stations' established throughout the region:

> A whole season can be most pleasantly spent by taking daily trips from one of the 'stations' or by taking excursions of a few days each, returning to the 'station' to get a new lot of supplies and to start out again. Once each month, on the 15th (unless it be a Sunday) the 'circuit trip' will leave the headquarters for a tour of the region. This will last two weeks, and will enable one to get a great variety of canoeing and fishing experiences.[28]

Rates were quoted on a weekly and a daily basis, for the length of a Temagami holiday might vary considerably. Group tours increased resort activity by introducing significant numbers of people for visits of short duration, often only overnight. The 1906 itinerary of the Canadian tour of the Duke and Duchess of Connaught and their entourage included a stopover at Temagami. In the following year, the American Institute of Mining Engineers held meetings in Toronto and then travelled to Cobalt, Sudbury, and nearby Moose Mountain. After visiting the Tritowns – Haileybury, New Liskeard, and the recently established community of Cobalt – the group spent a weekend at the Temagami Inn and the Lady Evelyn Hotel. The American Association of Passenger and Ticket Agents toured Temagami in 1908 on a promotional visit intended to familiarize tourist industry representatives with the Ontario northland, and the Associated Boards of Trade of Ontario were on the lake in 1912. All these groups and the other resort visitors, as well as most cottagers and summer campers, reached their destinations on the lake or points nearby using one of Temagami's early steamboats.[29]

O'Connor brought the first lake vessel, the *Marie*, by horse and sleigh in 1903. Completion of the TNOR and flatcar service made transportation a good deal easier, and several new steamers – *Wanda, Spry, Beaver, Queen, Bobs, Keego, Chance* – were soon plying Temagami waters. The *Belle of Temagami*, constructed locally around 1908, was queen of the fleet. These vessels emphasized transport only rather than accommodation and other tourist services.

The attractiveness of Temagami cottage sites may have increased in the 1920s as a result of improved communications on the lake. More commercial vessels then served the Temagami islands more frequently than in the past, and early outboards were becoming available. The boat lines that had originated with Dan O'Connor's efforts and the Temagami Steamboat and Hotel Company underwent reorganization. In 1918 Oderic Perron and Captain Fred S. Marsh entered partnership as the Perron and Marsh Navigation Company. Then in 1924 Captain E.T. 'Ted' Guppy obtained financial backing from several island residents for the Temagami Navigation Company and brought the *Iona* in from Lake of Bays.

In 1908, a different and earlier Temagami navigation company made a competitive proposal for another major resort hotel near the HBC post and Indian settlement on Bear Island. The new enterprise attempted to obtain land 'on the point now occupied by the Ontario Government Fire Rangers.' Although the Ontario government appeared sympathetic to the hotel venture, it was then in the midst of a long-standing conflict with the HBC concerning the latter's title to certain Bear Island property. For the HBC, Bear Island was but one of many land-title controversies lingering in the aftermath of the historic 1870 arrangements between the company and Canada to transfer the fur trade empire's authority to the new Dominion. On the assumption that HBC agreement was somehow required, the general manager of the proposed new venture wrote hopefully to solicit a favourable reaction: 'as the project will benefit your company practically as much as our own, we trust you will give the necessary instructions to have this matter looked into at once.' Recognizing that the Ontario government had attempted to use the possible advantages of Temagami Navigation's hotel plans to induce the HBC to modify or abandon its claims on Bear Island, HBC officials simply reversed the tactic. '[I]f you can induce the Minister of Lands and Mines to issue an official acknowledgement of the Company's claim,' HBC Commissioner Chipman replied, 'I have no doubt we could negotiate mutually satisfactory terms for a site suitable for your purposes.' But Temagami Navigation's hotel plans eventually failed to materialize.[30]

Accommodation less elaborate than that offered by the three major hotels of the Temagami Steamboat and Hotel Company was also available on the lake. A New York clergyman vacationing at Indian-owned Friday's Lodge on Point Matagama reported: 'Our luggage was speedily transferred, and we were soon in possession of our quarters, a spacious tent, its floor strewn with pungent branches of balsam, and fragrant with its aromatic odour – a charming invitation to a dreamless sleep.' On Bear Island, John Turner and his wife operated the modest Wisini Wigwam or Lakeview House with accommodation for up to fifty guests. Outfitting of canoeing and fishing parties was a major activity here. 'We were charmed by the friendliness of the islanders,' a 1909 visitor confessed, 'and although we told them frankly that we would not employ their guides, preferring to rough it alone, their demeanour did not change in the least, and they offered us every assistance.' The rustic atmosphere at these establishments was sustained by a menu that always included trout or bass and, on occasion, moose, venison or bear. And the frequent dances on Bear Island, which continued from fur trade days, were always popular with visitors and residents alike.

Bear Island in this era remained the centre of Lake Temagami's social activity. In addition to enjoying Turner's Lakeview House and the community dances, vacationers in the district could collect their mail at the post office, which opened in 1909; or they might come to shop at the Bear Island HBC post, which, as the company diversified away from furs, had begun to operate as a general store, selling fruits, vegetables, and camping supplies: 'We stock everything that the tourist could wish to ask for and our store is tastefully decorated, while all the delicacies of the season that are obtainable can be obtained here.' Although the opening of northern Ontario that accompanied railway construction increased competition from independent traders in the fur market, the financial position of the Temagami operation actually improved following the influx of tourists. Canoeists and vacationers at Temagami's youth camps, resorts, and cottages represented a valuable new source of revenue for the Bear Island sales shop. HBC officials concluded that 'there is a continued prospect of a considerable tourist trade being maintained' and, in anticipation of the arrival of the railway, briefly contemplated a passenger steamer service to accommodate sightseers on the lake. That possibility was not pursued because of uncertain profitability, 'the difficulties being chiefly the shortness of the season and the extravagant service the public look for from a reputedly rich Corporation.' Canoes rented for sixty cents a day or $3.50 a week, while comparable rates for a skiff were seventy-five cents and $4.00. Tents were available for between twenty-five and fifty cents a day; blankets ten to fifteen cents a day.[31]

A few miles to the south of the HBC operations, Wabikon – soon to be the largest adult resort on the lake – opened on Temagami Island near the site of the original HBC post around 1913. This resort – catering primarily to young middle-income vacationers – was established by John Orr, formerly a hotel operator in Stayner, Ontario, with the assistance of his two daughters. Up to two hundred guests, generally professional people from New York, Chicago and Cleveland, could be accommodated in buildings later described as 'substantial in character, and in appearance woodsy and rustic, in harmony with life in the Canadian North.' The staff was composed of about seventy employees – thirty-five male guides and thirty-five women responsible for housekeeping and kitchen facilities. When John Orr died in the fall of 1922, his daughter Laura assumed responsibility for running Wabikon. The camp invested heavily in advertising for space in the *New York Times*, the Cleveland *Plain Dealer*, and the Chicago *Herald Tribune*. George Lee of the TNOR was a regular and enthusiastic visitor who assisted with promotion in various ways. H.W. Wilson of Temagami village took over the Wabikon operation in 1926 or 1927 and ran the camp until the mid-1940s.[32]

A broad regional interest developed in the prosperity of commercial tourism on the lake. The contribution to northeastern Ontario's economic expansion and diversification brought by Temagami's seasonal employment opportunities, income from accommodation and services, and business related to hotel construction and supply was fully apparent to the Cobalt *Daily Nugget*, which urged that 'every resident of this north country should be an unofficial advertising agent for Temagami.' The paper unfortunately had to admit that northerners had never properly appreciated and made use of Temagami's assets: 'People will travel hundreds of miles to visit Temagami and find themselves well repaid for the trouble while people within 20 or 50 miles forget that the resort exists.'[33]

In a related campaign stressing the economic significance of Temagami tourism, the *Daily Nugget* supported a plea from Cobalt's Board of Trade to retain daily service to Temagami on the TNOR's local morning train, which was being rescheduled to run south from Englehart in the Little Clay Belt only as far as Latchford, more than twenty miles north of Temagami Station. The extended run to Temagami would not only have permitted the continuation of local tourism, but would also have preserved a convenient market outlet for dairy products and vegetables from the developing agricultural districts of the northeast. The TNOR's chairman merely expressed some willingness to consider the issues raised by the Board of Trade, but was evidently not very sympathetic to the suggestions made.[34]

The overall commercial importance of Temagami's recreational development is impossible to determine reliably. One contemporary estimate in *Rod and Gun* proposed $10,000 per day during the summer, apart from railway fares, as an amount approximating Temagami's financial significance. This figure was calculated on an expenditure of $5 per day by each of two thousand tourists around the lake at the height of the summer season. While this estimate has several uncertain features, it is nevertheless clear that substantial revenues – by regional standards – were involved. Transportation, accommodation, equipment and supplies, and personal services, all based on aesthetic resources or recreational assets, accounted for a large volume of expenditure and income.[35]

Tourism and wilderness recreation on a large scale could not have entered a northern Ontario region so abundantly suited as Temagami to extractive resource use – especially lumbering and pulpwood production – without occasioning conflict on several fronts. Aubrey White's concern about the fire threat from canoeists has already been mentioned. On the other hand, aesthetic values, environmental concerns, and the habits of vacationing campers were seldom in harmony with the priorities of the forest industry. Early-twentieth-century canoeists on the Sturgeon River complained: 'The water is stained brown by the logs, and this somewhat spoils the effect,' and concluded that 'there was no fishing on the Sturgeon, pulp logs driving the fish away.' Nor could the plans of pulp mill and power companies to control water levels in the Temagami Forest for commercial purposes be easily reconciled with the attitudes of the Indians and summer vacationers, particularly fishermen.[36] On Lake Maskinonge in 1904 an American canoeist lamented that 'this poor old lake has a fringed shore line,' the result of a lumber company dam that raised the water some six feet and flooded the trees at the water's edge. There were also fears that excellent fishing and spawning grounds at Temagami Falls above Cross Lake had been destroyed when the Sturgeon Falls Pulp and Paper Company constructed a short-lived dam.[37]

Dam building and artificial water-level control first became active Temagami controversies in 1899 when the Sturgeon Falls Pulp Company proposed to close the northern outlet of Lake Temagami flowing towards Lady Evelyn and the Montreal River and to regulate discharge from the south end in the interests of its own operations. The Booth, Bronson, and Lumsden interests depended heavily on Montreal River waters for log drives, however, and were apprehensive at the prospect of a Sharp Rock dam.[38] When G.E. Silvester reached the district in February 1900 as one of several government agents sent to examine the situation for Ontario's commissioner of Crown lands, he found construction underway on the south-end dam at Temagami Falls and learned that the northern dam at Sharp Rock Inlet had been completed the previous September. The water level, according to Bear Island residents, was at a thirty-year low.

Silvester ultimately concluded 'that it would not be detrimental to any public or private interests for the waters of Lake Temagaming to be dammed to ordinary high water mark ... during the former part of the summer and be gradually drawn off during the latter part' if certain conditions were met regarding the clearing of flooded trees or shrubs and some water were released at the north end during the spring log drive on the Montreal River. Beyond this, Silvester suggested that the damming would improve anticipated steamboat navigation on the lake and might eliminate the flooding of farmland on the lower Sturgeon River. Damming Cross Lake to Temagami's level, he added, 'would render accessible by steamboat a very considerable addition to Lake Temagaming.'[39] Twenty years later Mr Justice F.R. Latchford, who had been minister of public works in the Ross government at the time of Silvester's investigations, recalled another aspect of the episode that subsequently resulted in legislative action:

> I think there was a dam at the South end 20 years ago put up in secret, and when complaints were made to the predecessors in title to the Spanish River Company about the existence of the dam, the company denied that the dam was there, until I sent Mr. Joseph Rogers up and he, with half a box of dynamite blew the dam into the Temagami River, and then there was a very considerable complaint made to the other members of the Government for my actions.[40]

Water-level-management proposals in the Temagami Forest Reserve were under nearly constant criticism from the outset. An unsigned commentary, 'Lake Temagami Reserve,' in *Rod and Gun* stated in reference to the lakes of the region, 'Any raising of the level of these lakes which would destroy the trees along their edges and thus render them not only unsightly but exceedingly repellent to any person who had to effect a landing on their shores, should be strongly opposed.'[41]

Silvester's report itself provoked a direct response in the form of a lengthy letter to the Crown lands commissioner. The author, Archibald M. Campbell, a geologist from Perth, Ontario, raised three issues for further consideration: shoreline flooding, damage to the fish population, and impact on the fly season. He cited the Lake Kipawa area as a region that had been disfigured through lumbermen's activity in raising the water level, and he anticipated a similar fate for Temagami. Bass, he argued on the authority of Professor Ramsay Wright of the University of Toronto, are sensitive to environmental change and will be seriously disturbed by flooding. Campbell went on to predict that an increase in the insect population would result from newly created areas of 'comparatively stagnant water.' 'In view of the foregoing,' he concluded, 'I would most respectfully but strongly protest, as a citizen of Ontario and one immediately interested in preserving the natural beauties of Temagaming, against the proposed dam to be erected at Temagaming Falls.'[42]

Campbell's concern for the fish population of Lake Temagami was echoed in succeeding years by the well-known Ontario land surveyor James Dickson. 'It is well to impress upon our rulers,' Dickson wrote in *Rod and Gun*, 'the absolute necessity – in the interest of our fish – to disturb the level of our lakes as little as possible ... Alter the level of a lake by either raising or lowering the water and the spawning beds are injured. Let a margin of timber on a lake shore be killed by flooding, a drive of logs lose a portion of its bark, or some of the logs sink and the water becomes tainted and the finer varieties of fish soon begin to thin out and it is only a question of time when they disappear altogether unless the disturbing element has been removed'. Even the CPR pamphlet *Timagaming: A Glimpse of the Algonquin Paradise* warned about the dangers of dams and flooding in a surprisingly detailed account: 'A dam raises the water many feet, and when the fish return, as they assuredly do to the old beds, the eggs are deposited in water too deep for safety and are usually destroyed.'[43]

The initial dam controversy around the turn of the century appears to have become less pressing as a result of the financial problems of the

Sturgeon Falls Pulp Company, whose ownership shifted to Imperial Paper Mills and eventually to the Spanish River Pulp and Paper Company. During the period of reorganization by Imperial Paper Mills, initiative regarding water control shifted northwards into the hands of the Cobalt Hydraulic Power Company, one of several hydraulic operations established to supply compressed air and electric power to the burgeoning silver camps. In 1910, the hydraulic company applied for permission to erect two new dams on Lake Temagami and was authorized to proceed on condition that these would be removed at the request of the Department of Lands, Forests and Mines; that they would not interfere with the rights of those using the water for timber driving purposes; and that they would not raise the water level more than eighteen inches above the low water mark. Sturgeon Falls residents were immediately concerned about water-power shortages but were reassured by Frank Cochrane, who thought they had 'become unnecessarily alarmed over this matter.' When forced by repeated complaints from spokesmen for the local pulp operations to restate his assurances, Cochrane reacted with some hostility. 'I have been more than surprised at this in view of the fact that we have been most lenient in allowing the Company to run on, though practically in default. If these groundless and needless complaints are to continue, it may be necessary to return the compliment by taking up the question of cancelling the concession.' The pulp company spokesmen were suitably restrained by this rebuke and subsequently sought to demonstrate a sincere interest in restoring the financial stability and enhancing the value of their enterprise.

By the early spring of 1911, however – presumably following the installation of the Cobalt company's dams – the position of the pulp operations at Sturgeon Falls had deteriorated. The Temagami outlet to the Sturgeon River was now completely dry; the hydraulic company's northward diversion was estimated at sixty feet by two feet. E.R.C. Clarkson, representing Imperial Paper, requested permission to remove the offending south-end dam, while Aubrey White instructed Temagami's chief ranger, Clarence Hindson, to conduct an immediate investigation of the situation.

Hindson's report confirmed the northbound spillage and also provided a description of the two dams. 'There are five spillways in the north dam each ten feet wide and at noon yesterday there was twenty-four inches of water flowing. This dam is open to its fullest capacity.' No water was flowing out of the south end where all six spillways, five ten feet wide and one eleven feet wide, were completely closed. A Cobalt Hydraulic Power Company official was dispatched to restore the regular flow through the south end of Lake Temagami; however, 'there was only water enough to run the mills thirty-six hours last week,' Clarkson lamented at the end of March. Frank Cochrane was soon able to report the opening of the dam at the south end. High water levels that spring necessitated that the dams remain open at least until June.[44]

Cobalt Hydraulic's damming was soon under attack again. After the 1911 canoeing season, *Rod and Gun* published complaints about flood damage to shoreline trees. In a later issue of the same magazine, Aubrey White denied that any destruction of trees had occurred, although he admitted that the damming had been approved in order to ensure that year-round power would be available to the Cobalt mines.[45] There were thus at least two dimensions to the water-management questions around Lake Temagami. On the one hand, diverse industrial users centred at Sturgeon Falls and Cobalt contended for advantage. Simultaneously, an unorganized but persistent community of recreational users endeavoured to safeguard the natural environment of the forest from the impact of manipulated fluctuations or alterations in water levels.

Following the First World War, the needs of forest operations remained a source of continuing pressure for water-level controls in the district and on Lake Temagami in particular. After the Sturgeon Falls mills passed into the hands of the Spanish River Pulp and Paper Company, the new owners renewed efforts to regularize Lake Temagami's southward outflow in the interest of the mill at Sturgeon Falls. Negotiations during the war involving Spanish River Pulp and Paper, the Northern Ontario Light and Power Company (which had taken charge of power services for the nearby mining town of Cobalt), and the Ontario government led these parties to a satisfactory resolution of their water-management concerns in 1918. But land-use conflicts based on environmental values persisted. The hearings of the Riddell-Latchford Timber Commission, which the United Farmers' administration established to investigate alleged irregularities in the operations of the Department of Lands, Forests and Mines, brought to light much information on the range of industrial interests that continued to clash over the management of Temagami waters. The inquiry also contributed to an important early debate on the role of the wilderness environment in the modernizing province of Ontario.[46]

George H. Kohl, hydraulic engineer for the Spanish River firm, explained that since the very beginning of operations, the Sturgeon Falls mill had experienced a complete or partial shut-down of grinders every year during summer and winter, due largely to low water. Lake Temagami's importance to the mill operations may be seen from the fact that one foot of water in the lake could run a line of three grinders for nearly two months. Citing the report prepared for the Ontario Crown lands commissioner in 1900 by G.E. Silvester, Kohl argued that his company's work in closing the north outlet, building the Cross Lake Dam in 1918, and deepening the channel between Cross Lake and Temagami had reduced the variation in water levels from a range of five feet to between three and three and a half feet. In agreements with the provincial government, the company undertook to maintain water levels at between 965 feet and 963 feet, except after the tourist season or in late winter and then only with permission. Kohl expressed the opinion that 'the control of Temagami Lake by Cross Lake Dam had no effect at all on the spawning of bass, trout or whitefish in Temagami Lake due to the fact that the lake has never been down to its low water level.' A full examination of this episode by the timber commission revealed a more complicated and controversial sequence of events.[47]

In late August 1916, the Spanish River Pulp and Paper Company received word from the chief ranger, Clarence Hindson, that permission was granted to clear a channel in the Temagami River. The company continued to clear and blast the channel, which it had begun to work on before initially seeking a permit.[48] In a similar episode the following year, Hindson wrote to the department to ask whether the Spanish River company had permission to erect a dam they were in the process of building at Cross Lake and to cut logs in connection with this work. The department responded almost immediately that 'the company have been advised more than once that they should not construct any dams without first getting permission and getting the plans approved ...' But only a day before Hindson's inquiry to his superiors, the director of the Spanish River operations had written to Deputy Minister Albert Grigg in Toronto enclosing:

> as requested ... a blueprint of the dam which we are going to build at Cross Lake to replace the old timber dam now there. You will remember [the letter continued] that this old dam was built to regulate Cross Lake and Temagimi [sic] as one storage, and that it was agreed last year to allow us to remove the Temagami dam entirely and operate this storage from Cross Lake.

When the timber commissioners asked who had agreed, the company representative responded that the decision was reached during negotiations between the Spanish River company and the Northern Ontario Light and Power Company in interviews with the minister.

No document existed to record the Cross Lake agreement and, although construction had begun in 1917, no licence was issued until 1920. The timber commission learned that no flooded land was cleared in 1918, and that probably nothing had been done since then either. Moreover, there had been difficulty in collecting the province's costs for a survey of Cross Lake, despite frequent request from the Lands and Forests' survey branch. The company eventually paid for the survey in 1918, but since Lands and Forests had already paid their surveyors, the money was put as a deposit against the timber damage, estimated at $669 by Hindson.[49]

In 1916, the Toronto legal advisers to the Spanish River company wrote to Howard Ferguson – then minister of lands and forests, and later premier – to suggest that the company itself would like to nominate a candidate for a contemplated government position as supervisor of the Temagami and nearby Obabika dams. Ferguson's curt reply stated that the preparations for the Temagami dam were still only preliminary and that the Spanish River company should submit its plans. As for the second dam, 'the Obabika dam was erected by permission of the Department and on the understanding that the Department would control it. I cannot, therefore, see why it is necessary to appoint a second official for this purpose.' Only Hindson remained in charge of both dams. Mr Atkinson, the company forester, also reportedly told L.V. Rorke, the head of the survey branch, 'that they were erecting a dam at the foot of Tomaco Lake, or some Lake in there, for storage.'[50] These incidents show to what extent the deputy minister was ignorant of deals and negotiations with Ferguson, and the degree to which the Spanish River company had assumed control of the situation within the provincial TFR.

The department endeavoured to come to grips with its responsibilities on Lake Temagami in 1918. Rorke advised Deputy Minister Grigg that no damage had resulted to the shores of Lake Temagami from setting the limits of water supply. The dam at the foot of Cross Lake that raised the level of that lake to the elevation of Lake Temagami was 'a substantial concrete structure, well built and in good order.' When referring to the damage done to timber other than pine in two or three deep bays of Cross Lake, Rorke suggested that the department should insist on 'compensations for this timber and the rental of the lands flooded and the right to impound water as arranged.' Obviously, the company was not fulfilling the terms of the agreement.

Rorke also recounted an agreement whereby the Northern Ontario Light and Power Company relinquished to the Spanish River company the claim to Lake Temagami water in return for the right to create storage on Lady Evelyn Lake. Since no one now claimed rights to Lake Temagami's northern outlet, the Spanish River company had taken matters into its own hands; the dam was now 'partially destroyed and blocked up with earth and gravel.' Thus ended Temagami's northern outlet. Rorke told the timber commission that he knew an agreement had been reached, but had no knowledge of the terms. He had heard at one time of 'a proposition to divert the waters of that [Lady Evelyn] and the Anima Nipissing.' The old timber dam on the Lady Evelyn at Matawapika was not erected by the power companies, but they were using it, since there was no lumbering on Lady Evelyn Lake.[51]

However agreeable these arrangements for water management may have been to the power and forest industries of the Temagami district, other residents disliked them. The destruction of the natural northern outlet was cited as the reason given by the Indians for the high water problem in a letter of 31 May 1919 from Dr Murray McFarlane to Ferguson. McFarlane had been visiting the lake since 1900, travelling north two or three times a year for periods of four to six weeks. His testimony on the negative effects of the Cross Lake dam was considered 'radical' by the commission.

> Well, I complain of any dam from the standpoint of a lover of nature. I would sooner see every pulp and timber Company wiped out to save my one lake, so it is no good to ask about that [dams].
>
> In this specific case, Lake Temagami in my opinion, is a future fund of money for Ontario, and is worth ten small towns or villages where you have got to depend on the tourists. It logically cannot be a manufacturing country, because we have not got coal in Ontario.[52]

Dr K. McIlwraith, another critic who testified at the inquiry, had also previously written to the minister to advise him 'what an invaluable asset to the nation it is that these playgrounds and training grounds for our youth should be preserved in their beauty and freshness. No feature of our national life can be more important.' McIlwraith presented numerous examples of effects of low and high water. In Sucker Gut Lake, sand spits and bogs had been created, and one portage was unapproachable. Lost Lake was ruined by the stench from decaying animal and vegetable matter. All the cedars and many pine and birch were killed around Cross Lake, while trees along the Temagami River had also been drowned. A.L. Cochrane of Camp Temagami provided further evidence of the destruction along various shores and on the lack of clean-up on Cross Lake.[53]

The department heard numerous other complaints about high water levels throughout the 1919 season, and Mr Atkinson, the Spanish River company's forester, confirmed that the guardian of the dam had been holding a few extra inches of water. Meanwhile complaints were recorded of low water in August of that year and again in 1920. In the fall of 1920, cottagers complained that the water was too low. On this occasion, 'owing to the urgent necessity for power to keep in operation the power plants at Sturgeon Falls the Company requested to be allowed to draw the water down below the stipulated low water mark and it was considered advisable to allow this as the tourist season was over and any disadvantages following the low water would be more than offset by the relief afforded to citizens of Sturgeon Falls and the Power Companies interested.' In its annual report for 1918, the TNOR stated that 'on account of the Spanish River Pulp and Paper Company periodically raising and lowering the water in Temagami Lake' it had been necessary to build a new pump house and to renew the pipeline.[54]

The high water mark had been fixed at 965 feet above sea level while the level was held at or above 963 feet during the tourist season. Lower elevations, like that in the fall of 1920, were allowed by special permission of the department. Even Rorke testified against the system of fixed water levels, saying that if the water level was kept at one foot from high water mark during the hot weather, as the agreement allowed, many trees along the shores of Lake Temagami would be destroyed. Rorke was uncomfortable with his position as 'umpire or referee' between the summer tourists of Lake Temagami and the people at Sturgeon Falls. This latter group was always pleading for the Spanish River company to get more water on the grounds that otherwise they would be in darkness and without power for fire pumps. Indeed as Kohl had stated, the Sturgeon Falls mill closed every year because of water shortages. Counsel for the company asked witnesses at the timber inquiry whose interests they would choose if they were the government: those of the town of Sturgeon Falls or those of the seasonal tourists? Commissioner Latchford interceded that the dispute was not between the company and tourists, but between the company and the province. Counsel asserted 'that conditions as they exist today, are far better for controlling that lake than they were under natural conditions.'[55]

The final report of the timber commission commented at length on the problems of dams and water-level management. The Temagami situation demonstrated clearly that environmental problems in early-twentieth-century Ontario involved more than fish and game protection, for the commission concluded that 'the exploitation of the waters of this Lake [Temagami] by the Spanish River Pulp and Paper Company Limited has already seriously diminished the beauty and therefore the value of the Lake, and the adjoining Cross Lake.' Generalizing from the Temagami case, the commission continued: 'Of course, there will often be a conflict between the commercialization of waters and their conservation for aesthetic reasons, and sometimes the balance of convenience and advantage will be with the former – but nothing should be tolerated in that direction beyond what is reasonably necessary. In most instances it will be found, as it has in other lands been found, that the two are not inconsistent.' Legislation capable of controlling interference with natural water levels was likely required to prevent future abuses.[56] However important the problems of water management and environmental protection may have appeared to the timber commissioners, these questions failed to become prominent public concerns in provincial politics of the 1920s. Timber practices, political scandals, and, of course, Ontario's continuing preoccupation with prohibition dominated the agenda of the decade. It was clear nonetheless that environmental issues were of concern on at least a local scale and that some understanding of their general significance was gradually developing.

One further dimension of early environmental concern was a conflict between commercial recreation and wilderness travel. The Grand Trunk Railway argued in 1900 that Temagami was 'still the same untouched and uninhabited wilderness, with the addition that all the necessary accessories are at hand in the locality to make a trip of any length with comfort.' The GTR's reluctance to regard a dynamic and expanding tourist business as a major impact on the natural environment is in contrast with the remarks of some early canoeing enthusiasts: 'Temagami and Kippewa remain the peerless lakes for us – Kippewa is as wild as it ever was, Temagami is being tamed fast.'[57] A few years later, another wilderness paddler offered this advice: 'you will need the balm of this natural glory to heal the wounds of spirit you have received in your dealings with the powers that be in Temagami hotels, stores and steamboats, and the more nearly you go absolutely independent of these, the better off you are.'[58]

Conflict over land management involving recreational users and resources industries was thus an important element of the Temagami experience from the creation of the Temagami Forest Reserve in 1901 and indeed even a few years before. During the prewar era, reclassification of the district was contemplated on several occasions to recognize Temagami's prominence as a centre of tourism. In 1911 rumours circulated about the possibility of creating a game reserve in the area. By 1914, the Ontario Boards of Trade advocated provincial park status.[59] Although Quetico was reclassified from a forest reserve to a park in 1913, the Temagami case was not pressed vigorously and no similar adjustment was made. However, when the minister of lands, forests and mines withdrew the islands of Lake Temagami from further mineral prospecting, recreational spokesmen applauded the initiative: 'The beauties of Temagami are so entrancing that any interference with them, even from the material standpoint of increased wealth to the Province from minerals, would almost amount to desecration.'[60]

Temagami popularity among vacationers remained high in the postwar years as enthusiastic commentators extolled its charms and attractions. Harold C. Lowrey, in a contribution to *Maclean's* magazine in 1919, revived the wilderness experience for a war-weary readership: 'We were lifted above the every day, swept out of the sordidness of human discordances into a heaven of good thoughts bounded by rambling hills and sprinkled with sparkling lakes ...' The experience of the north 'touched the hidden spring within us that loosened our true natures and gave us back the care-free vivacity of youth.' 'This was Temagamie where every one was a friend and where the millionaire, awed by the tremendous wealth of Nature, travels incognito.'[61] Simultaneously, the Ontario government was becoming increasingly active in promoting tourism within the province.

By the mid-twenties, the government had perceived financial advantages to be derived from American cottagers located in the province and encouraged cottage site sales and leases with the assurance that 'there are no restrictions as to citizenship or nationality.'[62] After the publication of innumerable articles recounting very successful fishing expeditions and in spite of the existence of a short-lived commercial fishing industry, not to mention twenty years of dams and water-flow controls, *Ontario, The Lakeland Playground* referred in 1923 to 'the almost virgin waters of the Timagami Forest Reserve.' Moreover, the forest reserves had always been primarily regarded as areas in which successful lumbering, once introduced in an orderly manner, could be perpetuated. By 1923, commercial cutting of fire-killed sections was a well-established practice, and Temagami was on the verge of coming open for regular commercial licensing for pine timber. But *The Lakeland Playground* clearly conveyed the impression that the primary purpose of the Temagami district was recreational, 'unstained by the hand or the device of man': 'And such as it is today, so will it be for the latest generations, since this great excelling kingdom is forbidden alike to lumbermen and landgrabbers, forever consecrate to the nobler interests of the regeneration and upbuilding of mind and body, which it is obviously destined by Creative Hand to effect.'[63]

Perhaps we should take none of these descriptions too seriously: they may be highly subjective or biased to promote some calculated advantage, commercial or environmental, and some problems of credibility must be acknowledged in any discussion of the pleasures of sport fishing as seen by the participants. But disagreements between those engaged in the tourist business and resource users in forestry and mining were certainly not surprising. As well, many recreational canoeists were at odds with promoters with commercial interests in recreation on the question of the appropriate level of civilization to provide for vacationers. The response of the railways and the Ontario government to these rival interests was to try to reconcile divergent land use priorities by denying the existence of conflict – a tactic that has by no means been forgotten.

Nevertheless, Ontario's reaction to summer vacationers and wilderness travellers in the Temagami district had changed significantly in the first quarter of the century. At the time of the Forest Reserves Act and the creation of the TFR, the forest regions of the province were officially seen as a resource base to be devoted to productive uses. Algonquin Park (1893), although it had begun to attract summer visitors, remained an active centre of the lumber industry, and provincial authorities had been clear in their determination to minimize the impact of recreational canoeists on the Temagami region's principal purpose – a sustained-yield pine forest. Enthusiastic paddlers and persistent cottagers penetrated the district nevertheless and brought about the formation of a tentative and highly localized recreational land-use policy. By the 1920s, the province had recognized the economic potential of tourism in the Temagami district and – without fundamentally altering its perception of land-use priorities – had begun to promote the vacation industry as well as cottage sites in Temagami and certain other locales across the province. For their part, recreational users had begun to voice concerns about the manner in which the forest and waters of the district were being managed – and neglected – by the authorities responsible. With regard to another perceived obstacle to forest management, however, the provincial government maintained a more consistent course: Ontario's resolve to deny native land claims remained firm, and the Temagami Indians experienced increasing difficulty in pursuing their traditional occupations in the Temagami Forest.

CHAPTER SEVEN

The Temagami Indians and the Forest Reserve

Along with pulpwood, mineral development, and tourism, the Indian community within the Temagami Forest represented a challenge to Ontario's early plans for pine-forest management. With the support of the federal government, the Temagami Indians asserted legal and moral claims against the province and sought some clear resolution of the specific question of an Indian reserve within the TFR. Ontario firmly resisted the native claims that had been so clearly recognized by Aubrey White. Eventually the province undertook to apply its resource and wildlife policies to all occupants of the TFR, including the Indian residents. Although they adjusted somewhat in the early decades of the century to the modest economic opportunities presented by commercial tourism and appeared to have accepted missionary involvement on Bear Island, the Indians never abandoned their fundamental claims.

One year after the TNOR ended their relative isolation, the Temagami Indians used the new railway facilities in an attempt to protect their interests against the Ontario government's grand design for the northern forest. On 15 January 1906, the first recorded delegation from the Temagami band waited on Indian Affairs officials in Ottawa, urgently requesting an Indian reserve at the south end of the lake. The band was then willing to settle for a somewhat smaller territory even than that proposed by Abrey in 1885. As outlined it would not have included any of the McLean Peninsula or the big peninsula between Cross Bay and Cross Lake, but it would have contained the east shore of the Southwest Arm, the South Arm, Austin Bay, the south side of Outlet Bay, and the west side of Cross Lake, with the southern line remaining as before, for a total of 15,920 acres (twenty-five square miles), roughly equivalent to contemporary settlements under Treaty No. 9.

Federal Secretary of Indian Affairs J.D. McLean informed Aubrey White that he was sure the Temagami band would actually settle for a further cut to 9,436 acres, plus Bear Island (726 acres) exclusive of the lands used by the Hudson's Bay Company post (about 160 acres) for a total of seventeen square miles.[1] Yet Ontario remained opposed to any reserve arrangements for the band. Further petitions by the Indians and continuing attempts by federal officials to secure a reasonable outcome also failed. Indian Affairs continued to hold the view that no representative of the Temagami people had been present at the surrender meeting for the Robinson-Huron treaty and that 'the title of the Temagami Indians to the surrendered tract has not been fully extinguished.' McLean called for Ontario to recognize 'the absolute nature of such a claim.' If anything, however, the province's position stiffened, and the conditions facing the band deteriorated.[2]

Aubrey White somewhat condescendingly announced that 'when we set the Temagami region apart as a Forest Reserve, we found some Indians and half-breeds residing on the territory.' They were allowed to stay, White suggested, and a few enjoyed temporary employment as forest rangers. Ontario's approach to the area, however, now derived from the province's essential aim, 'the preserving of the timber.'[3] That goal underlay Ontario's clear rejection of proposals for an Indian reserve within the Temagami Forest and also supported a series of measures subordinating the life-style of the aboriginal residents to new administrative arrangements.

Shortly before the war, there were hopeful signs of moderation in Ontario's position. A casual suggestion by White at a meeting in Ottawa with Deputy Superintendent-General Frank Pedley that perhaps the Indians could have a small village in Austin Bay, where the Paul family already lived, raised the expectations of Indian Affairs officials and of the Temagami band. During the renewed discussions around 1912, J.D. McLean told Indian Agent Cockburn to go to Temagami to help Ontario survey a tract that would contain more than fifty acres for each of the estimated ninety-four band members. But Aubrey White cautioned that the Ontario government was not yet committed to a village. The Indians should not be led on, he said, and any arrangements worked out would have to be informal. No real Indian reserve was possible, White argued, because the local native people did not have 'any right' to one. When McLean tried to cancel Cockburn's proposed survey mission, Chief

Frank White Bear objected forcefully that some of the Temagami Indians had already set off on trips of one hundred miles or more to meet for the historic and long-awaited occasion at Austin Bay. Relenting, McLean told Cockburn to explain everything honestly to the band and to suggest that they might want to pick out residential land at the south end anyway. He also urged Aubrey White to reconsider, saying that anything less than a full reserve was 'unfair and unreasonable.'[4]

Cockburn met Temagami band members at Austin Bay, and the land selection of 1906 was reconfirmed. In fact, for many years nine dwellings, two barns, and three stables had existed on twelve cleared acres at the proposed village site. Naturally, White Bear soon wanted to know what Ontario had accepted. Could the Indians build? In the spring of 1913 Duncan Campbell Scott, Indian Affairs' newly appointed deputy superintendent-general, told Cockburn to have the Indians pick out a 'small area,' 'rather than being scattered all over the forest reserve.' Chief White Bear remained uneasy. Two years later, Cockburn again went to Lake Temagami to meet the frustrated Indians. He reported back that a real reserve was essential, that almost all Indians who had buildings had them at Austin Bay, and that without real land the band was making little progress.[5]

In September 1917, Second Chief Aleck Paul wrote personally to the minister to say that the Indians wanted to have the reserve they had selected. Chief Paul knew that Austin Bay had 'a few pines on the land,' and understood this to be the cause of Ontario's hesitation. But, he argued, 'we deserve to have something on our reserve. We have been here before any government was born in Canada.' Ontario's position remained unchanged throughout the war years. The province refused to consider an Indian reserve at Temagami to the extent applied for, but if the Indians really wanted a small residential and garden area on Austin Bay, they would definitely have to agree to leave Bear Island. Ontario officials were also emphatic on one further point: whatever the status of the Austin Bay site, it would not be a reserve.[6]

In addition to the continuing land-claims controversy, other prewar and wartime developments throughout the Temagami country had important consequences for the native people. The creation of the Temagami Forest Reserve, the arrival of the railway, and the influx of summer vacationers rapidly transformed the social and economic environment of the fur trade era. The traditional hunting and trapping territories now included within the TFR were patrolled by provincial government officials who administered and enforced regulations that reflected little sensitivity to the interests of the permanent inhabitants.

Ontario's objectives for timber management clashed with the Indians' long-standing aspirations regarding a reserve and with their established life-style.

Forest-management policy and resource-development activity resulted in many individual grievances, which arose from the day-to-day conditions facing Indians in the Temagami Forest. The Indians required permission from the chief ranger to cut firewood and were not permitted to 'cut timber for building purposes.' Fire rangers acting under Chief Ranger Hindson's direction stopped John Equana from cutting 'a few balsams on his little plot of ground.' Forestry officials tore down some buildings housing Indians and threatened White Bear's home, the former railway construction hospital near the station at Temagami village. White Bear's garden and some buildings were flooded around 1912 when the British Canadian Power Company of Cobalt dammed Rabbit Lake. In this instance, though, Indian Affairs interceded and was instrumental in effecting a compensation settlement. Years later John Katt was less fortunate when the A.B. Gordon lumber company dammed the channel between Diamond and Lady Evelyn lakes, flooding his small cabin. Chief Aleck Paul also complained to Indian Affairs that the chief ranger had forbidden Indians to erect shacks on Bear Island, although they obviously required accommodation while their children were obliged to attend school.[7] Most disrupting, though, was growing regulatory involvement in native hunting and fishing throughout the Temagami area as the province's use of wildlife-management legislation intensified.

Deputy Minister Aubrey White of Lands and Forests now reflected the firm provincial attitude at the highest level. Acknowledging in June 1911 that 'shooting and fishing' had been prohibited in the Temagami Forest, he nevertheless claimed that Ontario had treated the Indians 'in a very generous way' and asked 'by what authority' did 'they claim the right to fish and shoot there.'[8] White assumed that a short-lived prohibition on hunting and fishing in forest reserves across Ontario would be applicable to Indian residents of the Temagami area as well as to seasonal visitors.

This same senior official had earlier included in his formal recommendation for the creation of the Temagami Forest Reserve in 1901 an elaborate description of the Indians' position. That account not only stated frankly that 'by oversight or neglect' the Temagami Indians were not represented at the Robinson treaty and consequently did not receive a reservation, 'which would certainly have been done had there been anybody to press their claim,' but also explained the then current assumption regarding existing rights to wildlife, namely that: 'under the Robinson treaty these Indians are in common with other Indians in the territory surrounded, guaranteed the right of hunting and fishing there as long as the lands are in the Crown unsold and they can exercise these rights freely over all this territory.'[9] This clear statement fails to hint at the growing technicality of the law applicable to native rights to use renewable wildlife resources. If the situation in 1900 actually allowed the simple answer suggested by White's explanation for his minister, it was very soon true that detailed considerations of who, where, when, and for what purpose appeared to be relevant in determining whether an Indian had violated an applicable law in taking, possessing, or disposing of fish or game.[10] In Temagami the absence of an Indian reserve and the more basic problem of treaty status added further complexity.

After revising fish and game laws in 1892, Ontario took further steps early in the new century to respond to continuing concerns about wildlife in the province. Criticism of fish and game practices remained widespread, with Indians and settlers in the unorganized districts often singled out for commentary. Sportsmen's magazines frequently drew to the attention of their readers incidents with unfavourable implications. Settlers in the North Bay area faced frequent charges for out-of-season hunting or possession of game, although the exemption often claimed for two deer for personal use was reduced to one.[11]

Two Indians in the Nipissing district were said to have shot eighty-two deer in a four-day period, while forty carcasses were reportedly left to rot around Sturgeon Falls. *Rod and Gun* informed its readers in 1909 that an Indian 'attached to the Temagami Post of the Hudson Bay Company' dug seven pups out of a wolf den he came upon in May and claimed the bounty for them. An unidentified hunter who recounted the exploits of his party in Temagami noted a preponderance of cows over bulls. The animals had probably separated, he concluded, 'as it cannot be that the cows outnumber the bulls in this ratio in a country where the Indians are killing the cows at all seasons of the year.' Perhaps, though, the Indians were 'killing a lot of yearling bulls.'[12]

After an extensive inquiry into the current state of the province's fish and game, the Ontario Game and Fish Commission, in its 1909–11 reports, urged administrative reforms to strengthen the organization of the wildlife service.[13] Kelly Evans, the commissioner who conducted the inquiry, praised the provincial park preserves, in which category he included the Temagami Forest along with parks such as Algonquin. He spoke of these 'great tracts of land' as areas 'where nature may continue to hold undisputed sway, where the birds and beasts may thrive and breed, to spread in plentiful numbers over the surrounding territory, and where men and women may seek simple and healthy repose from the cares and worries of strenuous modern life.'[14] Despite his apparent ignorance of the principal purpose underlying the TFR, Evans's enthusiasm may have encouraged a more vigorous approach to wildlife protection within the forest reserve system.

By means of the Ontario Game and Fisheries Act of 1907, which was generally applicable throughout Ontario, the provincial government had revised its program of licensing, regulation, and supervision of wildlife. Like its predecessor, the Ontario Game Protection Act of 1892, this new statute was intended not 'to affect any right specially reserved to or conferred upon Indians by any treaty or regulations in that behalf made by the Government of the Dominion of Canada with reference to hunting on their reserves or hunting grounds, or in any territory especially set apart for the purpose.' Moreover, this legislation was not applicable 'to Indians hunting in any portion of the provincial territory as to which their claims have not been surrendered or extinguished.'[15]

The Temagami Indians faced a particularly awkward situation. They remained without a reserve under the Robinson treaty of 1850 despite Aubrey White's clear acknowledgement as late as 1901 that one should have been provided if they had not 'by oversight or neglect' been left out of the treaty; but they were also not regarded by the province as occupying lands subject to outstanding claims. This state of affairs seems initially to have produced uncertainty and inconvenience for the Indians rather than active and sustained interference, for when steps were taken to enforce an absolute prohibition of hunting and fishing in Temagami in 1911, this was actually done under the recently re-enacted Forest Reserves Act rather than by means of the general game laws.

In 1910 the provincial Legislature had re-enacted the Forest Reserves Act and prohibited, 'except under regulations,' a wide range of activities – including hunting and fishing – within the boundaries of forest reserves.[16] During 1911, actual administration of fish and game laws within forest reserves was, to be charitable, in disarray. In May of that year, Frank Cochrane accepted the advice of his deputy minister to transfer responsibility for game and fish in forest reserves to the Department of Lands, Forests and Mines from Public Works, which had been designated under the Game and Fisheries Act as the agency responsible for province-wide administration of that statute. In June, this decision was rescinded, and Public Works was again responsibie for the administration of fish and game laws within forest reserves. But regulations under the Game and Fisheries Act of 1907 could hardly authorize activity that was later explicitly prohibited by the Forest Reserves Act of 1910. It was in this context that Aubrey White denied that the Temagami Indians had rights of any kind to hunt or fish in their homeland. It was in response to 'numerous letters' from the 'general public' rather than the position of the Temagami Indians that White recommended to his minister, Frank Cochrane, late in 1911, that fishing and hunting should be allowed in forest reserves subject to the general legislation of Ontario until specific regulations for forest reserves were formulated.[17] The Indians appear to have benefited from the restoration of earlier arrangements. The prohibitions had been lifted. However, the status of the Indians' claims for wildlife use remained unresolved, and they continued to experience progressive disruption as a result of provincial resource-management initiatives.

Chief Aleck Paul expressed the general reaction of Temagami band members to the overall course of the developments in a conversation with the noted American anthropologist Frank Speck who was in the area in 1913, officially as a researcher for the Geological Survey of Canada:

> When the white people came they commenced killing all the game. They left nothing on purpose to breed and keep us the supply, because the white man don't care about the animals. They are after the money. After the white man kills all the game in one place he can take the train and go three hundred miles or more to another and do the same there. But the Indian cannot do that. He must stay on his own section all the time and support his family on what it produces ...
>
> If an Indian went to the old country and sold hunting licenses to the old country people for them to hunt on their own land, the white people would not stand for that ... What we Indians want is for the Government to stop the white people killing our game, as they do it for sport and not for support.
>
> We Indians do not need to be watched about protecting the game; we must protect the game or starve. We can take care of the game just as well as the game warden and better, because we are going to live here all the time.[18]

Thus, conflict persisted between the priorities of Temagami's aboriginal residents and the increasingly forceful influence of new interests. For both groups the goal of land management was maintenance of the resource base; yet no matter how much they appeared to share such a goal, at the practical level the interests of the native and non-native communities continued to diverge and conflict.

Speck's research for his *Family Hunting Territories and Social Life of Various Algonkian Bands of the Ottawa Valley* confirmed Aleck Paul's remarks about the land-tenure system then in existence. Speck found that each family within the band had a long-established hunting territory or 'lot' (mok i wak i, 'hunting ground') within which male members shared hunting and fishing rights (see map 5). Speck described the territories that he mapped in detail as 'more or less fixed tracts of country whose boundaries are determined by certain rivers, ridges, lakes, or other natural landmarks, such as swamps and clumps of cedar or pine.' Severe sanctions might be imposed against those hunting outside their own territory, but permission might be obtained on a temporary basis to use another's hunting ground:

> This happened frequently as an exchange of courtesies between families when the game supply of one or the other had become impoverished. These privileges were, nevertheless, only temporary, except in a few cases, where they were obtained through marriage. It was customary, for instance, in case a family had a poor season on its own domain, for it to obtain a temporary grant of a certain lake or stream from its neighbour, so as to tide over until a better season. When it was necessary in travelling to pass through another family territory, permission was generally sought at the owner's headquarters before passing on, and if by necessity game had been killed to sustain life, the pelts were carried to the owners or delivered to them by some friend. This gave the proprietors the right in the future to do the same in the territory of their trespassers ...
>
> The rights in the hunting territories were inherited paternally. Occasionally, to adjust matters, an old man would subdivide his district among several sons, thus creating new family groups, though, of course, these would recognize mutual privileges to a certain extent. For the most part, the territories were fairly rigid and permanent. Only a few changes are remembered to have taken place within the range of tradition.[19]

The Temagami people reportedly divided their hunting districts into quarters as a game-management or conservation practice. Each year on a rotating basis the family would hunt in a different section of the family territory. A 'bank' or reserve was always retained for emergency shortages; this could be used to permit other parts of the hunting territory to replenish themselves.[20]

In light of their understanding of a long-established system, it is easy to understand the enormous frustration and irritation the Temagami Indians experienced as provincial officials continued to introduce regulations to control the use of fish and game. These regulations affected the Indians not only as providers of 'country food' for their own consumption, but also as fur trappers in their commercial relations with the Hudson's Bay Company.

For its own part, the HBC monitored the evolution of wildlife legislation in Ontario (and other jurisdictions in which it operated) from at least the time of the introduction of Ontario's Game Protection Act of 1892. Sensing the impact of provincial actions on its commercial prospects throughout northern Ontario, the HBC eventually resolved to defend its position, relying in part upon legal arguments with respect to the constitutional position of Indians in Canada. In 1905, the province had placed limitations on the trapping of beaver and otter and on occasion had prosecuted violators, including the HBC manager on Lake Temagami, for accepting these furs from the Indians.[21] Vigorous reaction was provoked by two incidents elsewhere in 1910 that directly challenged long-standing practices in the fur industry and threatened to involve severe inconvenience and financial costs.

In February 1910, a special constable seized 123 beaver from the HBC warehouse at Biscotasing, and in less than two weeks a fine of $50 per skin had been imposed by the local magistrate. The post manager faced imprisonment. The company chose to appeal to clarify its rights under its Deed of Surrender (1869). With the appeal pending, provincial officials made a second and larger fur seizure at Montizambert in June. Again, conviction followed promptly, bringing the total in fines to well over $12,000. Relations with the provincial government deteriorated to the point where Attorney-General J.J. Foy, after acknowledging some uncertainty about his status to advise the HBC directly concerning its conduct, wrote to the company's legal counsel that, 'I would suggest they should try to obey the law and not give the Crown the trouble of prosecuting in such cases.'

The HBC, holding 'the strongest possible views of their rights,' denied that they had either disobeyed the law or acted illegally. The company defended the Indians' rights to hunt and sell and its own right to purchase from them, notwithstanding provincial game laws. There was no doubt that the law applicable to the fur seizures was 'in some respects very intricate,' as Commissioner Chipman explained to the

HBC's company secretary in London. Legal advisers focused on four basic arguments. Section 8 of Ontario's Game and Fisheries Act specifically preserved the rights of Indians – in this context, rights under the Robinson treaty; both in its regulation of Indians and as a consequence of its criminal-law dimensions, the act was *ultra vires* to the Ontario Legislature, as these matters fell within the sphere of federal responsibility; finally, the company relied on its Deed of Surrender, which was deemed to have the same force and effect as an imperial statute.[22]

The sabre-rattling in the aftermath of the 1910 fur seizure did not resolve the HBC's claims conclusively, but it encouraged a period of moderation on both sides. The HBC experienced continuing friction or 'molestation' as Ontario developed administrative arrangements and regulations for game management. The company monitored this process closely, and by 1916, although he was not satisfied that proposed regulations 'will work out in practice as expected by the parties responsible for their drafting,' N.H. Bacon, the HBC fur trade commissioner, concluded that it was necessary to 'choose between accepting them and agreeing to adhere to them, or practically going out of business.'[23]

In October 1916, five new sets of regulations relating to the Ontario Game and Fisheries Act were approved by order-in-council. Almost immediately the HBC fur trade commissioner wrote to the company's Ontario district managers requesting them to take the necessary actions to comply with the wishes of the Department of Game and Fisheries. Previously the company had refused to take out fur-dealers' licences as prescribed in section 49(d) of the act because of special privileges it claimed under its Deed of Surrender. Now, however, the company anticipated harmonious relations with the department and agreed, 'under protest,' to take out dealers' licences for each post manager as well as extra licences for clerks and those responsible for outposts. Licensees were required to provide monthly records to the Department of Game and Fisheries indicating all beaver and otter purchases from white or half-breed trappers. Bales of beaver and otter skins shipped by the company were to be accompanied by appropriate coupons, which were to be exchanged for export permits for furs being shipped out of the province.

The 1916 'Regulations Prescribing Terms and Conditions upon which Beaver and Otter may be taken or had in possession' specified that the open season for both species would run from 1 November to 31 March. Anyone operating under a trapping licence could purchase up to ten coupons at fifty cents each and exchange these at the time of sale at a rate of one for each beaver or two for each otter skin. Ten coupons was a maximum seasonal trapping allowance. The Hudson's Bay Company operations around Temagami and elsewhere in northern Ontario were most directly affected by 'Regulations Prescribing Terms upon which Treaty Indians living north and west of the French and Mattawa Rivers and Lake Nipissing are exempted from the operation of subsection 2 of section 9 of the Ontario Game and Fisheries Act, prohibiting trapping except under the authority of a license.' The position of the HBC fur trade commissioner was clear: '[A]s they should ultimately benefit the trading companies if properly enforced by the Department, it has been decided that it is to the Company's advantage to adhere to them.'

Treaty Indians with certificates from the federal Indian Affairs authorities would not require a trapper's licence. As most Indians were away at winter hunting grounds at the time the letter was written, managers were advised to obtain certificates for them from Indian Affairs or the nearest Indian agent. Unofficially, Ontario recognized the impracticality of enforcing trapping limitations against Indians and proposed to circumvent the political problem of preferential treatment by accepting Indian Affairs certificates for each member of the trapper's family irrespective of age or sex. Indian trappers enjoyed a further concession in that they were entitled to take ten beaver and/or otter without being bound to the coupon limit.

Section 3 of the new regulations promised the greatest advantages to the Hudson's Bay Company, as an ordinary fur-dealer's licence did not entitle the bearer to purchase furs from Treaty Indians. Only an authorized issuer of coupons could accept furs from Treaty Indians, and the Hudson's Bay Company planned to apply at once to secure these 'very limited' coupon-issuing privileges for its employees. Indians were definitely to bear the cost of attached coupons. Describing the new regulations as 'the outcome of many years of struggle with the Ontario Government, fighting for the Company's rights,' the fur trade commissioner concluded optimistically that they 'will enable us to carry on our business in future, not quite as freely perhaps as we should like, but at any rate unhampered by the fear of molestation from the authorities and the demoralizing influence consequent on the non-compliance with the Provincial laws to which our Post Managers have been subjected for years past.'[24] Uncertainty as to whether the Temagami Indians were Treaty Indians for purposes of the game regulations added further to their anomalous position.

The fur trade itself experienced major disruption as a result of the war, and the Temagami post's reported operating profit (including revenues from tourism) of $3,021 in the 1914–15 season made it the only post in the district to show a gain and one of the few in the country. In 1915–16 and in 1916–17, gains reported at Temagami were $3,888 and $7,725 respectively, but in the latter year, the Temiskaming District Annual Report indicated that the 'gross gain at Matagami, Biscotasing and Temagami is not considered sufficient, and will have to be improved during the current outfit.' The unsatisfactory level of revenues reflected the negative impact of the war on vacation travel, but the absence of several native trappers undoubtedly contributed as well.[25]

At the outbreak of hostilities, the Militia Department policy emphasized that Indians should remain in Canada to protect the Dominion in light of the greater risk and uncertainty they might face overseas. 'While British troops would be proud to be associated with their Indian fellow subjects, yet Germans might refuse to extend to them the privileges of civilized warfare.' Yet many Indians from across Canada including members of the Temagami band soon enlisted for service overseas. Indian Affairs commented in 1918 that:

> The manner in which the Indians have responded ... appears more especially commendable when it is remembered that they are wards of the Government and have not, therefore, the responsibility of citizenship, that many of them were obliged to make long and arduous journeys from remote localities in order to offer their services and that their disposition renders them naturally averse to leaving their own country and conditions of life.[26]

In many respects, though, native enlistment appears to have been an entirely predictable response to the disruptive impact of the war on the fur trade economy and, at Temagami, the sense of dislocation occasioned by the Ontario government's management of the forest reserve.[27]

The Ontario presence in Bear Island affairs was felt directly through the war years. In 1916 the province surveyed a formal village with lot and street allowances on the southeast corner of the island. The disruptive proposal bore little relationship then or later to the plots already established for Indian and Métis dwellings, yards, and gardens. Subsequently, in 1929, L.V. Rorke, surveyor-general for the province, argued that the town plots were necessary on Bear Island, 'owing to the summer resort business.' Indians, he said, could occupy lots and do business like other people, but they could not be allowed to 'hold up the development by refusing to pay rental.' Rorke dismissed the views of federal Indian Affairs officials about the need to safeguard the interests of the Temagami Indians. He argued that the Indians of Lake Temagami were 'more in touch with civilization than any other band,' that they guided and explored like white men.[28]

Property rights on Bear Island had never been satisfactorily resolved for anyone, including the HBC, whose claim was inextricably linked to the ongoing Indian land-settlement process. Thus, when Father Evain sought the company's permission to lease two acres of land around the site of the old Catholic church in 1906, and again two years later, when the Temagami Navigation Company inquired about a possible site for a proposed hotel, the HBC's position remained uncertain. A most unsuccessful interview with Frank Cochrane 'who positively refused to grant the Company a patent' had discouraged the HBC from pressing its ownership claims, but after W.H. Hearst became minister of lands and forests in 1911, it seemed worthwhile to seek a further interview on the Bear Island question. A letter from HBC Land Commissioner J. Thomson to the company's Toronto solicitors indicated that it was 'most anxious to have a settlement effected.' McCarthy, Osler, Hoskin and Harcourt then restated the HBC position that 'its claim to a grant of the Island is just and reasonable ... the acceptance of a lease [as the previous Minister had proposed] could not be entertained.' In the interview with Hearst, the new minister expressed no opinion on the Bear Island case, although Aubrey White, still deputy minister, vigorously advanced the old Cochrane position.

The lawyers put the Hudson's Bay Company case in 'writing' for the consideration of Hearst and Aubrey White. White's response was rigid and predictable. 'It is found,' the deputy minister answered, 'that there is nothing upon which the company could found a legal claim to have a grant of 170 acres made to them.' The issue was raised many times 'and pressed by Mr. Larratt Smith a long time ago.' White himself prepared a memorandum, indicating forty acres as the maximum area that could be leased or granted. When the lawyers had tested the issue of a land grant in November 1905, Cochrane had said he could not sell land within a forest reserve and took the matter to council. The council 'came to the conclusion that the offer of a lease of 40 acres was entirely too generous, and that the lease would not be issued for more than ten acres.'

The lawyers passed on White's letter to HBC Land Commissioner Thomson, and reported further that Hearst had now accepted his deputy minister's position. They did feel, however, that a long lease at a nominal rental might be obtained for a considerable area on Bear Island if not the full 170 acres claimed by the company. At this stage, in view of the matter's seriousness, Thomson referred the question to his board in

London for consideration. 'The point has now been reached where the Company must decide whether to accept a Lease or institute proceedings in the Exchequer Court,' a course of action Thomson felt the governor and committee would not welcome, possibly because of other continuing sources of friction with the provincial administration. He recommended instead that the law firm be authorized to negotiate for the best lease terms possible.

The board concluded that 'while the position taken up by the Deputy Minister was unreasonable, looking to the length of time the Hudson's Bay Company have been in possession of a large proportion of Bear Island, it would be undesirable to institute proceedings in the Exchequer Court, as there would doubtless be a considerable amount of opposition to the Company acquiring so large an area in what had already been set aside as a Forest Reserve.' The committee thought it might be possible to effect an exchange from its other holdings in timber reserves, but Thomson thought this possibility not worth pursuing. 'The title to Bear Island is vested in the Province of Ontario, and it is improbable the Dominion Government could effect an exchange which would be acceptable to the Government of Ontario.'[29]

The HBC eventually regularized its position on Bear Island in 1917 by accepting a ninety-nine-year lease on about half the lands it had claimed in lieu of the patent it had originally sought. The company immediately allocated $10,000 towards the construction of a new store and salesshop facilities suitable for what had become the Temagami post's principal summer activity – serving the tourist trade. After 1917 the Oblates and the Anglican missionaries, who had recently established St George's chapel, were also able to clarify the status of the lots they occupied on Bear Island.[30]

With white trappers (and many Temagami Indians) absent during the war years, game had become plentiful, apart from those sections where 'railroad trappers' had been active. But demobilization and postwar unemployment in northern Ontario greatly increased competitive pressures on Temagami's traditional native fur trade. Some described the postwar situation as a 'beaver stampede' or a 'fur rush,' which lasted for a few years – until animal populations became seriously depleted. Bill Guppy, called around Temagami 'King of the Woodsmen,' reported buying $140,000 worth of beaver pelts one year from trappers in the area. The fur trade activity of the HBC's Lake Huron district to which the Temagami post belonged did not recover to prewar standards, perhaps because of unsatisfactory district managers. The Temagami post's tourist sales revenues maintained the post's profitability during the

1920s while fur collection declined. HBC competitors accounted for some of the decline in the company's fur business, but by 1925–6 game scarcity – possibly attributable to disease – was recognized as a contributing factor. In that season, Temagami sales rose to $42,689, but fur-collection totals had fallen $9,150 to $12,211, following a decline of more than $5,000 in the previous season.[31]

Offsetting the impact of regulatory constraints – at least in terms of income potential – were the new opportunities for seasonal employment related to tourism. Opportunities for guides became available at the youth camps, lodges, and resorts of the Temagami region. Fishermen, hunters, and camping parties arranged, either privately or through their hotels, for the services of guides – often Indians – on a daily or weekly basis. The demand for guides far exceeded the limits of locally available manpower, and additional 'Temagami' guides from communities such as Mattawa, Gogama, Timmins, and Chapleau travelled annually to Temagami for summer work. Guides attached to particular resorts were not generally part of the overall complement of salaried summer staff, but were considered to be on call when work was available. Ordinarily, two or more fishermen would share a guide during a day outing from a resort base. Camping parties, particularly those embarking on extended trips, were advised to hire generously: 'A canoe and guide should be provided for each of the party, and an extra guide with canoe to carry supplies, cook and attend to camp, leaving the "sports", as those visiting the country for pleasure seem to be invariably called, and their personal guides, free to get away from camp in the morning or come in late at night, without the domestic economies being upset thereby.' Guides were certainly not essential, but their advantages were well recognized: 'The Indian guides who reside in the district know every nook and corner and are the best judges as to where the haunts of game are, and are reasonable and can be depended upon.'[32]

Guiding, which was made subject to a licensing regime before 1900, was one of the earliest features of the tourist industry to be put under strict government regulation. The first (1902) set of regulations under the Forest Reserves Act also included a provision for the licensing of guides: 'no person shall act as guide or accompany any tourist or visitors or party of tourists or visitors without being in possession of such license under a penalty not exceeding fifty ($50.00) dollars for each offence.' Four years later, salary levels for guides were fixed at a rate of $2.50 per day as a result of complaints that 'guides sometimes make an arrangement with one party and another comes along and offers them a higher rate of pay and they desert the party they first engaged with and leave them helpless to get about.' The rate established seems to be entirely consistent with other reports of wage levels for guides, although Baedeker's 1907 edition of the travel guide *The Dominion of Canada* indicated that the cost of a Temagami guide and canoe could range as high as $3.50 per day.[33]

Attitudes and impressions formed on the basis of this new form of Indian-white economic interaction found their way into canoe-trip reports, diaries, and tourist accounts. Observations from these sources present a range of generally favourable opinion. 'Reliable Indian guides are obtainable throughout the Temagami country, – wise old woodsmen who can lead you to where the wild things live.' A party of women who hired Bear Islanders to assist on a one-day outing emphasized that the guides were 'not inferiors; they serve, but are not menials, may be taken to your friendship as unreservedly as any product of our civilization.' But less enthusiastic responses were occasionally voiced. A regular traveller on the Temagami steamer *Belle* referred to the presence of 'the inevitable Ojibway, possibly with his frowsy squaw, looking for engagement as a guide to some timorous or lazy tourist.'

The guides' perception of the tourist community is even more difficult to determine reliably, although 'Grey Owl' (Archie Belaney) discusses the transformation of the guiding profession in the Temagami area where he spent much of his early career. 'Grey Owl' observed that in the early years guiding was a 'strange, new, interesting job,' and the tourists appeared as 'our comrades on the trail.' But the passing of time, he suggested, altered this relationship dramatically: 'Guides were no longer companions, they were lackeys, footmen, toadies; a kind of below-stairs snobbery had sprung up among them – kid-glove guiding; some of them actually wore white cotton gloves at their work.'[34]

Guides at Bear Island were earning $3.00 in 1918, but pressures for change in the nature of guiding within the province generally may also have affected Temagami. In June 1920, *Rod and Gun* announced 'Ontario Guides Will Organize.' In accordance with a proposal from F.C. Armstrong of Cochrane to form an Ontario Guides and Outfitters' Association, the following goals were presented:

a) To ensure the securing of competent and qualified guides for sportsmen;
b) to ensure, as far as possible, that uniform rates shall be charged by the various guides and outfitters;
c) to provide disciplinary measures for guides charging exorbitant prices to any sportsman;

d) to prevent guides trespassing on the rights of other guides who are now established;
e) to require each guide to do his best in protecting the game, and to give information to the proper authorities if this protection is not given by others.

Under the heading 'Northern Ontario Outfitters and Guides Association,' *Rod and Gun* continued to announce new developments in succeeding months. Rates in October 1920 as established by a meeting of the Trans Continental District Chairmen were: head guide, $6.00 a day; others, $5.00 a day; canoe rental, $1.25 a day; tent, $0.75 a day; fly, $0.25 a day. The camp outfit would be $1.50 a day for a party of two and would increase with the size of the party. The guides' transportation was to be paid for by the sportsmen who hired them. Presumably, arrangements along these lines were used when a crew of Temagami guides took Premier Howard Ferguson and the lieutenant-governor to Moose Factory in 1923.[35]

Seasonal employment in the tourist industry, whatever economic attractions it may have had for the native residents of Temagami, was modest compensation indeed for the dislocation they had experienced as individuals and for the continuing refusal of the provincial government to acknowledge their claims as a community following the establishment of the Temagami Forest Reserve. The native people's mobility through the TFR and their use of the area's natural resources had been restricted or inconvenienced by provincial administration and increasing commercial activity throughout the area. A tourist community had become well established on Lake Temagami, while mineral exploration and development, water controls for industrial purposes, and pulpwood cutting had all taken place in various sections of the forest-management area. Meanwhile, the Temagami Indians remained without a reserve and with at best questionable security of tenure on Bear Island. Curiously, as late as the 1920s there was little evidence that Ontario's commitment to pine-forest management was resulting in meaningful policies intended to place the pine lumber industry on a sustained-yield basis.

CHAPTER EIGHT

Lumbering and Pulpwood Operations in the Temagami Forest between the Wars

The Ontario system of forest reserves in its simplest form constituted a land-classification program involving the dedication of selected and suitable woodland areas to pine timber production on a perpetual-yield basis. Two elements were considered essential for success. First, it was necessary to eliminate (or at least to control) alternative land uses to the extent that these were inconsistent with timber production. The second requirement was a forest-management plan ensuring sustained yield. The latter requirement, as foresters, senior Crown Lands officials, and members of the Canadian Forestry Association recognized at the turn of the century, entailed consistent and regular supervision of the forests to produce a reliable inventory and assessment. It entailed, as well, a determined effort to monitor or perhaps even to assist the regeneration process as it was then understood, and an orderly program for cutting mature trees. At Temagami, the pre-eminent pinery of the original forest reserve system, neither element of success had been achieved twenty years after the original dedication. Potentially incompatible land uses persisted in the form of recreational activity, a well-entrenched native community, and substantial pulpwood operations. (Although often flourishing briefly the mineral sector experienced a period of decline.) And, despite a small army of rangers and surveyors, there was never a satisfactory management plan designed to produce sustained yield in the Temagami Forest, still less an ongoing commitment to carry out such a program. In practice, the Temagami Forest became an area in which the relative importance of various legitimate uses could be regarded as a matter of some debate, even though pine production remained the principal purpose of the TFR from an official perspective.

As the interwar period began, the managed forest once contemplated by Aubrey White and his contemporaries remained an unfulfilled promise. If orderly cutting of pine according to the degree of maturity had been a central factor in the program of sustained-yield forestry conceived at the turn of the century, the actual pattern of development around Temagami demonstrates that other factors had had a greater influence on the exploitation of pine lands. Most notable among these was the economic geography of the area, especially the distribution of watersheds and the introduction of rail access. Accordingly, most cutting to the mid–1920s was on the periphery of the TFR and away from Lake Temagami itself. It was usually initiated after fire damage had occurred, major burns in 1916 and 1923 being prime examples. The economic requirements of small lumber firms established in the Temagami Forest or dependent upon Temagami pine for continued viability or expansion also came to influence the pattern of development. In addition, the proximity of pine and licensed pulp lands in the TFR frequently affected the location and timing of lumber cutting. From about 1926 on, attempts were made to introduce improved forest-management techniques, but their application was intermittent and inconsistent.

Access routes to and from the Temagami Forest were fundamental to the pattern of timber licensing and development. Rail and water routes or, on occasion, a combination of these, constituted the interwar transport system and were not supplemented by extensive roadways before the 1950s. These routes contributed to the evolution of five separate or distinct sub-sections within the TFR, each associated with its own local service centres, markets, and distribution network: the west and southwest, based on the Wanapitei River and the CNR; the south-central, oriented along the Sturgeon and Temagami rivers; the eastern corridor, utilizing the TNOR and the Timiskaming–Ottawa River route; the eastern and central regions tributary to the Montreal River, and the northern region, based on such northward-flowing rivers as the Grassy and Mattagami.

In the southwest corner of the Temagami Forest, the Marshay Lumber Company of Sudbury was established before 1920 along the Vermilion River and upper Wanapitei watersheds. Relying heavily on the CNR for support of its mill at Laforest, Marshay ran lumber camps in Frechette,

Lampman, Marshay, Beulah, and Moffat townships along the border of the TFR. The company's rights to forty-two square miles in the latter two townships, obtained without public competition, came under close scrutiny from the Riddell-Latchford Timber Commission, as did its trespassing on Lampman.[1] Slightly to the east of the Marshay limits, Manley Chew of Midland cut red, white, and jack pine on limits acquired between 1914 and 1919 in four townships bordering the upper Wanapitei River. Chew's logs were driven and towed downstream via the Wanapitei and French River system to Georgian Bay.[2] Arnold and Bell, another significant pine operator in the southern part of the Temagami Forest, also used the Wanapitei system to transport logs to the village of Spanish Mills for sawing. Arnold and Bell's timber limits in Valin, Cotton, and Beresford townships inside the TFR represented only a small portion of the 920 square miles the company controlled at the time of the Riddell-Latchford Timber Commission inquiry through an extensive network of associated Georgian Bay firms selling into the United States.[3] Other small companies, including John Campbell and Sons[4] and Acme Timber of Sudbury, also obtained cutting rights in the southwest during the 1920s and early 1930s.[5] Forest operations in the Wanapitei River–CNR section of the TFR were thus quite varied. Marshay, Campbell, and Acme represented local enterprise, while Manley Chew and Arnold and Bell linked the area to the older Georgian Bay trade and more widespread markets. Combined river and rail access permitted comparatively intensive logging in this southwest section of the TFR.

Timber cutting in the south-central section of the TFR was oriented to the Sturgeon River. Pine operations here were in effect an extension of those in the lower valley of the river. Most lower Sturgeon valley pine operators were also active in the Georgian Bay area and around Sudbury. The Field Lumber Company, however, confined its activity exclusively to the Sturgeon watershed, eventually extending its cutting territory into the Temagami River area of the TFR.[6] Gillies Brothers of Braeside on the Ottawa River obtained rights in two Sturgeon valley townships, including McConnell within the TFR, in a 1918 sale, but abandoned plans for a mill in the face of poor market conditions.[7]

From as early as 1913, pressure for disposal of pine south of the TFR and within its lower confines was as closely linked to the requirements of the pulp mills at Sturgeon Falls as to actual demand for pine or to the maturity of the species. Even before the TFR was established, the Sturgeon Falls pulp agreement of 1898 had embodied the then prevailing priority of pine over pulpwood.[8] When Spanish River Pulp and Paper acquired the Sturgeon Falls concession shortly before the First World War, it confronted, according to its counsel at the Riddell-Latchford Timber Commission, 'the difficulty of having no townships upon which there was no pine' and, by virtue of a recent modification to the operating agreement, it was required to work strictly under a permit system.[9]

The question of boundaries and area was directly related to the question of supplies. Once closer adherence to the permit cutting system became the practice, it became impossible to overlook pine cutting on pulp lands. Apparently company officials realized by 1913 that the Spanish and Sturgeon rivers' limits were not inexhaustible. The seriousness of the position was made clear to the government, but negotiations were interrupted by the war. From 1917 to 1919, the company repeatedly asked for permits to cut on pine-bearing lands in the townships of McCallum, Sisk, Kenny, Notman, Fell, Blythe, Macbeth, and Sheppard. Claiming that the Sturgeon Falls operation could only cut two-thirds of the necessary quantity to keep the plant going for the season, company officials told Howard Ferguson in 1918 that, 'If permits are not granted us immediately so that we can start operations at once we will be in a worse position than ever this year and will without doubt have to close the Sturgeon Falls plant in the near future for the want of wood.' While Spanish River Pulp and Paper was applying pressure to have some of the pine-bearing townships open, more especially Kenny, Sisk, and McCallum, they actually trespassed on these three townships, cutting without a permit.[10]

The Spanish River company claimed that at one point it had been cheaper for the old Sturgeon Falls company to buy pulpwood from jobbers than to cut it. However the Spanish River company was now forced to purchase half the wood it used at the plant because of lack of permits, paying four dollars a cord for it, a price that made it more expensive than other kinds of pulpwood. Since there was little difference between 'rail wood' bought from farmers and the 'rail wood' cut on their concession, they needed to get permits to cut 'watered wood,' as on the three named townships. The company's claims were questioned by the Crown counsel at the timber commission for, when Spanish River Pulp and Paper was trying to attract financial support and new shareholders, spokesmen bragged about a 'perpetual supply of highest grade of pulpwood.'[11]

The timber commission was often diverted from consideration of appropriate supplies for the Sturgeon Falls mill by the broader policy argument arising from a 1918 memorandum written by Deputy Minister Grigg. In an extended commentary on the inadvisability of having two forest operations in the same area, whether they were cutting the same or different species of timber, Grigg presented Howard Ferguson with two possible solutions: pine sales to the highest bidder in a public competition, or disposal to the holders of pulp concessions following evaluation by the department. Grigg's memorandum expressed the opinion that:

> the cutting of all timber can be more economically done in one operation. If this were adopted as a policy, proper restrictions should be made that the pine be cut only on the areas from which pulpwood is being removed. This would prevent any possibility of large areas being cut over for pine timber in advance of the requirements of the pulp companies for the pulpwood timber necessary to keep their mills in operation.[12]

This was a recommendation in favour of a reversal of policy with respect to the superiority of pine over pulp, with a hint of patronage thrown in – more than sufficient material for argument at the inquiry. The Spanish River company claimed that, with respect to pine: 'We don't want it, never asked for it, and when we were asked to put in a bid on this reserve, we would not do it.' However, they did submit a bid of six dollars per thousand feet board measure, supposedly not to be taken seriously, and pine rights were later sold by public competition at much higher prices. The significant point remains that 'one of the objects' in selling these townships was that 'the pulp company could get their pulp.'[13]

The pine of the Temagami Forest's southeast corner was made accessible by the TNOR, which paralleled the long-established Lake Timiskaming and Ottawa River water route. The Gillies firm of Braeside continued to operate on this side of the Temagami Forest, adding the extensive Temagami Limit in 1919 to the Montreal River Limit (Gillies Limit) that the firm had acquired in 1895. This firm, with rights to red and white pine as well as jack pine and spruce lumber, was a major exporter to the United States, England, and South America.[14] Several other companies with roots around North Bay and the Ottawa valley also advanced along the TNOR corridor.

Before 1920 George and A.B. Gordon had established several small lumber firms around the TFR. The Tomiko Lumber Company worked the lower Sturgeon valley and in 1916 obtained rights (subsequently transferred to Manley Chew) in Grigg Township on the Wanapitei. The A.B. Gordon company owned a sawmill at Callander in the North Bay area. Like Gillies, the Gordon interests were seeking further opportunities for northward expansion. They formed the Timagami Timber Company and built a small mill at Goward on Net Lake to service local woods operations. Through A.B. Gordon, Timagami Timber succeeded to a valuable timber berth by White Bear or Cassels Lake, which Lands and Forests offered for sale following a serious fire in June 1923. The twenty-five-and-a-half-square-mile timber berth contained extensive quantities of red and white pine: the damaged timber alone was estimated at 10 million feet. Timagami Timber's Goward mill doubled production from 30 thousand feet, board measure (Mfbm), to 60 Mfbm between 1924 and 1930 as the firm acquired new timber rights in Law and Strathy townships.[15] After 1927, George Gordon and Company operated in the southeast quarter of Law, using the railway to transport logs to its mill at Cache Bay on Lake Nipissing.[16]

The TNOR served numerous other pine operations in the southeastern quarter of the TFR. McNamara Lumber, a subsidiary of Union Lumber of Toronto, is a typical example. McNamara began work in the 1919–20 season at several small lumber camps close to the TNOR. A short siding (in Kenny Township) linked woods operations to the TNOR main line where flat cars were attached to passing freight trains for a fifty-mile trip to a mill on Trout Lake. Three observers who examined work at one of the McNamara camps remarked in 1921 that few seedlings for red and white pine were to be found. They concluded that 'pine in this region as a commercial tree will soon be gone' and that pulpwood had already achieved 'greater prominence.'[17]

William Milne and Sons also followed the TNOR. Indeed, development of the company's mill at Trout Mills was stimulated by the clearing operations along the rail line. By 1921, Milne was cutting inside the Temagami Forest in Askin Township. The centre of operations advanced steadily northward past Redwater (mile 57.75), Rabbit Point (mile 60.3), Doherty (mile 65.6), to Temagami Station (mile 73). Until 1935, when Milne relocated its sawmill on Link Lake just north of the village of Temagami, all the company's timber was hauled by rail to Trout Mills. Beginning in 1937, log booms towed on Lake Temagami became the principal means of delivering sawlogs to the mills.[18]

Like the lumber industry in the southern and eastern reaches of the Temagami Forest, pine cutting in the northern extremity of the TFR was confined to the periphery, as the most accessible townships were the first to be utilized rather than those designated most mature or in need of cutting for purposes of long-term management. The fact that the Mattagami and Grassy rivers flowed north towards James Bay meant that the far northern section of the Temagami Forest remained a part of the lumbering hinterland of the Timmins–Porcupine area. Only along parts of the Montreal River watershed did lumbering in this era extend toward the geographic centre of the TFR. Yet here, too, lumber activity had more to do with local necessity than with forest management.[19]

Around Gowganda the early mining activities had encouraged the development of local lumber operations that acquired a greater degree of permanence and legitimacy when two berths of fire-damaged timber were sold in 1909. Mining activity near Elk Lake also contributed to the proliferation of small sawmills, many of which were portable and short-lived.[20] In the mid–1920s when a small quantity of partly fire-killed pine in the east half of Milner Township and the north half of Leith was offered for sale there was some hope that this would help to revive idle mills at Gowganda and at Elk Lake.[21]

In Charters and Nicol townships, immediately east of the Milner and Leith limits, J.R. Booth bought the rights to pine in 1922 from the original licensee. The quantity of pine thus obtained was of minor significance to Booth's overall production in the area, which, according to one well-placed observer, peaked in 1921.[22] But it was a matter of some convenience to control pulp and pine cutting together. Booth's Ottawa sawmill produced 350 Mfbm of lumber in 1924. The company produced 150 tons of paper and 250 tons of pulp in the same year. Booth's pulp cutting near mature red and white pine in Auld and Klock townships within the TFR prompted pine timber sales in 1925.[23]

Along the Montreal River between Mountain Chutes and Bay Lake, A.J. Murphy cut jack pine for his mill at Latchford and pulpwood for Booth. The firms of Grant and Dunn and of D. McLennan also cut pine in the vicinity in order to supply their Latchford mills. These three Latchford mills (Murphy, Grant and Dunn, and McLennan) had a combined capacity of about 100 Mfbm in 1924,[24] the year in which provincial Lands and Forests officials clearly signalled the administration's willingness to consider regional economic conditions when designating Temagami pine for cutting. A 1924 timber sale in the westerly and southerly portions of Kittson township was in large part a concession to the needs of the village of Latchford. As Deputy Minister Cain stated, 'there are three saw mills that give employment to the people of that community, and tend to continue the life of that thriving little village, which is now in a good way of growing into a town of considerable dimensions, but which is dependent almost entirely upon the life of the saw milling operations there.' A timber sale, he concluded, would not only encourage Latchford but would also create traffic for the TNOR.[25]

By the mid-1920s, several practical limitations on scientific and sustained-yield pine management in the TFR had become clear. The willingness of lumber companies to cut was dependent upon convenient access to resources via rail or water transport and, quite naturally, upon markets. Thus, with only isolated exceptions, lumbering was confined to the periphery of the Temagami Forest. The requirements of the pulp industry and the mix of pulp and pine lands had also influenced the pace and location of pine cutting such that townships within the Spanish River and Booth pulp concessions were often offered to the lumbermen as they were needed by the pulp producers. Indeed, Deputy Minister Grigg had gone so far as to recommend 'that the pine be cut only on the areas from which pulpwood is being removed.' In addition, once established in the area, small communities with local mills such as Latchford, Gowganda, and Elk Lake introduced new pressures for employment stabilization, a use of Temagami's pine lands not easily reconciled with the original concept of scientific forest management. These constraints were certainly not of the department's making. Nor were they readily avoidable in the general context of Ontario's competitive economy and later the social climate resulting from postwar unemployment. On the other hand, it was increasingly apparent that Ontario still had no orderly plan to dispose of mature timber in the Temagami Forest. Instead, fire damage or fire hazard and the threat of destruction by wind in partially burned areas were customarily cited as the basis for cutting specially authorized by order-in-council during the early 1920s.[26]

The 1923 Cassels Township fire and subsequent licensing to A.B. Gordon's Timagami Timber Company suggested that the acknowledged success of rangers in preventing or suppressing fires had not been matched by effectiveness in inventory and assessment of the forest resources. The area offered for sale in Cassels and adjacent townships contained an estimated 22.5 million feet, board measure, of red and white pine.[27] Industry spokesmen and forestry professionals lamented the government's apparent failure to identify and dispose of mature timber. Severe criticism emerged from these quarters in the mid-1920s. William Milne, after twenty-five years of industry experience from his North Bay base, told the federal Royal Commission on Pulpwood in 1922 that there were 'millions of feet of excellent pine going to waste in the northern country.' In Temagami, he said, there was old timber that should have been taken out forty or fifty years earlier, and he argued that the blocks of mature pine should be cut to permit young timber to grow. Another observer who examined the Temagami Forest during a visit to the North Bay and Sudbury areas in 1925 described the red and white pine as 'overmature' and 'deteriorating rapidly.' He urged that it be cut 'as rapidly as the market will absorb it.' 'It is quite evident,' the criticism continued, 'that had this timber been cut 70 years ago, nothwithstanding the slightly smaller diameter of the trees, probably twice as much actual raw material would have been obtained from this limit owing to the greater density of the stand.' Pathological research also pointed to the deterioration of Temagami pine.[28] Indeed, the Ontario forest reserve system itself came under attack as W.N. Millar expressed the view that the legislation 'does not appear to contemplate the employment of the lands contained in reserves for continuous production of timber.' He concluded that the province's Forest Reserves Act embodied outdated forestry principles and 'plainly has as its purpose not the production of timber by cultural processes, but merely the hoarding of a supply against an envisaged period of scarcity.'[29] The experience at Temagami, with sales occasioned largely by fires, the progress of the railway, the advance of the pulpwood industry, and the needs of small communities, was generally consistent with Millar's analysis of 'hoarding.' This situation awaited the Conservative Party under Howard Ferguson, which returned to power in 1923 after the interlude of the United Farmers of Ontario.

In 1926, Premier Ferguson appointed William Finlayson as minister of lands and forests. In the next eight years Finlayson presided over a period of change in Ontario forest policy and, in some respects, in the management of the Temagami Forest. The Department of Lands and Forests expanded and soon had three deputy ministers. Changes in administrative practices and forest law followed.[30]

During the late 1920s Finlayson brought in three pieces of legislation that became significant for Temagami: the Forestry Act (1927), the Pulpwood Conservation Act (1929), and the Provincial Forests Act (1929). The Forestry Act[31] of 1927 repealed the Reforestation acts of 1921 and 1923, integrating their contents into a single statute. Formerly, the minister of lands and forests had been authorized to acquire lands for reforestation; now these lands were placed 'under the control and management of the Minister, who may develop, protect, care for, and manage such lands.' the Minister also gained the power to remove settlers from unsuitable farming lands, and to set apart lands for such displaced settlers. Townships with less than twenty-five resident freeholders could be detached from any union of townships to form part of a municipal corporation. Lands suitable for the creation of a Crown forest reserve could be set apart by order-in-council 'under the Forest

Reserves Act, notwithstanding the fact that such lands may be valuable or used for the preservation or reproduction of timber other than pine.' This latter clause indicated the new weight given to the pulp industry and to reforestation. Thus the original Forest Reserves Act, first intended to create pine reserves, could now formally be used to create pulpwood reserves.

The 1927 Forestry Act also established the Forestry Board, a five-man committee appointed to conduct research in connection with Ontario's forestry lands and to investigate 'the planting, growth, development, marketing and reproduction of pulpwoods' on Crown lands or in the hands of private operators. Several members of the Forestry Board (among them J.A. Gillies of Braeside, whose firm had lumbered in the district since the nineteenth century, and Dr C.D. Howe, dean of the University of Toronto's forestry school, which conducted research programs around Temagami) were already familiar with Temagami before their appointments to the new agency.[32]

Almost immediately after it was established, the Forestry Board made five recommendations: that a forest experimental station and a forest nursery be established in northern Ontario so that data could be collected as a basis for reforestation policy; that demonstration forests be established to determine the best cutting method to allow natural perpetuation of the crop; that a yearly program of forest stock-taking be started; that forest nurseries be established as co-operatives; and that a percentage of the department's income be directed to planting and silvicultural schemes. Several of these worthwhile suggestions were reminiscent of the turn-of-the-century goals of an earlier generation of foresters. But, like its forerunners, the board did not remain active for long. By advocating higher pay for foresters, reforestation in northern Ontario, and administration of provincial lands by the Forestry Branch, it had gone 'too far too fast.'[33] Only two meetings were held after the stock-market crash of October 1929.

In spite of its short life, the Forestry Board played an important role in drafting the two other significant pieces of legislation introduced by Finlayson, the Pulpwood Conservation Act and the Provincial Forests Act, both passed in 1929.[34] The first required pulp operators to submit detailed information to the board and to provide a plan for sustained-yield production. Under the Provincial Forests Act, existing reserves (now reclassified as provincial forests) and other lands set aside were protected from agricultural settlement and were placed under the management and control of a forester, whose duty it was to preserve them 'according to the best forestry practice, and to gradually bring them under a sustained yield basis.' The timber in the provincial forests could be sold if it 'has been damaged by fire or has attained commercial maturity.'[35] Three new provincial forests were established under the legislation: the Wanapitei Provincial Forest, to the southwest of Temagami, the large Georgian Bay Forest, and the small Kawartha Forest north of Peterborough. The Provincial Forests Act also slightly increased the official size of the Temagami Provincial Forest by adding to it the oddly shaped and partly cut-over townships of South Lorrain and Gillies Limit north of Temagami village.

In his first report as minister, Finlayson in 1926 had enumerated the purposes of Ontario's forest reserves, an elaborate rationale somewhat broader than the original goals. To the growth of timber under advanced scientific management, the protection of timber areas from agriculture, and watershed maintenance, Finlayson explicitly added wildlife protection and propagation, 'opportunities for uninterrupted nature study and experimental forestry,' and enlargement of the 'health and recreation centres' of Ontario. In sum, the minister presented forest reserves as a means of perpetuating the province's natural wealth 'that it may be judiciously developed for the benefits of present and future generations.'[36] The province's forest reserve system was nevertheless under attack, as the charge of 'hoarding' demonstrated. Perhaps not surprisingly, Finlayson's subsequent package of legislation was regarded as 'window dressing' with political rather than administrative objectives, for in several respects Finlayson failed to follow through with the programs and expenditures necessary to achieve sustained yield.[37]

Despite criticism of his legislation, Finlayson's interest in forestry was sincere. By designating the head of the Surveys Branch, L.V. Rorke, as a deputy minister and by encouraging the activities of the Forestry Board, Finlayson demonstrated his commitment to research. The relationship between forest reserves and research was also articulated by the Forestry Board, which suggested the creation of the Wanapitei Provincial Forest north of Sudbury 'for the sole and express purpose of carrying on under the direction of the forest research section such research as may be from time to time decided upon.' The recommendation also stated, however, that the area contained 'little commercial timber' and that the agreement should be made 'with the understanding that if in the course of time any timber is cut on the area it shall go to the pulp and paper company that relinquishes its cutting rights for the purpose of establishing the above experimental area.' The sincerity of the minister and the sympathetic efforts of the Forestry Board ultimately proved wholly inadequate to withstand the impact of the Depression, which imposed severe constraints on financing and personnel.[38]

The Provincial Forests Act was supposed to protect valuable pulp and pine lands from agricultural settlement and to encourage silvacultural research and reforestation, even in the north. But Finlayson really believed in natural regeneration rather than 'artificial reforestation' in provincial parks and forests, including the valuable Temagami Forest. He confidently asserted in his department's 1928 annual report that 'artificial reforestation ... has its limitations' and that 'natural reforestation is our salvation.'[39] The minister largely staked the future of Ontario's northern resources on the land-classification model that excluded competing uses while protecting the existing forest from fire. Assistance for regeneration and other sophisticated management techniques apparently had little or no contribution to make. In southern Ontario, where the wastelands were so obvious, the idea of artificial reforestation was more easily popularized. Moreover, the idea of reforestation in the north was not consistent with the lingering image of a limitless frontier, the New Ontario mentality. Hence the Forestry Branch emphasized reforestation in southern Ontario while continuing to rely on fire protection in northern Ontario. Several flying boats – HS2LS from the fleet of the Ontario Provincial Air Service, and, after 1927, DeHavilland Moths equipped with pontoons – were regularly stationed on Lake Temagami. These planes were used for reconnaissance and for transporting men, supplies, and fire-fighting equipment, as well as for general forestry administration. Fire towers on Bear Island, near Temagami village, and atop Maple Mountain further strengthened the surveillance capability of Temagami rangers.[40]

Even the naming of a dedicated forest engineer, Frank Sharpe, to take charge of all provincial forests did not result in an improved management system. The provincial forests in general never became important experimental grounds. In part of the Temagami Provincial Forest a surveying project had begun before 1929, concentrating on the types, ages, and estimates of timber. After the Forestry Act, the survey continued 'but with a more definitive objective of relating the forest conditions and timber estimates to a preliminary forest working plan for the areas.'[41] In this way, a small-scale timber-management plan was instituted three decades after the TFR was established, but never fully implemented over the entire Temagami Forest. Given both the economic crisis that unfolded in the 1930s and the obvious lack of political will, the extent and diversity of the Temagami Forest made the task too demanding. Temagami did not become a distinct forest district. Indeed, the discrete significance of all provincial forests rapidly declined, and the once ambitious Ontario forest reserve system largely came to naught.

In addition to the forest policy initiatives already noted, Finlayson opened up the Temagami Forest before the Depression to more rapid commercial exploitation. Heeding professional advice and perhaps the criticisms of Milne and others, the minister had initiated a policy of allocating numerous timber limits over extensive accessible areas of the Temagami Forest that contained over-mature and mature stands of white and red pine. Finlayson certainly increased the pace of licensing of Temagami limits, even though the Department of Lands and Forests never formulated an overall forest-management policy for Temagami. The decisive move on licensing came in 1927, when Finlayson's department opened for tender a large block east and southeast of Temagami village along the TNOR. Gillies Brothers submitted the only tender at the sale of this block of 115 square miles covering parts of five townships, the single largest pine limit granted as one berth in the Temagami Forest up to 1940. Previous negotiations had been carried on 'for some time' with the former minister. In reopening the negotiations in 1926, J.A. Gillies based his claim on the reputation of his Braeside mill and his need for Ontario timber. Only about a third of the firm's six hundred miles of licensed land in Ontario contained 'any considerable quantity of timber which is merchantable,' Gillies explained, and there was some pressure from Quebec, where the Braeside company also held limits, to have all timber cut in that province manufactured there. He wrote of 'precedents for exchange of timber under such conditions' and indicated that some of his licensed lands in Ontario were reforesting rapidly. In the 1927 Temagami sale, Gillies did surrender various limits in parts of Ontario, including the peculiar township of Gillies Limit (originally the firm's Montreal River Limit), which was later added to the Temagami Forest as part of the 1929 reorganization.[42]

Gillies defended the old system of licensing timber limits for a lump sum, and criticized the overpricing of Ontario white pine in comparison to international prices. He obtained the extensive Temagami Limit by paying a deposit of $25,000. Finlayson defended the sale to Gillies as amply justified, 'based upon the principles of rotation of crop and perpetuation of forest wealth,' as well as on the fact that 'the purchaser ... is an active operator and owner of a going concern.'[43] This general policy seems to have applied to timber sales both inside and outside official forests; that is, established operators who provided stability and regular employment could expect to be favourably regarded in applications for additional supplies of sawlogs. This attitude towards major lumber firms was entirely consistent with the favourable treatment accorded pulpwood operators as a consequence of Premier Ferguson's well-known belief in supporting a small number of major producers in the pulpwood industry.

A second large Temagami pine stand covering 108 square miles was sold as one berth in early 1928 to the Spanish River Lumber Company, the lumber production arm of the huge Spanish River corporate empire. The sale covered the townships of Unwin and Leask, the west half of Haentschel, and the east half of Lampman, all in the central-west part of the Temagami Forest, straddling the upper Wanapitei River. Though the areas were not contiguous, they were merely separated by the township of Valin, in which the existing timber berths were already licensed to Arnold and Bell, the two main shareholders of the Spanish River company. Cutting was limited to red and white pine in the east half of Lampman, the southwest of Leask, and the west half of Haentschel, the three areas covered by the Spanish River and Montreal River pulp concessions. In the rest of the township of Leask and in the township of Unwin, the cutting of jack pine for sawlogs was permitted. This use of jack pine marked a shift from the tree's earlier application to railway ties, but no clear indication exists of a relationship beteen the use of jack pine for lumber and a perceived decline in pine timber supplies.[44]

These two sales of large timber berths represented exceptions to the pattern set in the province. Though pine operators rarely had the long-term lease arrangements used by the pulpwood industry, these two large and well-established firms obviously now benefited from departmental consideration and an emerging concern for stabilized employment in the lumber industry. In the case of Spanish River Lumber, it is also likely that the department expected to encourage co-ordination between pulp and pine cutting in the five townships.

Between 1927 and 1930, Lands and Forests sold numerous other timber limits in the Temagami Forest. The consideration given to established firms was clearly acknowledged in the department's 1928 annual report. As the department explained, timber limits were offered 'by public competition to provide opportunities, however, only for those individuals or companies with important vested interests concerned in continuing their established businesses.' In certain cases it turned out that the successful tenderer was not the prospective buyer. 'This fact alone justifies advertising the areas and requiring sealed tenders.'[45]

In 1927, Strathy Township, north of Temagami village, was offered as a limit and awarded to the Timagami Timber Company of Goward. Three years later this same company asked the government to open a section of the township of Best, north of Strathy and adjacent to their two licensed areas, which were now becoming depleted. Timagami Timber used as argument the fact that it had made a large financial outlay, that this was the only adjacent pine left, and that the timber was fully mature. The land was put up for tender, and the company did obtain the rights. The department also sold off Leo, the township surrounding the northern main part of Lady Evelyn Lake, and Speight, the township surrounding Mendelssohn Lake; neither of the notices for the sale asserted any fire damage. The George Gordon firm strengthened its position in the south of the TFR by acquiring limits in Macbeth, Afton, Sheppard, Scholes, Clement, and Law townships between 1927 and 1929. Production at Gordon's Cache Bay mill increased from 100 Mfbm of lumber per day between 1924 and 1926 to 220 Mfbm between 1927 and 1930.[46]

In addition to its efforts to dispose of some of Temagami's mature pine timber during Finlayson's tenure, the department also created or expanded pulp concessions in the Temagami Forest. These actions were part of the Ontario government's encouragement of the province's pulp and paper industry through the 1920s. They were consistent with what Premier Ferguson's biographer has described as his belief that it was 'to the mutual advantage of the people of Ontario and the pulp and paper producers that the industry be provided with an assured supply of raw material and that large units of production be encouraged in the interests of conservation, stability, and permanence.'[47]

Before Finlayson took over at Lands and Forests, J.R. Booth had been lobbying to secure a twenty-one-year extension for his Montreal River Pulp Concession. This included the Montreal watershed north of Latchford, upstream beyond Matachewan and the watersheds of the West and East Montreal rivers and of the Macobe. Booth had not been producing pulp up to previously agreed levels. The company excused this, noting the shortage of labour during the First World War, the heavy fire losses caused by prospectors, the disruptive effect of salvaging burnt timber, and the loss of valuable timber through flooding. Certainly the distance from the pulpwood stands to the Ottawa mill was an important reason for Booth's interest in the extension. 'As conditions are at present,' the deputy minister explained, 'the distance from the central logging operations to their plant at Ottawa, is from three to four years' drive and this means a considerable period elapses before they secure a return on their operating investment.' To reduce the time required for delivery, Booth proposed a pulpwood mill at Latchford. In view of the capital expenditure, though, the company sought an assurance that the present lease would be extended.

Lands and Forests finally granted the extension on 12 January 1928, but Booth's prior anticipation of success is reflected in the fact that the company 'built a pulpwood storage and railway loading plant in 1927 at South Gillies.' Under the new agreement the concession was adjusted to 1,662 square miles, and later to 1,616 square miles. Some territories on the west were removed, while more territory was added in the north, on both sides of the original vortex.[48]

In 1927, the vast Spanish River Pulp and Paper Mills organization, which ran the Sturgeon Falls mills, was itself absorbed into the still larger conglomerate known as the Abitibi Power and Paper Company Limited. Signs of over-production in the Ontario pulpwood industry were then already evident, and corporate restructuring had been advanced as one solution. After a period of uncertainty, the boundaries of the Spanish and Sturgeon concessions had finally been settled with the passing of an order-in-council on 27 July 1926. The Spanish River Concession was enlarged beyond the western boundary of the Temagami Forest from its supposed 2,833 square miles to 3,627 square miles of the Spanish, Vermilion, and Onaping watersheds. Through negotiations, the Sturgeon Falls Limit was set at 2,369 square miles, up from its usually stated area of 1,723 square miles, the area upon which the minister had determined fire charges.[49]

In 1929, a fourth pulp limit was established within the boundaries of Temagami Forest. Cutting rights to 965 square miles in the west-central section of the forest were sold by private agreement to Howard Smith Paper Mills Limited of Montreal. This company, with plants at Cornwall, Georgetown, and Merritton, manufactured a wide range of paper products. The agreement covered the rights to spruce, balsam, poplar, and 'whitewood' pulpwood. In 1935 Smith also secured permission to cut spruce sawlogs. Under the 1929 agreement the company agreed to increase the capacity of the Cornwall mill, to employ 650 men in its three plants, plus 250 men in the bush for seven months, and to manufacture a finished product other than pulpwood. It seems, however, that the Howard Smith company did not actually cut any licensed lands in Ontario; rather it continued to cut on its Quebec lands. It then purchased the remainder of its supplies from privately owned lands. The success or well-being of the Howard Smith company and the other pulpwood operations of northern Ontario was again emerging as a significant concern for the provincial government.[50]

In 1926, in correspondence with a representative of the Spruce Falls Pulp and Paper Company concerning another pulpwood agreement, Premier Ferguson had called for 'cooperation between the contracting parties.' He argued that one purpose of major timber sales was to facilitate 'perpetual industries' and that the province was 'just as deeply interested in the success of your Company as its shareholders. In fact, we are in a way the largest shareholders, because we contribute the power and the timber at a very reasonable price, that will undoubtedly enable your organization to flourish.' Yet in the Depression, neither Premier Ferguson nor his minister of lands and forests was able to prevent the collapse of the over-extended pulp industry. Indeed, as the condition of the industry deteriorated in the later 1920s, both men favoured industry measures rather than government intervention to rectify the situation. In the early thirties co-operation between the 'contracting parties,' as Ferguson had described them, seemed to mean that 'the government of Ontario, as the largest shareholder in the pulp and paper industry, had to bear the brunt of its collapse.'[51]

Finlayson's concern with achieving sustained yield on pulp limits had been genuine. Now, however, there seemed little the government could do but wait out the Depression. Thus, when the agreements for the Sturgeon Falls and Spanish River concessions came up for renewal in 1930 and 1932, the process was delayed. The huge Abitibi conglomerate fell into receivership, and in 1933 cabinet declined to renew the Abitibi agreements. The preferred response was some form of tentative agreements with the liquidator rather than a long-term renewal.[52] During the Depression, pulp cutting in the Temagami Forest almost disappeared. Although a few other Abitibi mills that were in receivership still cut on their limits and operated their mills at reduced capacities, this was not the case with the Sturgeon Falls and Spanish River concessions. These mills entirely shut down.[53]

The Depression also affected the lumber industry, which, according to Lands and Forests, had fallen into a tenuous position as early as 1927. The department expressed the view that the lumbermen's 'former determined activity to produce, come what may, has given way to caution in the face of so many competitive factors.'[54] The government also later acknowledged the deteriorating financial situation facing many companies as the banks tightened credit following the onset of the Depression. The department concluded that, 'notwithstanding the large supplies of lumber and other products within their yards,' many companies were unable to liquidate their indebtedness to the government. In response to the companies' claims that they could place men in the bush if fees were lowered, the department reduced the Crown dues. However, it refused to lower the bonuses bid by the companies during the productive twenties.[55]

As a further consequence of the unstable lumber market at the start of the Depression, the number of timber berths sold dropped significantly. Only two general logging berths were sold within the Temagami Forest from 1931 to 1934. In awarding William Milne the rights to six square miles of Milne Township north of the Marten River, the reasons given were the need for more timber for Milne's Trout Creek mill, the maturity of the timber, and the desire to relieve regional unemployment. Notices of timber sales during this period specified that companies should use 'as far as possible, local labour.' More specialized permits for railway ties and for cedar poles were also granted in the vicinity of Temagami, again mostly to relieve unemployment.[56]

In 1934, the flamboyant Mitch Hepburn led the provincial Liberals in turning out the Conservative regime, then ineffectively directed by George S. Henry. Committed to retrenchment rather than to genuine policy changes, the new premier set out to reduce costs and to replace Tories. His minister of lands and forests, Peter Heenan, from the northwestern region of the province, energetically led Hepburn's campaigns within the department. Although Deputy Minister Cain survived, Heenan's new deputy minister of the Forestry Branch, Frederick Noad, proceeded to review almost all district and assistant district foresters; many were demoted or fired. Clarence Hindson, the chief ranger for Temagami, did not escape. In retrospect it all seemed like a crude political purge of the public service. The fire protection service, which had long been the chief concern of foresters in northern Ontario, had its budget cut nearly in half. C.D. Howe, dean of the University of Toronto's forestry school, regretfully concluded that: 'In some cases governmental grants for the maintenance of forestry have been reduced far out of proportion to reduction in other public services. The cynic might say this was done because the governments know that it could be done with less protest than in any other field of public endeavour. Forestry controls few votes.'[57]

The change of government in 1934 represented an administrative break from the pattern of the twenties and early thirties in more ways than one. Hepburn claimed that he was only against the 'monopolists' and 'mismanagement' and that he 'would revive the forest revenues, and put men back to work.' Whereas the Conservative government had refused to reduce the bonus paid on cut timber, the Hepburn administration claimed that the previous concessions on the level of Crown dues had 'not been a sufficient incentive to the operators in the high-priced stumpage to proceed with any extensive operations.' In order to stimulate employment of 'thousands of bush men accustomed to such line of work, who have been thrown out of employment and made subject to relief,' as well as to re-establish a provincial revenue and to help the lumber industry out of its 'harassed condition,' the Hepburn government met all the lumbermen's demands and actually gave a bit more.[58]

Reductions of 50 per cent on Crown dues were made in 1934 along with 50 per cent reductions in the bonus over a minimum of $3.00 for red and white pine and spruce board measure, and $2.50 for jack pine. The order-in-council covered one year and sustained Ontario's manufacturing clause on sawmill production. The reduced rates were renewed for the remainder of the decade, while the Crown dues on spruce pulpwood were reduced from $1.40 to $1.00 per cord in 1936. In a complete reversal of established policy, the pulpwood manufacturing condition was suspended in 1935. An important proviso on employment practices was introduced at the same time: 'Fair wage rates shall be paid to workmen, reasonable prices charged for van and other supplies ...' This was one response to the serious labour and unemployment problems of the previous winter and part of the Hepburn government's efforts to minimize dislocation and unrest in the forest industries.[59] But as the Depression dragged on, the overall situation in the two forest industries did not improve. Lands and Forests attempted several rescue tactics, including favouring pulp companies and allowing them, under the 1936 Forest Regulations Act, to cut pine on their concessions. But it required the stimulus of the Second World War to revive the pulp and paper industry.[60]

The broad-ranging economic and social problems in the forest industry during the early 1930s dictated that sustained-yield management of the Temagami Forest would remain a subordinate consideration. At the start of the 1935–6 season, however, the Department of Lands and Forests did announce the introduction of a 'progressive scheme of forest management ... within a portion of the Temagami Provincial Forest.' Later described as 'a definite working plan involving the utilization of 600 million feet of white and red pine,' the program allocated timber for cutting on a basis 'related to the requirements of the established mills.' Thus 'no group is to have an advantage to the detriment of another.' The department contemplated a cutting cycle extending over a period of twenty-five to thirty years and now made some provision to support regeneration. 'All brush will be burned and a progressive planting program has commenced with the object of filling in where nature failed to restock. By brush burning the hazard is removed and the ground that would have been covered by slash for 10 to 20 years is made available for seeding or planting.'[61] This particular measure was a clear departure from the Finlayson era, in which natural regeneration was the favoured method of reforestation in the north.

After 1935 (the year in which pine cutting began in close proximity to Lake Temagami itself), the conditions of sale contained special restrictions:

> No lumber camps or buildings of any description to be erected along the shore of Timagami Lake. No land will be cleared for skidways or rollways along the shore of Timagami Lake. Trees within 300 feet of portages and shorelines of inland lakes are reserved, excepting where these are marked to be cut by a representative of the Department. No booming or towing operations will be permitted in Timagami Lake during the months of July and August.

This shoreline protection was supplemented by a 'Skyline Reserve,' a no-cutting belt that was enforced from the shore of Lake Temagami to the top of the surrounding ridge.

Deputy Minister Cain echoed Finlayson's enthusiasm for 'health and recreation centres' when he stated that 'the preservation of scenic values in relation to popular tourist centres ... is becoming general over the entire province. Crown timber along highways, around lakes, and paralleling portage routes will not be sold, nor, if licensed, be allowed to be cut, if by doing so it conflicts with popular tourist routes.' The policy applied in Quetico, Algonquin, Nipigon, and the Lake of the Woods areas and had been promised by Finlayson for Temagami in the early 1930s.[62] In timber sales dating back many years no cutting had been allowed on islands, except when considered advisable for the purpose of salvaging damaged timber or in emergency situations.

Because pine cutting directly adjacent to Lake Temagami did not begin until 1935, the shoreline reserve for that lake technically did not exist before that year. But the idea of shoreline reserves to preserve recreational attractions was not new. The original Sturgeon Falls pulp agreement of 1898 prohibited shoreline cutting. Under the new arrangements, a penalty of twenty-five dollars was imposed for each unmarked tree cut in a prohibited area. The minister could also cancel any licence for infractions of these regulations. This was a strong disciplinary measure, considering that heretofore trespassing was controlled only by the threat of double rates. It would appear, however, that the zone near Lake Temagami placed under this strict management scheme was only a narrowly conceived 'Tourist Area' in the southeast portion of the forest. The rest of the Temagami Forest, which was apparently not regarded as recreational, came under more general rules.[63]

In 1938, 5,000 trees were planted through the auspices of the Temagami ranger headquarters. In 1939, of the 74,000 trees planted by the various provincial ranger headquarters throughout the north, 52,000 were planted by the Temagami office. In 1940, 127,000 trees were planted by the Temagami headquarters alone. Relating this reforestation scheme to the management scheme, Lands and Forests highlighted the vicinity of Lake Temagami. Although the northern planting program was a new initiative in which the Temagami Forest figured prominently, reforestation in Ontario remained overwhelmingly a southern Ontario priority. It was carried out primarily in the south in county and municipal forests, on demonstration plots and woodlots, along highways, and to some degree on privately owned lands. Cain estimated in 1939 that 22 million pine seedlings were being supplied by three provincial nurseries, all in the south.[64]

An important aspect of the management plan of the late 1930s was reflected in the phrase 'Temagami Tourist Area,' sometimes used by Lands and Forests officials to describe the portion of the Temagami Forest where the new approach was being implemented. Was the area around Lake Temagami now a management unit because of its high tourist visibility, because it was in a provincial forest, because its timber was mature, or because some study of white pine regeneration in cut-over lands was the only research work not suspended by governmental restraints? Since research work and reforestation were neither confined solely to provincial forests, nor carried out in every forest, nor spread out over the whole of the Temagami Forest, it would seem that the existence of the Temagami Forest was not central in determining that a limited area around Temagami village was being singled out as a management unit. Thus, shoreline, portage, and island preserves in the immediate vicinity of Lake Temagami seem to have been related to the economic importance of the tourist trade and the potential for friction.

The protection of forest lands from agriculture, in order to guarantee them for industry's later use, seems to be the main reason behind the original system of forest reserves – or provincial forests, as these districts were known after 1929. Woods were still being set aside for both pine and pulp cutting in the 1930s. Cain claimed in 1939 that 'extensive areas of immature timber are being set aside and created into Provincial Forests or added to forests already existing.'[65] Cain defended the existence of Temagami and other provincial forests before a select committee of the Legislature in 1940–1, 'because theoretically speaking, there is a fence around each one of them and we do not allow so-called farmers to go into these vast areas, and we maintain that land in and by ourselves.' He concluded that the unsatisfactory conditions resulting from marginal agriculture in Old Ontario should not be allowed to recur in New Ontario.[66] Thus it appeared that the department continued to regard marginal agriculture, along with fire, as the principal threat to Ontario's northern forest resources. Notwithstanding some limited initiatives related to inventory, reforestation, and the disposal of mature timber by Finlayson and his successors at Lands and Forests, the province's underlying attitude had not shifted significantly from the era when criticisms of 'hoarding' had been made against it. Temagami pine had been defended in some respects, but it was not managed with any serious commitment to sustained yield.

Some challenges to Temagami pine and in particular to pine management for sustained yield were accommodated rather than resisted as multiple uses entered the district. Thus, the exclusion of agriculture did not preclude the release of some Temagami Forest lands for other resource exploitation, for railway development by the CNOR and TNOR, and for recreational development on the islands of Lake Temagami. A basic precept of the original system was also compromised from the outset by the mix of pulp limits alongside pine stands in much of the TFR.

In 1940 the Royal Commission to Investigate and Report upon the Affairs of the Abitibi Power and Paper Company heard the company's appeal for 'generally speaking, a renewal of all operating rights as to timber concessions and power, except those which would be no longer of value owing to the non-operation of the mills at Espanola and Sturgeon Falls.'[67] Severe problems relating to pulp and paper led in some parts of the province to a partial integration of lumber and pulp operations in the hopes of avoiding conflicts. In the Temagami area, however, this did not occur, although pulpwood requirements had often influenced the timing of pine licensing. Perhaps the suspension of the pulp operations in the forest on economic grounds and the comparatively slow pace of the lumber industry during the Depression permitted the introduction of the modest management plan outlined for part of Temagami.

The number of pine operators remaining active in the Temagami Forest at the close of the interwar years was rather high. They did not operate on many berths, nor did they come in quickly and leave. The duration of the licences indicates the relatively small size of many of the operators, as well as the amount of time they needed to cut an area. The actual area under pine licence was surprisingly small, considering that the creation of the pine reserve was related to permanent forestry. In a sense, it was astonishing not how much of the Temagami Forest was cut over between 1925 and 1940, but how much had not as yet been exploited. The forest wilderness that survived included the entire watershed of the Lady Evelyn River above Lady Evelyn Lake. An extensive stretch west and especially southwest of the Lady Evelyn Lake–Obabika Lake axis, beyond Smoothwater and the upper East Montreal, and across it into the Arctic watershed had also escaped commercial use – at least to the edge of the Timmins-Porcupine hinterland. As a result of high transportation costs and limited demand, the pine of these headwaters and the spruce and jack pine forests northward still awaited the lumbermen.

Although pine and pulp cutting were concentrated in a few areas of the Temagami Forest, the lack of overall administrative integrity and the limitations of provincial direction were reflected in the essentially ad hoc nature of the development that had taken place. The forest industries had clearly penetrated the Temagami Forest on the basis of geographic accessibility and local convenience rather than provincially supervised 'scientific forestry.' The earliest licences were initially associated with fire damage or the presence of pulpwood operators. Until Finlayson's reform after 1926, Temagami pine cutting largely took the form of salvage work, only very loosely related to sustained-yield management. Similarly, regional economic conditions operated more or less independently of a comprehensive resource-management plan to perpetuate or extend the tenure of licensees.

As an administrative superstructure, the Temagami Provincial Forest was unable to provide unity to a territory divided by three watersheds, organized around five different service centres, and occupied by two overlapping and frequently competing forest industries. Lands and Forests recognized these inconsistencies and never formally designated a forest district whose boundaries corresponded to the limits of the Temagami Forest. The management plan drawn up in the mid-1930s illustrated the possibilities of a logical utilization scheme on a very small scale, but the profession of forestry had neither the inclination, the manpower, nor the political influence to propose or implement an administrative strategy that corresponded to the size or diversity of the Temagami Forest.

With war again on the horizon, the constraints working against sustained-yield in the Temagami Forest were more readily apparent. Nothing in four decades had strengthened public support in Ontario for a perpetual-yield forest system. Moreover, the Temagami Forest was a potential source of some immediate relief from the severe problems of regional unemployment in northeastern Ontario. From a practical perspective the mix of pulp and pine lands, the number of small operators, and the natural barriers created by several adjacent watersheds increased production costs and made close supervision difficult to achieve. But it would not be until the Kennedy inquiry following the Second World War that the impact of these constraints and limitations would again be drawn to public attention. Recreational users of the forest had also begun to exert some influence on forest management, at least around Lake Temagami itself and along the more travelled waterways of the district.

CHAPTER NINE

Recreation and the Temagami Wilderness

From at least the 1890s, Temagami's potential for recreation had been recognized by railway promoters and other commercial interests. Gradually the provincial government responded to the needs and economic opportunities of tourism around Temagami and vacation centres elsewhere in Ontario, but the possible implications of tourism for resource management and particularly for forest policy were only dimly understood in the first quarter of the twentieth century. The resort, cottaging, and tourist constituencies remained largely unorganized and for the most part unaware of resource exploitation, which took place in the winter season. Commercial air travel was also largely undeveloped in the tourist districts and provided few opportunities for summer visitors to observe forest use away from the main lakes and canoe routes. Later in the century, recreational land users established a rudimentary organizational base and demonstrated some willingness to protest those aspects of resource use that impinged directly upon their enjoyment of the Temagami wilderness.

Mayors, members of the Legislature, and officials of boards of trade and transportation companies mingled freely with the general public in front of the Ronnoco Inn at Temagami to mark the completion of a highway link to the south on 3 July 1927. The Hon. William Finlayson, minister of lands and forests, who had recently completed the two-and-a-half-hour drive from North Bay, declared open northeastern Ontario's first gravel highway to the Tritowns. Finlayson named the highway after Premier Howard Ferguson, 'our distinguished chief,' and announced the introduction of a permit system to monitor car travellers in the northland for the purpose of reducing the risk of forest fires in 'one of the richest stands of timber left in North America.' Forest rangers constantly would patrol the road, and the careless would be prosecuted: 'the fair name of Temagami must be preserved.' Nevertheless, the Ferguson Highway would open the north to southerners who had begun in increasing numbers to acquire automobiles. Indeed, a few hardy motorists had already travelled the uncompleted road in the summer of 1926.[1] Despite occasionally hazardous road conditions,[2] the Ferguson Highway reduced the isolation of northeastern Ontario and brought Temagami to within one day's drive of Toronto. If the railway had inaugurated the age of commercial recreation and tourism at Temagami, now in the age of the private automobile the level of recreational travel and cottage use increased substantially. This increase added complexity to the task of serving a diverse recreational clientele with differing expectations and varying levels of commitment to wilderness, landscape, and the environment.

By the mid-1920s Lake Temagami had already become well known for its youth camps, particularly A.L. Cochrane's Camp Temagami and the American-owned Keewaydin, both established on the lake at the turn of the century. With highly skilled and mature staff, these organizations continued to emphasize the potential character-building contribution that rugged wilderness canoe-tripping could allegedly make to the next generation of leaders in the two North American democracies. Although the young campers still arrived in Temagami by train, the opening of the highway in the prosperous mid-1920s increased visiting opportunities for parents and distinguished guests, thus enhancing Temagami's reputation. As concerns about threats of social dislocation and challenges to traditional values occasioned by increased urbanism spread, the youth-camp movement expanded throughout Ontario and the eastern United States. Youth camping was also good business, at least for the 1920s; later, camp directors would have to decide between the conflicting aims of 'good business and good education.'[3]

Keewaydin Camps, Limited, acquired a network of camps and lodges across North America, becoming in the mid-twenties, a 'conglomerate,' '*the* camping consortium.'[4] In 1927, besides Keewaydin of Temagami and its associated Ojibway Lodge, the company operated Keewaydin of Dunmore in Vermont; also in Vermont it operated a girls' camp and a family camp. That year it opened Keewaydin of England, a short-lived bicycling camp. The dynamic 'Commodore' A.S. Gregg Clarke, who had been directing Keewaydin since before it had arrived on Lake Temagami, gave up his seat in the Connecticut legislature and a teaching position at the Gunnery School to establish a corporate office for Keewaydin in Philadelphia. But he spent many months each year in Temagami, still Keewaydin's flagship operation. Here, despite stern disapproval from friends and associates, the married 'Commodore' became involved with Josephine Grundius, a Métis. He was eventually forced to resign and leave Temagami. In 1926, a distraught Clarke lamented that he could not live without 'the flutter across his face' of Temagami's 'keewaydin' (the northwest wind) and committed suicide.

To replace Clarke, Keewaydin's board named John Harland 'Speedy' Rush as president at the then fabulous annual salary of $23,000. 'Speedy' Rush, who had been on the camp staff and was an ex-football coach and a track star, exchanged his controlling interest in a Philadelphia propane bottling company for Clarke's 52 per cent interest in Keewaydin. Sulton Douglas, Keewaydin's treasurer, became director of the Temagami operation, which was already in progress with 150 campers when Clarke left. Within weeks, two campers were drowned on a Keewaydin canoe trip at the La Cave Rapids on the Ottawa River, following an argument between an inexperienced young guide and a headstrong member of staff. Douglas now lost the directorship to the distinguished educator and experienced canoe-tripper 'Major' William K.Gunn, who was then directing the Dunmore operation.[5]

Keewaydin quickly recovered from the crises of mid-decade and for a few years reached new heights of prosperity and achievement. By 1929 the company had acquired four more camps including both boys' and girls' ranches in Montana, a boys' camp near Cleveland, and another in Vermont. Then the Depression struck and enrolments fell drastically. 'Speedy' cut off the commissions and instead offered discounts to encourage camper registration. The staff, many of whom were also shareholders and had been earning more than $3,000 a year in commissions, resisted.[6]

A male-oriented ethic prohibited women from living on the Keewaydin site at the south end of Devil's Island. Wives and daughters of staff stayed near the lodge at the north end. Gunn refused to allow staff to visit their wives, from the day campers arrived until they left at the end of the season, or to frequent neighbouring cottages on other islands. Keewaydin was to be male and dry. Staff, on occasion, defied these strictures by visiting their wives or canoeing surreptitiously to neighbouring islands for a social drink. A staff protest in 1929 failed to bring about change, but in the summer of 1931, several Keewaydin staff including Dick Lewis, Bill Roberts, and Bill Russell formally rebelled against the regime. Together they had accounted for more than 50 per cent of the camp's enrolment. In 1932 Colonel Creelman, the director of Ojibway, Keewaydin's adult operation, tried unsuccessfully to work out a compromise. The dissenters leased a portion of the northwest side of Garden Island from Harry Smith, owner and operator of Kakena Inn on the southwest side. In 1933, they opened Wabun (the east wind or the dawn) with more than half the former Keewaydin campers. Rival recruiting efforts at American prep schools became intense, and Keewaydin enrolment fell to eighty campers. Wabun was as dedicated as Keewaydin had been to high quality wilderness canoe-tripping involving challenging white water.

Astonishingly, both Wabun and Keewaydin survived the depths of the Depression. Within a few years Keewaydin of Temagami was back at 150 campers. In 1935 the corporation bought a Cape Cod sailing camp and in 1936 constructed a large adult lodge on Lake Fairlee in Vermont. Also in 1935 it took over the luxurious Keewaydin Club in Naples, Florida, from the estate of Chess Kittredge, Sr, a board member who owned a Temagami summer home in Devil's Bay. Tensions persisted between the business of camping and the educational thrust of the Keewaydin legacy as well as between the president and the camp directors. After another major internal controversy, Rush agreed to dissolve the company in 1938, and to allow the camp directors first rights of purchase over the individual operations. Jointly, Gunn and Creelman obtained the two operations on Devil's Island, while Rush carried on at Dunmore.[7]

Throughout its tribulations, Keewaydin's strength had always been with its canoe trips. Keewaydin was never an all-purpose camp with a general program. It was dedicated to extended wilderness travel. In-camp activities, which were minimal, consisted mainly of relaxation and elaborate ceremony. Campers, nearly all of whom were American, spent most of the summer on the waterways. Most instruction in canoeing and woodcraft, especially axemanship, took place 'on the trail.' The Trout Streams, that is the Lady Evelyn-Smoothwater wilderness, and the small lakes north and east of Lake Temagami were the heartland for the younger Keewaydin 'sections.' The Dumoine River and the Lake Kipawa district in western Quebec provided the regular intermediate white-water routes. Interrupted by the First World War and the camp's internal crises of the mid-twenties, Keewaydin revived the tradition of James Bay trips in 1928 with a voyage via Grand Lake Victoria and the challenging Nottaway River to James Bay followed by a coastal paddle and the ascent of the Abitibi. Later expeditions travelled the Harricanaw (1931), the long Albany River (1932), and the Marten-Rupert (1934). By this time, campers could return to Temagami on the newly extended line of the TNOR from Moosonee. Although very extensive tripping continued throughout the thirties, especially in Quebec on the Waswanapi, James Bay trips – with the exception of a Rupert expedition in 1938 – were suspended.

The Wabun-style canoe trip, with its focus on deep wilderness, white-water skills, self-reliance, co-operative living, and some distinctive equipment, came from Keewaydin. Wabun's red canoes traversed the same waterways of the Temagami country as Keewaydin's green ones. The Dumoine River was also a special white-water favourite. Numerous Wabun James Bay trips traversed various routes that ended up on the Rupert River.[8]

Meanwhile at Camp Temagami in the South Arm, A.L. Cochrane continued to develop a different canoe camping tradition.[9] By 1921 Cochrane had resigned as physical education instructor at Upper Canada College to devote himself almost exclusively to Camp Temagami and the Royal Life Saving Society. At Cochrane's camp, the wilderness canoe trip was very important, but so was the development of certain in-camp skills. Not that he would have disagreed fundamentally with the Keewaydin-Wabun philosophy, he merely put some of his emphasis elsewhere. Character building for boys and future leadership came, he thought, from a more rounded experience. With a charter from Britain, Cochrane had established the Royal Life Saving Society of Canada. Thus formal life-saving instruction was considered to be an essential element of the camp program. So were structured nature study, environmental concerns, calisthenics, diving, golf, and Indian lore. 'In real camping,' argued Cochrane, 'boys and girls meet the wind and rough water, rain and rough going. They learn to take it, maintain a cheerful disposition and work for the good of the whole camp, not just themselves.' 'The great virtue in camping,' he asserted, was 'in teaching young people to be socially effective.' Only on a canoe trip, he noted, can a young person 'endure so much hardship and discomfort – and learn so much about good citizenship.' Here, in part, Cochrane continued to reflect some of the influence of the Boy Scout movement with which he had become familiar early in the century.[10]

During the twenties, Cochrane spent at least four months of each year at the camp. His purpose was more clearly to educate, 'not to make money.' With official endorsements from both Upper Canada College and the University of Toronto Schools to promote enrolment,

Cochrane's camp catered to the Ontario establishment. Many Camp Temagami alumni went on to be counsellors and senior staff. More than a few later became leading professionals and businessmen. Several became federal or provincial cabinet ministers, and one – for a few months in 1984 – became prime minister of Canada. Nevertheless, Cochrane believed that camping should be for all boys and girls, not just an élite. He therefore played a major role along with Taylor Statten, Ernie Chapman, Mary Edgar, and others in the establishment of the Ontario Camping Association, a Toronto-based professional organization for youth camps. He became its first president in 1933.[11]

The effects of the Depression were more severely felt by Cochrane's camp than by its American counterparts on Lake Temagami. In the thirties, Camp Temagami could no longer afford enough canoes for all campers to be on trips at once; the camp often paddled three to a canoe. Nevertheless, its trips were on virtually all the popular waterways of the Temagami country, and young canoeists also travelled eastward deep into northern Quebec. With an in-camp program, Cochrane's trips tended to be modestly shorter than those out of Keewaydin and Wabun and, if expeditions to James Bay were ever attempted, they were certainly not emphasized.

At the onset of the Depression the only youth camps with major sites on Lake Temagami had been Keewaydin and Cochrane's camp. A dozen years later, at least seven youth camps were dispatching their canoe fleets to various remote haunts of the Temagami country. But only one of the new operations was Canadian owned. Before Wabun emerged out of the turmoil of Keewaydin, another significant American operation became established. Wigwasati was opened in 1930 by Homer H. Grafton and his wife, Eva. By then Homer Grafton already had behind him a distinguished career in Christian social gospel education; he had worked for the YMCA in naval, college, and overseas positions.

While the long wilderness canoe trip was an important aspect of the Wigwasati program of character building, spiritual guidance and inspiration from a mature staff with significant 'scholarly tastes and athletic attainments' received equal emphasis. Wigwasati existed for American teenage boys 'from Christian homes.' Campers came for the full eight-week summer season and paid in 1930 the very substantial sum of $350 plus transportation. In the wilderness, the boys were encouraged to absorb the spirit of vigorous outdoorsmen like John Muir, Theodore Roosevelt, Ernest Thompson Seton, Jack Miner, John James Anderson, and John Burroughs. 'Boys like leaders who are well read, have travelled, have seen adventure and are gentlemen.'[12]

The second Canadian camp on Temagami initially reflected the interests and background of its founder, Ed Archibald, and in several respects resembled the Canadian-owned Camp Temagami more than the American operations on the lake. Captain Ed Archibald, the owner of Camp Wanapitei, had been an Olympic pole-vaulting star, winning the bronze for Canada at the London games in 1908 and later serving on Canada's Olympic Committee. After graduating from the University of Toronto and canoeing and snowshoeing about the Gowganda–Shining Tree areas as a prospector, he had served with the YMCA in France during the First World War, as director of recreation, sports, and social work with the Canadian Army. After the war, Archibald returned to prospecting and then opened a youth camp in the mid-twenties on the isolated northwest shore of Lake Wanapitei by the mouth of Parkin (sometimes called Mountain) Creek. By the time of the 1930 season, Archibald had learned that a hydroelectric dam was to be constructed at the outlet of Lake Wanapitei, northeast of Sudbury. This would flood much of his property. As recompense, Archibald hoped to secure an option to lease a sixty-four-acre site of partially cleared mainland property on Lake Temagami's Sandy Inlet. This beach location had previously been the site of Father Charles Paradis's retreat.

During the 1930 season, Archibald led a canoe excursion from Lake Wanapitei to Camp Keewaydin. From Keewaydin, Archibald travelled by motor boat to Sandy Inlet, a 'magnificent arc of sand stretching for at least a mile.' Archibald obtained the Sandy Inlet option in 1931, despite the general prohibition against mainland development on Lake Temagami, and erected several log buildings, later including the two-storey 'Château.'

By 1932, patrons of the new Camp Wanapitei included such distinguished figures as General Sir Arthur Currie, then principal of McGill; Sir Robert Falconer of Toronto; R.Y. Eaton; Dr George Pidgeon, first moderator of the United Church of Canada; T.P. Loblaw; Brig.-Gen. John A. Gunn, and Morden Neilson of chocolate bar fame. The 1932 fees for the full summer were $200, a significant amount during the depths of the Depression but, as was typical of Canadian-owned camps, far less than the rate charged by the American camps. Besides the ever-important canoe trip, Archibald naturally emphasized track-and-field athletics. Out on the wilderness waterways, the crew of each canoe had to function self-reliantly as a discrete unit, cooking its own meals and pitching its own tent – all in preparation for a future that might, Archibald thought, involve the Ontario gentleman in prospecting for precious metals by canoe. Moreover, he argued, the deep-wilderness

Temagami canoe trip would be 'the realization of that glorious dream of boyhood.' 'No challenge,' he asserted, 'is so strong to youth as the challenge of the Northland, and its very beauty and purity demand high response in every thought and deed.'[13]

Most Temagami youth camps were privately owned and operated. But in 1937 the Cleveland YMCA established Northwoods, a boys' canoe-tripping camp, deep in the south end. Despite its initially small size, Northwoods undertook many canoe trips throughout the Temagami country, and in the late fifties joined the Temagami tradition of canoe tripping to James Bay. Eventually Northwoods grew to accommodate more than one hundred campers.[14]

With relatively easy road access to Temagami, it was not simply summer youth campers who paddled extensively in the district. In the late twenties the mystique of Temagami and general promotional material, both public and private, on the joys of canoe-tripping encouraged adult and family holidays in Canada's lake country. For Canadians, wilderness travel offered access to the landscapes depicted by Tom Thomson and the Group of Seven, and it reflected, for some, involvement with one continuing thread in their sense of national identity.[15] For visiting Americans, it seemed to recapture a happier time of national innocence. The chief ranger of the Temagami Forest believed it to be one of his responsibilities to encourage canoeists (and incidentally to prevent them from setting the forest ablaze). Rangers kept the main historic portage routes cleared and even erected discreet 'yardage' signs at portage landings. Such open trails would also facilitate fighting those fires that broke out periodically or spread despite the tower surveillance program. In this respect, at least, Ontario's commitment to the pine woods of the Temagami Forest produced co-operation and even harmony with recreational uses.

Some of these adult canoeists had learned their skills at the youth camps. One such man was Dr Hubert Brown, who had served on the Keewaydin staff from 1909 to 1911. During the four summers between 1926 and 1929, he took first his wife and subsequently his entire family on four typical Temagami canoe trips. Hubert Brown, who did not wander very far from the main lakes, kept meticulous records. Such unsung voyages of personal discovery and relaxation were not particularly expensive. The Browns' nineteen-day trip in September 1926 cost $88.72, including train travel to and from Toronto. Visiting Keewaydin, the trip passed through Emerald, Obabika, and Diamond lakes. The next year, with relatives, the Browns travelled a bit further. Then in 1928 they drove the family car in a twelve-hour trip from Toronto to

Temagami, averaging about '30 miles an hour.' They had five young children. They hired a taxi-launch to take them to Sandy Inlet, where they set up base camp for almost a month. This vacation cost $275 including $90 worth of new camping gear, $93 worth of food, and $25 for the water taxi. This experience was repeated in 1929.[16] Private adult canoe-tripping in Temagami appeared to decline somewhat in the early thirties, but it nevertheless survived. In 1934, for instance, Ruth Terborg and three other young women drove from New York City to Temagami for a canoe trip that may have been the first all-women, unguided, recreational canoeing expedition in the Temagami country.[17]

During the Depression, material promoting canoeing and wilderness travel continued to appear. Railways, including the TNOR, published brochures emphasizing the physical and mental therapy of the wilderness vacation. The writings of Grey Owl, especially *Tales of an Empty Cabin* (Toronto 1936) and the 1937 film on his exploits, romanticized the theme of canoe-tripping. The tales were often set in northeastern Ontario, even though Grey Owl's true identity as the Englishman Archie Belaney and his early wilderness training and experience as a guide at Temagami were not widely known until after his death in 1938. In such publications as *Canoeing in Canada*, which was revised and updated almost annually, the federal government's Department of the Interior and its successors urged non-Canadians to experience the Canadian bush. 'The carefree, take it easy life on a Canadian canoe trip,' the brochure declared in 1934, 'is a splendid tonic for worn nerves and minds dulled by care of office, mart or study.'[18]

In the late 1930s canoeing in the Temagami area revived significantly. Lands and Forests reported 'increasing tourist traffic' among the Temagami islands; at the HBC Bear Island post, Hugh Mackay Ross ran an active outfitting service. The HBC offered canoes, camping and cooking equipment, supplies, and a guide service. Bookings for the summer season were arranged by correspondence during the late winter or early spring. Trips lasting from one to three weeks were typical, and repeat business was common. In May, fishermen were among the first canoeists, with the last paddlers gone by mid-September. Of the sixty-five battleship-grey canoes available from the HBC, the seasonal average usage was something in the range of 90 per cent.[19]

Lodges and resorts on the islands of Lake Temagami and on the mainland near the village flourished in the interwar years, especially in the period immediately after the opening of the Ferguson Highway. These establishments suffered somewhat during the early part of the Depression and even more severely during the Second World War before another prosperous era in the fifties. Transportation to Temagami by rail and continuing improvements in highway access were factors in the fate of the various resorts. On the lake itself, until the late fifties, commercial boat services remained the principal lifeline moving guests, staff, and freight to the lodges.

Those lodges that had a major impact in the years before the Second World War and did not have links with a youth camp were the Ronnoco Hotel, the Temagami Inn, Wabikon, White Bear, Chimo, Acouchiching, Friday's Lodge, and Turner's Lakeview House. Friday's, run by the Indian family of that name, continued to provide inexpensive holidays at a mainland site north of the Northeast Arm and Fasken's Point. 'Granny' Turner, Métis widow of former Hudson's Bay Company employee John Turner who died in 1926, owned and managed a modest resort for up to fifty guests and operated a popular dance hall on Bear Island.

In 1926, Arthur Stevens, who had come to Temagami in 1905 with the railway and obtained the first concession to operate the station restaurant and newsstand, bought the Ronnoco Hotel. Stevens also operated the Temagami Outfitting Company a few hundred metres north of the station and, as highway traffic expanded and train travel continued, he was ideally situated to accommodate 'first night' visitors. In 1929, boasting a new '100 foot verandah' and a 150-car garage, the Ronnoco charged five dollars a day.[20]

After its founding in 1905, the Temagami Inn had remained for a few years under the control of Alex and David Fasken. Around 1914 the American Baldwin Locomotive Company acquired the property as a private retreat for the firm's executives, although it was closed for several seasons before 1920. Under new management and with an expanded plant, program, and clientele, the inn flourished from May to October through the twenties. It boasted one hundred canoes, guest cabins, a 'Marine Lounge,' bathrooms, a sewage system, a power plant, and riding horses and stables. Featuring great fishing, the inn regularly employed twenty-five guides. In the evenings there were ballroom and square dancing, the former often led by famous American musicians. In 1929 the Temagami Inn had accommodation for two hundred guests at rates ranging from four to seven dollars a day. But the Depression brought collapse for this American-oriented luxury business, and in 1933 the inn was again sold to Toronto entrepreneurs who continued the operation on a more modest scale into the forties.[21]

Wabikon, purchased from the Orr family by Herbert and Sarah Wilson in 1926, operated successfully as an adult lodge until the end of the

Second World War. Still described as 'a colony of detached cottages and floored tents' in 1929, Wabikon could accommodate up to 125 guests at daily rates ranging between four and five dollars or from twenty-four to thirty-two dollars a week.[22]

In 1926, Arthur Judson leased Island 488. There, in 1929, he established Camp White Bear as a private resort; accommodation at White Bear was by invitation only. Many early guests were executives or actors from the CBS network or the motion-picture industry. Movie stars Cary Grant, Carole Lombard, Bob Hope, and Jimmy Stewart were guests at White Bear. By 1935 Judson had constructed a two-storey lodge at a reported cost of $85,000, and the operation went public. Judson purchased five neighbouring islands in 1945 shortly before selling the entire operation to Mel Hundert of Toronto.[23]

In 1926, on Island 665 at the entrance to Lake Temagami's South Arm, Gordon S. Gooderham leased a ten-acre site to establish Camp Chimo for adults. Gooderham's decision to undertake this commercial venture actually re-established a long family association with the Temagami area, for twenty-three years earlier Gooderham himself had been with A.L. Cochrane on the canoe trip that led Cochrane to the founding of Camp Temagami. In addition, Gordon's father, William George Gooderham, had been an early backer of Dan O'Connor's Temagami Steamboat and Hotel Company, serving as vice president before withdrawing from the enterprise in 1914. At Chimo, Gordon and his family created a 'colony of cabins and floored tents' around their principal buildings and by the late 1920s charged guests thirty to forty dollars per week. The camp also specialized in outfitting for 'camping out parties.'[24]

Camp Acouchiching, another adult lodge, opened in 1920 on Islands 938 and 939 deep in the South Arm. The owner, George N. Allabough of Omaha, Nebraska, had also been involved in the steamboat business and in a prosperous but short-lived enterprise called the Temagami Fur Company. About 1927, J. Reginald McConnell of Toronto acquired Camp Acouchiching where he had previously worked as a guide. Acouchiching offered visitors an excellent beach and, by 1929, several substantial log structures and numerous floored tents, all with running water. Rates that year were twenty-eight to thirty-five dollars per week. Like Chimo, Acouchiching operated an outfitting service to complement its residential facilities. Acouchiching employed both Indian guides and a few experienced non-Indians from southern Canada and the United States. Angèle Belaney (Grey Owl's first wife) and two of her children worked here for several years.[25]

Commercial steamboats and motor launches served the lodges as well as the cottages and youth camps. In so doing, these picturesque vessels – the *Belle of Temagami*, the *Modello*, the *Iona*, and others – provided Temagami residents and visitors alike with a common experience on the lake and thus helped to integrate the summering community. Captain E.T. 'Ted' Guppy became a familiar figure to a generation of campers on the lake, first as the principal member of a group operating the Temagami Navigation Company and subsequently as lead skipper of the *Belle*, after John L. Sproat's Temagami Boat Company took control in 1936. In 1929 (and for many years thereafter), the *Belle* left Temagami at 10:15 AM and proceeded down the Northeast Arm to reach Bear Island at 1:15 PM. The daily journey continued to Keewaydin where the *Belle* arrived at about half past two, returning to Temagami by 6:30 PM. With the opening of Archibald's Camp Wanapitei in 1931, the service was extended to Sandy Inlet. A southerly circuit took travellers as far as Acouchiching.[26]

As well as resort visitors to the lodges of Temagami and canoeists who came to explore the waterways, the interwar years witnessed the arrival of a new group of cottagers who established and gradually developed summer residences on the islands. Before the opening of the Ferguson Highway, approximately 170 leases for cottages, lodges, and youth camps had been issued. In the late twenties, new leases were issued, and by February 1933 the official number of leases had reached 223, of which a significant proportion were held by American residents. In determining the total number of residential and commercial leases on the lake, however, some allowance must be made for the fact that on the larger islands adjacent parcels were sometimes issued to different people under the same lease number and that new numbers were usually used when property was reissued after cancellation of the original lease.[27]

The selection of a cottage site naturally involved very personal preferences, and the reasons for such decisions were seldom recorded or disclosed. It is possible, though, to describe a series of patterns common to different groups of Temagami cottagers. Several island families, especially those who obtained leases in the early days, are located on sites identified by canoe-tripping ancestors as 'the perfect spot.' Whether or not those early paddlers were in search of a cottage property or were transformed by the experience of the Temagami landscape from canoe-trippers to summer residents remains a mystery. Clearly, however, they felt some strong attachment to the local environment, for no community drew them to Temagami and no sense of fashionable summering propelled them to these remote islands.

Other long-time summer residents or their forbears first experienced

Temagami as campers and staff at a canoe camp and later returned to a nearby island to establish their own summer homes. The clustering of associated cottagers around Keewaydin, Cochrane's camp, and later Northwoods is particularly noticeable. Members of these families often remained an integral part of the canoe camp community; occasionally a family member continued to serve on the camp's staff. For these people, the ties to Temagami were reinforced by the camp network, an association that might also be fostered in the off-season by reunions and other camp gatherings in Toronto or the urban centres of the northern United States. To a lesser extent, the same pattern of building Temagami roots through an original social connection is repeated for the adult lodges such as Wabikon, Chimo, and White Bear. In other cases, extended cottage visits led guests to seek leases of their own on nearby islands, a process that also produced clusters of interlocking relationships. The general phenomenon of this form of community development in the cottage districts of Ontario has been described quite appropriately as 'clannishness.'[28] A few families simply heard of Temagami or made an excursion on one of the steamers or launches and decided subsequently to lease property for a summer home.

The reputation of Temagami as a wilderness sanctuary continued to grow through much of the interwar period, as articles, books, and pamphlets praised the glory of Temagami in a seemingly endless stream of superlatives and metaphors. In 1929, Ernest Voorhis, author, public servant, and occasional Temagami island summer resident, described the region for readers of the *Beaver* as 'one of nature's gardens,' offering 'fascinating scenery and exhilarating atmosphere.' Adventure stories and legends set in Temagami also contributed to the allure of the region. Cy Warman's *Weiga of Temagami* (Toronto and Boston 1908) was the first full volume in the tradition for which Lampman's poem 'Temagami' had provided firm foundations. *Bill Guppy: King of the Woodsmen* (London 1940) by Hal Pink was a further contribution to the genre, and *Temagami Guide* (Longmans 1954) by the popular writer Jack Hambleton probably found a still broader audience in postwar Ontario. More explicitly promotional efforts were also common in this period: John Turner, for example, made visits to the Sportsmen's shows in Boston and New York to attract vacationers to the Canadian northland.[29] Such literary and commercial promotion helped to sustain the interest of North America's urban population in the Temagami wilderness.

Films also furthered the association between Temagami and the Canadian wilderness, less directly perhaps than publications. *Silent Enemy* (1930), a feature-length presentation about the Algonkian peoples' prolonged struggle for survival, was set in the Temagami district. *Captains of the Clouds*, a 1941 propaganda film intended to encourage American involvement in the Second World War, opens with scenes shot around Jumping Cariboo Lake. James Cagney starred as one of a number of boisterous American bush pilots in northern Ontario who decided to enter the Canadian forces. The Temagami bush pilot was too rebellious for prolonged service with the RCAF but made a valuable contribution to the war effort by logging unarmed fighter planes from Canada to Britain: By crashing his plane into a deadly Messerschmitt, Cagney saves several of his buddies.[30] By the time *Captains of the Clouds* was ready for general distribution, Pearl Harbor had brought about the U.S. entry into the war. *Captains* was the last feature production to use the Temagami environment to promote the rugged men–rugged landscape relationship, but thousands of young Ontarians who saw the Lands and Forests film *Temagami Ranger* in the 1940s were left in no doubt about the continuing prospect of adventure in the province's northern wilderness.

Significant numbers of new summer vacationers in the 1920s, increased recreational activity on the lake, and the growth in value of camp and cottage properties to more than half a million dollars stimulated concern about an organization for residents. Cleveland lawyer and long-time cottager Robert B. Newcomb and Sherman R. Thorpe, who had been post manager for the HBC since 1922, together with Frank Todd, the Cochranes, and George Cecil Ames, were the leading figures behind the effort to organize an association of – as they described themselves – 'settlers,' 'the permanent residents of Lake Temagami and the Temagami Forest Reserve.' In August 1931, this group convened at Granny Turner's on Bear Island where about one hundred people gathered to form the Temagami Association, forerunner of the present Temagami Lakes Association, with Newcomb as president.

In addition to property protection, navigational improvements, and other direct services, the Temagami Association was clearly oriented towards the preservation of the natural environment of the lake and the forest reserve. The welfare and protection of the Temagami Forest was described as 'a sacred obligation resting on every member,' and the association report to prospective members noted the need for a certain amount of 'missionary work' in the sanitation field. Conveniently, about 1930, the Hon. William Finlayson, Ontario's Conservative minister of lands and forests, had become an island cottager in Lake Temagami's South Arm. Cynthia, Joan, and Phyllis townships in the central portions of Lake Temagami were named in 1933 after Finlayson's daughter and two of her friends, Joan Parmenter and Cynthia Jaffray. At the founding meeting of the Temagami Association, the minister pledged 'his earnest support' to the extent that the executive of the association advised, 'Mr. Finlayson has authorized us to say that no harm will be done to the forest.' Visual impact, the main environmental concern, was directly addressed: 'Selective timbering may be undertaken, but it will not be noticed from the shore, and will not offend settlers.' At the time of the second annual meeting in 1933, Finlayson had become the honorary president of the association. His relationship with the cottagers at Temagami no doubt assisted the association in securing year-round police surveillance and in launching a program to restock the lake with fish in 1932.[31]

Finlayson not only promoted the Temagami Association but maintained close relations with many resort and youth camp operators as well. As minister of lands and forests he was also in close touch with departmental officials in the region. Working with them, and in anticipation of the future needs of car campers in the province, Finlayson was responsible for setting aside a large public camp ground on a mainland site south of the village. Finlayson's efforts on behalf of the Temagami region were overshadowed, however, by rumours of extravagant weekend parties at the minister's luxurious cottage retreat. The reputation of these events was enhanced by the prominence of the guests and the gossip of the boat drivers who delivered them to Island 857. Finlayson had his staff, with the assistance of a naval architect from Ditchburn boatworks, build a 'forty foot mahogany inboard,' the *Wasp*, for the department's use on Lake Temagami. During the 1934 provincial election campaign, the *Wasp* and Finlayson's general behaviour became a minor scandal. There were allegations of extravagance and of misuse of public funds for the Finlayson summer home; some said that the *Wasp* had been brazenly used for private recreation. This was all part of Mitch Hepburn's ultimately successful technique of focusing the election campaign on government waste and alleged corruption in a time of economic suffering and depression. Hepburn and the Liberals defeated the regime of Premier George S. Henry, who had in 1930 succeeded Howard Ferguson. Out of office, Finlayson appears not to have returned to Lake Temagami for any significant period of time.[32]

Finlayson was by no means the only public figure to enjoy the splendours of Temagami in the interwar years. The region attracted a good many prominent Canadians for brief visits and was favoured by a number as a regular retreat. Premier Henry spent several weeks as a guest on the lake in 1932 around the time of the official opening of the TNOR extension to James Bay. Other cabinet ministers and public figures, including former Ontario premiers E.C. Drury and Howard Ferguson as well as future premier Tom Kennedy, also visited at this time.[33] Similar visits by legislative delegations took place after the war.[34]

Opportunities to gather and socialize often arose from the presence of such dignitaries on the lake, but other activities helped to integrate the summering community in the interwar years. The scheduled boat service with its regular route and daily stops provided one basis for common experience on the lake and the exchange of daily greetings. Regattas also provided a vital link among cottage dwellers, the youth camp community, and the Indian residents of Bear Island. In 1935 the Temagami Association assumed responsibility for the annual Civic Holiday Weekend event, which had traditionally been organized by the HBC at Bear Island. Canoe and swimming races were featured on the program, the latter having been recently introduced as the participation of the youth camps increased. Friendly rivalries developed around the keenly contested four-man guide canoe race and the mixed doubles.

Although the Second World War generally stimulated economic activity, northern Ontario recreation was naturally restricted. Gas rationing in the final years of the war helped to reduce traffic on the Ferguson Highway to below prewar levels. Wartime conditions also severely restricted youth camp operations. At one point, registration at Keewaydin fell to only thirty campers; the buildings on the site deteriorated severely. Camp Temagami was also greatly reduced in size during the war, while Wanapitei did not function as a boys' camp during the war period and for eleven years thereafter. Following the war, however, youth camping in Temagami gradually revived. Most established facilities recovered earlier levels of enrolment while new camps, including several for girls, began operations. In a generally buoyant period of economic growth lasting until the late sixties, youth camps in Temagami flourished and preserved the wilderness canoe-tripping tradition of the district.

In 1946 with enrolment now at fifty-five, Gunn and Creelman were persuaded to sell Keewaydin for $25,000 to the Thomas-Jones Foundation run by two families with established ties to the camp. In 1947 the foundation named the veteran trip leader and prep school teacher Howard Chivers as director or 'Chief.' Over the next fourteen years, the new owners engaged in a major reconstruction program on the site. By 1949 camper enrolment was back up to 100 and soon reached the maximum 150. Between 1941 and 1950, Keewaydin's only major northern expedition was a Rupert River trip led by Warren Chivers in 1948. In 1951 the tradition of the annual James Bay canoe trip was restored. That year and each summer until 1960, when George Herberton ('Heb') Evans and veteran guide Nishe Belanger explored the Nakina area of north-central Ontario, Keewaydin campers followed the Harricanaw to James Bay.

In 1960 with reconstruction completed, the Thomas-Jones Foundation agreed to sell Keewaydin to Howard Chivers, who would finance the purchase out of operating profits. Chivers agreed with the philosophy his predecessors had articulated and implemented for the Keewaydin program. Clarke had written in 1921 that Keewaydin had to be much more than a summer boarding place; it had to offer a disciplined educational experience close to nature, the bush, and the Indians. Creelman had affirmed that to 'know a man's true character, you must camp with him.' Chivers wanted Keewaydin to remain physically and socially demanding. Participants had 'to produce,' he asserted, 'under trying circumstances; work co-operatively for the good of the group; and build a real sense of pride and accomplishment as each physical obstacle or social problem was overcome.'[35]

At Wabun, Richard Lewis, who remained as president-director from 1933 to 1949, was followed briefly by Bill Roberts, Walter McLellan, and Bill Russell – all members of the original group of Keewaydin dissenters. Then in 1959, Wabun Limited appointed Herbert 'Stokie' Stokinger as director. Stokinger had been on staff at Keewaydin from 1929 to 1931, but had not been heavily involved in the rebellion nor in the establishment of Wabun. He had also worked between 1941 and 1950 on the Wabun canoe-tripping staff. Having friends in both camps, he was determined to end the enmity. Early in the summer of 1959 Stokinger and Howard Chivers reconciled ancient differences, though they did not eliminate a friendly rivalry.[36]

In the postwar years, A.L. Cochrane returned Camp Temagami to full operation. In 1948 with the camp at capacity with one hundred boys, he turned over administrative responsibility to his son Gilbert, director of athletics at the University of Toronto Schools. But serious tension developed, based in part on differences between Cochrane's own modest life-style and that of his middle-aged son. The camp was also in trouble financially. Two weeks before his death in August 1959, A.L. sold Camp Temagami to Douglas Gardner who had had Algonquin camping experience at his Camp Douglas.

These were difficult years for Camp Temagami, but Gardner persuaded

Bill Russell, one of the Wabun founders, to assume responsibility for the new Camp Temagami's canoeing program. By that move, the major distinctions between the American and Canadian tripping techniques out of Lake Temagami were blurred. Wanagans, tump-lines, and very rigorous voyages became ascendant at Camp Temagami. Gardner almost immediately purchased the Acouchiching site and there established Camp Metagami for girls. It too emphasized high-quality canoe-tripping. There were great camping years but, in the late sixties, the camp, like others in the years following Expo 67 at Montreal, experienced serious financial difficulty. Metagami closed after the 1970 season and Temagami after 1971.[37]

The high costs of upgrading wilderness facilities to provide adults with the standards of comfort and convenience that came to be expected after the war presented the owners of rustic Temagami resorts with a serious challenge. The task of modernizing no doubt helps to explain why several adult lodges and resorts were replaced or converted in the postwar period to children's summer camps, which were far less demanding in terms of accommodation and on-site facilities. Along with Acouchiching, Wanapitei, Wabikon, and White Bear made the transition from adult operations to youth camps, although in the case of Wanapitei, this was a reversion to an earlier pattern.

In wartime, Wanapitei had struggled on as a small adult operation with spring and summer lake-trout fishing and the fall deer hunt at the core of the program. After the war, Ed Archibald expanded the adult side of the business rather than attempt to revive the youth program, and in 1956 he sold Wanapitei. The new owners, Stanley and Laura Belle Hodgins, were already familiar with the Temagami area, having paddled extensively through the district during the late 1920s. They also arrived with a background in education and the Christian youth camping tradition, for Stan Hodgins was a public school principal from Kitchener with twelve years' experience directing Kitchener's YMCA youth camp. The Hodginses retained Archibald's adult operation and re-established the youth camp, which from the outset enrolled both boys and girls at the same time. Like Cochrane's camp, the reorganized Wanapitei, though never large, emphasized both diversified in-camp activities and deep-wilderness canoe trips.[38]

In 1943, on the advice of his friend Deputy Minister of Lands and Forests Frank A. MacDougall, Irwin Haladner visited Temagami in search of a site for a Jewish-oriented youth camp. He began operation of Temagami's first co-ed camp on the Wabikon site. Soon the new Wabikon had more than one hundred campers at a single period, which was either three or four weeks. Unlike the other camps on the lake, wilderness tripping at Wabikon played only a very minor role in the program. Instead, Wabikon featured swimming instruction, diving, sailing, riding, dramatics, nature lore, and, of course, flatwater canoeing.[39]

As already noted, Camp White Bear on Island 488 at the mid-point of the Southwest Arm had also begun as an adult lodge, opened in 1929. In 1961 Ron and Mickey Johnstone of London, Ontario, purchased the site from Mel Hundert and opened a camp that operated for boys in July and girls in August, with a 'family camp' around Labour Day. Ron Johnstone already had behind him twenty-four years of experience in the youth camping movement, connected initially with the YMCA. As a full-time Y secretary, he had served on staff and directed camps in both Ontario and Saskatchewan. Although never large, White Bear was a considerable success during the sixties, offering a high-quality general program. Like Wabikon, wilderness canoe trips were not central at White Bear. Instead, the focus was on 'wholesome ideals and attitudes' and 'leadership.'[40]

The expansion of camping for girls was among the most notable developments in Temagami youth camping in the postwar era. In fact, in 1940 Henry Woodman and his Métis wife, Margaret, established the first girls' camp on Lake Temagami. Cayuga had been established in 1925 as a small Canadian boys' camp by Dr Frank Wood. Most of its twenty-five or so campers had come from St Andrew's and Upper Canada College and from University of Toronto Schools. About 1932 the original Cayuga closed. The Woodmans' Camp Cayuga, situated on the northern tip of Island 1088 in the Northwest Arm, was soon sending American teenage girls into the Obabika system and up the Lady Evelyn River. Henry Woodman, a Quaker and biology teacher at Friends' College in Pennsylvania, was a consummate wilderness naturalist who emphasized environmentally sound practices in wilderness travel long before such an approach became common in camping circles.[41] Temagami camping for girls was also available at Camp Metagami, in the coed programs at Wanapitei and Wabikon, and each August at the Johnstones' White Bear. Briefly in the 1960s a small girls' camp, Pinecliffe, operated as an offshoot of the Graftons' Camp Wigwasati.

In the base camps, all operations preserved a rustic wilderness atmosphere. Until 1963 hydroelectric power did not reach Wabun and the other camps near the centre of the lake (and has still not been extended to more distant sites). The camps encouraged a generalized appreciation of the natural environment, but their essential purpose seemed always to be to instil leadership skills in a wilderness group setting. The camps claimed that their aims were primarily educational. Apart from Wabikon and White Bear, both comparatively late arrivals, the emphasis in Lake Temagami youth camps was on rigorous wilderness canoe tripping. It was assumed that challenging wilderness experiences would help to sustain young campers upon their return to disorienting urban settings and would produce leaders. All but Northwoods had to be self-supporting. Although 'camperships' attempted to broaden the social base, Temagami camps were clearly not able (nor in this era were they especially designed) to serve many of the disadvantaged.

During the 1950s and early 1960s, following the trauma of war and in the midst of the controversies of the cold war, youth camping in parts of Ontario and beyond went through much soul-searching. In most Haliburton-Muskoka summer camps, heavy physical challenges and intense competition were out of favour. Furthermore, high adventure and all life-threatening challenges were discouraged. Organized camping seemed more and more to stress social development; skill acquisition, while important, was secondary. 'Democratic group living' in the out-of-doors rather than the rugged wilderness canoe trip was in vogue. Youths in their mid-teens were urged to serve as 'counsellors-in-training,' then junior leaders and activity instructors, rather than to participate themselves in adventuresome wilderness experiences. Long portages, heavy travel days, and extended periods of isolation were also generally avoided. Above all, many leaders of the camping movement in southern Ontario regarded white-water canoeing as anathema.[42]

Despite the force of this broad movement, most Temagami camps, especially those that could loosely be placed in the Keewaydin–Camp Temagami traditions, resisted the pressures. River work, rapids and hard portages, and deep-wilderness travel with Lake Temagami providing the geographic base for expeditions much farther to the north remained the emphasis. Thus, from the outset, the Temagami youth camps made a distinctive mark on canoe-tripping throughout the north.[43] In the early 1970s, the Temagami tradition merged readily with the general revival of the appeal of wilderness travel for adults and youths concerned about the impact of technology on comparatively undisturbed terrain.

After the war, adult interest in Ontario's lake country, including Temagami, revived: increasing numbers of vacationers frequented provincial waters, for the seclusion and measured pace of summer life in the landscape of the Canadian Shield had great appeal. But in the aftermath of war, Canadians appeared slow to return to the rigours of the wilderness canoe trip. Comfort and relaxation at lakeside resorts and cottages were again fashionable, and – with renewed prosperity and better or extended roads – growing numbers of people enjoyed 'a new summer mobility.'[44]

Even before hostilities ended overseas, the role of tourism in Ontario economic reconstruction was under consideration. Leslie Frost, as Ontario's provincial treasurer, chaired a postwar planning conference organized by the new Conservative government of George Drew. Delegates from various sectors of the industry around the province attended the planning conference. Harry Leonard represented the resorts section of the Hotel Association of Ontario from Temagami. John L. Sproat of the Temagami Boat Company also participated. Discussion at the conference emphasized the diversity of economic opportunities associated with pleasure travel throughout the province, opportunities that should not be missed when wartime restrictions were eliminated. The chief of the Canadian Government Travel Bureau stressed the need for continued road improvements to facilitate access to recreational attractions and urged further efforts to sell cottage properties to American visitors: 'They are a permanent asset, because they return year after year, employ local labour in building and maintenance, purchase supplies, entertain guests, pay taxes, and in other ways benefit the community in which they are located.' Alongside these more or less familiar refrains, there was a concern for standards of service and government efforts to maintain them in the interests of the industry as a whole. Some steps had been taken as early as 1936 to regulate construction and sanitation standards for northern Ontario tourist camps, and additional temporary measures had been introduced during the war. George Martin, president of the resorts section of the Hotel Association of Ontario, cautiously set out the rationale for acceptance of public regulation: 'While the Resorts Association has no desire to see the resorts put in straight-jackets with a lot of government restrictions, and we look forward when the war is over to many necessary war restrictions being lifted, we are in favour of forward steps to raise the standards of service to meet the demands of the travelling public.' At the convention, Leslie Frost announced the Ontario government's new tourism policy, which included the creation of a special committee 'to study during the coming year and later report upon the advisability of bringing all forms of tourist catering places under government licensing, supervision and inspection.' Frost also announced 'a wide-scale advertising campaign as soon as war requirements allow' and other measures to promote tourism in the province. The Department of Travel and Publicity was established in 1946.[45]

Further gatherings, including a Dominion-provincial tourist conference in 1947 and a series of annual conferences on Ontario tourism beginning in 1949, demonstrated the deepening involvement of federal and provincial public officials in the well-being of commercial tourism and in its potential contribution to postwar economic prosperity. Arthur Walsh, Ontario minister of travel and publicity, established tourist reception centres around the province and, in keeping with the diverse composition of the developing tourism services sector, suggested the desirability of a general promotional theme: 'We are, in a sense, a gigantic department store purveying travel and recreation. Let us get our customer into the store, mentally at least, before we endeavour to sell him shoes or a necktie or a suite of furniture. Once he is "sold" on Canada, then we can all be sure that we will get our share of his trade.'[46]

The Ontario government's interest in the well-being of the province's tourist industry, however, went beyond concern for private resort and hotel operators whose livelihoods depended on commercial travellers and vacationers. The Ontario government itself took part, through the Temiskaming and Northern Ontario Railway, in the ownership and operation of tourist facilities at Temagami after the railway's authority was enlarged to permit involvement in these new services. In the mid-forties, the TNOR assumed responsibility for commercial transportation on the lake and ran the boat service as a Crown-owned public enterprise, the Ontario Northland Boat Lines. The ONBL responded to and promoted increased postwar demands for service. The loss of the *Belle of Temagami* in 1944 was partially compensated in 1947 by the diesel-powered *Aubrey Cosens VC*. The ONBL then had ten other boats, including the *Ramona* and several landing barges. The sleek *Naiad* launched in 1890, joined the ONBL fleet in the 1950s.[47]

The ONBL's aims included tourist promotion in general rather than profitability alone. Modest losses were common in the late forties and mid-fifties. By and large, however, the ONBL maintained or even extended services, adding a convenient launch service to the regular daily routes linking Temagami village with the distant arms of the lake. An afternoon departure from Temagami in the *Ojibway* brought late arrivals to Wanapitei at Sandy Inlet and various points en route. Leaving Sandy Inlet at 7:00 AM, on its return run the *Ojibway* could deliver travellers to the highway in two hours. This additional service presumably contributed to the decline of village accommodation for 'first nighters' and often added another night's business to the camps and lodges on the lake. An overnight grocery order and delivery service also offered to camps by the ONBL helped Temagami resorts to move 'up-market' with fresher produce, milk, and the mid-summer wilderness luxury of ice cream. The government boatlines provided ten year-round jobs and more than forty seasonal jobs for Temagami residents in 1957, including positions at a stylish second-storey restaurant overlooking the harbour from the ONBL's new terminal building.[48]

For a brief period after the war the Ontario Northland Transportation Commission (as the TNOR was renamed in 1946) also ran the Ronnoco Hotel and White Top Cabins. These modest public ventures into the resort business neither involved the criticism nor entailed the expense associated with the Minaki Lodge project several decades later. There were moments, though, when certain inconsistencies emerged between the public ideals of Conservative Ontario and the realities of the hotel trade. The potential for embarrassment was particularly acute in the immediate postwar years. A controversial amendment in 1946 to the liquor-licensing act represented a new advance in 'wetness' by permitting the sale of liquor in cocktail bars and hotels. Previous legislation dating from the then liberalizing moves of the early Hepburn era had authorized beer parlours where beer and wine were available by the glass. Pressure from the ever-vigilant 'drys' temporarily deterred the Drew government from proclaiming the 1946 legislation, with the result that bootlegging, hotel-room drinking, and disrespect for the law threatened to increase.[49]

The Ronnoco's total operating income of $21,921.28 for the first ten months of 1946 included $13,664.86 from the beverage room. Roland Michener, then provincial secretary and registrar en route in his career to Rideau Hall, was responsible for the ONTC. He considered it prudent to make other use of the Ronnoco facilities. 'I think you will agree,' he wrote in the early spring of 1947, 'that it is undesirable for the government to be operating beverage rooms. Perhaps some of our enterprising friends in Temagami will find it profitable to endeavour to satisfy the needs of the locality.'[50]

Recovering shortly after the war, the Temagami resorts probably reached a peak of activity in the mid-fifties. Prices for accommodation at Temagami were up sharply in the postwar years in comparison with interwar levels. White Bear, charging between $12 and $15 per day or $75 to $90 per week in 1957, was the upper end of the scale. Chimo, with accommodation for ninety guests, set its 1957 tariff at $10 per day or $60 per week, as did Acouchiching. More modest rates of $8.50 per day prevailed at Keewaydin's Ojibway, Wabun Lodge, and the Château at Wanapitei, all at some distance from the principal transportation routes to Temagami. At about $40 per week, housekeeping cabins offered a more readily affordable option to vacationers. These arrangements were available at Bambi Lodge on the Lakeshore Road and at Tadassack, which could also be reached by car.[51]

The Temagami Inn, the grandest of the early hotels on the lake, no longer operated as a commercial resort. Led by Samuel Lunenfeld, a group of Jewish families from Toronto acquired the inn in 1943 and ran it as Temagami Lodge Limited on a co-operative basis for their own use. The restrictions faced by Jewish Ontarians in obtaining access to resort and recreational facilities in the era before the 1944 Racial Discrimination Act and the Ontario high court decision of 1945 (which struck down discriminatory property covenants purporting to prohibit certain land sales to 'Jews or persons of objectionable nationality') would have increased the attractiveness of a Temagami retreat. Members of the group used the Temagami Lodge property until the mid-sixties, and several individuals purchased nearby properties for cottage sites.[52]

Of the eleven lodges serving the general public, White Bear, Chimo, Acouchiching, and two new small lodges, Canusa and Adanac, situated near the 'Hub' of the lake, seem to have been the most successful. White Bear, at least in the immediate postwar years, set the standard for luxury and expense on Lake Temagami. Mel Hundert, who purchased the property in 1947, obtained a provincial liquor licence the following year, added new cabins to the site, and installed a grand piano for the regular visits of Percy Faith. In 1952, however, fire destroyed the principal lodge, and the grand style never quite returned. White Bear, like Acouchiching before it, was converted to a youth camp in the fall of 1960.[53] Immediately after the war Chimo flourished, although it remained resolutely 'dry.' The camp hosted Governor-General the Earl of Athlone and Princess Alice and many cabinet ministers.[54]

As before, Lakeview House and Friday's were much more economical places to stay. So was the new and comparatively small Rabbit Nose Lodge in the North Arm, where a fishing and hunting camp opened in 1945. In Temagami village itself, Harold and Fran Shannon may have relieved Roland Michener's concerns about provincial involvement in the hotel trade when they bought and refurbished the Ronnoco Inn, renaming it the Minawassi. Along with Goddard's Place Hotel (1934), Amich Lodge (1939), and Kenmar Lodge (1924), the Minawassi primarily served 'first nighters' and the ever-increasing highway traffic.[55]

Highway 11, after the Second World War, had become 'the most important recreational route in Ontario,' and Lake Temagami was 'the ultimate area to which Torontonians follow that road in important numbers.'[56] *Ontario in Your Car*, a travel guide for mobile vacationers, described the attractions of summer travel in the province. The northland remained a source of adventure, an atmosphere still capable of inducing mild delusions: 'As we headed north from North Bay, we seemed to have entered a land that was untouched by man, except for the paved highway on which we were travelling.'[57]

Highway travellers who reached Lake Temagami had the opportunity to stay at one of the roadside camp grounds set aside by the provincial government for recreational use. Finlayson Point Provincial Park, named in the early fifties after the former Lands and Forests minister, served this purpose for Highway 11 travellers in the Temagami district. On the jut of land between the harbour (Portage Bay) and the southern approach (Inlet Bay), Finlayson Park in 1957 attracted about 6,500 visitors for periods of one night to two weeks. Nearly all 'tenters' were Ontario residents, mostly from Toronto, including many recent immigrants. The park then had 72 tenting sites and 9 trailer sites. With the number of camping sites increased to 130 by 1966, Finlayson Park contributed significantly to expanded use of Lake Temagami's recreational attractions.[58]

Temagami village itself continued to develop in the somewhat haphazard fashion typical of small northern centres in the difficult terrain of the Canadian Shield. A succession of access points including the old portage, the railway station, the waterfront, and finally the Ferguson Highway channelled growth in several directions, always subject to the constraints of a poorly drained and rocky landscape. Thus, the 1957 population of the unincorporated village exceeded 1,000, but this included 150 townspeople at the Milne lumber company site and a further 95 at the Gillies location. Five restaurants or snack bars and the Brewers' Retail catered to the food and beverage needs of travellers and residents alike. Four service stations operating in Temagami in 1957 attested to the significance of the highway for the well-being of the district.[59]

Improvements in road access and relaxation of building regulations in the fifties led to a proliferation of isolated service points along the periphery of the Temagami Forest and at some interior locations. By 1957 seventeen lodges or roadside camps with housekeeping cabins and several service stations existed along Highway 11 near Marten River, Angus Lake, Jumping Cariboo, and other points along the route from North Bay to Temagami. Most of these were small, but Beaverland

Camp at Marten Lake had a capacity of 124, and several other operations could each accommodate about 50 guests. To the northwest small lodges, fish camps, and service stations sprang up in the fifties along what became Highway 560, and in the following decade the languishing villages of Elk Lake, Gowganda, and Shining Tree flourished again briefly as tourist centres.[60]

Roads in the periphery of the Temagami Forest and improvements along established routes during the fifties had less impact on recreational activity and the environment than roads that penetrated more directly into the interior, particularly when new points of water access were created. The Temagami Mine Road running into the Hub of the lake from Highway 11 but well inland from the southern shoreline of the Northeast Arm was completed and opened to the public in 1958 despite protests from many Temagami merchants and island residents. As its name suggests, the new road was originally intended to provide access to a new mine site within the Temagami Forest.

The Temagami Mining Company had been established in 1954 by Dr N.B. Keevil of Toronto who consolidated scattered holdings to facilitate development. For a time the Temagami Island property was among the richest copper deposits in Canada; its success encouraged prospecting and drilling efforts throughout the area. The Temagami Island site employed about one hundred residents of the district, while the mine shipped valuable ore by barge to the train at the village and from there to Noranda for smelting. Cottagers, while not enthusiastic about the presence of the mine at the centre of the lake, did not express strong objection to its existence. Yet, as in the case of summer log booms across Lake Temagami, they did protest the manner in which the industrial activity was carried out. C.E. Rodgers, the president of the Temagami Lakes Association (as the Temagami Association had come to be known), protested to Ontario's deputy minister of mines on behalf of TLA members that 'if surface blasting, diamond drilling and other work is carried on in the midst of the summer season, it will destroy what pleasure is left to Temagami residents in this area.' Senator Joseph Sullivan added his influence in Ontario Conservative circles to the protest by writing his own letter to the deputy minister. Sullivan denounced 'this indiscriminate, unseasonal, and obnoxious exploration and mining activities,' adding, 'if necessary, I propose to take it up with the Premier.'[61]

Although the mining operations were extensive, the visible impact of the mine was relatively minor because both the main plant and tailings from the production process were located in a basin in the interior of the island. The most visible and immediate consequences of the mining development stemmed from the road.[62] Small private docks and a parking lot appeared on the lakeshore immediately after the twelve-mile road was opened. Cottagers were soon driving the Mine Road to the Hub and then completing the trip to the cottage by outboard, thus avoiding Temagami village and the commercial boatlines. Within four or five years, hydro wires were extended down the new road and out to the mine. Power cables soon linked up Bear Island and virtually all the lodges and some of the cottages in the central portions of the lake. Henceforth, the lake and its residents would be divided between those with hydro and those without. Limited telephone service followed hydro, again using the access corridor provided by the Mine Road.

In addition to these developments in access and communications, Temagami Mine lobbied for a workers' village on Denedus Point near the landing on the mainland. Opposition by cottagers restored Ontario's commitment to Temagami's recreational future and mainland preservation. This was a significant but not sustained initiative by cottagers to participate in development planning or control. A less optimistic appraisal of the mine's long-term future averted further pressure for such a radical alteration in policy regarding development of the lake.

Nevertheless, the significant local changes that did occur had the effect of reinforcing current recreational trends throughout Ontario and neighbouring U.S. states, the places that supplied Lake Temagami with its summer guests and its summer residents. More and more people wanted a private summer home of their own. By 1960 fewer vacationers seemed prepared to visit the traditional but now rustic resorts. Luxury accommodation in more exotic places was in vogue; more people were flying off for short winter holidays in the Caribbean or summer visits to Europe. Furthermore, those who had acquired or who sought relatively remote cottages in settings without direct road access, such as the islands of Lake Temagami, or those near Pointe au Baril and Honey Harbour or on islands in the Muskoka lakes, expected to reach their destination by their own boat at a time convenient to their own schedules. Once ensconced in these comparatively secluded retreats, cottage dwellers expected to enjoy a high degree of privacy. In an era of cheap gasoline, fast automobiles, and powerful outboards, weekend excursions to the cottage increased dramatically while the communal tradition of the lodge declined.

If they could not easily offer the privacy of cottage life, several Temagami lodges at least attempted to upgrade their facilities to meet the new demands for comfort. This often proved difficult or virtually impossible for camps without hydro. Most Temagami resorts were also severely undercapitalized and suffered from long-term cash-flow problems. Several soon closed or changed hands. The survivors tended to be the more modern but hardly grand resorts in or near the Hub where convenient road access and reliable electricity were available. Manito, Ket-Chun-Eny, White Gables, Canusa, and Malabar enjoyed such locational advantages.

These local developments and the broad changes in recreational life-styles sent the ONBL into long terminal illness. Very few sightseers now took the scenic cruise through the Temagami islands. For a few more years, well into the sixties, the parade each morning of the majestic fleet, with the lead horn sounded by the *Aubrey Cosens* steaming out of the harbour in full view of onlookers and busy highway traffic, remained a most impressive if already nostalgic sight. Even the casual observer could see the 'waste' and inefficiency of all those boats proceeding bow-to-stern down the Northeast Arm. In 1963 service was modestly cut back amid rumours that the ONTC was attempting to offload the growing liability of its boat lines.[63] Temagami lodges and youth camps seemed to have little political influence when it came to prolonging the full boat lines operation, which the Ontario government sold to Shell Oil after the 1965 season.

The Temagami Development Company at first leased the boat lines from Shell Oil and constructed new dock and parking facilities at Boat Line Bay. This completed the bypassing of the village begun in 1958 when the Mine Road was opened to the public. The historic flagships of the fleet were, of course, gone. The *Aubrey Cosens*, after ramming a dock, was trucked south to the Marten River to be transformed into a land-based restaurant. Fire rescued the boat from this inglorious fate. The *Naiad* was taken up for scrap and partly burned. A new and much-vaunted *Belle of Temagami* was promised but never launched. It remained tied up for several years in legal hassles. The *Vedette*, the *Ramona*, the classic *Ojibway*, a recycled Second World War crash boat, and other smaller boats, plus a Second World War landing barge were used instead. Passenger service was drastically reduced; round-trip excursions declined, and freight became the focus. The sheds and repair facilities in Temagami village deteriorated rapidly.

As the era of public boat service ended, Temagami resorts were also adapting to new demands and expectations from recreational visitors in order to remain commercially successful. With rising costs in the postwar years, including new capital expenditures for hydro, water transportation, and the general upgrading of facilities, the limited duration of the summer vacation season was a major problem. Spring and fall activity modestly extended the annual operating period for a number of lodges, and by the late fifties or early sixties efforts were underway to develop winter tourism in the district.

Spring fishing, favoured more by sportsmen than the family orientation of summer, had always been a Temagami highlight. Every one of the fourteen lodge operators in business in 1957 regarded fishing as the primary attraction for guests, and spring fishing had a distinctive appeal. In late May and early June, lake-trout fishing was at its best. The annual fall deer hunt, conducted in November just before freeze-up, was also important to the financial success of several lodges, notably Friday's, Adanac, Broom, Wanapitei, and Rabbit Nose. This event also provided welcome employment for the guide community from Bear Island. In the late fifties when red deer were especially plentiful around Temagami, guests could almost be guaranteed one kill per customer during the course of a seven- to ten-day hunt camp.

Bear Island guides led a group of hunters, using dogs to run the deer across a cleared line, either a summer portage or a trail specially cleared for the purpose. As some guides placed the hunters a short distance apart at designated stations on the trail, other guides with the dogs would run any deer in the area towards the line, where they would eventually emerge in the open.[64] Between 1962 and 1964 the deer totally disappeared from the district. Most commentators attributed their disappearance to a combination of a series of severe winters and disease, although over-hunting may have been a secondary factor. Moose had already begun to move into the Temagami area and became much more numerous when the deer were gone. They were especially common north of Lake Temagami and in the headwaters of the Lady Evelyn. Moose hunters soon entered the district in increasing numbers, but their preference for fly-in hunting and their use of the logging roads of the Temagami interior meant that the moose hunt would never replace the deer season either for the lodge owners or the Bear Islanders.

Efforts to extend commercial use of Temagami's recreational facilities and accommodation into the winter season were made initially by village residents rather than by resort operators on the lake. To focus attention on Temagami's potential for winter sports, the Temagami and District Chamber of Commerce organized the first of a series of annual winter carnivals in January 1958. Snowmobiling also became popular after Bombardier marketed its first Ski-Doos in 1959. These winter activities increased use of the Temagami environment without significantly affecting the summer activities of the lodges and cottagers.[65]

Indeed, to the extent that the earnings of participating lodges increased, more revenue was available for the general upgrading of facilities and services. Ice fishing, however, soon became a subject of controversy, particularly when operators at the Hub of the lake got involved in what had initially been a village activity based in the Northeast Arm. Cottagers and lodge owners who were not open in the winter season vigorously objected to the development of ice fishing. During the sixties, a noticeable decline in the average summer fish catch was widely attributed to winter use of the resource.

'Improvement of fishing conditions by all reasonable means' was one of the Temagami Lakes Association's three stated objectives in 1959. Perhaps the fish of Lake Temagami were actually the major preoccupation of the small core of summer residents who directed the affairs of the association. Dewey Derosier of North Bay, whose experience on the lake extended back to at least the 1920s, was an active chairman of the TLA Fish Committee before replacing Earl Rodgers as president on an acting basis in 1961 and officially in 1962. Derosier spearheaded campaigns to improve stocks of game fish, to establish a hatchery at Lake Temagami where lake trout and pickerel could be encouraged, and to eliminate the winter fishing. As president, he criticized the Department of Lands and Forests for its practices regarding the planting of fingerlings, and he assured members of the TLA that 'we will continue our pressure to abolish, or at least curtail, ice fishing.' The 1968 campaign went so far as to link ice fishing to the cottagers' long-standing concern about property damage: 'The Association motor toboggan is again available for police winter patrol for possible vandalism and a close check is kept on winter fishermen.'[66]

The nature of recreational activity, particularly in the Temagami summer, had altered after the Second World War. Few changes were sudden; none appeared to be dramatic. Yet the cumulative effects were such that the framework of life on the lake and the nature of human relations with the environment became significantly different. In the camping movement, the Christian tradition, never dominant in Temagami, receded further – a reflection perhaps of more general secularization in North America. With Gardner's move to Camp Temagami and Wanapitei's increasingly ambitious canoe-tripping program, earlier distinctions between Canadian and American camps were far less pronounced. Coed camping and the introduction of girls' camps were further indications of shifting values. At Temagami's lodges and resorts and at many cottages change was also evident in modernization and the arrival of power. Touches of comfort were introduced to rustic settings that were ever more readily accessible from parking facilities near the centre of the lake by outboard or, increasingly, by short commercial float-plane flights. The leisurely introduction to the lake during a steamer trip down the Northeast Arm and the familiar circuit routes with their scheduled stops at various central points, but particularly at Bear Island, were gone. These changing patterns and methods of access as much as any other alteration affected the character of the Temagami experience. The annual regattas had also disappeared. As recreational use of Lake Temagami and parts of the surrounding district gradually intensified after the Second World War, emerging resource-use issues set the stage for a new phase of management, planning, and attempted control of the Temagami wilderness. Decision makers would eventually have to take into account the established and growing recreational importance of the Temagami area as well as the continuing presence of the Temagami Indians. Thus, paradoxically, as overall recreational activity increased, other changes made the Temagami summer a less communal and more private affair for cottagers.

Since 1906 individuals had been able to lease the smaller islands or portions of larger islands at nominal rates and to erect cottages as well as lodges and youth camps. This situation changed in 1942 when a provincial order-in-council formally removed the islands of Lake Temagami from the forest reserve and authorized the conversion of existing leases and the sale of other islands to the public. This action was one aspect of a comprehensive effort by provincial officials to respond to widespread criticism of the land-management policy of the Department of Lands and Forests and to growing demand for resort properties.[67] Some island residents converted shortly after the ownership option became available. Helen Klingman, for example, patented in 1943 the property that her father, Samuel Haserot, had initially selected in 1908. Also in 1943, Grace Pleasance purchased Whispering Pines, the island that her father, Charles O. Anderson, had first leased in 1911. Others were content to wait, there being no sense of urgency about the matter. Thus, Gladys Glenn, daughter of John Trethewey, did not buy Silver Birches (Island 1003) until 1949, although she took over the lease at the start of the decade. Yet in the postwar period most cottagers converted to freehold. A surge of new arrivals and land sales on new island properties in the late forties and throughout the fifties increased the summering population significantly. By 1957 there were about 400 cottage families on the lake. By 1972 the number of island patents and leases had risen further to more than 700.[68]

The distribution of cottagers throughout the lake was far from uniform. However, the concentration of summer occupants – later of considerable interest to land-use planners and always central to the islanders' own perception of the quality of summer life – was increasingly evident. Cottage clusters were most obvious close to the locations of lodges and youth camps because of the continuing tendency of families to preserve some form of association with familiar routes and locations. Because transport by means of the boat lines was so important in the early decades of the century and remained vital for many into the fifties, location near a regular stop of the boats was also an important influence on the concentration of cottage sites. Sites near Temagami village were also popular. These could be quickly and conveniently reached and offered some sense of association with the year-round community that many found a further attraction.

A concentration of Americans in some parts of the lake and of Canadians in others could also be noted. American ownership of lake properties declined gradually in the post-Second World War period, although this group still constituted 40 per cent of cottage owners in the early 1970s. It was possible to identify concentrations of people from Cleveland in one bay, from Cincinnati in another, and from Toronto – the predominant source of Canadian residents – in a third. The concentration of Canadian-owned cottages in the Northeast Arm, especially close to the village, probably indicated considerable weekend use of the facilities.[69]

Elsewhere in the district, modest cottage development was taking place in other nearby lakes. The pattern, however, remains unclear. The TNOR had initially received, as a grant from the province, a belt of land on either side of the right-of-way. This belt was normally 150 feet wide, but where the track ran fairly close to a lake, the railway usually received all the land between the track and the lake, at least up to 400 feet. Such land was not covered by the various forest reserve acts. The railway frequently leased lots in these bulges of its land belt for cottages or even for small lodges. After the war the railway allowed these leases to be converted to sales. A small surge in land grants for remote cottages and a few small lodges also occurred on various nearby lakes, especially Cassels (White Bear), Rabbit, Anima Nipissing, Lady Evelyn, Angus, and Jumping Cariboo. By 1960, about 150 Crown land sales had taken place for all non-mining purposes, including cottages, residences, lodges, service stations, marinas, and stores, in various townships close to Lake Temagami. Sales took place under the Public Lands Act despite their apparent prohibition under the Forest Reserves Act and the subsequent Provincial Forests Act.[70] Certainly, until the abolition of provincial forests in 1964,[71] the granting authority lay legally in a very grey area. Cottagers off Lake Temagami obviously had a commercial impact on merchants in the village, but they played little role in affairs centred on the main lake.

CHAPTER TEN

The Temagami Indians, 1929–1970

'We never signed no treaty with no Government.'
Chief John Twain, 5 April 1954

As recreational and resource development activity intensified during the middle decades of this century, the Temagami Indians faced their most traumatic times. Although for the most part they resided on Bear Island at the geographic centre of the lake, the Temagami Indians were certainly no longer at the psychological centre of life in the region. They served as guides – often highly regarded for their wilderness skills – and performed other functions for the summer residents and vacationers, yet many saw the community as decidedly marginal and in decline. Years of transition required serious modifications in life-style and social adaptation to changing circumstances and conditions. Some Bear Islanders adjusted successfully; others did not. Especially in the early postwar years, individual and family breakdown along with alcoholism seemed rampant. Then as provincial governments across Canada became more involved with welfare services for native people, Ontario officials came to play a more direct role in the social life of the Temagami Indians. But for the long-term future, the community's controversial claim of aboriginal title over the lands of the N'Daki Menan remained central. Although the province resisted pressure to resolve the land-claims issue, the Temagami Indians never entirely abandoned their aboriginal claims; by the early 1970s, young men and women were ready to launch a political, social, and cultural renaissance.

Throughout the 1920s, despite the fact that most of the Temagami Indians resided on Bear Island when they were not on the traplines or guiding, the community had no reserve and no official home. In the summer of 1929, Walter Cain, Ontario's deputy minister of lands and forests, wrote to three Bear Island residents – Chief Alex Mathias, Chief William Pishabo, and John Katt – to demand rent for use of land where their homes were situated on Bear Island. When news of the provincial claim reached Ottawa, A. MacKenzie, assistant deputy minister at Indian Affairs, took up the old case with Cain, pointing out that the Indians still awaited their legitimate reserve. As MacKenzie explained, Pishabo had been born on Bear Island and had lived there for all his fifty-eight years; any attempt to obtain rent from him and others in similar circumstances was surely unjust. MacKenzie argued that the Indians should be allowed to remain on the island without payment, either until a reserve was established or the land was needed. He concluded that they were Treaty Indians, wrongly denied a reserve.[1] Ontario rejected the position taken by Indian Affairs. L.V. Rorke, the provincial surveyor-general, argued that Indian Affairs was out of touch with reality. Indians on Lake Temagami, he asserted, were 'more in touch with civilization than any other band'; they guided and explored like white men. They could not hold up development on Bear Island, but if they wished to settle somewhere else, perhaps something could be done.[2]

After interviews on Bear Island, Indian Agent George Cockburn reported that most residents would not pay rent to Ontario. The community would, however, relocate to Austin Bay where a few families had been living for fifty years, but only if that area were made a reserve. MacKenzie passed this information on to Rorke and asked for action. Chief Pishabo grew restless in the absence of a serious reply. Eventually, he rejected both rental payments and an Austin Bay reserve. Rorke later expressed the opinion that as time passed there was 'less and less reason why lands should be set apart for the Temagami Indians in Austin Bay.'[3]

Chief Pishabo wrote to Cockburn again in January 1932 to plead for a reserve. He protested Ontario's demand for taxes that most of his followers simply could not pay. Pishabo claimed that the community had even lost control over trapping because Ontario sold licences to anyone who applied: as a consequence very little fur remained. They were 'not allowed to net fish or shoot moose or deer,' and apart from trapping there was no winter work. In July 1933 after visiting Bear Island, Thomas McGookin, the inspector of Indian agencies, corroborated Pishabo's descriptions. Without a reserve, the Indians squatted on Bear Island, existing mainly 'on relief' and a little trapping, with some guiding and boating in summer. Even the school was closed.[4]

Indian Affairs put renewed pressure on Ontario, again to no avail. Federal officials outlined the situation at Temagami and prepared a partial list of families of status Indians, including the location and size of their current dwelling-place. The list indicated that thirty-seven families lived on Bear Island. These included most of the Katt, Mathias, Potts, and Moore families. The families of Chief Pishabo and Peter Misabi were inexplicably omitted. Five persons, including widowed Mrs White Bear and the deserted Mrs Belaney (Angèle), lived in Temagami village, while Aleck Paul and his family were at Austin Bay. Twelve members of the Mathias family lived at Larder Lake. Fifteen of the Twains were at Gogama and six at Elk Lake.[5]

Once more, in October 1935, chiefs Pishabo and Mathias formally petitioned Indian Affairs concerning the Austin Bay site. Ontario ignored the request, and late the following year Cain proposed that the Temagami Indians should make rental payments to the district forester, then the pre-eminent local representative of the province. Cain claimed that only William Pishabo, Peter Misabi, and Aleck Paul were old and without funds to make rental payments. Almost in fatalistic resignation, MacKenzie asked the new Indian agent at Sturgeon Falls to urge the Indians to pay rent on a temporary basis. Then H.W. McGill, the new director of Indian affairs, made a further retreat; he told Cain that Indian Affairs would pay for the indigent members of the community, but he indicated that neither Peter Misabi nor William Pishabo were on the Temagami list!

'You surely must have some record of the Chief of that tribe,' Cain exclaimed in rejoinder with reference to Pishabo. And Peter Misabi was certainly a status Indian, but one on the Parry Sound band list ('Shawanaga, No. 34'). Ontario's Department of Lands and Forests now seemed to know more about the Temagami Indians than Canada's Indian Affairs, where new personnel were in place. McGill sheepishly admitted his error about Misabi, but claimed that with an annual federal grant of fifty-six dollars, Misabi was not indigent. Although he wrote to Indian Affairs as if he were chief, Pishabo was not in the records and would have to be checked out; the only adult male by the name of Paul resident on the island was described as 'a half-breed.'[6]

The administrative advantages in this prolonged intergovernmental sparring match over an obscure aboriginal claim had clearly shifted. Cain used the opportunity in April 1938 to review the matter for McGill from the Ontario perspective. He asserted that the province would probably never set aside a reserve inside the Temagami Provincial Forest, and that Indian Affairs would have to pay the rent for the Indians who could not do so. If it objected, the federal government could move the Temagami Indians onto 'a proper reserve.' Spiritedly, if somewhat inconsistently, McGill replied that they definitely deserved their own reserve, that they had not signed the Robinson treaty, and that their claims were 'never extinguished.' It could hardly be considered 'a relief matter' to pay 'rent for lands which these Indians have a moral, if not a legal claim to.'[7]

The firmness of this federal response finally elicited an offer of compromise from the province. If the Indians would relocate to a 'small reserve' off Bear Island, Ontario would consider it. At this point, however, the federal principals changed again. J.A. Marleau replaced an ineffective predecessor as Indian agent at Sturgeon Falls, but obviously did not appreciate the past story as much as Cockburn had. Marleau suggested a new Indian reserve outside the Temagami Forest, or a splitting up of the Temagami Indians who could be sent back to what he described as their 'original bands.' More members would help, for example, to sustain a school at Matachewan. Marleau also reported his conclusion that the Temagami Indians had 'big ideas,' that all were northern Indians, that none were on Robinson lists, and that Chief Pishabo was actually a Treaty Nine Matachewan Indian. Marleau even claimed that the Pauls and Twains were from Matachewan and the Katts from Timiskaming. Based on Marleau's misguided observations, the chief of the federal government's Reserves Division urged full co-operation with Ontario: if the Indians did not come from Temagami, let them be moved back to wherever they originated.[8]

Inspector Thomas McGookin set the record straight in 1938 for McGill, who was still the director of Indian affairs. McGookin emphasized the legitimacy of both the band's separate and unique existence and its right to a reserve of its own. He took Marleau with him to Bear Island, where Chief Alex Mathias explained that the Temagami people had existed long before the Robinson treaty. At the time of the visit the band had 106 members, most of whom resided on Bear Island in 'nineteen very creditable homes of frame and log construction, kept in good repair and clean.' An Indian day school with 27 pupils then operated from mid-April to mid-October. Band members survived by guiding 'tourists and huntsmen in summer and fall,' plus some trapping, 'but their old hunting grounds' had become 'overrun by whites' so that the maximum fur catch had been only $1,500. In winter, relief was necessary to prevent starvation. Most could not pay the $10 rental fee for land and were constantly 'harassed' by Forestry officials and 'treated as trespassers.' Although Mathias acknowledged that some Temagami Indians originally came from Matachewan and Timiskaming, they had intermarried 'and are considered members of the Band.' McGookin believed that 'on the whole they are a good type of Indian, quite intelligent, law abiding and industrious. Their demands are not unreasonable.' But with fur in decline and competition from white men 'as guides and caretakers of the local summer camps' growing, 'they feel they will have to turn to the soil more and more.' The status quo regarding rent was quite satisfactory and it was 'out of the question' to expect Indians 'to pay rent for lands occupied by their forefathers for over a hundred years.' Unleased parts of Bear Island were available, but there were complications connected with the Hudson's Bay Company lots (ninety-nine-year leases beginning October 1917) north of the surveyed 'village' and with the homes and properties of whites and Métis on the island. If Ontario wanted the Indian community to leave Bear Island, McGookin understood that they would vacate the place any time they got their reserve. Otherwise, they would stay 'for the simple reason they have no where else to go.'[9]

Various individuals and organizations subsequently lent their support to the claims of the Temagami native people. The Canadian Legion reminded Indian Affairs that several members of the band were veterans and that they surely deserved their reserve. Walter Little, the local Liberal MP from 1935 to 1953, completely endorsed the Indian position and obtained an actual copy of the Robinson treaty for the band. A strong letter by Tom Saville written for Chief Mathias appeared in the Ottawa *Citizen*. Saville stressed that seven Temagami band members whose ancestors had had 'implicit faith in the Great White Mother Queen Victoria' had fought in France for British institutions and the 'traditional policy of fair play,' the sincerity of which was now in doubt. Later in the *North Bay Nugget*, under the Indian pen name of Wan Che Koe, Saville pointed out that now that the band finally had a copy of the Robinson treaty, which they had not signed but which was said by Ontario to cover their lands, they would demand 'at least a million dollars as their share' from wealth derived from ore production 'in Ojibway lands.' The treaty had stated that if 'without incurring loss' the Crown could give a higher annuity because of wealth produced by the territory, then it would do so. Chief Mathias reported to Walter Little that all present at a recent band meeting had expressed a desire to have Austin Bay and to move there. He regretted that authorities had prevented them from presenting 'in person our handicraft to their majesties' on their current visit to Canada. Agent Marleau, for his part, while condemning Saville as 'a good-for-nothing hanger-on, who seems to have a lot of influence with Chief Mathias' wife,' 'an Englishman and a friend of the late Grey Owl, from whom he takes his pattern,' nevertheless urged his superiors to press hard and quickly to secure from Ontario both sides of Austin Bay as a reserve. The Indians were ready to leave Bear Island.[10]

Ontario totally rejected the use of 'any portions of the Township of Vogt in this way.' The township, which included Austin Bay, was 'altogether too valuable from a timber point of view to even consider the question.' The province's original interest in timber resources from the Temagami region clearly had a strong residual significance, at least in relation to Indian claims. Indeed, Ontario expected federal authorities to pay $1,200 for the removal of 'dangerous slash' that Indians had cut on Bear Island. Why not, Cain now argued, settle the matter and have the Temagami Indians 'allotted a portion of Bear Island'? Cain supported his suggestion by reference to well-established ties to Bear Island, and to the fact that the overall community included some who would never move to Austin Bay. Indian Affairs was weary of the prolonged dispute and wanted a resolution. Ottawa's support for the Indians had clearly faltered somewhat, and federal authorities agreed amongst themselves to settle for most of Bear Island and to add several resident non-Treaty Indians to the band list. Agent Marleau opened direct links with Ontario's district forester in North Bay, and a federal land surveyor was charged with handling on-the-ground details.[11] So, after almost sixty years of frustrating discussion, a formula for settlement was emerging, but the idea of a reserve at Austin Bay was dropped – unfortunately without any consultation with the Indians.

Following completion of a lengthy report by the federal land surveyor in 1939, McGill began detailed negotiations with Cain and other Ontario officials about the possibility of a reserve covering most of Bear Island. Ontario agreed to a reserve that would exclude lands leased by the HBC, subject to the condition that Canada would hold the reserve lands under a lease rather than through a full transfer. When faced by severe federal criticism of these arrangements, however, Ontario relented and reluctantly agreed to a transfer of the proposed reserve lands.[12] Having been totally excluded from the negotiations, the Indian community refused to accept this federal-provincial agreement. John Twain, who was elected head chief in 1939 following the death of Alex Mathias and the retirement of William Pishabo, firmly told MP Walter

Little that his people wanted Austin Bay, not Bear Island, and reminded him that Austin Bay had been picked and promised 'long before there was any forest reserve.' Little raised the matter with McGill, who replied that Twain's view was probably not representative and that the sole hope was Bear Island. Early in 1941, while Canada was still waiting for the transfer, John Twain reiterated the band's interest in Austin Bay. Twain warned that if his people did not get Austin Bay, the Ontario government was 'going to have a pretty bad headache in the near future.'[13]

Although the Temagami band criticized Indian Affairs for complacency, Ontario was also stalling on the transfer. In the fall of 1942 Lands and Forests again suggested that all the land, including that leased by the Hudson's Bay Company, but excepting the land of the Forestry Station, should be transferred as a lease not a grant. Not surprisingly, Indian Affairs continued to insist on a grant, although officials suggested that if the band ever became extinct Bear Island could revert to Ontario. Federal officials assured the province that Canada would honour the leases of the Hudson's Bay Company and others.[14]

Ontario eventually agreed to a transfer in 1943 if Canada would pay $3,000, and if the Indians would agree to cut timber and firewood on Bear Island only with the permission of Lands and Forests and to pay for it. Ontario refused to give the timber to the Indians, on the grounds that the Temagami Association of cottages and tourist operators would be furious if the scenic shoreline reserve was destroyed. The province insisted that it was not out to make money and agreed to allow the Indians freely to cut wood for fuel and to set a low price for timber used for 'personal and for their own domestic use.' But the management of timber removal over a long period of time required that the trees remain in provincial hands. Canada ultimately acquiesced and also agreed that no shoreline 'Indian shacks' would be built outside the surveyed subdivision. Thus, in early October 1943, Ontario agreed to transfer to Canada all of Bear Island, except the two Forestry Station lots (which would also be transferred when no longer needed), for the creation of a reserve, subject to conditions.[15]

Bear Island did not become an Indian reserve. John Twain denounced the entire agreement and repeatedly told MP Walter Little that the band wanted Austin Bay. Twain expected the Temagami Indians to get their proper reserve 'whether the Province or the Dominion Government likes it or not': Bear Island was unacceptable. In a period when native law – and especially aboriginal rights – was far less visible than it has since become, Twain hired a solicitor to inquire into the status of the

Robinson treaty. Indian Affairs advised the solicitor of the contemporary view that the Robinson treaty technically survived but that, like others, it had been reduced in significance by judicial decisions and that the Indian Act had become the more important document.[16]

John Turner, Jr, and other Métis and non-Indians, especially those running businesses on Bear Island, also objected to the plan for the island to become a reserve. Turner feared a ban on liquor that would seriously affect his business at Lakeview House. Indian Affairs offered the reassurance that liquor would only be banned in the unlikely event that Bear Island ever became a formal Indian reserve; even then it would be possible to exclude Lakeview House and other lots from the reserve.[17]

So from a promise by Canada in 1885 of a reserve of one hundred square miles, the Temagami Indians were assigned for their partial use in 1943 considerably less than seven hundred acres. Bear Island was not a real reserve, and even within it the Temagami Indians had no secure rights to its commercial timber or the right to build outside a very restricted area. Nothing really had been settled. The Temagami people continued their quest for recognition of their distinctive status relative to the treaty framework applicable to other parts of northern Ontario.

After the war, the Indian leadership made further assertions concerning their rights. Chief John Twain bitterly complained to the fur office of Indian Affairs in 1954 about constant harassment by provincial game wardens and lack of support from federal authorities. The provincial officials, he argued, had no supervisory rights over the Temagami Indians, who had never signed a reservation agreement and whose 'hunting grounds' had never been relinquished. In fact, Twain emphasized, 'we never signed no treaty with no Government.'[18] The Temagami Indians thus remained a small but persistent irritant on the federal-provincial agenda.

In social and economic terms, the Depression and the postwar era involved continuing pressure for transition and an uncertain integration into a new framework of institutions and relationships. At the end of 1943, Harold Shannon, vice-president of the Temagami Association, complained to Indian Affairs about illegal alcohol consumption on Bear Island and the potential hazard that the unhealthy condition of the Indians posed for cottagers. 'Tragedies and near tragedies' were happening year after year, he argued, especially relating to boating accidents. These were all traceable 'directly to intoxication on the part of their Indian guides.' Shannon called for increased police supervision, a medical clinic, and regular medical examinations. At the time, health care was provided on a voluntary basis by 'public-spirited doctors' of the association to both Indians and Métis, and supplemented by a welfare fund established by the association. The Sturgeon Falls Indian agent was not particularly sympathetic to the Temagami Association's complaints. Marleau concluded that in response to criticism over the previous six years, 'the Temagami Band has been cleaned up considerably.' Members had received immunization against typhoid and diphtheria, had been vaccinated, and had been given Wasserman tests. 'Every case of syphilis has been followed and compelled to take treatment'; none existed at present. Dr Wilson of the Haileybury Sanatorium had checked over all children and taken many to the hospital for X-rays, and no tuberculosis currently appeared to exist on the island. Dr Arnold was visiting Bear Island fortnightly. Personally, Marleau thought that the male and female 'half-breed' and white employees of the lodges and other establishments were the real problem and that these people were also the source of all liquor.[19]

The Indians on Bear Island were affected not just by contacts with the lodges and the cottages, but by the influence of church, school, and the Hudson's Bay Company. Most priests and other Catholic officials tried to help ease the adjustments that accompanied accelerating resource and recreational activity in the region. In an age, however, before either the development of a consciousness concerning the psychological nature of cultural values or the acceptance by the dominant society of multiculturalism generally and the aboriginal heritage in particular, their presence did little to prevent social breakdown.[20]

Most members of the native community had converted to Catholicism under Oblate influence in the 1890s – nominally, at least. In 1928, the Diocese of Sault Ste Marie with headquarters in North Bay completed St Ursula's, a frame church situated on Bear Island. This replaced an old log edifice behind the HBC post where Father Evain had long ministered to his parishioners. Father Evain and the various Oblate priests who succeeded him merely visited the parish. In 1936, Father I.C. Wittig was assigned by the bishop to St Elizabeth's Church in Temagami village; his duties also included ministering to St Ursula's. The bishop of Sault Ste Marie visited Bear Island about every three years, at which time people put on their best; papal flags were displayed and fir trees were transplanted to the pathway up from the shore. The religious influence of the Hudson's Bay Company had been in an Anglican direction. In 1911, St George's, a small Anglican church, was built south of the post. The Friday family came to Temagami as Anglicans from the James Bay Cree tradition. The Petrants and some of the Moores were Anglican, but this denomination represented only a small minority. St

George's, linked with St Simon's in Temagami village, held summer services that were frequently attended by cottagers. The last service in St George's was held in 1971, whereupon the building was destroyed and the premises transferred to the band.[21] The religious division of families on Bear Island was carried to the grave, where adjacent Catholic and Protestant cemeteries were preserved until relatively recently. In such a way did the religious values of the dominant society permeate the lives of the Temagami Indians.

Formal education was introduced on Bear Island in 1915 when a tiny one-room school was erected. Classes were held only in the summer months. After a long period of service by the devout Honan sisters from North Bay, Father Wittig and a number of his successors taught part-time at the Indian school. Following severe difficulties, the Ontario government agreed to assume control of education from Indian Affairs in 1950. This was part of a general trend towards greater provincial involvement in the social life of native communities across Ontario. The 'School Area of Joan and Phyllis' provided schooling to Indian and non-Indian children from grades one to nine. Ontario's regular curriculum and the standard provincial school year were introduced, thus centralizing the community and disrupting the traditional cycle of Indian trapping life: a winter camp in the bush involving all the family was now quite impossible. 'Deviant' behaviour on the part of older children increased. The building itself had never been designed for winter use, so frost lifted the floor. In 1957, the school had twenty-seven pupils, all Indian or Métis. No one from Bear Island was going to high school. The next year a new one-classroom school with attached teacher's quarters was completed under the auspices of both the province and Indian Affairs. In the years that followed, the school population increased as the birth rate soared.[22]

Apart from trapping, the principal employment of the Temagami Indians was 'guiding,' a generic occupation involving a wide range of work and activity at the lodges and camps around the lake. Guides were available to lead fishing parties by daily arrangement or on a more extended basis. They might accompany canoe trips for summer campers, and in the fall many guides participated in hunt camps throughout the district. When not directly engaged in activity of this kind, guides were generally on call at Bear Island or engaged in maintenance, supply, and construction work at the camp to which they were most closely tied. Dr Ernest Voorhis, who saw much of the lake in his many years as a canoeist and cottager in the district, estimated that 40 Bear Island Indians were among the 150 persons employed as guides in 1929.[23]

Guiding, if not often a transitional form of employment for Temagami Indians moving from land-based and independent subsistence activity to wage employment, nevertheless did provide opportunities to earn income from outdoor work similar in nature to the traditional pursuits in which they were highly skilled. In this way the familiar presence of the Temagami Indians became an essential part of the popular vision of Temagami as a wilderness area of adventure and escape.

It was no accident that the makers of the film classic *Silent Enemy* (1930) chose the Temagami area as their setting.[24] Two Harvard classmates – Douglas Burden, a dedicated naturalist and explorer who produced the film, and William Chanler of the New York bar who provided financial support – were determined to depict the struggle for survival and the eternal quest for food of the pre-contact Algonkian-speaking peoples. Burden and Chanler examined the territory between Temagami and Abitibi to find suitable filming locations and to select Indians for group scenes in the movie. In 1928, Tem-Kip Camp at the mouth of the Kipawa River on the Quebec side was the site of many of the summer scenes, while autumn and winter scenes were shot in the vicinity of Rabbit Chutes at the Matabitchewan outlet of Rabbit Lake. The majority of the 150 Indians who gathered by Rabbit Chutes with 'hundreds of canoes' came from Bear Island; others came from Abitibi, Kipawa, and Mattawa. For salaries of sixty-five dollars per month plus room and board, the Temagami Indians helped to erect a full-sized traditional Ojibwa village as well as accommodation for the cast and production crew. Non-Indian woodsmen from the district, such as Bill Guppy, also obtained construction or transportation contracts in the film project.

Silent Enemy was filmed in 1928 and the bitter northern winter of 1929 under the experienced direction of H.P. Carver. Carver's camera crews recorded extensive footage of the Temagami Indians shooting the stretch of rapids below the main pitch at Rabbit Chutes. But the residents of the area had limited involvement as identified characters in the drama. From Bear Island, only John Turner, Jr, had an individual part, although a young Ojibwa from Lake Abitibi especially distinguished himself in the role of Cheeka, the son of old Chief Chetoga, who was played by Chauncey Yellow Robe, an elderly relative of Sitting Bull. Paul Benoit from Golden Lake played the villain Dagwan, while Mollie Nelson, a Penobscot from Old Town, Maine, played the beautiful young heroine. Chief Buffalo Child Long Lance, whose autobiography *Long Lance* had just been published in New York, starred in *Silent Enemy* as the hunter Baluk, suitor of Chetoga's daughter.

Long Lance claimed to be a Blackfoot of the Blood Tribe from Alberta who had been raised by Cherokee in the American West prior to studies at West Point and service in the Canadian Army. It eventually came to light that Long Lance's acting was not confined to the silver screen. After his death in March 1932 – a suicide, in the view of the inquest – it was learned that the star of *Silent Enemy* was really Sylvester Long, a 'coloured man' from Winston-Salem, North Carolina. Few suspicions preceded the revelation, but in Temagami village Long Lance's dark skin and cultural mannerisms raised doubts in the mind of Agnes Belaney, the innocent progeny of another great hoaxer claiming to be a Canadian Indian. Agnes's father, Grey Owl, who was himself only a few years from death and unmasking, did not suspect. After reading *Long Lance*, he praised its author as a 'splendid savage.'

Silent Enemy opened at the Criterion Theatre in New York in May 1930. Despite favourable reviews praising the film for educational merit and authenticity, the production was not a commercial success. *Silent Enemy* had been eclipsed by the arrival of 'talkies.' Financially, the film could not be redeemed by the addition of a short prologue delivered by Yellow Robe and a synchronized scene of native Indian music. Paramount, having agreed to distribute the film, did so without enthusiasm, although German, French, Spanish, Polish, Swedish, and Dutch versions were also prepared for international audiences.

Silent Enemy's later opening in Cobalt, Ontario, was a less gala affair than the original New York release, but the audience was keenly interested in the production. For many Temagami and Bear Island Indians, *Silent Enemy* was their first movie, and they and their Temagami country were in it: 'The pines, the lakes, the rushing creeks, white water roaring down the rapids, smoke trailing up from the fires in the Indian camps, they were all there.'

Trapping was the main independent activity of the Temagami Indians, especially in wintertime. Until 1939 and apart from a brief period following creation of the TFR, the Temagami Indians trapped according to their traditional family hunting territories, regulating the activity through customs and procedures that Lands and Forests appeared unable to comprehend. Virtually all furs were sold to the local Hudson's Bay post. The Indians regarded free trapping to be their continuing right as untreatied Indians. It appeared, however, that Ontario merely allowed such action under its interpretation of the Robinson treaty. In 1916 mandatory 'sealing' or identification of furs was introduced to prevent illegal trafficking. Licensing of non-native and non-status Indian trappers was introduced in the early thirties.[25] As the decade wore on, these measures gave rise to considerable tension in the Temagami area. In March 1939, Henry Hopkins, the provincial game warden on Bear Island, informed Chief Alex Mathias and those Indian trappers who were not then out on their traplines that Ontario had decided to include status Indians in the licensing scheme. In the ensuing uproar, the Temagami Indians complained of lack of backing from Ottawa on their aboriginal claims. Hopkins agreed to leave blank licence forms for sale at the HBC post and to postpone enforcement until the time of marketing. The Indians acquiesced.[26]

The enforcement of Ontario game regulations contributed to further friction between the Indians of the Temagami area and regional game wardens in 1954. Chief John Twain complained to Premier Leslie Frost that the game wardens 'have made a criminal out of us for eating wild game meat and fish which we have always thought it our God given rights to use to feed ourselves and families.' Twain cited the confiscation of fish and game by wardens from Temagami and North Bay from the home of Ben McKenzie and his family of nine as an illustration of discrimination. The charges were subsequently dropped. A reply to Chief Twain from Lands and Forests Minister Welland S. Gemmell denied any wish to discriminate against the Indians and argued that 'on the contrary, in matters relating to fur, fish and game, the Indians are given first consideration, as it is appreciated that as a group they are more dependent upon these resources for their livelihood than is the average white man.' Although he acknowledged that departmental field officers sometimes acted without full knowledge regarding a certain case, Gemmell firmly defended their interventions:

> we usually find that they have been given information whether reliable or not, that indicated a need for unhesitating action. I am confident that our officers take great care in not accusing anyone unjustly of a violation of the Game and Fisheries Act. I know you will appreciate the fact that there must be some regulation for the taking of game and fish, or in a comparatively short time there would not be any left for anyone, neither Indian nor white man.[27]

To a community whose family hunting territories had provided conservation controls long before the introduction of provincial game management programs, the minister's observations must have appeared somewhat patronizing.

In the Temagami country and throughout much of Ontario during the late twenties and thirties, the quantity of beaver, which was the principal animal trapped, appeared to be in severe decline. Some observers feared that extinction was a serious possibility. Grey Owl attributed the threat to over-trapping, and non-native trappers came under severe criticism. In 1943, Indian Affairs reported that depleted resources in some areas were the result of 'the wrecking of aboriginal conservationist practices by uncontrolled White infiltration into traditionally Indian hunting grounds.' Although this argument suited the vocal lobby that perceived all trapping of wild animals to be barbaric, there may have been some substance to the accusations. Fur prices during the Depression were much lower than in the twenties, but still adequate for a skilled woodsman to survive in a period of mass unemployment. Poaching in Algonquin Park was reported to be quite common. Trends in beaver production figures for Canada certainly seemed to indicate a decline from a high in 1922 of 232,134 pelts to an alarming low of 44,600 in 1936. Average pelt prices fell from $26.61 in 1919 to a low of $8.05 in 1934. Perhaps more significantly, although beaver prices were not as drastically affected in the thirties as were prices for other fur-bearing animals, in actual dollar value of production beaver dropped back by 1932 to fourth place behind fox, mink, and muskrat.

Federal officials expressed their concern for the decline in the beaver population with the announcement in 1929 of new conservation measures and long-term studies. Then in 1937, in co-operation with the Quebec government, Indian Affairs embarked on the first of a number of major programs that included the restocking of depleted areas and the restriction of trapping, particularly by non-natives. Ontario agreed to co-operate to a lesser degree in 1941, and subsequently, in 1947, sought assistance from Indian Affairs towards setting up a province-wide program. The Fur Conservation Agreement was instituted in 1950 on a cost-sharing basis. The result was an increase in Ontario beaver trapping from approximately 40,000 pelts in 1947–8, to more than 100,000 by 1956. Ontario Indians were responsible for between 60 per cent and 70 per cent of this fur crop.

The beaver population began to increase again in the late thirties. Soon the Ontario government appeared to be having second thoughts about the over-trapping argument. In the late fifties and sixties other factors that could adversely affect the natural propagation of this popular fur-bearing rodent were more commonly discussed: food supply, predators, environmental factors, and diseases such as tularemia.[28] However valid each argument may be in explaining the decline of the beaver from the mid-twenties to the late thirties, Ontario, which led all other regions in Canada in beaver production, was unlikely to promote the argument of over-trapping as the major cause.

The Temagami district followed the general Ontario pattern with regard to the beaver trade. The net profit for the Bear Island Post in 1939–40, that is 'outfit 270,' was 'very satisfactory' at $3,622. In the calendar year of 1940, the post 'sealed' 268 beaver pelts, up 55 from 1939. This represented a percentage increase comparable to that shown by Canadian production overall. Despite the increase in fur prices and beaver population, the HBC manager at Temagami observed that winter trapping by the Temagami Indians had become a 'sideline,' taking second place to 'cutting ice and cordwood for the many camps and cottages on the lake.'[29] The beaver population expanded gradually during the forties while prices recovered quite dramatically during the war years: from $10.50 in 1938, beaver prices reached $37.01 in 1943.

On the initiative of Deputy Minister Frank MacDougall and the group that in 1947 became the non-Indian-dominated Ontario Trappers Association, Lands and Forests instituted a system to allocate fur-bearing areas by means of registered or licensed traplines. These had already appeared in certain areas south of North Bay in 1943; they spread and were confirmed by order-in-council in 1947 and made general in 1950. At first a designated trapline covered a geographic township, then more appropriately it became a sub-watershed of roughly the same size. Trapping quotas were soon instituted, and an Ontario legislative committee was moved to observe in 1954 that 'the Indians quickly caught on to the quota system and have become fine conservationists.' The Temagami Indians, like native trappers in other parts of the province, were unhappy that the new arrangements did not clearly recognize their traditional family hunting grounds. In practice, however, where white or unassociated Métis trappers were not involved, Ontario pragmatism prevailed: in these areas many of the traditional trapping grounds remained more or less intact within the registered trapline system. Yet under the new arrangements, when Indian trappers failed to approach their quotas, they sometimes lost their traplines to another Indian or even to a non-Indian. In the fifties the problem as perceived by Lands and Forests was under-trapping not over-trapping.[30]

A further change of great significance to the fur industry occurred in 1951, when the Ontario Trappers Association broke the near-monopoly of the Hudson's Bay Company by establishing and running its own fur auctions. In 1953 the first of the annual northern auctions run by the association was held in Sudbury. Later auctions took place in North

Bay.[31] By 1957 a few Temagami Indians were auctioning their pelts in North Bay and elsewhere, but most still found the credit and convenience of the local post more appealing. In that year, the Temagami office of Lands and Forests administered forty-two traplines. More than 500 beaver were trapped, including over 400 'sealed' on Bear Island. Other Temagami pelts that year included 800 mink, 100 otter, almost 100 fisher, 35 lynx, and at least one marten. The price for a prime beaver pelt had fallen from a one-time high in 1946 of between sixty and seventy dollars, to only twenty dollars, which for a time made local fur trapping an economically marginal activity.[32] Beaver meat was also cooked and eaten by local inhabitants and certainly was a mainstay as dog food.

Beaver prices recovered again in the sixties as both the harvest and the beaver population had a decade earlier. In the middle of the decade the beaver population in the Temagami district may have reached an all-time high. Concern was expressed that over-population would increase the susceptibility of beaver to disease. Warnings were repeated that trappers not reaching 75 per cent of their quota might lose their traplines. In the early 1970s it was reported that, on average during the preceding half-decade, trappers operating twenty-three registered traplines in the immediate vicinity of Lake Temagami had taken only 53 per cent of the allowable harvest. Fourteen of those traplines were held by Indians. In 1973, with the HBC post on Bear Island shut down, the Ministry of Natural Resources (as Lands and Forests was redesignated) granted one comprehensive licence, to the newly formed Bear Island Trapping Co-operative. The co-operative thus obtained community control of trapping rights to 1,131 square miles or 20 per cent of the old N'Daki Menan, although the ministry still set the regulations and established the quotas.[33]

Apart from the vacation season between late spring and fall, and excluding the unique experience of war, the HBC had provided the principal economic link between the Temagami Indians and the external environment. The basic pattern of post-contact native life in the Temagami district, while modified, had preserved its basic integrity despite continuing change in Ontario and beyond. In general, the process of adaptation to external forces had been gradual and intermittent; it had not caused major disruption. Following the Second World War, external social and economic pressures increased as a result of the wider popularity of cottaging, a new boom in mineral and pulpwood development, and more comprehensive and regular intervention on the part of the federal and provincial governments. These latter changes in the institutional context were, of course, part of the implementation of the welfare state that touched all Canadians in varying degrees. Meanwhile, the local influence of the HBC was decidedly on the wane. When the Hon. J. Wilfrid Spooner, the acting minister of lands and forests, unveiled a plaque in July 1958 to commemorate the historic founding of the Bear Island post, the disappearance of the company from Lake Temagami was only a few years away.[34]

The visits of successive federal Indian agents, such as Cockburn, Lévesque, Maclean, Marleau, and their successors, continued to be of some significance on the lake. Indeed until 1974 the Indian agent, in theory as far as Canada was concerned, retained wide discretionary power over band affairs. Cockburn in the late twenties and early thirties directly concerned himself with 'irregularities.' Acting on information from Granny Turner he took it upon himself to see to it that any young men who had put young women 'in a family way' were marched off to Father Evain to have a marriage quickly arranged. With equal resolve he acted with the help of the chief ranger and the law against any tourists who mistreated Indian women.[35] Yet by 1960, the influence of the Indian agent, like that of the HBC post manager, had declined as far as the Temagami Indians were concerned. A broader group of federal officials, those more oriented toward housing and other social problems, was more important.

With regard to the Ontario government, the chief ranger and his game wardens, in addition to the provincial police, retained a high degree of visibility in the area, but the elimination of legally based provincial discrimination against Indians' drinking somewhat altered the relationship. During the 1950s and 1960s, other officials concerned with the regulation of health and water quality, for example, gradually assumed a more regular place in the pattern of activity around the lake. These developments at Temagami coincided generally with changes in the administration of native affairs in the postwar period. As explained by the authors of the 1966 'Hawthorn Report,' *Survey of the Contemporary Indians of Canada*, the federal Indian Affairs branch at the end of the war 'had primarily a custodial approach to its tasks,' while the provincial governments 'played almost no part in contributing their services to Indian communities,' apart from wildlife management. A shift in policy at Indian Affairs and a growing acceptance of a positive role for the state in social and economic matters was combined with a greater willingness on the part of federal authorities to accord provincial governments an opportunity to extend services to Indians. Through what the Hawthorn Report described as 'a convergence of increased federal attempts to involve the provinces and the development of a more receptive atmosphere in the provinces,' provincial education, child welfare, and community services were introduced to native communities.[36]

In the case of Ontario, this more receptive atmosphere emerged under the leadership of Premier Leslie Frost, who took a personal interest in native affairs within the province. A select committee of the Legislature was appointed in 1953 to study the civil liberties and rights of the Indian population of Ontario and to consider measures that would contribute to 'improved standards of living and equality of opportunity.' Committee members regarded their work as constituting 'the first survey of conditions among the first Canadians, under the auspices of the Provincial Government.' Their report, presented to the Legislature in March 1954, recommended equality for Ontario Indians in terms of access to intoxicants as proposed in the Indian Act revision of 1951 and urged the full extension of the provincial franchise. In addition, the report proposed changes in health, welfare, and education to increase native participation in several established provincial programs within these fields.[37] For Temagami, though, a secondary effect of the process of postwar evolution in social policy was that the relative importance of the federal government, the Indians' long-standing ally in the land-claims controversy, declined during the fifties and sixties in comparison with the stature and involvement of the provincial antagonist. Indeed, when the Trudeau government dismissed native land claims based on aboriginal title in its 1969 White Paper on Indian policy, the prospect of continuing federal support for the Temagami community seemed remote.[38]

As the 1960s drew to a close, life in the Temagami country was very different in many respects from what it had been when the Ferguson Highway opened four decades earlier. The level of recreational and resource activity had increased significantly, while hydro, telephone, and air communications services were much more readily available. For the Temagami Indians these changes in the physical environment had had a comparatively limited immediate impact, even though the cumulative effect of forest access roads and mining projects was profound. Isolated on Bear Island, much of the Indian community was not directly affected by commercial and resource development on the mainland or in the Temagami Forest interior; other members of the community, though, had moved elsewhere to seek new opportunities for education or employment. Social change, while gradual, had involved some fundamental adjustments in the Temagami Indians' relations with the external world. The more active involvement of provincial social services following the Second World War and a seemingly corresponding decline in federal concern was particularly important. After the major efforts of 1943 to resolve at least the reserve issue, federal officials during the fifties and sixties appeared to have less enthusiasm for the struggle than in earlier days. A focus of attention on the 1951 Indian Act revisions and on departmental restructuring in Ottawa may have been a contributing factor. In any event no conclusion to the reserve arrangements was reached during these years. When the land-claims issue re-emerged in the 1970s, the Temagami Indians' claim was one of several unresolved aboriginal title questions in a country where native people were becoming far more visible than ever before.

CHAPTER ELEVEN

Forest Operations and Resource Development in Temagami, 1940–1970

The image of Temagami as a summer playground for campers, cottagers, and anglers dominated the general public impression of the district. In 1943 an article in the *Beaver* noted that the area remained 'practically unspoiled' even though 'thousands of city dwellers' visited each year. As the war ended, the same magazine referred to Temagami as a 'forest sanctuary,' one that had 'somehow managed to preserve the beauty and freshness of the virgin wilderness.' Railway advertising of this period presented Lake Temagami as a 'gem among northern lakes,' a lake of 'transcendent beauty which combines ready accessibility and remoteness from mundane influences.' The Temagami Chamber of Commerce promoted tourism with a brochure entitled 'Temagami: Nature Unspoiled in the Great Outdoors' while other observers continued to refer to 'the primeval forest' surrounding 'a miracle lake.'[1] The reality, of course, was rather different.

There had been a decline in resource activity in wartime, but the postwar impact of lumbermen and mineral development on the environment was extensive. While the shoreline and skyline reserves advocated by the Temagami Association protected Lake Temagami, and the shoreline reserve buffered other principal lakes and a few rivers, lumbering and pulpwood operations now reached many of the most remote areas of the forest. Later revolutions in lumbering technology and in the transportation of sawlogs and pulpwood – especially the move to summer cutting and from river runs and lake barging to truck hauling on long all-weather bush roads – challenged the remaining

Temagami wilderness and threatened to undermine opportunities for non-extractive enjoyment in parts of the district. Indeed, in the late fifties, as the end of an abundant supply of Ontario pine approached – as Bernard Fernow had long before forecast that it would unless strict conservation measures were enforced – the Temagami Forest supplied a very significant percentage of the province's best domestic pine to mills at Temagami, Goward, Latchford, Field, Sturgeon Falls, and Timmins. Major new mining ventures in the Temagami Forest – on Temagami Island and on the mainland near the village – provided further contrast between public impressions of a rugged wilderness and the reality of northern Ontario resource development.

After 1940, the cumulative pressures from the forest industries, from mining, and from the burgeoning recreational use of the Temagami landscape continued to erode the concept of the Temagami Provincial Forest as an entity with administrative, environmental, and policy integrity. Ironically, shifts in government policy and organization in the direction of strengthened forest management across Ontario also undermined the distinctiveness of the forest reserve model and culminated in the eventual abolition of the provincial forest system.

The decline or collapse of significant parts of the forest industries in Ontario and the economic hardship of the Depression had focused provincial government attention during the 1930s on means to revive production and to increase employment. Yet critics charged as a consequence that for several outstanding forest issues a well-articulated policy was still lacking. Following a proposal by George Drew, newly elected leader of the Conservative opposition in the Ontario legislature, a select committee was created in 1939 to examine 'the administration, licensing, sale, supervision and conservation of natural resources by the Department of Lands and Forests.' This inquiry led ultimately to the resignation of the Honourable Peter Heenan and of Walter Cain in 1941 as minister and deputy minister of the department.[2]

Frank A. MacDougall, the new deputy minister, a forestry graduate of the University of Toronto, had extensive field experience as district forester at Sault Ste Marie and as superintendent of Algonquin Park. MacDougall and N.O. Hipel, who replaced Heenan as minister, initiated a departmental reorganization that was followed in 1946 by a comprehensive public review of policy and practice. The inquiry was appointed by Conservative Premier George Drew after the provincial election of June 1945. Drew named the well-respected Major-General Howard Kennedy as commissioner in charge of the investigation with instructions to 'report upon the forest resources of Ontario and their conservation, management, development and beneficial utilization for all purposes.' The broad mandate included specific responsibility to examine the extent and value of Ontario's forests; industry practices including cutting, marketing, wages, and working conditions; education of forest-industry personnel and the public, as well as 'the closer integration of the various types of forest operations and of the industries utilizing forest products.' Kennedy accepted his task with enthusiasm and launched a thorough study of forest industry practice and regulation.[3]

In the wartime and postwar era there were four methods through which an operator could obtain access to Crown timber in Temagami or elsewhere in the province. In the case of large pulp concessions, negotiated agreements were invariably used. As J.F. Sharpe, the head of the Timber Management Division, explained to the Kennedy inquiry, 'Interested parties appear before the Minister, discuss their proposition, and if given encouragement, further discussion on the terms of the agreement which might be entered into take place.' Actual bidding was unusual, and the discussions were generally secret. Inhabitants of the area often found out about the existence of an agreement some time after the final signatures were in place, and even then the discovery was often made by accident.

In the case of lumbering operations, authorization to cut was obtained through the licensing process, commencing ordinarily by application. A call for tenders in local papers followed. In some circumstances, a licence might result from negotiations, as in the case of pulp concessions. This was common in the Temagami Forest: 'There was a substantial stand of pine in the Temagami section which is not sufficient to maintain the mills already established, but we did not see that we should invite outsiders to come in, to shorten the life of the mills already there.' This recurring consideration for established operations reflected a concern for stability in forest-industry employment that paralleled, but potentially contradicted, continuing interest in the ideal of the sustained yield.

'Permissions' and 'permits' were two alternative means to authorize cutting. In the case of permissions, 'used in special cases,' a company that found it had a market for a product not covered in its licence or agreement could seek to include it in the terms of operation. Around Temagami, cedar or red pine poles fell in this category, as neither of these was usually covered in the original licence or agreement. Permissions also added flexibility in that they could be used to extend an existing licence for a short period or to authorize cutting when a licence was in the final stages of negotiation. Yet the flexibility offered by the permission could be abused. 'Permits' were issued locally by the District Office if the stumpage involved was under $500. In all four processes there could be considerable negotiation about stumpage rates and, if applicable, about the bonus.[4]

The lumber industry operated widely in the Temagami Forest during the 1940s, supplying wood to several mills within the forest or nearby and providing regular and seasonal employment for hundreds of men. The lumber business of William Milne and Sons, which had begun regular operations in the Temagami Forest in the twenties, continued. Cutting to supply the firm's Link Lake sawmill northwest of Temagami village expanded during the war. Milne's existing limits were inland from the north and south shores of Lake Temagami's Northeast Arm. These were extended, and in 1943 the company also obtained a ten-year arrangement for yearly licences to cut behind the shoreline reserve on the west side of Lake Temagami. The 1943 agreement required Milne to produce a working plan for the limit in conformity with the Provincial Forests Act. Milne also had to provide the department with a map of its proposed cutting areas by August of the year of the cut. No buildings were to be visible from the lake, nor could skidways or rollways be cut into certain shorelines. The company was not allowed to tow booms on Lake Temagami during the months of July and August. All these conditions represented an earnest effort to place cutting on a more orderly basis and to accommodate the scenic and recreational virtues of the Temagami district within a forest-use plan.

Kennedy's team visited the Milne operation on the south shore of the Northeast Arm in Briggs Township. The inspectors reported that Milne's jobber ran a winter operation, sleigh-hauling his logs as much as five miles to Shiningwood Bay. From Shiningwood they were boomed, in the spring season, up the Northeast Arm to a jack-ladder below Turtle Lake. There the logs were again put in booms for the short trip to the mill. Stumps were very high, an average of forty inches, and the distribution of seed trees was very poor. There was no visible reproduction or advance growth on the cut-over terrain, but a three-hundred-foot reserve had been left along the lake. The reporter for the inquiry concluded that 'this should be gradually cut over, preserving the scenic value but utilizing the old pine before it dies.'

The Milne limits covered a total of 102½ square miles in 1946, with an average annual cut of 3 square miles, and an annual output of 700 Mfbm. In his submission to the Kennedy Commission, Vice President

David Milne complained that the biggest problem faced by middle-sized operations such as his own was the small operator with a portable mill. Small lumber operators, he argued, would flood the market when prices were good and could afford to close instantly when they dropped. He called for co-operation between the industry and government in reforestation and fire protection work.[5]

Like Milne, the Timagami Timber Company began operations in the Temagami Forest in the 1920s. Just after the war ended, the mill at Goward employed about 80 men while 125 worked in the woods operations to cut between 3½ and 5½ square miles a year. The company's principal limits extended over about 100 square miles across a belt from Cassels Lake, just east of the railway line, through the base camp and westward past Kokoko Lake to the shoreline reserve on the North Arm of Lake Temagami. The Kennedy inspection team reported after visiting Timagami Timber's cutting area near Wasaks Lake that high stumps had often been left and that large tops containing merchantable material had been abandoned by the piece workers. There was no evidence of pine reproduction or advance growth, nor were any seed trees left. However, a 150-foot reserve had been left around Wasaks Lake.[6]

A.B. Gordon and Company continued to operate a large mill at Latchford in the forties. At the time of the visit of the Kennedy inspectors, when the company's total limits were eighty-one square miles, A.B. Gordon was cutting 3,500 to 1,500 Mfbm per annum on its own limits, though the overall mill run was increased by logs purchased elsewhere to about twice this amount. A.B. Gordon employed 125 men in the woods during the winter. On part of its limits A.B. Gordon sleigh-hauled logs to Mendelssohn Lake and then drove them down the creeks and the Montreal River to Latchford. The inspectors' report asserted that stump heights were not bad and that, although some spruce had been used illegally for skidways, in general it was a good clean cut. They suggested that the company should develop a road system in order to avoid the shores of Mendelssohn Lake. Besides the area visited by the Kennedy Commission team in 1946, A.B. Gordon had obtained, in 1944, a second major limit for white and red pine sawlogs. This was in Le Roche, Cynthia, and Belfast townships, inland from the north half of Lake Temagami's western shore.[7]

Latchford was also the mill site for the A.J. Murphy Lumber Company, whose somewhat irregular dealings with Lands and Forests concerning cutting privileges stand out in the records of otherwise largely routine transactions.[8] In a meeting at Latchford between the department and all local operators in 1941, an allocation of licence areas had been negotiated. The department planned to grant to Murphy (and ultimately did so) a sixty-eight-square-mile area around Diamond Lake, west to Wakimika, and north, including Willow Island Lake halfway up the south channel of the Lady Evelyn River. As negotiations about the dues and the actual area of the limit on which ground rent and fire tax had to be paid dragged on, Murphy began woods operations anyway. On 20 October 1942, J.F. Sharpe, chief of the Division of Timber Management, wrote to the district forester at North Bay, giving him permission to issue a work permit.[9] The ten-year arrangement covered a ninety-square-mile area with dues set at $9 Mfbm including $1 Mfbm for brush burning. The company was expected to provide collateral of $10,000. The 'special operating restrictions' were similar to those required of Milne and included a prohibition against cutting on lake shores and portage routes, which were withdrawn to protect scenic values.

After MacDougall and the minister approved the arrangements, negotiations continued through to 25 August 1944, when Sharpe advised the North Bay district forester that Murphy had been allowed to operate in the 1942–3 and 1943–4 seasons without making any payments whatsoever. Murphy was then cutting two to two-and-a-half square miles per year and from 1,500 to 2,000 Mfbm per year plus some pulpwood. Sharpe had little success in inducing Murphy even to pay ground rent and fire tax on a five-square-mile assessment for the two past seasons while negotiations on the rate for dues continued. Sharpe eventually informed Murphy in May 1945 that the department was lifting its agreement with the company and holding it in abeyance. Cutting would be allowed to continue, however, but only if Murphy began payments and complied with other conditions.

Murphy employed fifty to sixty men in the bush and ran a mill with capacity of forty to forty-seven Mfbm per day to produce lumber and ties. But in addition the company wanted to install a picket and box-board plant. J.H. Murphy told the Kennedy inspection team that: 'We are operating the last available timber area to come to Latchford that has not been cut over before.' How this may have affected the company's attitude to its financial obligations arising from use of Ontario's forest lands remains a mystery. Murphy's statement indicates, nevertheless, how much cutting had already taken place in this corner of the forest and the economic complexity of sustained-yield forestry.

The Kennedy inspectors' report on Murphy's wood operations noted very high stumps. Merchantable red pine tops and knotty logs were left behind. Jack pine and spruce were used for skids and left to rot. The slash had not been burnt, but the regeneration was reasonable. This was one of the few areas in the Temagami Forest so noted by the Kennedy inspectors, who had expected 'fairly good stands of young pine following operations.' The trees cut were about 200 years old, and fire scars showed that the area had been burnt about 80, 100, and 135 years previously, to which the inspector credited the good natural regeneration. A 300-foot preserve had been left around Willow Island Lake.[10]

The limit holdings of the George Gordon Company in 1946 extended over 271 square miles in the southwest section of the forest, on both sides of the Sturgeon River running west, southwest, and south from Obabika Lake. The annual cut averaged 9 square miles. With a capacity of 140 Mfbm per day and a work-force of 150 men, the George Gordon mill at Cache Bay on Lake Nipissing was the largest in the area, although the Gillies mill at Braeside on the Ottawa River could produce 200 Mfbm per day. George Gordon employed a forester whom the Kennedy inspection team described as being keen on regeneration. On visiting the 1946 cutting area along the south shore of Wawiagama Lake, where a 500-foot preserve had been left, and east to Obabika, however, the inspectors found high stumps, and there was no advanced growth or regeneration. Regeneration on a three-year-old cut-over nearby was good, though patchy. Cull white pine had been left standing and were wrongly called seed trees. The inspectors anticipated that balsam fir would most likely take over the area.[11]

Gillies Brothers continued in the 1940s to hold large sawlog limits containing 150 square miles east and southeast of Temagami village; these limits were later enlarged to 204¼ square miles, and after 1945 Gillies also had the right to cut pulp. Though its holdings took the form of a negotiated pulpwood concession, Gillies could cut sawlogs and also fuel wood. The Gillies cut-over examined by the Kennedy team was on the east shore of Cassels Lake. Gillies' crews sleigh-hauled logs to Cassels Lake on a network of good winter roads and towed them across the water to be transported by train south to the Braeside mill. The report of the operation was very positive – the 'best seen to date' – with only low stumps. Gillies had a professional forester in charge, a man who expected to cut in the area for many years and so was careful. While not required to do so by its agreements, Gillies Brothers was voluntarily leaving a reserve around the various lakes. The operation, the team concluded, was on a 'sustained yield basis.' 'This Company intends to carry on woods operations to keep the mill going in perpetuity.'[12]

Many small lumber companies also remained active in the Temagami Forest, providing considerable though intermittent employment for local residents. Mountjoy Lumber and Feldman Lumber cut spruce and jack pine sawlogs as well as pine in the Timmins area in the northwest corner of the Temagami Forest. The existence of the provincial forest had absolutely no effect on their operations, which were severely criticized for wastefulness by the Kennedy Commission's inspectors. These companies were under no obligations to burn brush, to maintain scenic values, or to refrain from booming in the summer, for regulations maintained around Lake Temagami were not applied in the vicinity of Lake Kenogammissi, which Mountjoy and Feldman used for towing.[13] M.J. Poupore on the upper Wanapitei River, J.D. Cockburn of Sturgeon Falls around Emerald Lake, and the Field Lumber Company in the area south of Lake Temagami and west of Red Cedar Lake were probably typical of the smaller firms in this era. Neither condemned nor lauded by the Kennedy inspection team, their economic ambitions were comparatively limited and they often performed useful salvage work. In 1946, for example, Poupore was cutting an old red and white pine stand, 15 to 20 per cent of which – according to Kennedy's inspection – had been killed by sulphur fumes from the Sudbury mines.[14]

Markets for Temagami lumber cannot easily be determined with precision, and this is particularly true of end markets, which linked wholesale dealers and overseas buyers. Information recorded during the Kennedy inquiry, however, supports some general observations. The Kennedy inspectors identified local sales, wholesale dealers, and exporters as the three categories of distribution. Most of the firms surveyed distributed through all three outlets, though in widely varying proportions. Local sales rarely exceeded 30 per cent of a firm's production, although Poupore sold half its lumber in the local market. A great many wholesalers distributed lumber from the Temagami producers. These included the National Lumber and Laidlaw Lumber companies of Toronto and the Clark and Smith Company of Weston, which disposed of some 80 per cent of Timagami Timber's production. Although numerous dealers shared the Temagami wholesale lumber market, much more concentration was evident in export dealing. Robert Cox and Company of Ottawa exported Temagami lumber for Timagami Timber, A.B. Gordon, and George Gordon.[15]

In May 1946 Kennedy himself met at Temagami with the forest operators of the district to review his interim findings and conclusions. The commissioner's assessment dealt with existing resource-use practices and with general prospects for the industry. Kennedy noted the considerable variation in the standards and practices of different operators. Forestry methods were 'reasonably sound' in general, but very good operations were in a minority: few operators left seed trees or practised selective cutting. Kennedy pointed to several forms of waste, including high stumps, the use of good spruce logs in corduroy roads, and the abandonment of many small areas of pulpwood in the midst of cut-over pine lands. In one stand of white and red pine, about one-third of the stumps were under accepted diameter limits, while the tendency of local operators to seek a high percentage of sixteen-foot logs resulted in the neglect of valuable tops: 'Many White Pine tops were noticed which could easily be floated to mills.' Despite these and other criticisms, Kennedy and the commission staff were in general very supportive of the Temagami forest operators and anxious to ensure the continuation of the industry if at all possible.

Kennedy acknowledged that the loss of trained and experienced lumbermen to the armed forces meant that the previous four years were not entirely representative. He also agreed that as a result of the uneven terrain, with its hills and valleys, rigid enforcement of strict timber diameter measurements was not appropriate. However, drastic measures were required in the commissioner's view to prolong the life of the industry locally. Much more efficient utilization of the woods cut was essential, perhaps involving agreements between lumber and pulpwood operators and the replacement of the piece-work system with 'a more sensible method of payment.'

Failure to take measures to eliminate the most wasteful practices would lead to a situation in which 'the country may very well be turned over to the tourist and fishing trade within twenty years' time.' Tourists, Kennedy argued, endangered the forests, but the prospect that they might eventually become the chief source of local revenue required that they be encouraged nonetheless. Kennedy, who saw no possibility that Temagami hardwoods would ever support sawmill operations, concluded frankly 'when the pine is through, local operations are through.'[16]

Kennedy's conclusions about Temagami, where sustained yield had been a formal but unattained objective for years, corresponded in many respects to his observations on industry practices across the province. Wastage was common in the bush, conflict and tension between pulpwood and sawlog companies was all too frequent, and current measures aimed at regeneration showed little prospect of success. Thus, in presenting his report in 1947, the commissioner proposed new approaches to timber administration and government management with a view to achieving sustained yield throughout Ontario. The amount of timber cut each year should correspond to new growth. Discrepancies in forest regulations between various operators should be eliminated, but those adopting sound silvacultural practices should certainly be encouraged. Cutting procedures required reform to ensure that all usable species were harvested – at least up to the level the market could absorb; new growth needed to be promoted on cut-over areas. Kennedy also advocated a broadly representative provincial advisory committee to counsel the minister, a strengthened force of field officers to monitor compliance more closely, and a completely new allocation of Crown lands that would allow what he considered to be a more rational apportionment of forest resources in terms of watersheds and company requirements.[17]

Certain recommendations of the Kennedy Commission were implemented after consideration and review. In particular, the Forest Management Act of 1947 introduced a series of management procedures and requirements applicable to all companies in the province. The management arrangements contained in the 1947 legislation corresponded with goals provincial forest officials had held for some time. Firms would be required to submit maps and long-range as well as annual plans for the use of their limits, and these were subject to alteration by the minister. Departmental officials hoped that the resulting framework for operations would stabilize the forest economy and permit a careful check to be introduced against the ongoing process of resource depletion.[18]

Understandably, the Ontario industry had resisted pressure for the level of monitoring and control embodied in the Forest Management Act. At least one precedent had been established, however, by the 1945 Abitibi agreement, applicable to the company's pulp limits, including its Temagami holdings. Abitibi had five years from the date of the agreement to provide an inventory by species, size, and age classification and to propose a cutting plan for ministerial approval.[19] In this sense, the Temagami Forest experience provided a model for future use in the province, but it is equally true that the proposed application of sustained-yield forest-management practices to timber holdings throughout Ontario signalled the end of efforts to maintain the forest reserves or provincial forests as distinctive management units. The elimination of the reserves as a special category of forest land was then only a matter of time.

The dismantling of the provincial forest system in fact began in the same year as the Forest Management Act, when the small Sibley Forest, which had been designated a provincial park by order-in-council in 1944, was removed from the list of provincial forests in Ontario.[20] In 1952, an amendment to the Crown Timber Act specified that the lands remaining in the system 'shall continue to be set apart and known as provincial forests ... and shall be used primarily for the production of timber.'[21] Alternative uses could thus clearly be accommodated within the official conception of provincial forests, although the precise nature of such activities remained unspecified. Four years later, further legislation conferred considerable new discretion on the minister, who was authorized, subject to cabinet approval, to 'sell, lease or otherwise dispose of land in a provincial forest for any purpose that is not inconsistent with the purpose of such forest.' In addition, where it was considered 'expedient to establish a townsite in a provincial forest,' the minister could withdraw land necessary for that purpose.[22] A good deal of flexibility was thereby introduced to the management framework for provincial forests, in keeping with growing postwar recognition of other public purposes, such as recreational and mineral development, that might be accommodated within areas previously set aside for timber conservation. Other general legislation of the fifties and sixties regarding parks and forest management across the province continued to diminish the vestigial significance of provincial forests as special territories. In 1964 the result implicit in the Kennedy Commission's report occurred: the entire provincial forest system was abolished.[23]

While Ontario's overall approach to forest and land management gradually evolved, advances were still being made in forest-fire protection. The provincial air service undertook experiments, including some on Lake Temagami, that revolutionized the role of airplanes in fire fighting. As a result, the surveillance and logistical support role of aircraft developed into front-line responsibility for what has become known as water bombing. Initial experiments at Lake Temagami involving a Fairchild KR34 and a somewhat modified Norseman appeared promising, and the water-bombing technique was successfully demonstrated on a lightning fire in a remote part of the Elk Lake area several years before the practice became widespread.

In the Lake Temagami area, the functions of the province's Air Service and those of the private bush-plane operations were frequently interconnected. Pilots formed an informal fraternity, often moving back and forth between the public and private sectors. As general bush pilots, the Temagami flyers transported lumbermen, prospectors, fishing parties, and a few guests of the commercial lodges. Lands and Forests contracts and winter delivery of the Bear Island mail broadened the base of operations. Forest fires, such as a series of serious burns in the Chapleau area in 1948, kept pilots busy airlifting men and supplies.

From 1935 to the outbreak of the war, Sudbury-based Austin Airways stationed a couple of planes at Temagami for the summer season. Small independent operators, including some from Latchford and Haileybury, used Lake Temagami for commercial flights after 1946. Then in 1948, the Temagami Air Service (later Lakeland Airways) was formed. By 1957 Lakeland had a five-passenger Gull Wing Stinson Reliant and two Cessna 180s available for charter at fifty cents per mile.

Lakeland's principal pilot was RCAF veteran Lou Riopel, who rapidly developed a reputation as an expert and knowledgable flyer. In February 1951, *Time* magazine credited Riopel with a daring winter rescue in Quebec's Kipawa district. When a flyer from North Bay put down to deliver supplies to two Indian trappers and discovered that his Piper Cub had become frozen in surface slush, Riopel managed the rescue. To avoid the dangerous slush, Riopel slowed his Stinson to 'about 30 m.p.h.' and skimmed just above the surface, allowing the stranded pilot to grab a strut. This was apparently 'the first on the fly, ground-to-air rescue old time bush pilots could recall.'[24]

In the late 1940s, Ontario's Royal Commission on Timber was not the only source of concern about long-term management procedures for the Temagami district; nor was the Temagami Forest itself the exclusive focus of attention. The Temagami Chamber of Commerce advocated municipal status for the community as a means of increasing local influence. Although this early quest for municipal status failed, local pressure did arouse the interest of various components of the provincial administration in the Temagami situation. The departments of Municipal Affairs, Highways, Health, Travel and Publicity, Lands and Forests, and Planning and Development became involved, along with the Ontario Northland Transportation Commission (ONTC), in a series of discussions and proposals.[25]

W.A. Orr, the acting deputy minister at Municipal Affairs, met in April 1948 with residents of Temagami who were interested in municipal status. A new school and water and sewage facilities were immediate objectives. Yet the estimated cost of establishing such services greatly exceeded the capacity to finance them of the village itself – which had a population of between 400 and 500, including approximately 100 individual taxpayers. In addition, as Orr was careful to remind village inhabitants, a new municipality would also be responsible for policing, fire protection, relief, and hospitalization. Orr advised his minister that although the services – particularly sewage – were needed, most of the buildings in the townsite were of frame construction and not originally built for year-round use. 'I am of the opinion,' he concluded, 'that if these services were installed that a number of the ratepayers would pick up their houses and move them out of the area.' To alleviate the financial burden, community representatives proposed a government grant covering at least 50 per cent of the capital costs of sewage facilities and, in addition, suggested that if a municipality were to be organized it should include ten or twelve townships around Lake Temagami. This would allow municipal officials to levy taxes on the cottage and resort community. The proposal was defended – in the absence of summer residents – on the grounds that all the cottagers used townsite facilities and had an interest in controlling pollution.

A few months after the Temagami meeting a group of officials from several departments and the ONTC met at Queen's Park to review the situation. The sewage problem was central, as it was then widely recognized that 'the minimum requirements for public health' were not being met and, in the words of an ONTC official, 'there is a very serious danger of the occurrence of disease of epidemic proportions which would be highly detrimental to the whole area.' The departmental officials rejected municipal status as a solution and proposed instead a far more comprehensive and ambitious response, based ultimately on the designation of the entire forty-two-township region as a provincial park. A parks commission consisting of government officials and local residents and equipped with municipal powers would administer the community and surrounding area.[26] This proposal was never implemented, in part no doubt because Ontario still lacked an overall framework for a parks system within which Temagami might have been placed. Nevertheless, the proposal was noteworthy in itself and a forerunner of several subsequent attempts to provide some system of accountability.

The interdepartmental response to Temagami residents' concern over water and sewage facilities represented the first co-ordinated effort to implement a comprehensive framework for or approach to resource-management issues in the area. Significantly, in contrast with both the original purpose of the forest reserve and Kennedy's emphasis a few years previously, the interdepartmental group acknowledged tourism as a legitimate and desirable forest use. If anything, the ONTC report of the discussions suggests that recreation was a favoured use. Having described the Temagami area, as 'still generally unspoiled,' the report noted the danger that water-level regulation and 'rather extensive lumber operations' might mean that this condition would not be permanent. Thus, the goal became a balanced approach to the future of the forest: 'The principles of forest management should be strictly applied in this whole area to permit a continuance of existing lumbering operations while preserving the beauty and safety of the area.'[27]

These interdepartmental discussions on means to reconcile the extractive forest industries of the Temagami district with recreation were in part a reflection of a broader concern with long-term land-use planning in postwar Ontario. Significant interest in summer resort or cottage properties and increasing recreational travel stimulated efforts by the Ontario government to offer a more vigorous and coherent response to the provision of recreational facilities, including parks.[28] The work of the Ontario Select Committee on Conservation in 1950 laid foundations for measures to clean up or preserve a number of watersheds, and in 1953 provincial foresters were dispatched on an inspection tour of U.S. parks. A general statement of principle on Ontario parks appeared the following year: 'All provincial parks are dedicated to the people of the Province of Ontario and others who may wish to use them for their healthful enjoyment and education, and the provincial parks shall be maintained for the benefit of future generations.'[29] The legislation established several categories of parks within Ontario and allocated responsibility for them to several government departments.

Between 1954 and 1960 the number of parks in the province grew from eight to forty, and the Parks Branch was created within Lands and Forests to manage the system, which became the exclusive responsibility of the department in 1958. The Wilderness Areas Act created a new parkland classification in 1959, although 'utilization and development' of several resources was permitted in wilderness areas larger than one square mile. The 1963 budget address announced a $200 million program to acquire parkland over the next twenty years.[30]

The significance of these developments for the Temagami Forest was indirect for, until the abolition of provincial forests in 1964, the forest retained its original status. However, the debate about land-use planning and the classification of parklands in Ontario no doubt broadened understanding of the issues and the conflicts in land-use management. The parkland classification system that evolved in Ontario after 1967 introduced five categories of parks: primitive, wild river, natural environment, recreation, and nature reserve.[31] These categories helped to provide points of reference or a series of models to ground an intense debate in the 1970s on wilderness management in parts of the Temagami country where forest industry use and recreation were in actual or potential conflict.

Throughout the 1950s, as forest-management and park-planning policies evolved at the provincial level, the lumber industry remained active in the Temagami Forest. Indeed, this decade saw the peak of traditional sawlog lumbering in the Temagami Forest, for by the sixties the west side of the forest was largely cut over so far as accessible sawlog timber was concerned. Pine cutting, especially by Milne, did continue throughout the sixties, but costs of extracting the surviving virgin pine increased. Significant transformation occurred, however. Woods technology and transportation procedures altered quite dramatically in the ten- to fifteen-year period following the Kennedy Commission's report. In addition, the make-up of the local industry changed as several long-established firms were consolidated with other operations or were replaced by new companies.

Gillies Brothers established a new mill on Cassels Lake near Temagami village on an extensive freehold property obtained in April 1948. The grant covered more than 500 acres, included significant stretches of Cassels Lake shoreline, and was the largest single freehold property in the area. In 1955, Gillies' Temagami sawmill shipped 14,250 Mfbm. This was the busiest year of operations.[32]

The A.B. Gordon Company entered its limits in Le Roche Township in Temagami's North Arm about 1950 and subsequently renegotiated an expanded pine limit. In the first season, a boom of 25,000 logs towed from Devil's Bay on the North Arm to Temagami village destroyed so many private docks that other arrangements were required. Accordingly, Gordon decided to construct a jack-ladder to haul logs from Sharp Rock Inlet across to Diamond Lake en route to the company's mill at Latchford. By the mid-fifties A.B. Gordon's bush operations employed hundreds of men whose winter work involved horses and trucks on an expanding network of bush roads along Lake Temagami's western shores. Despite the scope of operations, the A.B. Gordon Company faced dwindling timber stocks. That shortage made it impossible for Gordon to raise capital to allow the introduction of the more mechanized logging methods that were required to stay competitive. Several operations soon faced similar constraints. Thus, when A.B. Gordon died in 1956, his sons opened negotiations with Milne.[33] Milne incorporated the A.B. Gordon limits and equipment into its own increasingly successful operations. Milne concentrated its cutting activities for some time after 1947 in the area between Temagami's western shore and Obabika and Gull Lakes. Logs were boomed by tug from Obabika Inlet and other drop points across the lake and up the Northeast Arm to the jack-ladder. Until 1953 and again in the 1960s, Milne also cut in its old limits along both sides of the Northeast Arm in Strathcona and Briggs townships.[34]

The Murphy operation also remained active during the 1950s. Initially, cutting spread northward across the 'island' lying between the south and north channels of the Lady Evelyn River and eastward through the peninsula dividing Willow Island and Lady Evelyn lakes. In the late fifties the firm shifted its efforts to the area around Wakimika Lake and then to the region east of that lake and south of Diamond. About 1964 Murphy ceased operations.[35]

Somewhat farther west of the Murphy limits, the George Gordon Company expanded its cutting area along the Sturgeon River and its Yorston tributary. George Gordon began to cut jack pine and spruce pulpwood as well as pine and spruce for lumber. By the late 1950s, an intricate network of private bush roads reaching far up the Sturgeon valley from Glen Afton had largely supplanted traditional river transport for the Gordon operation. As Gordon continued to cut in Temagami in the 1960s, the company's road network expanded significantly, while to the south the Field Lumber Company established a fairly extensive system of bush roads northwest from River Valley to Baie Jeanne on Lake Temagami itself. Others of the earlier pine lumber operations, including Gillies, carried on through the fifties and into the early years of the next decade.[36] Increasingly, though, pulpwood cutting returned to prominence in parts of the Temagami Forest and accelerated the pace of change in forest technology and transport.

After 1930, pulpwood cutting in the forest was relatively limited until well into the fifties. During most of the Depression and the early war years, Abitibi Power and Paper retained the Sturgeon River concession but did not reopen the Sturgeon Falls facility. In 1946 a new Sturgeon River concession agreement specified that if any area within the concession was let for sawlogs by the department, it was automatically removed from Abitibi's holdings. A similar clause in the three other agreements covering the forest – Booth's Montreal River, Gillies' Temagami, and that of Howard Smith – explains why Milne, Murphy, Gordon, and other pine lumber companies were able to obtain sawlog licences in areas nominally within a pulpwood concession. Abitibi cut pulpwood extensively in its Sturgeon River concession during the early fifties, but in 1956, when the lease expired, it let the limits go to other companies.[37]

Meanwhile, a new kind of forest exploiter had appeared on the Temagami scene in the form of the multinational Johns-Manville Company operating in Ontario with a large, modern mill in North Bay. In 1956 Johns-Manville obtained an extensive concession to cut poplar and jack pine for pulpwood and chipboard production. The limit stretched in a wide belt from just west of Highway 11 north of Net Lake across the north of Lake Temagami, past Sharp Rock Inlet. This area coincided, in part, with a large pine limit licensed to Milne. To extract its timber, Johns-Manville encouraged use of the latest heavy equipment. The company constructed all-weather roads to transport the trees (usually in full lengths) to the various mills. Using a main access road in from Highway 11, Johns-Manville initially and into the mid-sixties cut in an area north of Net Lake, where it established a large bush camp. To spread its costs, the company entered into agreements with Milne to cut white pine and with the Princess Pine Lumber Company to process the jack pine and spruce that Johns-Manville cut. The Milne and the Princess Pine contracts helped pay for Johns-Manville's poplar and jack pine extraction.

In 1964 Johns-Manville extended its main access road as far as the jack pine stands of the Eagle River valley north and east of Lake Temagami's Sandy Inlet. The road extension was controversial because of its 'permanent' quality, its location immediately alongside Red Squirrel Lake and several other previously isolated wilderness lakes, and its proximity to Lake Temagami. Furthermore, Johns-Manville introduced clear-cutting and summer logging. These practices were not new to the forest industry, but they were new to the Temagami area.[38] In 1962, amendments to the Crown Timber Act relieved Johns-Manville and all other forest industry operators of responsibility for ensuring the continued productivity of the Temagami Forest. Once again, the province became directly involved in reforestation of cut-over lands, although regeneration agreements could assign licensees responsibility for performing the work.[39]

In another sense, the Johns-Manville operation was symbolic of changes in the forest industry. Until the fifties, lumber and pulpwood extraction in Ontario had been remarkably resistant to technological innovation, though changes in occupational structure had occurred.[40] In 1950 most operators in the Temagami Forest still relied on heavy draught horses for skidding and other bush work. Cutting was almost exclusively a wintertime activity, a fact that greatly reduced direct conflicts with recreational users. Most cutting roads were narrow winter tracks that quickly 'grew back in.' The cutting and skidding season was still followed by river drives and often lake booming. Bush labour was thus largely seasonal.

Workers traditionally engaged in other activities during the summer. In northern villages such as Temagami and Latchford these included serving the tourist and recreational operators and working for Lands and

Forests or perhaps in the mills. In the southern reaches of the Sturgeon valley and around Elk Lake, winter bush workers frequently engaged in marginal farming activities during the summer, on land outside the Temagami Forest. Even pulpwood operators at the time of the Kennedy Commission (when only 30 per cent of Ontario woods workers were 'professional lumberjacks' and 50 per cent were part-time farmers) had invested very little in equipment. They relied instead 'on labour-intensive methods developed earlier by the traditional family firms of the lumber industry.'[41] By 1960 all wood cutting was by chain-saw, and by 1965 mechanized harvesters were utilized in some pulpwood areas. Horses were replaced by mechanized skidders and trucks. Although Milne and several other lumber operators continued for some time to transport logs using tugboats, by 1965 the 'all-weather roads' of pulpwood and clapboard operators increasingly penetrated the Temagami interior. As mechanization continued, summer cutting increased; the overall work-force declined in size but became more specialized and less transient. More and more workers either lived with their families at home in the villages or towns of the district or in regularly serviced camps some distance from the scene of the cutting.[42]

Once again mining also became an important component of the economy of the Temagami district. Copper mining on Temagami Island had greatly accelerated changes in transportation and communications along the Northeast Arm of Lake Temagami and at the centre of the lake. But by 1972 production ceased. On the other hand, extraction of local iron deposits finally got underway in the 1960s and appeared to offer longer employment prospects.

The extensive iron deposits had been known about at least since the Barlow Report for the GSC and subsequent work by Ontario's Willet G. Miller around 1900. They were prospected and promoted by Dan O'Connor at the turn of the century, but development of the dispersed deposits along the Northeast Arm and by Iron and Vermilion lakes awaited the discovery of a pelletizing process to make extraction economical. Development of the Sherman Mine – controlled by Dominion Foundries and Steel and named after Dofasco's long-time president – began in the mid-1960s. Road access, some construction, and preliminary clearing were completed in early 1966. Contracts were then awarded for the concentrator facility and the pellet plant. Production started in the following year for shipment to the south via a spur line across Highway 11 to the ONR main track.

The Sherman Mine, ultimately representing an investment of some $40 million, contributed significantly to employment in the district, as the labour force was drawn not only from the village of Temagami but from North Bay in the south and the Tritowns up Highway 11. Eventually, some five hundred people were employed in the Sherman operations. But there was some apprehension about the impact of the new venture on the environment and the community.

While the location of the pits was such that 'their operation is not expected to damage the scenic beauty of Lake Temagami,' they were clearly visible to the growing numbers of vacationers who entered the Temagami interior by float plane from the highway. There was also concern about the impact of drainage from the tailings basin into Temagami waters, and constant monitoring was undertaken to produce information on the outflow.[43] The residential impact of the mine took two forms. Several properties on the western extremities of Temagami village were thought to be too close to blasting. These were purchased. In addition, because sections of the ore body extended underneath the village itself, pressure mounted to relocate the community to a new townsite near Net Lake. By about 1970 nearly two hundred people lived at the New Temagami Townsite, soon to become known as Temagami North.

Overall the local population had reached 1,500. In addition to the residents of Temagami North, 900 people lived in the village of Temagami, 100 at the Milne Townsite on the north shore of Link Lake, and 75 at the Gillies Townsite (now owned by Consolidated Bathurst) on Snake Island Lake. A further 125 people lived in trailer parks near Link Lake and along Highway 11. The population of Bear Island was estimated at between 100 and 150.[44] For residents of these communities and for many others commuting along the Highway 11 corridor, Ontario's decisions about the management of provincial resources were of great significance, since resource use, and especially resource extraction, appeared to be the economic foundation of the district that had once promisingly been designated as a forest reserve.

At the turn of the century the forest reserves concept introduced by the Ontario Liberals had appeared to be an ambitious and advanced approach to resource conservation and land management for the pine forests of Ontario. But the initial promise had never been fulfilled, and implementation efforts were continually subject to exclusions, exemptions, and reservations. The maintenance of the Temagami Forest never enjoyed sustained leadership and political commitment. Varied and expanding resource activity was both cause and consequence of the absence of consistent and comprehensive planning. Following the 1941 reorganization and MacDougall's arrival as deputy minister, the need to manage a wide range of land uses within the forests of Ontario came to be recognized as a general policy goal within the Department of Lands and Forests. With this development, the provincial forests of Ontario were less distinctive and in two decades even the classification disappeared.

Although valuable pine stands remained to be exploited in the seventies, when the Temagami Forest was formally abolished in 1964 it was no longer the magnificent pinery that had been set aside in 1901 and expanded in 1903 for perpetual use. Official commitment to sustained yield had been far too weak and intermittent to resist short-term economic pressures and persistent lobbying from the forest industry. Ontarians, in the north and south both, would for generations have to pay for the persistent failure of their democratically elected governments to implement and enforce comprehensive forest-management procedures. When the future of the Temagami district became the subject of public debate in the 1970s, other long-time users – particularly vacationers and the aboriginal inhabitants – would seek a greater direct role in the land-use and management decisions from which they had historically been excluded.

CHAPTER TWELVE

Crises, Confrontation, and the Lake Temagami Plan

> 'I also wish to stress that we are well aware that planning is a dynamic process and there may be good reasons to revise this plan from time to time. This we are prepared to do but only if the proposed revisions are the result of a planning process similar to the one that led to this plan.'
>
> Leo Bernier, minister of natural resources, 8 February 1973

A ruinous flood in the Sturgeon valley, a devastating fire, and a brief but violent tornado all left their mark on the Temagami landscape during the 1970s. Yet the major forces affecting the evolution of the district were of human origin. The provincial government made greater efforts to manage the pace and direction of development than at any time since the creation of the forest reserve. The remaining representatives of the forest industry aggressively asserted their interest in continued access to the pine and other species. Simultaneously, however, a revitalized Temagami Lakes Association aided by the canoe camps vigorously advanced an environmental perspective and insisted upon the rights of Temagami's 'appreciative' or recreational users. And under a dynamic new leader, the Teme-Augama Anishnabai (as the Temagami Indians were now known) demonstrated a renewed determination to resolve their aboriginal claims and preserve their homeland.

In March 1972, shortly after he assumed office as premier of Ontario, Bill Davis introduced measures to reorganize the structure and operation of the provincial government. Davis intended the reforms to contribute to the coherence of government initiatives in an increasingly complex society. The creation of the new Ministry of Natural Resources out of the old Department of Lands and Forests was one element of the restructuring. This aspect of the overall reorganization drew little comment in the Legislature, although Stephen Lewis of the New Democratic Party remarked that 'one of the sorriest things' about the reorganization was 'the maintenance of something called Natural Resources and the imposition on the member for Kenora [Mr Bernier] of the simultaneous responsibilities for the extraction of mineral wealth and the preservation of the environment.' The *Globe and Mail* noted that while Lands and Forests was 'schizophrenic,' the new MNR was expected to combine 'totally incompatible' responsibilities. R.G. Hodgson, Conservative backbencher from Victoria-Haliburton, voiced a common sentiment about the disappearance of the familiar Lands and Forests name: 'throughout northern Ontario ... it has stood for something that has been very meaningful in the people's lives. So that to change it, seems to me to be somewhat regrettable.'[1]

However regrettable the change in nomenclature may have been, the search for coherence and comprehensiveness underlying the Davis reorganization of government simply mirrored at the provincial level pressures that had already appeared in individual departments, including Lands and Forests. The background to the Ontario Conservative government's initiatives affecting Temagami lay in administrative developments of the late 1960s, including an interest shown by Lands and Forests in long-range recreational planning and a parks classification system. Planning and classification measures represented the department's continuing response to the public interest in amenities and a variety of recreational facilities that had evolved since the Second World War. They also reflected the province-wide debate on regional development and the trend towards planning and land-use control that was apparent in municipal affairs across the province. Comprehensive resource management – including recreational uses – within the context of official plans or some equivalent framework gradually emerged as a formal objective.[2]

Cheap energy and better highways had produced great pressure on the outdoor recreational facilities of southern Ontario. Too many southern lakes had too many cottages. Algonquin Park had too many car campers along its highway 'corridor' and too many canoeists along its best-known canoe routes. Ministers René Brunelle and then Leo Bernier (the first with the new title) were charged, among other things, with increasing the number of 'vacation days' in Northern Ontario, including Lake Temagami.

The new ministry estimated that Lake Temagami had provided 250,000 vacation days in 1968, made up of roughly 145,250 days at cottages, 30,000 at commercial lodges, 30,900 (including, curiously, staff) at youth camps, 9,000 at Finlayson Point Park, and 33,500 at the year-round village-based motels and hotels. In 1970, even before the governmental reorganization, all land disposals were stopped, pending completion of a long-range plan that would increase by 50 per cent the number of Temagami vacation days.[3] Public hearings were announced for the summer of 1971.

An early result of the governmental initiative was a revival of the almost moribund Temagami Lakes Association. The revival was led by young or middle-aged summer residents primarily from families long established on the lake. The group's members, many of whom lived and worked in the Toronto area, were representative of citizens concerned about environmental deterioration throughout North America. Threats of air and water pollution – primarily from the mineral industry – questionable forestry practices, and seemingly uncontrolled road penetration aroused feelings of alarm in a previously complacent community. Most of Temagami's recreational users were also apprehensive about future subdivision projects, the risk of overcrowding, and mainland developments with road access – in a word, 'muskokafication.'

A virtual *coup d'état* took place at the TLA's annual meeting over the August Civic Holiday Weekend of 1971. With the new wave dominating elections for the incoming board, only Ron Johnstone, allied to Dewey Derosier, survived from the old regime. The basic objective of the new guard was clearly more political than that of the previous regime: to influence the outcome of the Lands and Forests / MNR hearings, and thus the nature of the proposed Temagami plan. The new guard was by no means opposed to all development, although extensive mainland development and a proliferation of new road access points were anathema.[4]

The area covered by the 'Lake Temagami Plan' encompassed only the twenty townships in and immediately around Lake Temagami itself, that is, the area outlined for years on the many editions of Ontario's special 'Islands in Lake Temagami' map. The planning area did not officially extend north even as far as Lady Evelyn Lake, the Trout Streams, or Maple Mountain, even though these areas had always been integrally linked to the economic and recreational development of Lake Temagami itself. Ultimately these exclusions would become problematic. Ministry officials referred to the plan as 'a dynamic document meant to handle the dynamic planning process.' This attitude was welcomed by most of those interested in Temagami's future, although few could have anticipated at the time just how dynamic the implementation might become.[5]

The *Lake Temagami Plan* was released in 1973, although its contents were well known in the previous year. Its main thrust called for the lake to remain 'primarily a recreation area, but with discreet resource production and other minor uses.' Over a period of twenty years, 135,000 more annual 'recreation days' were to be obtained. The plan proposed two 'cottage clusters' with a maximum of one hundred units each, one on the Northeast Arm near the village of Temagami and one on Shiningwood Bay south of the Mine Road. A camping park at Sandy Inlet was contemplated as a possibility for the future. Otherwise, mainland shoreline 'incursions' would 'not be permitted.' Nor would additional roads for public access be allowed, apart from two short branches off the Temagami Mine Road that would be required to service the proposed cottage 'clusters' and perhaps a short link from the Johns-Manville Road to Sandy Inlet if a need for a camping park was eventually demonstrated. The planners intended the road-access restrictions to preserve the 'aesthetic values on Lake Temagami.' Three new youth camps, all in the North Arm, would be encouraged; they would be on 'either islands or mainland' – a point in direct conflict with the general mainland prohibition. Up to six new lodges would also be encouraged. All new youth camps and lodges would receive their land only on long-term leases – once again becoming the norm in Ontario.[6]

In terms of resource production, the development policy outlined in the *Lake Temagami Plan* indicated that existing industries were to be accommodated 'in order at least to maintain their present job levels.' Moreover, the plan's authors noted, some seven decades after the designation of the original Temagami Forest, that 'opportunity must be provided for the management of the renewable resources.'[7] Six different licensees held timber rights in the 'planning area.' Only Milne, which had rights to most of the red and white pine north and west of the lake, focused its efforts on Lake Temagami, and only Milne towed logs on the lake. The plan estimated that 300 million board feet of pine existed in the lake's skyline reserve, 200 million of it in marketable locations, a supply that alone could keep the Milne mill going for fourteen years.[8] Some experimental cutting had taken place within the skyline reserve since 1969. According to the plan's authors, these tests indicated the possibility of successful regeneration. But much of the pine was overmature – about 250 years old – and 2 per cent to 3 per cent was dying annually. Without cutting or fire, 'little' regeneration was taking place. On the other hand, the plan reported that Milne had enough pine in the licensed area to 'sustain operations at the present rate for the foreseeable future.' The plan described the activities of the Field Lumber Company and J.B. Smith and Sons of Marten River operating around Baie Jeanne and Cross Lake in the south, and the minor activities of Morrison Brothers operating to the southeast.[9] The Rabbit Lake limits of Consolidated Bathurst were outside the lake's 'planning area.'

By 1972 the Johns-Manville Road gave direct access to the north end of Lake Temagami and to Diamond Lake by crossing over the blocked-off former northern outlet at Sharp Rock and passing within a mile of Sandy Inlet. The plan, though equivocal on the future of the road, claimed that 'public use' was 'restricted at all times.' Milne's road network linking its Obabika Inlet operations and the secondary Highway 805 running north from River Valley were also mentioned in the plan. Public use of this route, although not prohibited, was rare because of the poor quality of the road. The same was said of J.B. Smith's very rough road to Baie Jeanne from the Marten River settlement on Highway 11. This road intersected with the route north from River Valley.[10]

Despite the logic of scientific forestry, pine cutting on the skyline reserve would occur, according to the plan, only 'for scenic improvement purposes,' even if this meant a reversion to other species on some stretches of the shore. Other lakes and streams in the planning area would also receive 'adequate' shoreline protection. Otherwise, scientific or perpetual use forestry was supposed to prevail. Portages too would be preserved from cutting – 200 feet on either side on major routes, 100 feet on minor routes. Mining exploration would not be restricted geographically, but 'water quality and aesthetic values' would be paramount in determining the nature of mining development. An advisory committee, representative of major economic interests and reporting to the district forester, would review the plan at five-year intervals.[11]

Challenges to the MNR's Lake Temagami plan emerged unexpectedly from two sources: the Ontario Ministry of Industry and Tourism and the Teme-augama Anishnabai. In a division of provincial governmental responsibility unfathomable to most people familiar with Temagami, it was the responsibility of Natural Resources to plan the development of the area, including the drastic expansion of recreation, yet it was the responsibility of Industry and Tourism to promote tourism throughout the province.[12] The latter ministry was especially anxious to promote development in economically depressed northeastern Ontario where unemployment was persistently high. Industry and Tourism had received northern criticism for the amount of public funds expended to build and promote Ontario Place on the Toronto waterfront; some compensatory northern diversion was obviously desirable. Maple Mountain – just outside the area covered by the MNR plan – although clearly an integral part of the Temagami country as understood by vacationers, the forest industry, and the Indians – attracted the attention of Industry and Tourism's minister, Claude Bennett, and his advisers.

In 1972 the Special Projects Branch of Industry and Tourism was developing plans for a major resort and recreation complex in the Maple Mountain area at the very heart of the Lady Evelyn wilderness. The proposal contemplated an urban centre with accommodation for 3,500 people, shopping facilities and other services, an eighteen-hole golf course, tennis courts, a heated pool, riding trails (snowmobile trails in winter), and downhill ski slopes on Maple Mountain itself. The first phase alone was expected to involve an expenditure of $82 million of public money. When a two-man study team making a secret preliminary survey became lost near the mountain and required rescue assistance the proposal came to light late in 1972. Nearly a year of bureaucratic effort had already been devoted to background planning.[13]

At the TLA annual meeting in August 1973, Ed Havrot, the Conservative member of the Legislature for Timiskaming and now the project's loudest political promoter, defended the resort concept against the criticisms of the new environmentalists who regarded the project as a major violation of the spirit of the Temagami plan. Reflecting a not-uncommon perception that natural resources, while constitutionally the responsibility of the province, are always available for locally designated uses, Havrot accused the TLA representatives of being absentee southerners intent on telling northerners how to run their own affairs. Havrot had not recognized in his audience Gary Potts, the newly elected chief of the Temagami band, who rose to reply. Potts calmly informed Havrot that he had no doubt about his own status as a northerner, that he vehemently opposed the resort project, and that he would work unceasingly to have it stopped. Furthermore, he reminded his listeners, as so many of his predecessors had done before, that the Temagami Indians had never surrendered their aboriginal land title.

The new TLA board soon joined the Temagami band in opposition to the resort proposal and issued a press release condemning the Maple Mountain project and endorsing the critical views expressed by the Indians and the canoeist lobby, the latter including not only Temagami camps but supporters from elsewhere in the province and the Ontario Camping Association.[14] With encouragement and some preliminary financial support from the TLA, a separate organization, the Save Maple Mountain Committee (SMMC), emerged to take charge of a campaign in response to the Ontario government's plans for commercial development at Maple Mountain. Hugh Stewart, a year-round resident on the lake and a principal in a new canoe-tripping venture called Headwaters, assumed early leadership of the SMMC and carefully gathered support from area residents and camp operators. The SMMC directly challenged the procedures and the assumptions of Industry and Tourism, especially the ministry's unsupported projections of long-term prosperity and increased employment flowing from the project.[15]

Although municipal councils and chambers of commerce in the communities to the east and north of Maple Mountain, such as Temagami, Latchford, and Elk Lake, generally supported the project, local opposition grew; the centre of SMMC activity shifted distinctly to the Tritowns. At its peak in late 1974, SMMC had more than a thousand members who sent a steady barrage of letters to politicians and newspaper editors, ran an advertising campaign, and maintained a liaison with numerous conservation and environmental groups. These activities succeeded in bringing the underlying and long-term issues into the public eye at a time when government secrecy in the handling of the project had precluded or eliminated most opposition. Hugh Stewart posed the fundamental question: 'what will be more valuable fifty years from now? another resort or a wilderness area preserved in its natural state?'[16] Gradually the press became less enthusiastic about the project. The *Toronto Star* and the *Globe and Mail* condemned the exercise in editorials titled 'Maple Mountain Makes a How-Not-To Lesson' and 'Maple Mountain Madness.'[17]

But in fact the Maple Mountain project was not stopped by the SMMC, the TLA, the Temagami youth camps, or the sceptical views of the *Globe and Mail.* It was stopped by Chief Gary Potts of the Teme-augama Anishnabai.

Immediately after his election in 1972, the dynamism and political acumen of Gary Potts were felt. He participated in TLA affairs. He secured federal funding for local improvements on Bear Island, most of which had been officially designated as a reserve in 1971, almost three decades after it was transferred from Ontario to the federal government. It did not, of course, even come close to the traditional size of reserves for comparable bands. Potts spoke against the Maple Mountain project, and his efforts helped to restore the pride of a people who had never signed a treaty with the Crown. To assert the land claim three legal cautions were filed in August 1973 on behalf of the Bear Island

Foundation in the land titles offices of Temiskaming, Nipissing, and Sudbury. The cautions covered Crown land (not land already in private hands) in 110 townships, an area of nearly 4,000 square miles.[18] Except in the northwest, the land claim area was remarkably similar to the Temagami Forest Reserve of 1903, with Maple Mountain not far from the centre (see map 1).

When the existence of the cautions became public,[19] the Ontario government admitted that although existing private landholdings could be transferred, the cautions would prevent new Crown grants in the area until they were lifted or cleared away by the courts. They also severely curtailed those aspects of the MNR's Lake Temagami Plan that involved the granting or selling of Crown land into private hands either by long-term lease or by freehold. However, the legal controversy appeared not to affect 'temporary' grants of timber limits or the continuation, under certain circumstances, of mineral prospecting. At Industry and Tourism, Claude Bennett reluctantly acknowledged that the Maple Mountain resort proposal was left 'just sitting on the shelf doing nothing.'[20]

The TLA had now reached an early peak of its environmental activity. On 13 August 1971, only one week after the 'coup,' the new board broadened the mandate of its Committee on Land Use and the Environment (CLUE). CLUE had been responsible for relations with Lands and Forests regarding the Temagami plan. But CLUE was now also charged with 'direct concern with the ecology of the area.' Through a sub-committee, CLUE was also expected to initiate action and research with regard to 'the Sudbury air pollution source.' TLA President Ron Johnstone wrote to INCO and Falconbridge, with a copy to Queen's Park, expressing 'concern and dismay' at the continuing air pollution affecting the entire area.[21] Thus, Temagami summer residents set in motion an institutional study and lobbying effort with regard to acid rain – some years before the issue received continent-wide prominence as perhaps the primary long-term environmental hazard for North American life, and a significant issue for Canada-U.S. relations.[22] The continuing deterioration of the Temagami environment was particularly unfortunate in light of the 1902 regulations, which had specified, long before 'acid rain' was discovered, that 'no ores containing sulphur or other deleterious substances shall be roasted in the open air in any Reserve or treated in such a way as to expose the trees and other vegetation therein to injury.'[23]

Reports of low pH counts or high acidity levels on many lakes west of Lake Temagami reached the floor of the Ontario Legislature in 1971, shortly before the TLA established a 'Sudbury SO_2 sub-committee' to examine the local situation. In May 1972, a delegation from the TLA attended a conference sponsored by Sudbury labour and environmental groups to gather information on SO_2 pollution from the new INCO 'super stack,' 'the world's highest chimney.' Water-quality studies were initiated on Lake Temagami to develop vital baseline data to support long-term monitoring and analysis. There was some liaison with groups such as the Canadian Environmental Law Association, and TLA representatives intensified pressure on the Ontario Ministry of the Environment.[24] The TLA's impact is hard to measure, but it was not negligible in furthering the gradual evolution of a more substantial acid-rain coalition.

The Ontario government responded slowly to criticism of the nickel industry's SO_2 emissions. Numerous delays and unexplained postponements of efforts to enforce some cutting back of INCO's allowable emissions from the high stack took place. Later studies revealed a steady fall in the pH levels in lakes such as Florence, Yorston, and Bobs, where fish life eventually disappeared. The effects of acid rain had penetrated the Temagami country, even if only the waters of Sharp Rock Inlet and Obabika Inlet on the lake itself seemed to be immediately threatened.[25]

To provide a framework for response to government initiatives under the plan, CLUE prepared a statement entitled 'Man and the Environment.' The statement reasserted opposition to mainland development around Lake Temagami and acknowledged the Temagami country overall as the 'home' of the Temagami Indians whose 'rights and interests' were recognized. This reflected a major shift in attitude from the sentiments of the Temagami Association founders of the 1930s and was some indication of a temporary coalescence of native and environmental interests during the decade. From a procedural perspective, the CLUE document accepted land-use planning and regulation as appropriate means of managing the inevitable conflicts of 'multiple use' in the area. Several specific policies were also advanced, including the desire to keep lumbering 'out of sight of the lake' and to minimize road access to water. The statement condemned 'subdivision whether by government or by private individuals' and opposed 'conversion' of use of property, especially to 'commercialism in a cottage area.'[26] 'Man and the Environment' provided a foundation for TLA involvement in the series of local environmental and development clashes that followed. These saw the association and its members drawn ever further into the intricacies of environmental planning, lobbying, and decision making about land use in northeastern Ontario.

Meanwhile the youth camps and lodges of the Temagami area experienced the impact of economic and social changes in all phases of their program and operations throughout the 1970s. Significantly increased costs for new 'light weight' camping equipment, provisions, and especially transportation placed severe pressure on the traditional fee structures of businesses whose annual income was almost totally dependent on receipts from a short summer operating season. Rising energy costs after 1973 were particularly worrisome for northern youth camp operators, far removed from the major urban centres that constituted their core market areas.

Changing social values also presented challenges. Within youth camps, for example, life-style differences were reflected in more liberal attitudes to drugs and sex on the part of many university students who often staffed children's summer camps and sometimes called for a difficult mix of discipline and diplomacy on the part of camp directors. Yet there were also positive developments for the camping movement in the ferment of changing values that emerged from the late 1960s. Interest in wilderness living and a return to nature and widely expressed concern for the environment were all indicative of at least a partial shift away from postwar consumerism and conventional assumptions about economic progress. Canoe travel was on the verge of a great rise in popularity, unprecedented for several decades. No less a figure than the new prime minister celebrated 'the tough but satisfying life of the voyageurs,' while the legacy of the 1967 centennial canoe festivals and races also strengthened popular awareness of the pleasures of paddling.[27] On Lake Temagami, the cross-currents of economic and social changes presented both a challenge and an opportunity for camp and even resort owners.

For most Temagami-based youth camps, canoe travel remained the central feature of the summer program. Trips from Keewaydin and Wabun, both camps still oriented to the American market, explored the Temagami district as well as more remote waterways. Both camps frequently travelled the Rupert River in northwestern Quebec and the Ogoki-Albany waters of northwestern Ontario. Wabun sections were often found on the Attawapiskat, while Keewaydin trips emphasized Quebec's Eastmain River watershed until about 1978, when the area was devastated by the James Bay hydroelectric power project. Following a corporate reorganization in 1971, Wanapitei's youth camping program expanded rapidly to include regular James Bay trips in Ontario and Quebec. Headwaters, a new operation launched in 1972 by several former staff from Camp Temagami, also concentrated on northern expeditions, as well as canoe travel in the Temagami country. In mid-decade, both Wanapitei and Headwaters started to outfit canoe trips in the NWT. But the Temagami country itself continued to provide the setting for most of the canoeing programs sponsored by these and other youth camps.

From Garden Island, Wabun, which was directed after 1976 by Richard Lewis, a grandson of one of the camp's founders, continued to operate an extensive canoeing program. Lorien Wilderness expanded rapidly on the old Cayuga site and attracted hundreds of young American campers to the Temagami Forest before branching out with satellite camps elsewhere in Canada. Gordon Deeks, a veteran of Camp Temagami and an early associate of the group that founded Headwaters, formed Pays d'en haut and ran successful boys' canoe trips for several summers before acquiring a permanent site on the lake. Youth camps from several locations in southern Ontario also used the Temagami area for canoeing. The Taylor Statten camps – Ahmek and Wapomeo – established a Temagami 'outpost' on Maskinonge Lake on the Chinuguchi system to take advantage of the readily available canoe country. Among youth camps in the area, one notable exception to the canoe-tripping emphasis was Canadian Adventure Camp, which opened in 1975 in the North Arm opposite Rabbit Nose. The program at Canadian Adventure revolved around water skiing and gymnastics and surprised sceptics with its success.

Each summer the Sturgeon and its tributaries, the Trout Streams of the Lady Evelyn and the intricate network of Temagami's other lakes, waterways, and portages, welcomed thousands of travellers; they were young and old, men and women. Temagami's popularity as canoe country was enhanced by the publication of *Temagami: Canoe Routes*, a handsome and detailed guide to the district's attractive and accessible routes.[28] The enthusiasm for canoe camping and whitewater travel reflected in this guide was typical of a renewed interest in recreational paddling throughout the 1970s. C.E.S. Franks drew this phenomenon to the attention of *Queen's Quarterly* readers in 1975: 'Canoeing enables Canadians to recreate, for themselves, part of their heritage; it lets them see their countryside from a different angle; and it enables them, if they want, to explore new frontiers in themselves by developing their physical and mental capacities to the utmost in wilderness or competitive river canoeing.'[29]

The Temagami landscape and environment were regarded by many canoeists as a significant element of Canada's natural heritage. Not surprisingly, as land-use controversies unfolded – particularly where wilderness preservation was involved – youth camps and canoeists were keen participants. These groups were active in efforts to block the Maple Mountain project. In 1976 the newly formed Association of Youth Camps in the Temagami Lakes (AYCTL) introduced 'Minimum Environmental Standards,' guidelines designed to minimize the impact of their canoe camping program on the local environment. Drawing on their first-hand knowledge of several northern rivers, Temagami-based canoeists also became involved in environmental issues beyond the borders of Temagami country. Heb Evans, for example, celebrated historic waterways in *Canoeing Wilderness Waters* (Cranbury 1975) and lamented the detrimental impact of Quebec's James Bay power development in *The Rupert that Was* (Cobalt 1978).

The experience of canoeing Temagami waters led many to an increased awareness of the Bear Island community and its contribution to the heritage and character of the district. Lovat Dickson's *Wilderness Man*, a biography of Grey Owl, and a fine CBC feature documentary on Grey Owl's life renewed popular interest in this legendary conservationist's ties to Temagami and its Indian residents.[30] Acknowledgment of the aboriginal heritage of the area took many forms. The 'Indian Night' program at Wanapitei evolved into Temagami Heritage Day. A Keewaydin project promoted to celebrate the ninetieth anniversary of the camp's founding and eighty years of operations on Lake Temagami resulted in a published history that included a helpful glossary of canoe-tripping terms and local geographic names.[31] And at Langskib, the successor since 1971 to Windshift at Sharp Rock Inlet, David and Karen Knudsen expanded a survival-oriented canoe-tripping camp for boys to include an adult program stressing a serious study of Indian lore that focused on the experience of 'the vision quest.' Others began to gather a record of native place names from remaining elders of the Temagami band.[32]

Despite a resurgence in the popularity of canoe travel, camps continued to face the significant challenge of economic survival. Competition from Expo 67 and other centennial attractions had helped to undermine several operations. Camp Cayuga and Camp Wabikon had closed by 1970, although Gordon Wolfe bought Wabikon the following year to begin a very successful decade. Camp Metagami, the girls' branch of Cochrane's old Camp Temagami, ceased operations in 1971. The year 1971 was also the last year for Camp Temagami itself, the oldest Canadian-owned summer camp in the country. Northwoods, established by the Cleveland YMCA, also closed early in the decade; in 1975 the Northwoods site was sold to Ron Johnstone, who was searching for a suitable new location for Camp White Bear where sewage disposal would be a less costly problem. Wigwasati survived a little longer, yet it too went out of business in 1977.

Changes were also evident at the lodges around Lake Temagami. Road access contributed to a shift in the focus of activity to the centre or Hub of the lake. Year-round use, including ice fishing and cross-country skiing, became more common, although there had been a drastic decline in the yield of lake trout at the time of the plan, and the ice-fishing season for this species was shortened to two and a half months in 1975 and further reduced to one month the following year.[33] Camp Manito Hotel, with its strategic location and picturesque Nordic architecture, became a central rendezvous. A few hundred yards across the channel, White Gables also flourished. New owners reorganized Ket-Chun-Eny and emphasized ice fishing, north up toward Kokoko Bay. Boake Haven also operated year round, while Camp Canusa developed a prosperous summer business. In 1974 the Plumstead family bought Malabar, which they renamed Loon Lodge, and also took over much of Lake Temagami's water taxi business as the boat lines continued to decline.

At Temagami Lodge, the Metcalfes made effective use of the newer buildings and offered year-round service. For several years Bill Metcalfe endeavoured to preserve the original structure, possibly as a public institution. But the years of rain pouring through the decaying roof and down to the hardwood floors of the great lobby had taken their toll. Finally, in the spring of 1980 when all efforts at restoration had failed, the historic building was deliberately burned to the ground. Chimo, another long-established resort operation, reverted to the Gooderham family in 1970. The Gooderhams attempted a part-time revival for four years. But after the 1974 season Chimo shut down permanently. Bill Gooderham concluded that the era of the traditional summer-only fishing lodge, operating from a rustic, semi-wilderness site, was gone forever. The summer resort had become a victim of inflation, changing life-styles, and greater demands for comfort by its patrons. Thus closed what for many years after the Second World War had been Lake Temagami's largest and most successful tourist operation.[34]

The village of Temagami had operated under 'Improvement District' status since 1968. There was thus a local council, albeit one appointed by Queen's Park rather than elected. The territory over which it presided encompassed the new townsite on Net Lake (Temagami North), much of the Northeast Arm, and the Hub, as well as the Mine Road and Temagami Island. The Improvement District council wrestled unsuccessfully for several years with the long-standing and divisive issue of the design and financing of a badly needed sewage system, while criticism of its non-elected composition mounted. These issues came to a head in the mid-seventies.

Phil Hoffman, chairman of the Temagami Improvement District Board of Trustees felt that the estimated $2.5 million price tag for town sewage in 1974 was 'way out of line,' particularly when $800,000 had been considered sufficient four years earlier. Even with a 75 per cent government subsidy, at $2.5 million Temagami residents would be facing a $450 annual sewage tax compared with the $120 to $130 typical of other municipalities. The revival of the sewage-disposal controversy in the 1970s had been complicated not only by escalating costs but also by lingering dissatisfaction concerning a 1968 ministerial order freezing development in the old village and by persistent provincial efforts to relocate residents to the new townsite. The lack of elected officials increased local frustration in dealings with the several ministries whose representative appeared to exert excessive influence over the fortunes of the community.[35] The next stage in the village's battle for survival was concluded in December 1978 when the Township of Temagami was organized, with an elected council. The new jurisdiction included the old village, Temagami North, the Milne and Sherman townsites, the costly Mine Road – now restyled the Lake Temagami Access Road – and parts of the Hub area.[36]

Within the village many significant changes took place. In early 1973, it was announced that the Minawassi Hotel, Dan O'Connor's old Ronnoco Hotel, would reopen. Refurbishing had already begun when the property mysteriously burnt to the ground in September, removing a village landmark rivalled only by the train station. The same year major construction work began on the Kanechee Copper Mine, reached by a road south of Net Lake. Yet within a few years the buildings were abandoned, the equipment silenced. Economic uncertainty had not stopped the expansion of Lakeland Airways, however. After sustaining a tragic crash of its old Stinson, Lakeland acquired Beaver aircraft and new Cessnas. Recreational, government (for aerial fires and game surveillance), and industrial use of the bush planes expanded. Several camps abandoned the irregular boat lines operations and converted almost totally to plane service. In the late seventies, Lakeland expanded into the helicopter business, contracting out for assignments far afield from Temagami. Bob Gareh (while retaining control of Lakeland Helicopters) sold the bush plane operation to Ramsey Airlines of Sudbury in 1981, but he reassumed responsibility for the 'fixed wing division' of that expanding company a few years later. In one of the small ironies of economic development in the Ontario northland, Lakeland Helicopters of Temagami ventured into the Toronto market. Lakeland briefly became one of four operators in a consortium that formed Toronto Downtown Heliport Limited, running shuttle service between the Toronto Island Airport and Pearson International.[37]

The resource-production dimension of the Lake Temagami plan initially attracted less public attention than the recreational development proposals, which appeared to involve greater direct impact, socially and environmentally. But Ontario had failed miserably in its commitment to sustained yield, certainly with regard to pine, and rapidly declining pine stands confronted the Milne lumber company with a dilemma in the mid-1970s. Led by General Manager Fred McNutt and Forest Manager Doug Buck, Milne obtained new financing and diversified with the addition of new facilities for non-pine lumbering. About 1978, with Johns-Manville now gone from the district, Milne obtained spruce, jack pine, and poplar rights to an extensive area north, northwest, and west of Lake Temagami, beyond Diamond Lake, that included the 'island' between the south and north channels of the Lady Evelyn. A road system, including the Johns-Manville route, and trucks rather than water and tugboats would become the principal means of transporting the timber to the mill. The prospect of additional roadway development was soon to become intensely controversial.

The *Lake Temagami Plan* had indicated that the Johns-Manville Road was strictly closed to the public. Elsewhere there were suggestions that it would not be opened beyond the area north of Sandy Inlet. But while the *Plan* was in press, during 1972, Johns-Manville abandoned the route. Fall moose hunters entered the area and unofficially opened the road network, with little evidence of objection from MNR. For a time the ministry made half-hearted efforts to block the road at the Eagle River, and the overall surface deteriorated severely during the spring run-off. Yet some minimal MNR maintenance work meant that it remained at least passable in the mid-1970s. In about 1976 MNR officially took over the road and undertook more substantial upgrading. The bridge at the Eagle River was rebuilt, and a gate appeared farther west near Whitefish Bay. Beyond that point Milne was responsible for the road; the Milne sections were closed to vehicular public use. East of the MNR gate, the road soon acquired an official designation as the Red Squirrel Lake Forest Access Road. The MNR encouraged car camping and fishing by the roadside along Red Squirrel Lake. North of Whitefish Bay between Aston and Diamond lakes, Milne soon began extensive pine cutting. The road network expanded, though Milne continued for the time being to boom the logs out from Whitefish Bay in the traditional fashion.

The most devastating fires in decades swept across the Temagami country in 1977, raging northeastward from the Sturgeon-Obabika area to the shores of the Northwest Arm. Carried by balls of burning pine tops, the fire crossed the narrows of the Northwest Arm and roared to the very shores of the main North Arm opposite Rabbit Nose and up into Granny and Devil's Bay. Even a few island cottages were destroyed. Before fire jumped the Northwest Arm, the situation had been temporarily under control, but when Temagami fire-fighters were reassigned to help save lives and private property from a blaze in nearby Cobalt, the conflagration resumed. Altogether 27,000 acres were lost.[38]

MNR diverted Milne back to its earlier cutting area by the Northwest Arm to salvage as much timber as possible before insects ruined the dead pine. Milne then linked up its Sharp Rock road system (the extremities of the former Johns-Manville network) with the north end of its old Obabika Inlet roadways. From the south shore of Obabika Inlet, Milne also maintained a road system south to Highway 805 and River Valley. Thus, except for the gap (of less than a mile) across Obabika Inlet (in winter, trucks could even traverse the gap), Lake Temagami was now completely surrounded by road. Beginning in about 1979, MNR also spent heavily on the Red Squirrel road, especially its eastern section. Curves were widened and gradients were reduced. For much of the winter of 1979–80, Milne plowed the entire public system as it constructed a major private road from the Sherman property near its mill and north through to a mid-point on the Red Squirrel road, all in preparation for major spruce and pine cutting farther to the west. Highway 11 could thus be bypassed. In 1981 cutting of poplar and birch (neither species considered very desirable in the area)[39] began in earnest just off the Red Squirrel road north of Lake Temagami. The wood was machine 'chipped' into fine pieces near where it fell, for delivery to the Abitibi-Price plant at Sturgeon Falls. With various operators and jobbers, cutting along the road continued to expand in the mid-eighties.

While the survivors of the historic forest resource industry penetrated new corners of the old Temagami Forest and diversified through the extraction and processing of new species, the land claims of the Temagami Indians remained unresolved. The Indians revived the use of their old tribal name, the Teme-augama Anishnabai, 'People of the Deep Water.' And the Bear Island Foundation amassed extensive documentation to support legal proceedings anticipated in relation to the aboriginal title claim.

The historical and anthropological evidence indicated – in the bands's analysis – that the Temagami Indians were a distinct community, a border people formed from a blend of Ojibwa and Algonquin with later Cree migrants, all speaking a variant of Ojibwa. As a community the Indians had been around Lake Temagami long before the Robinson treaty of 1850 and prior to the Royal Proclamation of 1763. They also had aboriginal, clan-based hunting territories whose historic development throughout the N'Daki Menan had been carefully recorded by Frank Speck early in this century.[40]

As an offshoot of the land claims research, genealogical charts of virtually all band members and many related Métis were prepared. These no doubt contributed to the continuing revitalization of the Bear Island community. In 1974 the band assumed responsibility for functions previously performed by the Indian agent. Then a small community-run grocery store was opened in 1976 to replace the old post store, which had closed two years before after a brief period in the hands of an independent trader. Following several years of negotiations, the band council took over the lands previously leased to the HBC for the post and with federal financial assistance rebuilt and reopened the old store as the Bear Island Trading Post in 1981.[41] Operated by the Indian community and serving vacationers and residents alike, the trading post displayed and sold craft items and the work of local artists such as Hugh MacKenzie. Benjamin Chee Chee, another Temagami native whose highly regarded work was no longer available locally, died in 1977.

In the summer of 1978 the indigenous people of Temagami, including Métis and other non-status relatives, had a great gathering. The assembly adopted a constitution authorizing the Teme-augama Anishnabai to define their own membership. Gary Potts was elected chief of the tribe (as well as being chief of the band); Rita O'Sullivan, a Métis, was elected second chief. The new tribal council also signed on 7 September 1978 'Indentures of Accord' concerning the boundaries of N'Daki Menan, with authorized representatives of Anishnabai-Nipissing, Saugeeng, and Matachewan.[42]

Ontario, now fearing that major mineral and other development projects could be indefinitely delayed by the Temagami claim, responded firmly. In an attempt to establish that the province was entitled to manage and dispose of the lands in question without interference from the Indians, the Ontario attorney-general launched new proceedings against the Teme-augema Anishnabai in May 1978. Among other claims, Ontario sought a declaration that the Temagami Indians had no rights or interest in the disputed lands; or, if the Indians had rights of some kind, Ontario wanted these defined and the cautions lifted. For its part, the Indian community claimed to be entitled to all the lands and waters covered by the cautions by virtue of their outstanding aboriginal title as well as by virtue of the terms of the Royal Proclamation of 1763.[43]

Looking back from the end of the decade, the early 1970s appeared to be a period of relative calm and complacency, an almost naive era. MNR's planning initiative, environmental awareness at the TLA, the Maple Mountain controversy, and a comprehensively researched aboriginal land claim had produced a vastly different perspective. Yet the underlying issues associated with competing land uses in the Temagami Forest and the continuing tension between diverse local and external influences concerning future directions had all been in place when the 1970s began. Nor, after so many recent crises and confrontations, would the complex challenges of aboriginal rights, resource management, and the northern Ontario wilderness go away.

CHAPTER THIRTEEN

Aboriginal Rights, Resource Management, and the Northern Ontario Wilderness

The controversies of the 1970s had been intensely debated and, unquestionably, positions had hardened: the native community was firm in its resolve to pursue the fundamental claim of aboriginal rights; the environmental constituency was more experienced and fully determined to safeguard the Temagami landscape from the continuing threat of what it regarded as inconsistent and ill-considered decision making; and the forestry industry, having begun some difficult restructuring, was equally committed to survival. But with the Maple Mountain affair as one notable exception, land-use conflicts in the Temagami country had been essentially matters of local concern, apparently without much significance outside the district. In the 1980s this would change, and the Temagami dimensions of aboriginal rights, resource management policies, and the wilderness movement would become more closely intertwined with the broader aspects of these public concerns.

While the Ontario government and the Temagami Indians prepared for the trial of the aboriginal-rights issue, an attempt was made in 1980 to negotiate a political settlement of the matter. Talks were held under the aegis of Mr Justice Patrick Hartt's tripartite commission on Indian claims.[1] Although ultimately unsuccessful, these discussions reconfirmed the traditional view of the federal Department of Indian and Northern Affairs that the Temagami Indians had existed in 1850 and had not been a party to the Robinson treaty. The process confirmed that the aboriginal claim was not intended to apply to patented lands and also helped to establish that the Teme-augama Anishnabai would not be satisfied with a simple financial 'pay-off' that would leave them without influence on the management of their ancestral lands. A decisive Indian voice in proposals within the N'Daki Menan was a necessary – but unsatisfied – precondition for abandoning the judicial route.[2] The political route failed by mid-1982, and the trial proceedings finally began.

The chief trial witness for Ontario was Dr Charles Bishop, a noted Canadian professor of anthropology teaching at New York State University in Oswego. Bishop advanced the view that Iroquois invasions, starvation, and smallpox had dissipated the Indians living in the Temagami area during the French regime. He argued that in the early nineteenth century various Chippewa (Ojibwa) Indians from Lake Huron began moving into the vacant Temagami lands, and that relatives of these Ojibwa had accepted the Robinson-Huron treaty of 1850. The Temagami Indians were, he concluded, a 'post band' that emerged as a community only after 1850, a community that derived its coherence and focus from the Hudson's Bay Company fur post on the lake.[3]

Expert witnesses for the Teme-augama Anishnabai offered a different interpretation of the past. Their evidence indicated that the Indians had been living in the N'Daki Menan since 'time immemorial,' that they were a community of survivors who had always found sufficient food. They had escaped invaders and had intermarried with Indian families who at various times migrated into their homeland. Evidence was advanced to show that they had existed as a self-governing community in 1763 at the time of the Royal Proclamation, that they had not signed any treaty with the Crown, and that they therefore still had a valid aboriginal claim to the land.[4]

After reviewing the very extensive evidence in the case, Mr Justice Steele dismissed Indian claims to an aboriginal interest in N'Daki Menan on several separate grounds.[5] Indian aspirations for self-government or some form of authoritative participation in the management of their ancestral lands suffered a severe blow. Furthermore, with an argument that ignored nearly all recent historical research and relied heavily on restrictive decisions from late-Victorian cases before the Judicial Committee of the Privy Council and other courts, Justice Steele presented a severely confined interpretation of the extent and significance of aboriginal rights. Aboriginal rights had to be seen, Justice Steele ruled, as 'temporary' and of limited territorial extent. They were strictly 'usufructory' in nature, rather than proprietary, and limited to such surface uses as could be proved to have been exercised in 1763, that is hunting, fishing, trapping, and gathering – and only in areas not used for other sanctioned purposes. He considered it unproductive to attempt 'to penetrate the mists of an indefinite past before 1763'[6] and thus dismissed without comment the elaborate and well-documented evidence presented by Professor W.J. Eccles, English Canada's leading historian of the pre–1774 era, about the generous nature and long-term significance of French-Indian policy before the British conquest of Canada. Yet the rights to autonomous, territorial-based self-government, so carefully nurtured by the French, were the very rights that Britain's Royal Proclamation recognized and was intended to protect. Eccles publicly called Justice Steele's reasoning and decision 'bad history and worse law,' a 'rejection of the historical background' in a case where the evidence was convincing 'that the Indian claim was sound.'[7]

The trial judgment handed down in December 1984 placed Temagami temporarily at centre stage in the national constitutional debate over aboriginal rights, a debate that now included the concept of entrenched self-government described by the Parliamentary Committee on Aboriginal Rights (the 'Penner Committee') as a 'third order' in Canadian federalism.[8] As constitutional talks with federal and provincial authorities, as provided under the Constitution Act, 1982, proceeded, leaders of the Assembly of First Nations recognized the significance of the Temagami case. Chief Gary Potts was actively involved in the constitutional conferences of 1983 and 1984. The Bear Island decision seemed to challenge the political trend in matters related to aboriginal rights since the abandonment of the 1969 White Paper on Indian policy. It also raised again the profound question as to whether or not the judicial route was an appropriate means for resolving complex historical issues between Euro-Canadians and aboriginal peoples. Though hard pressed financially, the Teme-augama Anishnabai immediately announced plans to continue with what Chief Potts called their 'odyssey toward justice,' to appeal their case all the way to the Supreme Court of Canada and, if necessary, beyond it.[9] As the Teme-augama Anishnabai Council, representing the 700-member tribe, engaged legal advisers in Toronto to prepare argument for the Ontario Court of Appeal, there was some indication that full federal funding for the legal action would be available.[10]

The Conservative government of Ontario fell in May 1985 and was replaced by a minority Liberal regime led by David Peterson and backed by the New Democratic Party. New ministers assumed political responsibility for portfolios closely linked to the challenges of managing the Temagami wilderness. The new attorney-general was Ian Scott, an experienced and respected Toronto lawyer, who had additional duties as the minister responsible for Native affairs. In the autumn of 1985, Scott indicated that the province was prepared to open negotiations leading toward an out-of-court settlement of the Temagami situation.

A year later, in late September 1986, Scott flew to Bear Island and formally presented Ontario's proposal to the Teme-augama Anishnabai. In exchange for the agreement of the Teme-augama Anishnabai to abandon their appeal, to remove the cautions, and to release their claims to other lands (subject to the negotiation process), Ontario would grant the Indians $30 million in land, capital, and other considerations. This government offer was subject to federal approval and the latter's contribution of 50 per cent of the total. Up to $15 million of the local settlement value could be taken in the form of Crown land (excluding lands subject to private interests or such public right as highway use) within the N'Daki Menan. Lands transferred to the Indians within the Temagami Planning Area would be subject to the terms of a forthcoming official plan as administered by the council of the Township of Temagami and the Temagami Planning Board on which the tribe could have what Ontario described as 'appropriate representation.' The attorney-general emphasized that the rights of others in the district would be protected. He anticipated that federal and provincial legislation setting out and guaranteeing self-government would be a part of any final settlement. Scott requested a decision on the matter of negotiation by 9 January 1987 and specified that the negotiations should thereafter be completed in one year.[11]

This was the first serious offer made by Ontario since Confederation. Chief Tonené and the determined local leaders who had succeeded him had been effectively vindicated. Notwithstanding that Scott insisted that Ontario and the Temagami Indians would continue to take different positions on the relevance of the Robinson-Huron treaty, the government of Ontario now acknowledged that 'the Teme-augama Anishnabai are in a unique position in that they may be entitled to additional benefits pursuant to the Robinson Huron Treaty.'[12]

In non-aboriginal circles, various kinds of unease were expressed. Some wondered how (apart from preserving spiritually significant sites such as Maple Mountain and granting a proper reserve) a large tract of private land could serve Indian interests, except as potential development land. Some feared new commercial activity on the mainland of Lake Temagami or in back-country wilderness areas. Chief Potts was known to be personally dedicated to the preservation of the Temagami environment, but some observers were less confident about the future under other Indian leadership. The Ontario offer potentially threatened the informal but vital environmentalist-aboriginal alliance that had had considerable success in wilderness preservation. In contrast, others, especially in Temagami village, feared that lasting impediments to local economic development would result from the entrenchment of the Indian claims.[13]

Chief Potts responded to Ian Scott's initiative with a partial counter-proposal. Potts again reassured Ontarians that the Indians had no wish to disturb existing private landowners or municipal regimes. But in any of the lands and resources where they would be giving up exclusive aboriginal title, the Temagami Indians expected that the matter of 'shared use and shared future of the land claim area' would receive serious consideration. In general the Indians were 'grateful and appreciative' of Scott's initiative, which they felt had been made in 'a conciliatory and constructive manner.' There was, however, no hint that the appeal would be abandoned. Indeed, in February, the tribal council abandoned the negotiation process and resolved to proceed with the court action. Neither the amount of the financial compensation offered by Ontario nor the suggested provisions regarding land control and the relations between governing institutions appeared adequate to the native leadership.[14]

There had been no Canadian response approving funding for the double-track approach to resolution of the dispute, nor had the federal government unequivocally expressed its willingness to contribute to the financial settlement as outlined by Ontario's attorney-general. Yet wider moves both to entrench self-government as a definable part of aboriginal rights and to abandon the notion of total 'surrender' and 'extinguishment' of interests in the land was gaining ground with federal authorities after the publication of the 'Coolican Report' in December 1985.[15] Indeed, a few Indian communities were already working these matters out with appropriate federal and provincial authorities, and preparations for the final round of constitutional negotiations where these questions would be addressed on the national level were well underway. The Temagami case was of some significance to these proceedings.

In 1987, as the third first ministers' constitutional conference on aboriginal rights approached and with intense pre-conference negotiations far advanced, legal advisers to the Ontario government urged the province to maintain a firm stand on the issue of entrenching native self-government. The government was told that acceptance of the approach to self-government advocated by Native leaders would undermine Ontario's legal position in the Temagami appeal. Assistant Deputy Attorney-General Blenus Wright, QC, wrote in a confidential memorandum that 'If we were to adopt the Indian view of treaties ... we would seriously undermine, if not completely erode, our chances of success on the appeal.'[16] Ontario's unwillingness to resolve the Temagami situation decades earlier and at comparatively modest cost and inconvenience now threatened to have profound consequences for the province and – in light of Ontario's distinctive status in this round of constitutional amendment – for Canada more generally. The aboriginal constitutional conference did fail, and the federal-provincial Meech Lake constitutional accord that followed shortly represented a further setback for entrenching aboriginal self-government in the Canadian constitution.

While the Ontario government resisted the land claims of the Temagami Indians, the local office of the provincial Ministry of Natural Resources had been attempting, despite the caution, to administer district affairs and to implement the proposals of the *Lake Temagami Plan*. Under the 1972 departmental reorganization, Temagami, formerly a Lands and Forests division within the North Bay District, was redesignated as an MNR district within the Northeastern Region. The new district contained over 2,600 square miles (6,900 square kilometres), 13 per cent of it water. The historic titles 'District Forester' and 'Chief Ranger' disappeared: the area was placed under the direction of John Rumney, who assumed the title 'District Manager.'[17]

In terms of development decision making, the areas of major concern addressed in the *Lake Temagami Plan* were increases in vacation days, through additional commercial and cottage projects, and resource use, including road access and management procedures.

In response to the cautions' effective prohibition of sales or leases of Crown land for recreational use, MNR endeavoured to establish clear procedures for dealing with development proposals in the plan area. On 23 May 1975 an order under section 17 of the Public Lands Act provided that 'improvements' to property, including all new buildings, would require a permit from the district manager. To obtain a permit, the applicant would have to submit to a field inspection and secure a positive recommendation from the Temiskaming Health Unit and, when appropriate, from the ministries of Industry and Tourism, Transportation and Communication, and the Environment. It was anticipated that new cottages would be allowed only on islands near the proposed development clusters and that additional 'sleeping' cabins would rarely be permitted. The TLA – and apparently most summer residents – approved the section 17 order in principle.[18] Nevertheless, it was now abundantly clear that land-use management might involve more than abstract principles about environmental preservation. The 1975 order introduced direct governmental intervention into property development decisions in what many still regarded as the northern wilderness, a refuge from the complexity and regimentation of modern urban life.

In anticipation of a time when the caution would no longer be in effect, MNR continued to advance plans for the proposed mainland cottage cluster on the Northeast Arm. However, on account of poor drainage conditions, health and environmental approvals could not be obtained. Early in 1976 MNR raised with the TLA the likelihood that the scheme for the development of the Shiningwood Bay mainland cottage cluster would move ahead, but because of the caution little happened. At the TLA's annual general meeting that summer, President Gordon Lak expressed alarm about Shiningwood Bay and about a proposal from the former Camp White Bear interests to divide Island 488 into a twenty-four-cottage condominium, a proposal that had been accepted in principle by the district manager's advisory committee. The TLA opposed the condominium proposal, and at the AGM in 1977 it was announced that the Temagami Region Studies Institute (TRSI), a research offshoot of the TLA, would initiate a detailed environmental study of the Shiningwood Bay area and of lake development generally.[19]

Still expecting the caution to be lifted soon, MNR revived the Shiningwood Bay scheme in the early spring of 1978. The TLA responded vigorously by accepting a proposal from Hough-Stansbury and Associates for a comprehensive environmental assessment of Lake Temagami. The study concentrated on Shiningwood Bay and several major islands with possible potential for development, but it also brought independent expertise to bear on the issues of water purity, acidification, and other major environmental concerns.

The Hough-Stansbury report concluded that from a purely scientific point of view Lake Temagami could sustain very considerable development indeed without endangering water purity. Similarly, while acid rain would be a serious problem in the long run, most of the lake itself was not in immediate peril. The fundamental problems were not scientific; they were cultural and political. The land-use issues related to the quality of the Temagami life-style and experience. If major mainland development such as that proposed for Shiningwood Bay went ahead, the report asserted that significant social change should be expected. Yet several of the larger privately owned islands appeared to be capable of sustaining some severances and thus more cottage development, and when the caution was removed there would still be some potential for further cottage lots on Crown-owned island sites. The report pointed out that canoe travel and family camping were also raising the level of 'vacation days.' Greater occupation of existing cottages, because of extended family arrangements and more frequent off-summer activity had the same effect. What was needed, the report argued, was 'a clear set of objectives for the future development of Lake Temagami.' 'Certainly, what should be promoted,' the summary of the report concluded, was 'back country recreation and additional island cottage development.'[20]

By the time the Hough-Stansbury report appeared in early 1980, however, the attention of TLA members had been partly diverted by other matters. Extremely contentious were the White Bear condominium issue and a new proposal to subdivide Island 758, the choice, picturesque core of defunct Camp Temagami, into nine cottage lots. The TLA board continued to object to the White Bear development on the grounds of very serious existing sewage problems, poor drainage, potential for serious overcrowding, and major change in use. The main issue at the old Camp Temagami property was not the principle of subdivision but the number of lots that could be created without significant disruption. Despite TLA reservations, both subdivision projects were approved in principle when the district manager's advisory committee met on 25 July 1979, for the first time in two years.

In October 1979, the TLA sought outside legal advice and registered its objections with the Ontario Municipal Board. The association also retained Hough-Stansbury again to examine the two specific cases. Apart from the idea of nine lots and a few minor items, this assessment exonerated the Camp Temagami subdivision and found the project unobjectionable from an environmental standpoint. In May 1980 a compromise was reached providing for eight lots. The TLA withdrew its legal objection, and the first significant new development on Lake Temagami since 1970 got underway. In contrast, the White Bear condominium proposal came in for continued criticism, focused on the serious potential threat to the environment, even from only eighteen lots as contemplated in a revised concept. The White Bear project was eventually blocked at the Ontario Municipal Board.

In the spring of 1980, the TRSI and TLA presented a report entitled *Summary: Environmental Assessment* to MNR Minister James Auld.

Impressed by this initiative on the part of area residents, Auld congratulated them 'on a ... significant contribution toward future planning for Lake Temagami and the attainment of our mutual goals.' 'You have my assurances,' he concluded, 'that no major developments will be undertaken on Lake Temagami without consultation with your Association and other interested groups.' The TLA had established its credentials in the new era of environmental decision making. It had become 'a major environmental organization with expertise, considerable political responsibilities, and clout.'[21]

But where did all this leave the lake? Was even the section 17 order enforceable? How far had MNR exceeded its mandate by attempting to regulate private land? Was the 1973 plan dead? Was it legal? In the summer of 1980 Robert McGee replaced John Rumney as district manager. McGee indicated at the first and only advisory committee over which he presided that MNR intended to withdraw from the business of directly regulating private land use; the section 17 order was going or gone. Henceforth, the Ministry of Municipal Affairs and Housing (MMAH) would handle such matters. In the meantime, MNR would offer no objections to reasonable plans for severances or the construction of additional accommodation on suitable sites. MNR also agreed that any new cottages authorized on island properties would come off the target of 200 additional units that had recently been reconfirmed as the goal for Lake Temagami. It was clear then that while the caution remained in effect the plan could not be implemented.

The TLA had already moved to implement recommendations from its earlier environmental study and had encouraged the TRSI to prepare a plan for Lake Temagami. McGee's announcement changed matters somewhat, in that any new plan would also be subject to negotiations with the MMAH over private land regulations and to discussions with the Township of Temagami. The survey of residents' opinions carried out as part of the TRSI study found clear support for the concept of orderly development confined to the islands of Lake Temagami. Simultaneously, discussion got underway concerning a complex joint planning authority made up of representatives of the organized Township of Temagami and the 'unorganized' portions of the lake.[22]

Local development plans – of which the 1972–3 Lake Temagami plan had been an early example – were also to be gradually integrated into MNR's Strategic Land Use Planning (SLUP) process. The SLUP exercise covered all of Ontario and was MNR's contribution to the Ontario government's Regional Planning Program. The process involved public input on long-range planning from various interests.[23] For example, the

Conservation Council of Ontario, an amalgam of environmental and naturalists' groups, was generally satisfied with the northeastern Ontario SLUP when it appeared in 1978 – except with regard to what appeared to be high and arbitrary targets for 'vacation days' and cottages. Some lumbering interests reacted less favourably, however, because of the SLUP's acceptance of the value of wilderness preservation and other non-extractive uses for the northern forests. Within the framework of the regional SLUP, a document entitled *Background Information: Temagami District* was released by MNR in June 1980. The new document updated statistics from the old *Lake Temagami Plan* and extended the geographic coverage to the entire district, including fifty-six townships subject to the caution.[24]

The transition from the dominance of pine in the Temagami forest industry to a greater emphasis on jack pine and spruce was confirmed in MNR's 1980 report. While red and white pine had 'historically' been the most important species, 'large volumes of white and red pine no longer exist due to past cutting practices, over-maturity and decadence.' Here the ministry frankly acknowledged the failure of Ontario's eighty-year effort to achieve sustained-yield pine forestry in the former Temagami Forest. Hardwood, especially aspen and balsam poplar, which had previously experienced 'little harvesting,' were now being cut commercially. With demand for wood products rising, yields would have to increase, though all this would produce less and less 'management flexibility.' For softwoods, the annual 'available allowable cut' to the year 2000 was 'expected to be almost fully committed.' In recent years only about 25 per cent of the 'annual allowable cut' had actually been harvested. The concept of 'sustained yield' was reaffirmed as a goal.[25] In 1981 the ministry followed up the detailed *Background Information: Temagami District* with the more conclusive *Temagami District Land Use Plan: Proposed Policy and Planning Options*.[26] The TLA and others soon criticized the heavy emphasis on extractive resource use and the apparent willingness of MNR to see logging roads multiply and to facilitate additional road access to Lake Temagami and adjacent wilderness lakes. Similar reservations about MNR planning processes and overall priorities emerged during the work of the Royal Commission on the Northern Environment, which had been established in 1977 to review the application of environmental assessment principles to major developments in Ontario north of the fiftieth parallel.

RCNE staff examined planning processes similar to those used by the ministry around Temagami and concluded that 'the land use planning documents and the assumptions underlying them are so seriously flawed that they must not be implemented ... they should be discounted as a basis for informed decision-making about balanced development in the north.' The ministry's guidelines were criticized for perpetuating and extending into the north a pattern of development that was already recognized as unacceptable. The planning processes had simply failed to consider alternatives. Moreover, participation by those affected was generally inadequate. As a final ground for dismissing MNR's planning efforts, the RCNE staff observed that the ambiguous status of the planning documents had the effect of leaving too much discretionary power with politicians and the bureaucracy.[27]

Levels of actual recreational activity and proposals to achieve new target quotas of vacation days had been the most controversial elements of the 1970s' planning exercise and again provoked keen interest when the new MNR documentation was released. The 1980 *Background Information* document predictably argued that the number of cottages in the district should increase from the approximately 1,000 then in existence to about 1,300. The district office called for 275 new cottages, 200 of them on Lake Temagami, and supported this proposal with new economic data: existing cottages were estimated to bring in about $1,358 in annual revenue to the district. In 1976 the Lady Evelyn Wild River Park had provided vacationers with an estimated 105,000 hours of canoeing or '2500 man-days of camping.'

Furthermore, MNR was now seriously investigating the possibility of establishing a major wilderness park in the Smoothwater–Lady Evelyn River area in response to the northeastern Ontario SLUP's recommendation for such a development somewhere in the region.[28] The park proposal created an immediate uproar locally. Milne and other lumber companies were deeply disturbed. The Save Maple Mountain Committee, now known as the Alliance for the Lady Evelyn Wilderness, released a commissioned study, *Preliminary Environmental Overview of the Maple Mountain–Lady Evelyn Wilderness Area.*[29] This helped to document the environmental significance and ecological sensitivity of the area.

Shortly after MNR's detailed 'Smoothwater–Lady Evelyn Wilderness Park Proposal' became unofficially available, the alliance announced its firm support for the concept. The candidate park would cover 291 square miles or 186,250 acres (74,500 hectares) south of Gowganda and Elk Lake, including most of the Lady Evelyn Trout Streams (but not Lady Evelyn Lake), the headwaters of the East Montreal River, and the Stull Creek branch of the upper Sturgeon. Under Ontario's provincial park classification scheme, a wilderness park excluded all logging activities and any new road access. If the park were established, both the recently outlined cutting limits for Milne and others and the stalled Maple Mountain resort proposal would be permanently inoperative.

In a broadsheet prepared to encourage support for the park proposal, the Alliance for the Lady Evelyn Wilderness outlined the recent changes in local lumbering techniques, including clear-cutting, trunk roads, and summer operations; the alliance viewed these developments as severe threats to the wilderness experience in the Temagami country. Furthermore, the alliance observed that it was 'indeed, a strange contradiction that the very government department which is proposing the park is also planning extensive lumber harvesting in exactly the same place'.[30]

Representatives of the Federation of Ontario Naturalists, the Algonquin Wildlands League, and other provincial environmental organizations toured the area at the alliance's invitation. Public interest in the future of the Temagami landscape broadened.

Milne's response concentrated on economic issues. The company alleged that the park threatened to increase local unemployment and placed the very existence of the company in jeopardy. Milne had intended that its extension of the Red Squirrel road network would shortly reach the south shore of Diamond Lake. With barges on Diamond Lake and a bridge across the south channel of the Lady Evelyn River, Milne would then have access to the timber on the 'island.' Much of the multi-species harvesting on which the company now staked its future would involve clear-cutting. The perceived threat of economic loss persuaded several local community councils and chambers of commerce to oppose the park concept. Firm assurances by staff in MNR's local Lands and Parks Branch that alternative areas would be made available to Milne and other affected companies were discounted by the companies themselves, as were assurances that the 'no logging' provisions would most likely be phased in over several years.

In a classic example of the historic debate between preservationists and conservationists, Hugh Stewart of the Lady Evelyn Alliance and Doug Buck of Milne lumber debated the wilderness park proposal in the *Temagami Times*.[31] Buck was almost as critical of the Ontario government as Stewart, and they agreed that Ontario's forest policies had been and still were deplorable. Not enough money was available for replanting. Each believed in multiple use within the Temagami district. But Stewart denied that logging should exist virtually everywhere in the Temagami forest; an uncut mature pine was not necessarily a wasted tree. Moreover, he argued, wilderness recreation was incompatible with an expanding network of forest-industry roadways. Buck made the undeniable point that true wilderness conditions no longer existed in or near the Temagami district: forest-fire prevention was a form of management that had ended natural forest progression. Comprehensive forest management for resource and recreational use was now necessary. Stewart contended that the forest industry's commitment to multiple use really amounted to forestry priority: once the harvesting was done, government might or might not ensure regeneration when other 'users' could move back into the domain. This was hardly consistent with a serious recognition of the long-standing interests of wilderness canoeists and other outdoor vacationers.

Immediately after the 1981 election, Premier Davis called a temporary halt to all park expansion and, in a sense, to the whole, elaborate SLUP process that had encouraged broadly based public participation. He established a committee under the direction of Richard Monzon to review all park proposals and parks policy. G.B. Priddle, chairman of the government-appointed advisory Parks Council, protested that Ontario parks policy was 'now being circumvented, circumscribed and sabotaged to the point that it soon will be meaningless.' He defended wilderness as aesthetically, biologically, and economically important to Ontario: 'the Monuments, Cathedrals and Art Galleries of the country are our natural and unspoiled places.' He denounced the prevailing official attitude toward parks and wilderness and called for the immediate establishment of the Ogoki-Albany Wilderness Park in the northwest and the Lady Evelyn–Smoothwater Wilderness Park in the northeast of the province as 'the first-step' in the restoration of the province's parks policy. These and other wilderness parks represented only 1.3 per cent of 'our forested land.'[32]

Locally, the Lands and Parks Branch of MNR at Temagami continued to prepare documentation for an economic feasibility study of the Lady Evelyn candidate park. The branch also advanced a proposal for designating the Grays and Makobe rivers as a waterway park linked to the Lady Evelyn wilderness. The Grays, which flows into the Lady Evelyn, was within the area of the wilderness proposal, while only the very headwaters of the Makobe were so contained.[33] Ironically, the two MNR branches, the powerful Timber Branch and the weaker Lands and Parks Branch, seemed to be working at cross purposes right within the Temagami office. This was essentially what the Lady Evelyn alliance and other wilderness advocates had predicted.

Natural Resources Minister Alan Pope received the Monzon report, *Parks Systems Planning for Ontario*, in March 1982.[34] The report spoke favourably of the Lady Evelyn–Smoothwater Park and several other northern wilderness parks. Pope called upon those who believed in the importance of parks to attempt to prove their claim. Public meetings, often stormy, were numerous. The Lady Evelyn–Smoothwater proposal was widely supported by environmental and preservationist groups and criticized by the various forestry organizations.

In June 1982, the minister finally announced that the Lady Evelyn–Smoothwater Wilderness Park and five other proposed wilderness parks noted in the Monzon report would be added immediately to the Ontario park system. By the year 2000 park lands protected under the system would effectively be doubled. The efforts of the Lady Evelyn alliance and other wilderness advocates had proved fruitful. The renowned Trout Streams and the wildlands behind them would be withdrawn from commercial forestry, although at 29,300 acres (72,400 hectares), the park as approved was somewhat smaller than originally proposed. Road access remained a source of concern as the Liskeard Lumber Road, running south from Long Point on Highway 560 between Elk Lake and Gowganda and then diagonally through the park and across both branches of the Lady Evelyn River, was to remain open for resource-extraction purposes.[35]

Within a few weeks of Alan Pope's announcement concerning the Lady Evelyn park, the document *Temagami District Land Use Guidelines* was released. The guidelines dealt with cottage development, road access, and other environmental issues, and – most important for the long-term future of the district – with resource-production goals. MNR agreed that when the caution was lifted, it would proceed with dispersed, island-only cottage development. There would be no new access roads to Lake Temagami, and the Red Squirrel road off Highway 11 would continue to be closed to the public beyond Whitefish Bay. Lake Temagami's skyline reserve and the narrower shoreline reserves for Temagami and adjacent lakes were reconfirmed.[36] But these long-established sanctuaries were unilaterally down-graded in the MNR guidelines and described merely as 'areas of concern.' The lack of details concerning the extraction allowable within the former skyline and shoreline reserves rendered these areas more vulnerable. The possible sites for new cottage clusters on islands still held by the Crown were also not identified. MNR had already indicated that Municipal Affairs and Housing would take over responsibility for supervising residential development on patented land. Thus, the task of managing the evolution of the Temagami landscape within the framework of the guidelines remained a formidable challenge, particularly when new resource-production targets were considered.

In the 1983 guidelines for the Temagami district, MNR had renewed its commitment to sustained-yield forest management and had simultaneously called for an increase in the cutting of conifers from the current annual figure of 93,000 to 255,000 merchantable cubic metres by the year 2000. Furthermore, hardwood cutting was to increase by 400 per cent.[37] Higher production targets implied more road access to the heretofore remote central reaches of the Temagami Forest. Those concerned with other uses of this area demonstrated a determination to preserve what they regarded as vital parts of the diminishing wilderness. Thus once again the historic tension arose between timber extraction and the protection of northern Ontario's wilderness heritage. And again the Lady Evelyn area was the centre of controversy.

MNR proposed a westward extension of the Red Squirrel Lake Forest Access Road to link up with the Liskeard Lumber Road running south from Highway 560 across the recently established Lady Evelyn–Smoothwater Wilderness Park (see map 4). This would create a major arterial trunk line for the forest industry, giving access to relatively large quantities of mature mixed timber in Shelburne and adjacent townships and considerably to the west and north along what became known as the Pinetorch Corridor. The linkup would enable the Liskeard Lumber mill at Elk Lake to obtain logs from the Diamond Lake–Lake Temagami area. Milne Lumber in Temagami would gain direct access to mature pine and large spruce in Shelburne and Acadia townships.

Controversy over the proposed trunk road immediately brought into play most of the non-aboriginal interest that had been concerned for decades about the future of the Temagami country. In 1983 and 1984 MNR's district manager had surveyed and then cleared the 9.3-mile (15-kilometre) gap between the two roads. The new right-of-way began just south of Diamond Lake and continued westward into Shelburne Township, running alongside the main canoe route between Diamond and Wakimika lakes. Canoeists were alarmed by the presence of the work and by the impact of the road-building process, which left considerable debris and disorder.[38]

While clearing was underway in the Temagami district, the Ontario MNR was involved in the preparatory stages of the province-wide 'Class Environmental Assessment' concerning its timber-management policies. MNR's Temagami office intended to build the so-called 'extension' under an exemption order connected with the overall environmental assessment and after an informal public survey and internal review.[39] The launching of the clearing process in advance of these modest procedural checks neatly illustrated MNR's unfortunate tendency to minimize meaningful public involvement despite the evolution of public participation during the preceding fifteen years.

Shortly after he assumed office, Vincent Kerrio, the new minister of natural resources in David Peterson's minority government, agreed to the alternative 'bump-up' procedure with regard to the projected linking of the two roads. Thus, the proposal was redirected to an 'Individual Environmental Assessment' by which an MNR document would proceed after public input to the minister of the environment. The minister of the environment could then accept or reject the report, or call for a formal hearing before the Environmental Assessment Board of Ontario.

The various interests again geared up for conflict. Liskeard Lumber and the senior forest-management staff in MNR's Temagami office argued that the link was vital if logging in the area was to be increased and employment maintained in the surrounding communities. The canoeists, represented initially by the Association of Youth Camps (AYCTL) and Hap and Trudy Wilson of Smoothwater Outfitters, argued strongly that the trunk line and heavy truck traffic would severely reduce public enjoyment of the Temagami wilderness. Moreover, the canoeist lobby contended, the road constituted a fundamental violation of the spirit underlying the creation of the Lady Evelyn–Smoothwater Wilderness Park. MNR, which had postponed development of a master plan for the park in anticipation of the removal of the outstanding land caution, responded that a viable compromise in the form of a strictly enforced system of gates was available. MNR claimed that gates would prevent all but logging vehicles from crossing canoe routes along the inner portions of the trunk line. In light of previous experience with controlled access roadways in the area, few were convinced that the compromise was viable.

The significance of the road issue and the potential importance of the Temagami country in the long-term future of Ontario's wilderness attracted attention from outside the immediate vicinity. Soon, the Federation of Ontario Naturalists (FON), the Canadian Parks and Wilderness Society, and the Sierra Club joined local and provincial associations of canoeists in voicing opposition to the lumber road. On the other hand, following heavy lobbying from Liskeard Lumber and the Milne company, several municipal councils, including Elk Lake and Temagami, passed strongly worded resolutions favouring the link as a means to avert potential increases in regional unemployment. Then River Valley, which had coveted more direct access to the Lake Temagami and the Lady Evelyn interior for decades, as well as Sturgeon Falls and other communities immediately to the south of the district, entered the debate. They proposed northward extensions to one or two of the back roads linked to Highway 805 in order to form T-junctions with the proposed trunk roads.

The economic aspects of the conflict between the lumber and recreational interests intensified as a result of MNR's decision to close logging in Shelburne Township pending completion of the environmental assessment. Liskeard Lumber announced that it would be forced to shut down if the decision was not rescinded by the summer of 1987, and many Elk Lake residents blamed the canoeing lobby.

A draft environmental assessment report appeared in late September 1986.[40] On economic grounds it advocated both the road link and the Pinetorch Corridor offshoot under strict environmental controls and monitoring. The draft report acknowledged that one possible result of the road link could be that 'Canoeists and campers seeking back country "wilderness" experience may shift their activities to other parts of the region, elsewhere in Ontario or outside the province.' Consultants working on the assessment had estimated the gross income of the recreational/tourist sector at $8 million, of which $3.2 million was allegedly spent locally. In contrast the forest industry apparently contributed something in the order of $20 million to the economic activity. The forest industry provided 306 jobs in comparison with the equivalent of 175 in the recreational/tourist sector.[41]

Critics of MNR's plans formed the Temagami Wilderness Society (TWS) specifically to fight the road extension, to preserve the Lady Evelyn–Smoothwater Wilderness Park, and, generally, to campaign on behalf of wilderness values in the Temagami country. The TWS was the direct descendant of the Save Maple Mountain Committee and the Alliance for the Lady Evelyn Wilderness. The emergence of the TWS reflected serious public concern about the capacity of existing management structures to safeguard Temagami's wilderness heritage and to implement sustained-yield forestry.

Through the efforts of the TWS a longer-term and more general forest-management issue gradually surfaced. Was sustained-yield forestry actually being practised in the Temagami district? If so, on what basis? It was quietly being admitted that because of the shortcomings of past management practices there would probably be – in about twenty years – a long hiatus in pine cutting before recently planted and regenerating stands matured. Arithmetic might indicate a long-term theoretical sustained-yield future in pine, but not sustained delivery levels or stable employment. In this context the question did arise as to whether the virgin pine around Shelburne Township should be cut quickly.[42]

Then in late November 1986, largely through the efforts of the FON, the International Union for the Conservation of Nature and Natural Resources in Geneva placed the Lady Evelyn–Smoothwater Wilderness Park on its endangered parks list because of the proposed opening of the trunk road. Ontario's citizens, argued Don Huff of the FON, 'do not recognize the value of this park, but people who look at it from Switzerland and Africa classify it as being as important as poaching rhinos in Africa and ask why we are being so stupid?'[43]

In spring 1987, MNR submitted its final environmental assessment document – essentially unchanged from the draft – to the Ministry of the Environment, only to see the proposal attract greater public interest and become gradually enmeshed in the anticipated provincial election. Involvement of prominent Canadians (including writers Margaret Atwood, Timothy Findley, and M.T. Kelly, and wildlife artist Robert Bateman) in the Temagami controversy raised the profile of the issues and may have alerted the premier and other provincial officials to the potential political impact of the simmering dispute. A controversy concerning development on the Queen Charlotte Islands off Canada's west coast had become the subject of national interest, and there were enough points of comparison with Temagami to signal the importance of proceeding carefully, if at all, with road expansion.

For its part, the TWS now promoted the concept of a wildlands reserve between the existing wilderness park and Lake Temagami. The proposed designation would preclude further road construction and would entail a gradual phasing out of lumber operations. Local community councils and the lumber industry reacted bitterly to what they perceived as a direct threat to future employment.

In an attempt to mollify both sides of the increasingly intense debate just before September's provincial election, Natural Resources Minister Kerrio ordered a stop to any northward extension of the Obabika (or Delhi) road toward the site of a possible T-junction with the east-west link MNR hoped to complete. Kerrio also authorized Milne Lumber to cut pine in the narrow corridor between Gull Lake and Lake Temagami and to tow logs across the main lake. Despite this arrangement, Milne temporarily closed its Temagami mill later in the fall.[44]

To defuse a complex and highly volatile situation, the province established a citizens' advisory committee, the 'Temagami Area Working Group,' chaired by John Daniel, president of Laurentian University in Sudbury, to report to the minister of natural resources on land-use questions, including the proposed wildlands reserve and road extensions. But polarization had increased, and Daniel himself is reported both to have expressed concern that people who are not satisfied with MNR decisions 'take the political back door' and to have indicated that the appointment of the committee was 'probably not a very good idea.' Public hearings in Elk Lake and Temagami were comparatively uneventful, but in North Bay the emotional intensity increased. A spokesman for the Ontario Federation of Anglers and Hunters, a group concerned that public road access would be restricted in a wildlands reserve, suggested that violence was not unlikely. 'We've had people saying that if this [proposal] goes through, we are going to burn down tourist establishments. We've been fortunate so far in Ontario that we have not had that. However, if it's carried out, I really don't think that with the masses of people out there, the Ontario government will be able to prevent it.' Daniel's decision not to hold hearings in southern Ontario on the grounds that 'you have to weigh people's views by the importance that it represents to their own life' outraged provincial environmental groups and threatened to undermine the credibility of the working group's efforts.[45]

Daniel's own proposals for reconciling the divergent interests of the resource developers, anglers and hunters, local communities, cottagers, and conservationists represented on his committee were presented to the minister of natural resources in March 1988. Daniel's recommendations were premised on one central finding of the inquiry process: 'The [Temagami] area includes so many special features that it should be managed as a model area for forestry, recreation, earth and life science features and tourism that Ontario could hold up to the world.'

Unfortunately, but perhaps not surprisingly, more detailed measures to accomplish the objective failed to win the support of working group members. Dissenters, described by Daniel as 'going for the jackpot,' ultimately ensured that no clear direction would be offered to the minister. Industry representatives, the anglers and hunters, and the mayors of Elk Lake and Sturgeon Falls felt that the Daniel proposals placed excessive restrictions on logging and failed to provide road access for local sportsmen. Recreational and conservationist elements on the working group judged that the level of logging Daniel would have permitted around the Lady Evelyn–Smoothwater Wilderness Park would effectively undermine or preclude enjoyment by appreciative users. As the *Globe and Mail* observed. 'There is a basic incompatibility between telling one group it can admire the trees and animals and another group it can cut them down and shoot them.'

The Ontario government moved comparatively quickly, following the presentation of the Working Group's conclusions, to reject the creation of a wildlands reserve or buffer zone around the park, while the minister of the environment rejected an environmental assessment hearing into the Red Squirrel road extension on the grounds of undue delay. To lessen the adverse political implications for its relations with Ontario environmentalists, the provincial government announced the creation of fifty-three new provincial parks at the same time that the disheartening Temagami decisions were made public. As Margaret Marland, Conservative opposition critic in the Legislature, aptly remarked: 'This is akin to giving a child candy while stealing their tricycle.'[46]

The Ontario government's action deterred neither environmental interests nor the Teme-augama Anishnabai in their efforts to preserve the Temagami wilderness. For its part the TWS initiated a legal challenge to the minister of the environment's acceptance of the Red Squirrel environmental assessment. The group argued that in light of the number of requests for further review of the proposed development the minister had exceeded his statutory authority in denying a public hearing as contemplated in the Environmental Assessment Act. In addition the TWS directly challenged the validity of MNR's environmental assessment, relying in part on criticisms made by the consultants who had carried out the original inquiry into the impact of the road proposal.

The Temagami Indians had also recognized the severity of the latest commercial intrusion into their ancestral homeland. The Teme-augama Anishnabai established an encampment along the proposed route of the road extension. Thus in the absence of a comprehensive settlement or provincial willingness to provoke direct confrontation, the development was – at least temporarily – forestalled.[47]

As controversy was unfolding in the interior, the TLA-TRSI had continued to press for a joint planning authority responsible for as wide an extent of territory as possible in and around the Temagami lakes. With the encouragement of Municipal Affairs and Housing and the formal approval of the Temagami Township Council, a joint steering committee composed of representatives from the township and from the various groups on the lake began regular meetings in 1981 to work out operational details for such an authority.

MNR successfully endeavoured to restrict the geographic scope of the new board's authority to the organized township, the islands of Lake Temagami (other than Bear Island), and any privately held mainland properties. The Township of Temagami, which included Temagami Island and most of the islands in the Northeast Arm, had its own planning by-law by the time the Temagami Planning Board came into existence in the fall of 1983. It was necessary, therefore, to integrate the rules for the township into the wider plan. This was accomplished in part through the composition of the planning board, which included several township appointees along with ministerial appointees who were nominated by the user groups – the TLA, the permanent residents, the lodge operators, and the Association of Youth Camps.

The ultimate power of the new Temagami Planning Board in its ongoing and future relationship with MNR remained unclear. There were those who still saw the ministry's district manager as a direct descendant of the District Office of the British imperial tradition. Nevertheless, the establishment of the board represented a significant victory for many people who lived in the central portion of the Temagami country. Diverse – even conflicting – local interests would have a major influence on the rate and nature of development. This was a measure of the successful struggle begun with the TLA *coup d'état* in 1971 and aided by the stalemate that the caution had produced. In a move that foreshadowed its rejection of Ontario's later land-claims settlement offer, the Bear Island band declined an invitation to be represented on the planning board as minority participants in a management process that would affect their ancestral lands.[48]

In February 1984 the new board selected contractual advisers to help draw up an official plan.[49] They reported that the populations of the old village and Temagami North now were roughly the same, 450 and 438 respectively. Just under 350 people were resident elsewhere within the township boundaries, not including the occupants of the 1,254 islands in the lake's more than five hundred cottages, twelve commercial lodges, and nine youth camps, which accommodated 900 staff and campers. The two principal employers of the district, Sherman Mine and Milne Lumber, employed 455 and 154 people respectively, many of them commuters from elsewhere along the Highway 11 corridor. Diminished prospects for the resource sector were reflected in statistics. Whereas in 1971 there were four lumber companies and two mines in the planning area, only one operation remained in each sector; total employment in the two sectors had dropped by 216 persons. The Sherman Mine had recently experienced annual shutdowns of several weeks' duration due to low demand; it now had a life expectancy of only ten to twenty years. Milne had also begun to adjust to changing wood-supply conditions.[50] Social and economic information of this nature along with data about water quality and other environmental features was essential for planning purposes, but sensitive issues of judgment were also central. This was nowhere more evident than in the issue of visual impact, for aesthetic considerations had been controversial around the lake from at least the era of the original skyline reserve.

Recent American literature on landscape planning identified form, line, colour, and texture as the key elements comprising the visual character of an area. The more varied the landscape, the more 'pleasing' it was found to be, particularly where harmony was also displayed. Consultants attempted to apply these ideas to Lake Temagami. In order to preserve 'the existing mosaic' of landscapes, great care would be required. Planning should identify stretches of pristine shoreline that could best be appreciated 'at a slow pace, i.e., fishing, canoeing, picnicking and hiking' and should ensure that development did not take place in these landscapes. New cottages or camps should appear in areas that were already 'semi-modified' and their impact curtailed by careful spacing, set-backs, and aesthetically pleasing earth-toned buildings.[51] However difficult it would be to implement and maintain the process proposed, the consultants' study had provided the first clear statement of comprehensive principles designed to reconcile the competing claims of preservation, conservation, and development in a 'managed' wilderness.

The long-overdue facelift of Temagami village proceeded at a considerable pace. The township acquired the harbourfront property of the old Ontario Northland Boat Lines and tore down the dilapidated sheds. New docks and landscaping and decorating in this area and on nearby Forestry Island produced a significant change in the community's overall appearance. Prospects for further development nearby at the Gillies Townsite on Cassels Lake heightened a strong local sense that a new surge in recreational use could now be expected.

The Cassels Lake property – more than five hundred acres in all – had been sold to Gillies Brothers in 1948 and subsequently transferred to Consolidated Bathurst. With a lake frontage of approximately five miles (eight kilometres), the largest private holding in the vicinity represented a major opportunity for commercial development. By mid–1987 planning was underway for an initial development of seventy-five one-acre lots.[52] As the Cassels proposal came before the now fully functioning planning board, it appeared that, once again, the policy of moderate expansion in recreational activity and of measured growth in 'user-days' had been undermined by unanticipated private initiatives. Possibly though, the Cassels development would take some pressure off Lake Temagami and compensate for the employment lost through the continuing decline of the lumber and mining industries.

The challenges of land management in the Temagami wilderness in the eighties had evolved directly from those of earlier years. The enduring problems included the continued deficiencies in forest-management practices, the challenge to the back country of more and more access roads for resource extraction, and the problem of reconciling a desire for increased recreational use with the need to restrain development on the main lake if the recreational experience was to remain worthwhile. The insecure position of the Teme-augama Anishnabai both with regard to their historic claim for a viable land base and the increasingly prominent issue of self-government remained a central element on the local agenda. The ominous long-term threat of widespread devastation from acid rain added a further dimension to the complexities facing planners and residents of the district. Lake Temagami's condition had deteriorated, according to the Ministry of the Environment, and nearby lakes such as Diamond, Smoothwater, and Makobe had already reached levels of 'extreme sensitivity.'[53] Thus, many outside forces continued to press in upon the land and the people of Temagami. To an unprecedented degree, developments within the area – notably the land-claims controversy, forest management, and wilderness protection – now also had external repercussions.

Epilogue

In the late 1980s, loons – whose numbers around Temagami were seriously threatened in the preceding decade – were calling again. Other formerly diminished species were also recovering, in the case of the beaver to levels perhaps higher than in the early days of the fur trade. Trout were still found in the deep waters of Lake Temagami, and small pickerel were coming back with the assistance of an active restocking program. In parts of the old forest reserve the appeal of the pine landscape and the challenge of fast-flowing rivers remained much as it had when the first recreational visitors arrived in the late nineteenth century. Indeed, estimates by MNR suggested that canoeists' use of the district increased more than 60 per cent in the decade after 1975.[1] Under clear blue skies hardy winter visitors can continue to enjoy the pure white northern snow. These aspects of the Temagami experience thus survive, albeit precariously in the face of threats from the latest series of proposals for resource development. The situation is neither accidental nor the product of any clear and sustained intent.

For the past century, since the time of surveyors' reports on the resource prospects of the district, the processes of occupation and settlement by non-aboriginal people and the patterns of forest use and land management have been conditioned by a complex interplay between local interests and more distant influences. The strength of the aboriginal community, the resource industries, and recreational interests in determining the fate of the landscape at any given time has been a combination of the local and the external support for these perspectives.

Viewed historically, the varied and often conflicting objectives of the several constituencies interested in the landscape and resources of Temagami have preserved or been forced to preserve a balance. As a result of the determination of the various groups interested in the Temagami environment, as well as moderation, compromise, and on occasion neglect, no group has been able to sustain a position of exclusive dominance over the pattern of development. Despite intermittent conflict and tension among divergent groups and despite very different values, severe clashes were generally minimized or avoided – at least until recent years. Whether or by what means the historic balance between these groups with respect to their relations to each other and to the environment will be maintained now remains to be determined. Some combination of historical perspective and awareness of contemporary concerns in resource management may offer insight into the challenges ahead.

Early in the twentieth century the Ontario government designated Temagami, regarded at the time as primary pine land, as a forest reserve with the stated intention that sustained-yield forest management might be implemented there under the direction of professional foresters. The success of sustained yield appeared to depend on two essential elements. First, it was necessary to control alternative land uses insofar as they were perceived to be inconsistent with the goal of timber production. Second, as foresters, senior Crown lands officials, and members of the Canadian Forestry Association recognized at the turn of the century, consistent and continuous supervision of the forests was required to produce a reliable inventory and assessment. As well, a determined effort was needed to monitor or perhaps even to assist the regeneration process as it was then understood and to implement an orderly program for cutting mature trees. At Temagami, the pre-eminent pinery of the original forest reserve system, neither requirement for success was met. Thus in practice the Temagami Forest Reserve served several constituencies: extractive resource industries, a range of recreational interests, and a resident population that included the long-established native community. The relative importance of the varied uses could be regarded as a matter of some debate, even though pine production remained the principal purpose of the forest from an official perspective.

Ontario's failure to achieve a sustained-yield forest-management program for Temagami and elsewhere in the extensive system of forest reserves may be accounted for in several ways. Despite an initial burst of enthusiasm, sustained yield in forest reserves was not a public objective supported by firm political will at the provincial level. The major lumber interests of the Ottawa valley, professional foresters, and Ontario Liberal politicians who governed until 1905 backed the conservation policy but never secured popular approval in the way in which public ownership of hydroelectric power captured the imagination of the community. Smaller lumber firms, conscious of their unstable tenure on Crown domain, generally ignored conservation. But the presence of competing uses, notably canoeists and cottagers – who may be regarded as the forerunners of the more recent environmentalists – hardly interfered seriously with forest management if such management had actually been a clear provincial purpose. If anything, the presence of the recreational interests served to moderate the manner and pace of forest cutting in such a way that later generations have been given an opportunity to revisit the issue of sustained yield with the benefit of further knowledge of the scientific principles involved and with greater understanding of the risks of continued failure.

Fire is vital to the natural processes of white and red pine regeneration. Before the creation of the forest reserve, most fire in the pine belt killed some pine but did not permanently damage all or even most of the larger and more mature white pine, while it destroyed the deciduous underbrush, small trees and even the coniferous competition such as spruce and balsam. 'Shocked' by fire, the surviving pines produced an extra heavy crop of seeds the next year. Unlike jack pine, white pine does not need fire to germinate – though it certainly is important for the red. After they fall to the forest floor, if there is room and nourishment, the open cones of the white pine will allow the seeds to germinate and new growth will begin. The question remains: will the white pine seedlings survive? This is where fire, the absence of heavy competition, and shade determine the result.

The second crucial ingredient after fire is shade. Red pine is intolerant to shade (and thus generally grows in pure stands). White pine will tolerate and even thrive on light shade. Both species need sunshine. If young white pine have no shade in hot weather, the trees are usually killed off by insects. Too much shade will also kill white pine. Hazelnut, poplar, and other deciduous bushes and trees, along with balsam and white spruce, will grow faster under thick mature pine and kill off the very young pine seedlings. In mature stands of red pine, the underbrush is choked off, and a thick mat of nutrients, including rich needles, accumulates. Fire kills the underbrush and a lot of big trees, but ordinarily leaves some to produce cones for the future. Following germination, sunlight penetrates briefly and the stand is renewed –

unless the unburned trees are too old to produce or other species move in too vigorously.[2]

Government efforts over the last century have largely curtailed the extent of forest fires in the Temagami country. In this respect, as forest industry representatives are quick to point out, the wilderness is gone. But intervention to control fire was never accompanied by sufficient intervention in planting and harvesting techniques to ensure sustained-yield pine forestry. The replacement of red and white pine did not keep pace with cutting, especially in the mixed stands of forest that became the common focus for timber operations while Ontario continued to receive significant income from the resource.[3] Recently, attention shifted more and more to jack pine and spruce and to their regeneration, and even to fast-growing hardwoods such as poplar, which locally is never replanted.[4] Based on presumed market requirements and alleged oversupply of overmature stands of these species, the 1983 *Temagami District Land Use Guidelines* called for a dramatic increase – almost 200 per cent – in the cutting of conifers in the Temagami district by the year 2000, from 93,000 net merchantable cubic metres to 255,000, and even more of hardwoods, from 24,000 to 125,000.[5] Increases are also forecast in portions of the Temagami country within the Kirkland Lake and Gogama districts.

In a well-documented critique entitled *Forest Management in N'Daki Menan*,[6] C.A. Benson argued in 1982 that the cutting level was already too high, that MNR calculations based on a 'low intensity provincial ground survey' and faulty methodology had sadly overestimated the usual local yield per acre, and that the land base of the commercial forest was declining rapidly. In Benson's view, the ministry had underestimated the age when pine became overmature and therefore underestimated the rotation age. It was overly optimistic and outdated in its views on natural regeneration without fire and was determining the size of the allowable cut to suit the perceived needs of local industry rather than considering the ecological reality. The goal of 'continuous social and economic benefit' for the Temagami country, and indeed all Ontario, so clearly affirmed by planners was not being pursued. Modified harvest cutting methods and more site-selective methods 'such as strip cuts, selection cuts and shortwood cutting would reduce runoff, erosion, and leaching problems' and sustain 'the potential for an increase in wildlife abundance.' Comparing the Ontario forestry situation unfavourably with that of Finland and Sweden, Benson concluded: 'To retain the quality of the water, fish and wildlife, and timber, it may be necessary to either raise the cost of using the environment, the timber, wildlife, etc., or to subsidize the cost of maintaining it.'[7]

Late in the summer of 1986, the Ministry of Natural Resources received yet another report on the state of forest management in Ontario.[8] Prepared by Gordon L. Baskerville, dean of forestry at the University of New Brunswick, *An Audit of Management of the Crown Forests of Ontario* contains a severe critique of the Ontario Crown forest administration system.

Baskerville concluded that, while adequate, the basic structure of forest management across Ontario was not being used effectively. Management plans were 'so general as to defy evaluation.' Baskerville suggested that the existing management plans were assembled like a 'cookbook' – the right topics, but no 'application of intellect.' Objectives for forest management required urgent attention, for the vague principles of 'goodness' so routinely enunciated were typically accompanied by 'little technical substance, or biological and logistical realism.' These observations echoed Benson's assessment of the Temagami forest in its various forms of organization throughout the twentieth century.

The Baskerville report's account of MNR's integration of timber and non-timber uses was especially damning:

> The approach used to integration of timber with non-timber values is based on local judgement with no objectively measurable standards ... The approach to discovering public opinion about planning issues is open, but it is being used to justify actions (or inactions) rather than to determine what values the public expect from the resource so that management can be designed to achieve those values to the extent possible.

'Much of the planning material in this area,' Baskerville continued, 'would be better described as creative writing about the resource than as a realistic attempt to control resource development over time to achieve objectively stated values.'[9] Again, Baskerville's conclusions reflecting his survey of the province as a whole are well illustrated in the details of the Temagami experience of the past decades. The absence of historically consistent (or at least comparable) standards for the management of the Temagami forest has made it virtually impossible for interested citizens to hold public officials accountable for their performance. Accordingly, MNR and its predecessors have enjoyed a broad discretionary authority over land use while the provincial government's constitutional responsibility for natural resources in the province has largely been exercised by accommodating local producer interests.

It is an ironic consequence of the events of the preceding decades that the failure of the provincial government to devise and pursue a coherent strategy to sustain forest production on a continuous basis in the Temagami district made the presence of alternative uses that much more contentious and difficult to administer.[10] Increasingly, resource use practices such as clear cutting and the proliferation of permanent roadways have undermined the enjoyment of the Temagami country by its seasonal occupants and by the native population, whose status has remained precarious. Had efforts been made to devise and implement the kind of forestry management envisaged in general terms almost a century ago, by Aubrey White and his contemporaries, and to offer some rational or predictable pattern for the extractive industries, several of the more prolonged clashes of recent years might have been avoided. But performance standards have never been clearly established. Appreciative users who have been encouraged by government to enjoy Temagami since the turn of the century sought some indication that their long-term interests in the quality of the landscape would be respected.[11] Native residents sought the modest social and economic goals of a secure land base, dignity, and identity, which have come now to entail a role in management of the surrounding territory and its resources. Their patient insistence merited a respectful response from Ontario long before Ian Scott's hopeful initiative in 1986.

In the absence of provincial acknowledgment of the legitimacy of the aboriginal and non-extractive interests, relatively minor conflicts have gradually escalated, in the cases of the Lady Evelyn wilderness and Red Squirrel road, into a major confrontation on basic principles. The lack of an environmentally sound plan for forest use offering some certainty of continuous employment at a sustainable level for inhabitants of the region engaged in the lumber industry has increasingly forced its representatives into the trenches each time a specific management issue arose. The dangerous dichotomy between environment and employment is thus intensified.

During the 1970s the position of the various interests concerned with the future of Temagami hardened significantly. Environmentalists responded to the threats to wilderness posed by new resource activity, roadways, and grandiose commercial resort proposals with the awareness that throughout North America other local groups were engaged in similar causes. The Temagami Indians finally lost patience with their situation and undertook legal action to enforce aboriginal claims, as did other native communities across Canada in the wake of the federal White Paper on Indian policy and the landmark Nishga decision on aboriginal rights in the Supreme Court of Canada. The forest industries of the district, both lumber and pulp and paper, campaigned vigorously for access to new resources in the forest, including remote areas previously beyond easy water access or sheltered within shoreline and skyline reserves.

More than in any previous period, the various communities interested in the use and future of Temagami have had to address each other's concerns. Tentative alliances between members of the recreational community and the Temagami Indians have formed and been tested. Resource interests and environmentalists have engaged – only intermittently, it must be said – in an exchange of views, and inconclusive dialogue between senior Ontario government and native representatives is occasionally pursued. As the pace of extractive development has intensified, however, the issues that divide directly interested parties from each other and from decision makers have become more visible and contentious. Thus, the resource-management issues of the Temagami Forest, a territory described by HBC post manager James Hackland in 1857 as a 'most wretched' place, have recently entered the news with considerable frequency. National newspaper and television coverage of an Indian road block along the route of the proposed extension of the Red Squirrel road and of forestry workers and municipal councillors obstructing Labour Day traffic on the Lake Temagami Access Road to protest the construction delays dramatized the potential for severe discord.[12] The latter protest was short-lived, but on behalf of the provincial government Attorney-General Ian Scott eventually decided to seek a court injunction to remove the Indian barricades. The Indian community removed the road block in compliance with a court order that simultaneously prohibited Ontario and the lumber interests from undertaking further road construction, pending a hearing of the land claims appeal.

As these pages were being revised for the final time, the Milne lumber company – allegedly unable to obtain secure access to long-term supplies of Ontario timber – lost its financing and was forced into receivership. This development, together with the township council's decision to withdraw permanently from the planning board, has further widened the chasm between the people of the village and those of the lake. Some popular media and local authorities attributed Milne's problem of timber supplies to the pressure of the environmental lobby and the recalcitrance of the Temagami Indians. But the forest has declined in quality during the almost ninety years since it has been under provincial management; Milne has been operating in the area for most of that time and has observed the fate of Temagami pine. With or without the environmentalists, the Indians, and new roads, a serious interruption in pine cutting was no more than a few years away. As for the aboriginal land claim, the Ontario Court of Appeal is scheduled to hear arguments on behalf of the Teme-augama Anishnabai and the Ontario government early in 1989.[13]

Issues once perceived as local have merged rapidly with the global resource-management challenges of 'sustainable development' as outlined for the United Nations in *Our Common Future*, the report of the World Commission on Environment and Development.[14] Led by Chief Gary Potts, Temagami's original inhabitants, the Teme-augama Anishnabai, have declared the N'Daki Menan to be 'an experimental outdoor laboratory for 400 years' and resolved 'that the management plan for our Motherland for thousands of years to come, be finalized in the year 2387.'[15] Their vision – whatever else it may do – should help to put our collective responsibility for the Temagami country in perspective. The measure of success may well be that, like the original human inhabitants of the area, we too will some day be understood by future generations in Temagami to have lived in 'time immemorial.'

Appendices

A. Ontario's Chief Forestry Officers at Temagami*

L. Loughren 1901–6
S.C. MacDonald 1906–9
G. Clarence Hindson 1909–34
Wilfred Eckersley 1934–5
Major J.H. Bliss 1935–42
Philip Hoffman 1942–60
W.A. O'Donnell 1960–3
John Rumney 1963–80
Robert B. McGee 1980–5
James L. Hamill 1985–7
Warren Evershed 1987 (Acting)
Robert Griffith 1987–

---

*Titles vary: Superintending Ranger, Chief Ranger, District Forester, and, since 1972, District Manager

B. Presidents of the Temagami Lakes Association**

Robert B. Newcomb 1931–5
Frank R. Todd 1935–7
George C. Ames 1937–late forties
Harold Shannon late forties
Charles Earl Rodgers late forties–1961
Dewey Desrosiers 1961–71
Ron Johnstone 1971–3
Phil Greey 1973–4
Bill Allen 1974–5
Gordon Lak 1975–7
Tim (Gordon) Gooderham 1977–9
Bruce W. Hodgins 1979–81
Jack Glenn 1981–3
Bill Allen 1983–4
Ted Underwood 1984–6
Graeme Thompson 1986–7
Tom Romans 1987–

C. Chiefs of the Teme-augama Anishnabai, 1820–1988†

Head Chief		Second Chief
Enene (d. c. 1835)	c.1820–32	Wabbacou (or Wabimakwa, the White Bear, d. 1870)
Nebanegwune (son of Enene, d. 1884)	c.1832–55	Kekek (or Kakaka)
Kekek (d. 1868)	c.1855–68	Kabimigwune (eldest son of White Bear, d. 1880)
Kanecic (or Kanecjc or Cana Chintz, second son of White Bear, d. 1878)	c.1868–78	Tonené (eldest son of Kabinigwune and son-in-law of Nebanegwune)
Tonené	1878–88	Mathias (son of Nebanegwune, d. 1887 or 1888)
John Paul (Odakawasigewini, d. 1893)	1888–93	Frank White Bear (brother of Tonené)

**Originally the Temagami Association

†Compiled from various documents and expert testimony in the Temagami Trial Proceedings with assistance from James Morrison, former senior historical researcher for the Teme-augama Anishnabai

Appendix C (cont'd)

Head Chief		Second Chief
Tonené (continued before and after second term as honorary 'life chief,' d. 1916)	1893–1910	Frank White Bear
Frank White Bear (d. 1930)	1910–c.25	Aleck Paul (d. 1964)
William Peshabo	c.1925–35	Aleck Mathias
Aleck Mathias (d. 1939)	1935–9	Tom Potts (d. 1973)
John Twain (d. 1964)	1939–64	Frank Katt
Bill Twain	1964–71	During most of the sixties and seventies Laura McKenzie (Moore, d. 1979) served as 'First Councillor.' Then in 1980, Douglas McKenzie became first councillor; since 1978 Rita O'Sullivan (Moore) has served as second chief, elected by the tribal council.
George Mathias	1971–2	
Gary Potts	1972–	

Notes

Abbreviations Used in Notes

AO / Archives of Ontario
AO, Temagamingue / AO, Fur Trade Papers, HBC Temiskaming District, Temagamingue
Barlow, *Report 1899* / GSC, *Annual Report*, New Series, 10 (1897, Ottawa 1899), A.E. Barlow, Report 1 (*Report on the Geology and Natural Resources of the Area Included by the Nipissing and Temiskaming Map-Sheets*)
Bear Island Trial Decision / 'Attorney-General for Ontario *v.* Bear Island Foundation et al. Potts et al. *v.* Attorney-General for Ontario,' *Ontario Reports*, vol. 49 (Second Series, 353–490, [High Court of Justice,] 11 December 1984)
BTB / Ontario Burnt Timber Books
DLF / Ontario, Department of Lands and Forests
GSC / Geological Survey of Canada
HBC Archives / Hudson's Bay Company Archives
HBC, Temagami Post Journal / HBC Archives B488/a/1, Temagami Post Journals
Indian Affairs, Temagami / PAC, RG10, Vol. 7757, files 27043–9
LFM / Ontario, Department of Lands, Forests and Mines
MNR / Ontario, Ministry of Natural Resources
OBM / Ontario, Bureau of Mines
ODM / Ontario, Department of Mines
PAC / Public Archives of Canada
PAC, Timagami Post Journal / PAC, MG19, D21, Timagami Post Journals
Timber Commission / Ontario, *Royal Commission to Investigate and Report*

upon the Accuracy or Otherwise of All Returns Made Pursuant to the Crown Timber Act, Section 14, by Any Holder of a Timber License (1922)

TTP (Temagami Trial Proceedings) / Transcripts of the proceedings in the Bear Island Trial Decision (68 vols, unpublished), Bear Island Library, Lake Temagami

1 The Homeland and Its People

1 Craig Macdonald, 'The Nastawgan: Traditional Routes of Travel in the Temagami District,' in Bruce W. Hodgins and Margaret Hobbs, eds, *Nastawgan: The Canadian North by Canoe and Snowshoe* (Weston, Ont., 1985)

2 A. Boissonneau, 'Glacial History of Northeastern Ontario, II, The Timiskaming-Algoma Area,' *Canadian Journal of Earth Sciences*, 5 (1968), 97–109; V.K. Prest, 'Quarternary Geology of Canada,' ch. 12 in R.J.W. Douglas, ed., *Geology and Economic Minerals of Canada*, Geological Survey of Canada, Economic Geology Report No. 1 (Ottawa: Energy, Mines and Resources 1976), 675–764; John William Pollock, 'Ecological Perspective,' ch. 2 in his *The Culture History of Kirkland Lake District, Northeastern Ontario*, field work 1972, 1973, National Museum of Man, Mercury Series, Archaeological Survey of Canada, no. 54 (Ottawa 1976), 8–20; and Larry E. Hodgins, 'Economic Geography of the Lake Timagami District' (BA diss., University of Toronto 1958), 1–13

3 Prest, 'Quarternary Geology,' 714–25

4 C.A. Benson, *Forest Management in N'Daki Menan of the Teme-Augama Anishnabai* (May 1982), np, and his testimony at the Temagami Trial Proceedings (see n6 below), 6254–360. Henry A. Wright and Arthur W. Bailey, 'Red and White Pine,' ch. 13 in their *Fire Ecology: United States and Southern Canada* (New York 1982), 328–48

5 Thor Conway, *Archeology in Northeastern Ontario: Searching for Our Past* (Toronto: Ontario Ministry of Culture and Recreation 1981), 4

6 The judgment of Mr Justice Steele in the Bear Island Trial Decision is based on the evidence of twenty-seven expert witnesses, including anthropologists, historians, and other researchers whose testimony is recorded in the sixty-eight (unpublished) volumes of the trial proceedings.

7 Dean Knight, 'Montreal River Site,' primary research 1969, and 'Montreal River Salvage Project Progress Report,' primary research 1972, National Museum of Man, Archaeological Survey of Canada, nos 53, 899 (Ottawa 1970, 1972); Pollock, *Culture History of Kirkland Lake District*; Thor Conway, 'The Witch Point Site, Lake Temagami,' *Temagami Times* (Winter 1982), 5–6; Conway *Archeology in Northeastern Ontario*, esp. 46; record of Conway's testimony at the TTP.

8 TTP, Craig Macdonald, 4066; and Kirk Wipper, 2600

9 TTP, various witnesses

10 TTP, Macdonald, 4089, 4213, 4259–60, 4377, 4387–9, 4409. 'Maple Sugar may have been "post contact."'
11 F.G. Speck, *Myths and Folk-lore of the Timiskaming, Algonquin and Timagami Ojibwa* GSC, Memoir 71 (Ottawa 1915); TTP, J. Morrison, 8050, and Macdonald, 4421
12 TTP, Charles Bishop, 146, 210, 253
13 TTP, Conway, 1866–81, and 1937–9 and Macdonald, 4107, 4121, 4149. The argument that animal conservation predated the fur trade is strenuously attacked by Charles Bishop (at the TTP and elsewhere), who argues that fur-bearing animals were hunted out three times in the Historic period by the inhabitants of the Temagami country. Calvin Martin, in *Keepers of the Game: Indian-Animal Relations and the Fur Trade* (Berkeley, Ca., 1978), argues that the Algonkian-speaking Indians of eastern North America declared religious war on the animals, blaming them for the diseases brought in by the white man. This argument has not gone unchallenged. Note Shepard Krech, ed., *Indians, Animals and the Fur Trade: A Critique of Keepers of the Game* (Athens, Ga., 1981).
14 TTP, Conway
15 TTP, Morrison, 8214
16 TTP, Morrison calls it a 'process of great antiquity,' 8214
17 TTP, Edward S. Rogers, 2869. Note his three publications on the *Mistassini Crees*, 1963, 1967, and 1973, National Museum of Man, *Bulletin*, nos 195, 218, and *Ethnology*, 5.
18 TTP, Morrison, 7233–5 (quotation), Macdonald, 4436, and Rogers, 3104
19 F.G. Speck, *Family Hunting Territories and Social Life of Various Algonkian Bands of the Ottawa Valley*, GSC, Memoir 70 (Ottawa: Department of Mines 1915), 18; and TTP Rogers, 3404, Morrison, 7658, 8216, Macdonald, 7233–4; Conway, 2048
20 TTP, Rogers, 3104
21 Pollock, *Culture History of Kirkland Lake District*, 190–1
22 Speck, *Family Hunting Territories*, 20–2
23 TTP, Morrison, 8065
24 TTP, Rogers, 3013. In dissent, Bishop argues that around 1690 Timiskaming posts were feeding the starving Indians, and that after 1800 Timiskaming Indians had become dependent on trade items such as knives, blankets, and guns. TTP, 193
25 TTP, Morrison, 8119–20, citation from the Matawagamingue Post Journal 1889, HBC Archives, Winnipeg
26 Daniel Francis and Toby Morantz, *Partners in Furs: A History of the Fur Trade in Eastern James Bay 1600 –1870* (Kingston 1983), 96
27 TTP, Rogers, 2892, and Morrison, 8081. Note also Abraham Rotstein, 'Fur Trade and Empire: An Institutional Analysis' (PHD diss., University of Toronto 1967), and Christopher L. Miller and George R. Hamell, 'A New Perspective on Indian-White Contact: Cultural Symbols and Colonial Trade,' *Journal of American History*, 73, no. 2 (September 1986), 311–28

28 H.P. Biggar, ed., *Champlain's Works*, Champlain Society, New Series (Toronto 1922–36), vol. 3, 41–2

29 R.G. Twaites, ed., *The Jesuit Relations and Allied Documents*, 73 vols (Cleveland 1886–1901), vol. 18, Relation of 1640, 229; or *Rélations des Jesuites* (Montreal 1972), vol. 2, Rélation de 1640, 34

30 Conrad Heidenreich argues that this merely shows French confusion about 'Northern Algonkians,' whereas Bishop contends that the maps show the dispersal of the original Temagami population. TTP, Heidenreich, 3796, Bishop, 125–41; and note Macdonald, 4444, and W.J. Eccles, 5024–9

31 TTP, Heidenreich, 3679–86

32 TTP, Rogers, 2917. Bishop expresses the view that disease probably went north with the Nipissings, allegedly helping to wipe out the original Outimagami. TTP, 232–6

33 W.J. Eccles, *France in America* (Toronto 1972); Conrad Heidenreich, *Huronia: A History and Geography of the Huron Indians, 1600–1650* (Toronto 1973); Bruce Trigger, *The Children of Aataentsic: A History of the Huron People to 1660*, 2 vols (Montreal 1976); and Donald Smith, TTP, 4660–9

34 Eccles, *France in America*, 45, 66–7; his *Canada under Louis XIV, 1663–1701* (Toronto 1956), 42–6; and Francis and Morantz, *Partners in Furs*, 18–22

35 *Rélations des Jesuites*, Rél. de 1667, 24–6, and George F. Hunt, *The War of the Iroquois* (Madison, Wis., 1940), 106

36 Thor Conway, 'Temagami Oral History Relating to the Iroquois,' draft dated October 1982 in *Temagami Times* (Spring 1983), 21–3

37 Bishop discounts all this and claims that any Algonkian-speaking people left in the area by 1660 'would have fled' the Iroquois threat. TTP, 243. But note TTP, Eccles, 5119–20. Furthermore, Rogers suggests that because the Temagamis were hunter-gatherers, they were more 'elusive' than the Hurons and thus better able to survive Iroquois marauding. TTP, 3071–7

38 *Rélations des Jesuites*, vol. 6, Rél. de 1671, 35–6

39 W.J. Eccles, 'Sovereignty-Association, 1500–1783,' *Canadian Historical Review*, 65 (December 1984); and his testimony at the TTP, 5070–5, 5114–22, 5179–94. Note also Donald Smith, TTP, 4660–9.

40 Elaine Mitchell, *Fort Timiskaming and the Fur Trade* (Toronto 1977), 8

41 TTP, cited in translation by Eccles, 5034

42 Elaine Mitchell, *Fort Timiskaming*, 8; TTP, Eccles, 5059

43 TTP, Eccles, 1118–19 and 5394–6. Otherwise the Temagami lands would have to have been vacant, a position that Eccles and most others (except Bishop) reject.

44 W.A. Kenyon and J.R. Turnbull, *The Battle for James Bay, 1686* (Toronto 1971)

45 There is no way of knowing with certainty to which of the two waves of

the northern Iroquois raids the oral tradition of the Teme-augama Anishnabai refers. But the first is more logical. By the time of the second wave the Ojibwa frontier seemed more secure.

46 See P.S. Schmalz, 'The Role of the Ojibwa in the Conquest of Southern Ontario, 1650–1701,' *Ontario History*, 76, no. 4 (December 1984), 326–52. Schmalz, in contrast to Eccles, stresses that the 1701 peace was more a victory for the Ojibwa-Algonkians (and the English) than it was for the French, and that the Iroquois were the real losers. Schmalz makes particular use of Kah-Ge-Ga-Gah Bowh (George Copway), *The Traditional History and Characteristic Sketches of the Ojibway Nation* (Boston 1851). He also recounts (349, n364) oral traditions (with skull remains) in the Gogama area concerning earlier Iroquois raids that are very similar to those in the Temagami area. Concerning the humbling of the Iroquois, Bruce Trigger agrees with Schmalz; see his *Natives and Newcomers: Canada's 'Heroic Age' Reconsidered* (Kingston and Montreal 1985)

47 TTP, Eccles, 5430

48 Franquelin's map cited and exhibited by Eccles in the TTP, 5075

49 TTP, Appellant Factum, vol. 3, 15, 51, citing PAC, MG1, CIIA, vols. 19 and 27, 'Memoire sur la Baye d'Hudson 1701,' 247, and 'Chefs concernans le Canada pour l'année 1707,' 11 avril 1707, 83

50 TTP, Eccles, 5041, 5042, 5053 (quotations), and also 5060, 5180, 5299. Note also his 'Sovereignty-Association,' and his 'A Belated Review of Harold Adams Innis' *Fur Trade in Canada,' Canadian Historical Review*, 60 (December 1979) 419–41. Furthermore note an article (translated by Eccles for the TTP, 5081–99) by Jean Laflamme, 'Naissance de la traite des fourrures en Abitibi et en Temiscamingue, 1673–1798,' *Cahiers d'histoire et de géographie*, no. 5 (Rouyn 1976).

51 TTP, Eccles, 5005–118, 5174, 5179–80, 5421; reference to 'third richest' is on 5114; to 'Timagamingue' in quotation 5174, and 5179

52 TTP, Eccles, 5085–88.

53 Eccles, 5070, 5396, 5114 (for the quotations); also 5024, 5179–84

54 TTP, Morrison, 7595

55 TTP, Rogers, 3098

56 TTP, Eccles, 5053, 5180–94. At least as far as 'historical evidence' is concerned, Eccles, Rogers, Morrison, and others reject the position taken by Bishop and tentatively supported at the TTP by the historian Yves Zoltvany, that the N'Daki Menan, due to animal exhaustion probably from over-'harvesting,' became vacant 'again' after about 1725. For analysis and explanation of the legal principles of aboriginal rights, see Brian Slattery, 'Understanding Aboriginal Rights,' *Canadian Bar Review*, 66, no. 4 (December 1987), 727.

57 TTP, Morrison, 7678

58 TTP, Morrison, 7705–48

59 Mitchell, *Fort Timiskaming*, 10

60 TTP, Eccles, 5337

61 Ibid., 5406–30
62 TTP, Eccles, 5434, takes the warrior estimate from the DeBougainville Journal of 1757; Eccles himself, 5435, uses the word 'astonishing.'
63 TTP, Eccles, 5131, 5192, 5210–15, 5227, 5336–60, 5401–9, 5434–8, and his 'Sovereignty-Association'; TTP, Brian Slattery, 5653, 5887–918, 5942, 6091–3; his 'Ancestral Lands, Alien Laws: Judicial Perspectives on Aboriginal Title,' *Studies in Aboriginal Rights*, no. 2 (University of Saskatchewan Native Law Centre 1983), and his *The Land Rights of Indigenous Canadian Peoples, as Affected by the Crown's Acquisition of Their Territories* (D Phil diss., University of Oxford, published by Saskatchewan College of Law 1980); and Thomas R. Berger, 'Native Rights in the New World,' *Northern Perspectives*, Canadian Arctic Resources Committee (CARC), 1, no. 4 (Summer 1979), 1–6
64 Cited in Mitchell, *Fort Timiskaming*, 17
65 Ibid., 16–20, and TTP, Eccles, 5131–8
66 Mitchell, *Fort Timiskaming*, 18–32; TTP, Morrison, 7140, 7658–831, 7764–80, 7836, 7891. It is Morrison who refers to the red-coated Soushoagamys.
67 Mitchell, *Fort Timiskaming*, 33–58
68 TTP, Morrison, 7856 (and also note 7891), and Mitchell, *Fort Timiskaming*, 52–79
69 TTP, 7388–92
70 Cited in Mitchell, *Fort Timiskaming*, 94
71 Ibid., 98–9

2 Just beyond the Canadian Periphery

1 HBC Archives, B.135/a/124, Beioley's Journal, as quoted in W.S. Wallace, 'The Post on Bear Island,' *Queen's Quarterly*, 46 (Summer 1939), 187
2 AO, MS209, Angus Cameron Papers, Temiskamingue Journals, 1823–5, 18 and 30 July 1825, and letter, McBean to Allan McDonell, 14 January, 1827
3 TTP, J. Morrison, 7912
4 TTP, Morrison, 7929; and Elaine Mitchell, *Fort Timiskaming and the Fur Trade* (Toronto 1977), 153–9
5 TTP, Edward S. Rogers, 3065–7
6 TTP, Morrison, 7930–1
7 Mitchell, *Fort Timiskaming*, 159–60
8 Quoted in Wallace, 'The Post on Bear Island,' 187, and TTP, W.J. Eccles, 5430
9 TTP, Morrison, 7937–50
10 HBC Archives, D4/104 f. 3d, 16 August 1836, cited in Mitchell, *Fort Timiskaming*, 162. Note also TTP, Morrison, 7904–45, and quotation about the 'best deal,' 7992. On the other hand, Charles Bishop claims that the Temagami outpost was established to encourage Indians in the environs

of Temagami, Matachewan, Mattagami, and even Abitibi to congregate. This, he argues, led to the emergence later of a 'trading post band,' but not until the late 1860s. The fires of 1846 plus epidemics and game depletion from competition during the 1830s leading to starvation and egress meant that there was still no Temagami band, Bishop suggests, at the time of the 1850 Robinson treaties. TTP, Charles Bishop, 190–2, 214–19, 227–31, 329–30, and 338

11 'Report of the Commissioners on the Survey of the Ottawa River, etc.,' in Upper Canada, *Appendix to Journal, House of Assembly 1839*, 4th Session, 13th Parl., 2 Vict. (Toronto 1839), 87–97. The background to the Ottawa-Huron surveys of 1837 and the expedition of David Thompson who led one of the parties are discussed in Florence B. Murray, ed., *Muskoka and Haliburton, 1616–1875* (Toronto 1963), xlv–lii.

12 Dianne Newell, *Technology on the Frontier: Mining in Old Ontario* (Vancouver 1986)

13 PAC RG10, vol. 226, Vidal-Anderson Report 1849; AO, Diary of Thomas Gummersall Anderson

14 For material on the Anderson-Vidal expedition and the Robinson treaties note: Robert J. Surtees, 'Indian Land Cessions in Ontario, 1763–1862: The Evolution of a System,' esp. ch. 7, 'The System Tested, 1850–1862: The Robinson Treaties and Manitoulin Island,' 208–68 (PHD diss., Carleton University 1982); Anthony J. Hall, 'The Red Man's Burden: Land, Law, and the Lord in the Indian Affairs of Upper Canada, 1791–1858' (PHD diss., Toronto 1984), esp. 331–9; Douglas Leighton, 'The Historical Significance of the Robinson Treaties of 1850' (Paper presented to the Canadian Historical Association, Ottawa, June 1982); and E.M. Ellwood, 'The Robinson Treaties of 1850' (BA diss., Sir Wilfrid Laurier University 1977).

15 Canada, *Indian Treaties and Surrenders* (Ottawa 1891), treaty nos 60, 61, 1:147–52

16 Bear Island Trial Decision, esp. 443–9

17 See TTP, Appellant Factum, vol. 3, 34–7.

18 In connection with his work on Ontario-Canada arbitration issues, Aemilius Irving recorded his conclusion that Peter Na-ban-nay-quan-nay 'did not go to the Treaty, not invited – never went for presents after the Treaty.' See AO, Irving Papers, Box 26 / Package 30 / Items 10–13. The suggestion concerning 1855 and the link between the Temagami Indians and the Lake Wanapitei reserve are made by Mr Justice Steele (esp. 432–3 and 449–53). Mr Justice Steele lays great stress on an 1880 map in the PAC prepared for Chief Tonené. Justice Steele interpreted the map to mean that Lake Wanapitei was then part of the hunting territory of the Temagamis. The Teme-augama Anishnabai reject this conclusion. Note also Anthony J. Hall, 'The Ontario Supreme Court on Trial: Mr Justice Donald Steele and Aboriginal Rights' (unpublished paper, presented at Indian Heritage Conference, Walpole Island, 15 and 16 November 1985).

19 PAC, Timagami Post Journal, 5 October 1857

20 PAC, Timagami Post Journal, 8 December 1857
21 PAC, Timagami Post Journal, 17 November 1864
22 PAC, Timagami Post Journal, 29 October 1858, containing a letter from John W. Simpson to Hackland, transcribed by the post manager
23 PAC, Timagami Post Journal, 24 September 1865; 13, 14 October 1865
24 PAC, Timagami Post Journal, 27 October 1865; 12 February, 24 March 1866
25 PAC, Timagami Post Journal, 16 May 1866
26 PAC, Timagami Post Journal, 12 November 1866; 24 October 1866; 20 May 1867; 4, 26 October 1874. AO, Temagamingue, Arthur J. Ryder to C. Rankin, 15 October 1877; George H. Lennon to C. Rankin, 22 March 1875
27 AO, Temagamingue, Lennon to Rankin, 7 March 1875
28 AO, Temagamingue, Ryder to Rankin, 19 March 1876
29 AO, Temagamingue, Lennon to Rankin, 4 October 1874
30 AO, Temagamingue, Ryder to Rankin, 25 October 1875, 19 March 1876
31 AO, Temagamingue, Ryder to Rankin, 24 October 1876, 12 December 1877
32 AO, Temagamingue, Ryder to Rankin, 25 October 1875, 23 January 1876, 24 October 1876, 22 March 1877, 15 October 1877, 29 October 1877, 2 April 1878; John H. Cummins to Rankin, 21 March 1879
33 AO, Temagamingue, Lennon to Rankin, 26 February 1875
34 PAC, Timagami Post Journal, 25 December 1857, 29 December 1858
35 AO, Temagamingue, Ryder to Rankin, 23 January 1876, 24 October 1876, 12 December 1877
36 PAC, Timagami Post Journal, 26 May 1879
37 PAC, Timagami Post Journal, 16, 20 May 1866
38 PAC, Timagami Post Journal, 14, 16 October 1878, 27 December 1878
39 PAC, Timagami Post Journal, 16 October 1878, 18 May 1879; AO, Temagamingue, Ryder to Rankin, 12 December 1877
40 AO, Temagamingue, Cummins to Rankin, 1 November 1879
41 PAC, Timagami Post Journal, 1 January 1879
42 PAC, Timagami Post Journal, 1, 3 January 1879
43 PAC, Timagami Post Journal, 14 October, 3–24 November 1857 (a transcription of James Hackland's letter to John W. Simpson appears with the entry for 25 December 1857); AO, Temagamingue, Ryder to Rankin, 22 May 1876
44 PAC, Timagami Post Journal, 24 October 1858, 23 October 1859, 19 October 1860, 24 October 1864; AO, Temagamingue, Ryder to Rankin, 25 October 1875
45 PAC, Timagami Post Journal, 7–15 October 1866
46 PAC, Timagami Post Journal, 23 September 1858, and 16 October 1859
47 PAC, Timagami Post Journal, 16 October 1859, 30 October, 30 November 1866, 24 October 1874; AO, Temagamingue, Ryder to Rankin, 22 May 1876
48 AO, Temagamingue, Ryder to Rankin, 25 October 1875

49 PAC, Timagami Post Journal, 6 October 1857. A copy of Hackland's letter to Simpson is in the journal. A biographical sketch of John W. Simpson may be found in Mitchell, *Fort Timiskaming*, 244.
50 PAC, Timagami Post Journal, Simpson to Hackland, 12 October 1858, is copied in the journal at 16 October.
51 PAC, Timagami Post Journal, 19 October 1860; AO, Temagamingue, Lennon to Rankin, 4 October 1874, Ryder to Rankin, 25 October 1875
52 PAC, Timagami Post Journal, 17, 18, 26 January, 25 March 1861; AO, Temagamingue, Cummins to Rankin, 1 November 1879
53 PAC, Timagami Post Journal, 17, 18 May 1858, 25 September 1865, 3 June 1879; AO, Temagamingue, Cummins to Rankin, 1 November 1875
54 AO, Temagamingue, Ryder to Rankin, 25 October 1875
55 AO, Temagamingue, Ryder to Rankin, 22 March 1877
56 PAC, Timagami Post Journal, 17, 18 May 1858
57 AO, Temagamingue, Tonené to Rankin, 13 March 1877; Cummins to Rankin, 19 December 1879; John Turner to C.C. Farr, 26 October 1885. Cattle had been brought to trading posts in the region several decades earlier. See Mitchell, *Fort Timiskaming*, 88, 224
58 PAC, Timagami Post Journal, 1 January 1879
59 AO, Temagamingue, Lennon to Rankin, 4 October 1874; Lennon to Rankin, 26 February 1875
60 E.E. Rich, *Hudson's Bay Company* (London 1960), 880–90
61 Indian Affairs, Temagami, Charles Skene to L. Vankoughnet, 1 March 1880, and enclosures. Skene thought that one of his visitors in both 1877 and 1879 might have been Nebanegwune. This seems unlikely; Nebanegwune had ceased to be chief in 1855 and by the 1870s was very frail.
62 Ibid., and Tonené to Skene, 10 February 1880
63 Indian Affairs, Temagami, Vankoughnet to Rankin, 20 March 1880, and reply 3 April 1880; Vankoughnet to Skene, 19 April 1880, and reply 3 May 1880; Rankin to Skene, 2 April 1880; Vankoughnet to Skene, 8 May 1880, and Skene to Vankoughnet, 22 May, 12 June, early August, and 14 August 1880. See also *The New Topographical Atlas of the Province of Ontario* (Toronto: Miles and Co. 1879), 98.
64 Indian Affairs, Temagami, Skene to Superintendent-General, 28 February, 5 March 1881, and enclosures; Vankoughnet to Superintendent-General, Memorandum, 4 April 1880. Prime Minister John A. Macdonald held the position of superintendent-general of Indian Affairs from 1878 to 1885, when responsibility for the post was shifted to the minister of the interior.
65 Indian Affairs, Temagami, Walton to Superintendent-General, 5 September 1884
66 Indian Affairs, Temagami, Abrey to Superintendent-General, 12 February 1885, enclosing blueprint map
67 AO, Temagamingue, Piper to Temagami Fur Trade Lodge, 29 April 1885
68 Indian Affairs, Temagami, Department to C. Powell, Under-Secretary of

State, 8 May 1885, urging action by Ontario; Walton to Superintendent-General, 28 September 1885, enclosing sketch

69 Indian Affairs, Temagami, W.E. O'Brian to Department, 14 May 1887, with enclosure of 11 May 1887

3 Southern Forces in the Temagami Country

1 M. Zaslow, *Reading the Rocks: The Story of the Geological Survey of Canada, 1842–1972* (Ottawa 1975), and A.H. Lang, 'Sir William Logan and the Economic Development of Canada,' *Canadian Public Administration*, 12 (1969), 551–65, provide background on the GSC. Murray's account is in GSC, *Report of Progress 1853–56.*

2 CPR, *Progress Report on Canadian Pacific Exploratory Surveys, 1872 and 1877*, 5, 47; Canada, *Sessional Papers*, no. 123 A, 1880, 43 Vict,, App. 18, *Report Canadian Pacific Railway*, W.A. Austin, 'Reports on Examinations Made North and West of Lake Nipissing, in Connection with the Projected Railway Extension to the Eastern End of Lake Superior'; *The New Topographical Atlas of the Province of Ontario* (Toronto: Miles and Co. 1879)

3 Barlow, *Report 1899*, 7

4 GSC, *Report of Progress 1876–78* (Ottawa 1878), vol. 8, Robert Bell, 'Report on an Exploration in 1865 [*sic* 1875] between James Bay and Lakes Superior and Huron,' 299–306

5 GSC, *Annual Report*, New Series, 3, pt 1, (1887–8, Montreal 1889), Summary Reports, 'Exploration and Surveys' [1887], 22–4; Barlow, *Report 1899*, 8; 'Exploration and Survey' [1888], 77–8; PAC, Timagami Post Journal, 10 October, 1888

Considerable uncertainty has existed concerning the identity of 'Lady Evelyn,' the woman who had a lake, a river, a hotel, and eventually a wilderness park in the Temagami district named in her honour. She was, in fact, Lady Evelyn Catherine Campbell (1855–1940), eighth child of George Douglas Campbell, the eighth duke of Argyll (1823–1900), and thus sister of the man who served as governor-general of Canada from 1879 to 1883 and was then styled the Marquis of Lorne (1845–1914, the ninth duke of Argyll). Robert Bell's field notes for the expedition of 1887 long were missing. Those for the 1888 expedition do not refer to the naming, but A.E. Barlow states in his *Report 1899*: 'Lady Evelyn Lake (so named in 1888 by Dr Bell) is known to the Indians as Muskananing (the haunt of the Moose),' 265. Bell had upon occasion been a guest at Government House and probably met Lady Evelyn on a visit by her to Canada. In 1886 she married James Baille-Hamilton, whose brother, William, was private secretary to the secretary of state for the colonies (*Burke's Peerage*, 105th ed., London 1970). The link is confirmed in *The Grand Trunk Railway* (6th ed., 1910), 15.

The Ontario Government Names Board, however, records a different story, stemming from W.S. Wallace, *Encyclopedia of Canada*, vol. 3, 371. Wallace speculated that the Lake was 'probably' named by a prospector or tourist in 1879 after Lady Evelyn Louisa Salina, daughter of John Henry, the fourth earl of Erne (1839–1914), a prominent grand master of the Orange Association. Wallace admitted, however, that the origin was unknown when he visited Bear Island in 1896. Such a Lady Evelyn (1879–1955) is confirmed in *Burke's Peerage*, but the Wallace story is quite improbable; for one thing, the lake had not, in 1879, yet experienced either prospectors or tourists.

6 PAC, GSC, RG45, vol. 129, folder item 1732, 'Field Notes of A.M. Campbell'

7 Barlow, *Report 1899*, 5–6, 22–41. Notwithstanding Barlow's description of the area as 'untouched by the axe,' timber licences along the Montreal River dated from at least the 1860s. See MNR, Survey Records Office, Map S16–10, Wm Bell OLS, 28 February 1881. Bell's impressions of timber potential are in his 1887 notes, PAC, MG53, B198, Lawrence Lande Papers.

8 Barlow, *Report 1899*, 139–62; OBM, *Annual Report* (1900), 172–4

9 Ontario, Report of the Royal Commission on the Mineral Resources of Ontario (1888). Evidence of Edward Haycock, evidence of J.C. Bailey

10 Société historique du Nouvel-Ontario, document historique no. 41, *Field*, 13; Société historique du Nouvel-Ontario, document historique no. 18, Roger Bélanger, *Région Agricole Sudbury-Nipissing*, 15; George R. Rumney, 'Settlement of the Nipissing Passageway,' *Transactions of the Royal Canadian Institute*, 28, pt 1 (October 1949), 65–120

11 George Carruthers, *Paper in the Making* (Toronto 1947), 663; 'Sturgeon Falls Pulp Company Agreement, 6 October 1898,' Ontario, *Sessional Papers*, 1898–9, no. 74

12 Morris Zaslow, *The Opening of the Canadian North 1870–1914* (Toronto and Montreal 1971), 177; *Globe*, 11 April 1900

13 H.V. Nelles, *The Politics of Development: Forests, Mines and Hydro-Electric Power in Ontario, 1849–1941* (Toronto 1974), 113–15. An exchange between Ross and Whitney over the Spanish River agreement is in the *Globe*, 30 March, 11 April 1900

14 Morris Zaslow, *Opening of the Canadian North*, 158

15 Bruce Hodgins, *Paradis of Temagami: The Story of Charles Paradis 1848–1926* (Cobalt, Ont., 1976), 7, 13; T.T. Tait, 'Haileybury: The Early Years,' *Ontario History*, 55, no. 4 (1963), 194

16 Elaine Mitchell, *Fort Timiskaming and the Fur Trade* (Toronto 1977), 226

17 Tait, 'Haileybury,' 195–7

18 Albert Tucker, *Steam into Wilderness: Ontario Northland Railway, 1902–1962* (Toronto 1978), 2

19 Tait, 'Haileybury,' 198; C.C. Farr, *The Lake Temiscamingue District, Province of Ontario, Canada* (Toronto 1894)

20 Royal Commission on Mineral Resources of Ontario Report, 56; Ontario,

Commission of Crown Lands, *Report of the Survey and Exploration of Northern Ontario 1900* (Toronto 1901), 87, 90, 112

21 Hodgins, *Paradis of Temagami*, contains additional detail and notes on the following section.

22 *La Patrie*, Montreal, 20 August 1898

23 AO, Prime Ministers' Papers, George W. Ross, Box 3, 'Railways, Temagami Railway'

24 PAC, Wragge Papers, D.W. St Eloi to Wragge, 17 October 1893, and John C. Kennedy to the President and Directors of the Nipissing and James Bay Railway Company, 17 October 1893. Bell's observations are in his notebook from the 1887 Lake Temagami trip, which may be found in the Lawrence Lande Papers at the PAC, MG53 B198. See also T.W. Gibson 'The Hinterland of Ontario,' OBM 4 (Toronto 1894), 119.

25 PAC, Bronson Papers, vol. 837, J.M.Gibson to E.H.Bronson, 23 June 1899

26 AO, Pamphlet Collection, 1898, no. 13, *Re the James Bay Railway*, 9

27 AO, Pamphlet Collection, 1884, no. 11, *Nipissing and James Bay Railway*, 8–9; 1885, no. 24, 4; Ontario Commissioner of Crown Lands, *Our Northern Districts* (Toronto 1894), 56

28 Barlow, *Report 1899*, 263

29 *The Poems of Archibald Lampman*, edited with a memoir by D.C. Scott (Toronto 1900), xix–xx

30 [L.O. Armstrong], 'Timagami, Mississagua, French River and That Sort of Thing,' *Rod and Gun*, 6 (April 1905)

31 Ibid., and continued as 'Mississagua, French River and Temagami,' *Rod and Gun*, 6 (May 1905)

32 Barlow, *Report 1899*, 14; HBC Archives, Provincial Archives of Manitoba, *Annual Report*, Montreal Department / Temiskaming District, A74/1–11; PAC, MG53, B198, Lande Papers. Robert Bell, 'Notebook on Expedition to Lake Temagami,' entry for 14 August 1887

33 Barlow, *Report 1899*, 33

34 Indian Affairs, Temagami, John Turner to Walton, 31 May 1887; W.E.O. O'Brien to Department, 14 May 1887 with enclosure 11 May

35 Indian Affairs, Temagami, Walton to Superintendent General, 17 September and 12 October 1889, and 10 February 1890 and 1 March 1890; VanKoughnet to Walton, 27 September 1889 and 13 March 1890; Tonené to Walton, 11 February 1890

36 Indian Affairs, Temagami, Deputy Minister of Justice to Superintendent General, 28 February 1890 and Minute of the Privy Council, 18 March 1890

37 Indian Affairs, Temagami, 'Statement of Case of the Dominion on behalf of the Temagamingue Band of Ojibwa Indians,' 10 March 1896; W.D. Hogg to H. Reed, 11 May 1896

38 Indian Affairs, Temagami, D.C. Scott to A. White, 15 May 1896; H. Reed to A. White, 28 September 1896, A. White to H. Reed, 3 February 1897 and C. Sifton to J.M. Gibson, 26 March 1897

4 Establishing the Temagami Forest Reserve, 1897–1906

Much of the material in this chapter previously appeared in Bruce W. Hodgins and Jamie Benidickson, 'Resource Management Conflict in the Temagami Forest, 1898 to 1914,' Canadian Historical Association, *Historical Papers, 1978*, 148–75.

1 Richard S. Lambert with Paul Pross, *Renewing Nature's Wealth* (Toronto 1967), 162–3, 177–82, 525–7. R. Peter Gillis and T.R. Roach, *Lost Initiatives: Canada's Forest Industries, Forest Policy and Forest Conservation* (New York: Greenwood Press 1986); B.W. Hodgins, R. Peter Gillis, and Jamie Benidickson, 'The Ontario and Quebec Experiment with Forest Reserves,' *Journal of Forest History*, 26 (January 1982), 20–33

2 R.P. Gillis, 'The Ottawa Lumber Barons and the Conservation Movement, 1880–1914,' *Journal of Canadian Studies* (February 1974), 14–29; Lambert and Pross, *Renewing Nature's Wealth*, 161–2.

3 PAC, Department of the Interior, RG15, vol. 81, file 69113

4 Robert Craig Brown, 'The Doctrine of Usefulness: Natural Resources and National Park Policy in Canada, 1887–1914,' in J.G. Nelson, ed., *Canadian Parks in Perspective* (Montreal 1970), 46–62

5 Lambert and Pross, *Renewing Nature's Wealth*, 182–4

6 Ontario, 56 Vict. (1893), cap. 8. See Lambert and Pross, *Renewing Nature's Wealth*, 10, 78, 167–73, 277–81; and Audrey Saunders, *Algonquin Story* (Toronto, reprinted 1963).

7 James Dickson, 'A Glimpse at Ontario's Forest Reservations,' *Rod and Gun*, 7 (June 1905), 33–40; AO, Department of Lands and Forests, 'Memorandum for the Honourable the Commissioner of Crown Lands,' 7 January 1901, *Woods and Forests Report Book IV*, 102, and James E. Defebaugh, *History of the Lumber Industry of America* (Chicago 1896), 75, 190

8 Ontario, Clerk of Forestry, *Annual Report* (1896), 22–3

9 B.E. Fernow, 'Forest Resources and Forestry,' in vol. 28, *The Province of Ontario*, of Adam Shortt and A.G. Doughty, eds, *Canada and Its Provinces*, 23 vols (Toronto 1913–17), 595

10 *Globe*, 29 December 1897, 8; H.V. Nelles, *The Politics of Development: Forests, Mines and Hydro-Electric Power in Ontario, 1849–1941* (Toronto 1974), 205; Ontario, Bureau of Forestry, *Annual Report* (1899), 6–9

11 Ontario, Director of Forestry, *Annual Report* (1900–1, Toronto 1902), 6

12 AO, 'Re Forest Reserves,' 27 November 1900, *Woods and Forests Report Book IV*, 102

13 PAC, Timagami Post Journal, 1894–1903

14 PAC, Bronson Papers, 837, Gibson to Bronson 18 October 1899

15 Ibid., Davis to Bronson, 24 February 1901

16 *Rod and Gun*, 1, no. 2 (July 1899)

17 *Globe*, 20 February 1900

18 Ontario, Commission of Crown Lands, *Report of the Survey and Exploration of Northern Ontario, 1900* (Toronto 1901)

19 Ibid.
20 AO, 'Memo for the Assistant Commissioner: re Forest Reserve,' Thos. Southworth, 27 November 1900, in *Woods and Forests Report Book IV*, 102, attachment
21 AO, Aubrey White, 7 January 1901, *Woods and Forests Report Book IV*, 102, attachment
22 Ontario, Director of Forestry, Annual Report (1900–1), 13–14, contains the order-in-council.
23 Ibid., 6
24 AO, Prime Ministers' Papers, RG3, OC44/88, 8 March 1902, with enclosure
25 AO, Prime Ministers' Papers, RG3, OC46/160, 15 December 1902
26 AO, Prime Ministers' Papers, RG3, OC49/4, 16 December 1903, enclosed memorandum of T. Southworth, 2 December 1903
27 AO, 'Re Forest Reserves,' 21 March 1899, *Woods and Forests Report Book II*, 317–21
28 AO, 'Memorandum for the Honourable the Commissioner of Crown Lands,' 7 January 1901, *Woods and Forests Report Book IV*, 102
29 AO, Prime Ministers' Papers, Orders-in-Council, RG3, OC49/4, 16 December 1903
30 Ibid., 16 December 1903, enclosing Southworth, 2 December 1903, White, 8 December 1902, and Davis, 8 December 1903. Also, Ontario, Director of Forestry, *Annual Report* (1904), 12. In 1901 the Nipissing and James Bay Railway and the Timagami Railway had charter rights in the original forest. AO, *Woods and Forests Report Book IV*, 102
31 PAC, Bronson Papers, 699, Letterbook 1903–9, Bronson to Ross, 14 December 1903
32 'Lake Temagami Reserve,' *Rod and Gun*, 2 (February 1901), 454
33 *Globe*, 19 February 1904
34 J.B. Miller, 'Forestry from the Lumberman's Standpoint,' *Canada Lumberman* (February 1906)
35 Lambert and Pross, *Renewing Nature's Wealth*, 285
36 Albert Tucker, *Steam into Wilderness: Ontario Northland Railway, 1902–1962* (Toronto 1978), 1–27
37 AO, Irving Papers, 'Temiskaming Claims File'
38 PAC, Latchford Papers, W.B. Russell (Engineer) to A.W. Campbell (Deputy Commissioner of Public Works), 26 February 1902
39 TNOR, *Annual Report* (1903), 35
40 Tucker, *Steam into Wilderness*, 13, 18
41 AO, RG3, OC53/243, 14 August 1905, with enclosures from Frank Cochrane
42 AO RG8, I-7-B-2, Ontario, *Sessional Papers*, 1908, no. 65 (not printed)
43 Tucker, *Steam into Wilderness*, 193–4, n1
44 Ibid., 43–4, and n6, 196
45 'Henri,' *La Patrie*, 20 August 1898; and AO, Ross Papers, Box 3, 'Railways: Timagami Railway'

46 6 Edward VII (1906), cap. 136, 'Ontario Northern and Temagami Railway Company'

47 'Sturgeon Falls Pulp Company Agreement, 6 October 1898,' Ontario, *Sessional Papers*, 1898–9, no. 74; found in Timber Commission, Exhibit 348, Box 17

48 'Sturgeon Falls Pulp Company Agreement, 15 December 1901,' Ontario, *Sessional Papers*, 1902, no. 67; Timber Commission, Exhibit 348, Box 14; George Carruthers, *Paper in the Making* (Toronto 1947), 663–8

49 Carruthers, *Paper in the Making*, 670–1, 687

50 Carruthers, in *Paper in the Making*, states that 'about 25 men were employed at the mill, and about 300 in the pulpwood camps,' 368. Apparently the Sturgeon Falls Pulp and Paper Company built several camps on Lake Temagami before the reserve was established. See Larry E. Hodgins, 'Economic Geography of the Lake Timagami District'(BA diss., University of Toronto 1958), 54.

51 In a letter from the minister of lands, forests and mines to the lieutenant-governor, dated 6 June, 1902, the minister recommended a refund of $20,000 to the Montreal River Pulp and Paper Company in full settlement of all claims. AO, *Woods and Forest Report Book III*, 230. See also AO, Memorandum, 17 November 1903, Commissioner of Crown Lands to Lieutenant-Governor, *Woods and Forests Report Book III*, 59–61; AO, Letter, Commissioner of Crown Lands to Lieutenant-Governor, 2 February 1905, *Woods and Forests Report Book III*, 191–3. The Sault Industries episode is described in Nelles, *The Politics of Development*, 132–8.

52 'Spanish River Pulp & Paper Company Agreement, 21 September, 1899,' Ontario, *Sessional Papers*, 1911, discussed in Lambert and Pross, *Renewing Nature's Wealth*, 261. The agreement was renegotiated for twenty-one years in 1909; 'Spanish River Pulp & Paper Company Limited Agreement, 1 October 1909,' Ontario, *Sessional Papers*, 1911, in Timber Commission, Exhibit 350, Box 17.

53 Indian Affairs, Temagami, Pedley to Watson, 25 February 1905; Hanes to Pedley, 2 March 1905

54 Indian Affairs, Temagami, Pedley to White, 9 March 1905; Pedley to Hanes, 9 March 1905

55 AO, 'Re Forest Reserve at Lake Temagami,' 7 January 1901, *Woods and Forests Report Book II*, 441–50, quotation at 445

56 Indian Affairs, Temagami, 'Regulations,' received 8 August 1905

57 John Flood, 'The Duplicity of D.C. Scott and the James Bay Treaty,' *Black Moss* 11, no. 2 (Fall 1976), 51–63; Scott et al., *The James Bay Treaty* (Ottawa, 6 November 1905, 5 October 1906); D.C. Scott, 'The Last of the Indian Treaties,' *Scribner's Magazine* (December 1906); Pelham Edgar, *Across My Path*, Northrop Frye, ed. (Toronto 1952), 58–67; E. Brian Titley, *A Narrow Vision: Duncan Campbell Scott and the Administration of Indian Affairs in Canada* (Vancouver 1986), 60–74

58 Gillis, 'Ottawa Lumber Barons,' 24–9

59 Ibid.; see also Lambert and Pross, *Renewing Nature's Wealth*, 258–63. Nelles, *Politics of Development*, 132, and Charles W. Humphries, *'Honest Enough to Be Bold': The Life and Times of Sir James Pliny Whitney* (Toronto 1985), 58, note the emphasis of the Ross Liberals on northern Ontario resource development. For references to resources and northern Ontario in *Whitney*, see 58, 73–4, 79, 92

60 Thomas Southworth, 'Ontario's Progress towards a Rational Forestry System,' *Canadian Forestry Journal*, 3, no. 4 (December 1907), 157–63

5 Mining and Lumbering in the Forest Reserve, 1905–1914

1 8 Edward VII (1908); AO, RG3, OC53/243, 14 August 1905; AO, RG8, I-7-B-2, Ontario, *Sessional Papers*, 1908, no. 65 (not printed); and J.F. Turnbull, A.B. Doran, and A.C. Thrupp, 'Logging Operations on Temagami Forest Reserve in Ontario,' *Canadian Lumberman*, 41, no. 2 (15 November 1921), 42–3

2 AO, OC, 10 September 1912

3 D.O. Baldwin, 'Imitation vs. Innovation: Cobalt as an Urban Frontier Town,' *Laurentian University Review*, 11 (February 1979), 23–42

4 Quoted in H.V. Nelles, *The Politics of Development: Forests, Mines and Hydro-Electric Power in Ontario, 1849–1941* (Toronto 1974), 161

5 OBM *Annual Report*, 16, pt 1 (1907), 8–10; ibid., 17, pt 1 (1908), 19; ibid., 19, pt 1 (1910), 40–5; Nelles, *Politics of Development*, 160–66

6 OBM, *Annual Report*, 16, pt 1 (1907), 8–10; ibid., 17, pt 1 (1908), 19

7 The site of the Brown and McLaren findings may have been on a small portion of the Gillies Limit, which had been granted to one of the early applicants for mining lands who subsequently consented to government reorganization of the land. OBM, *Annual Report*, 16, pt 1 (1907), 8–10; ibid., 17, pt 1 (1908), 19

8 Ibid., 16, pt 1 (1907), 10; ibid., 18 (1909), 42; ibid., 19 (1910), 41–4

9 Ibid., 19 (1910), 41

10 Quoted in Nelles, *Politics of Development*, 165

11 'Opening of the Gillies Limit,' *Engineering and Mining Journal*, 94, no. 9 (31 August 1912), 394

12 E.S. Moore, 'Geology of the Afton-Scholes Area,' OBM, *Annual Report*, 45, pt 6 (1936), 45–6; J.D. Ramsay, 'The Maple Mountain Mining District of Ontario,' *Canadian Mining Journal* (1 September 1909), 526

13 W.H. Collins, 'Geology of Gowganda Mining Division,' GSC, Memoir no. 33 (1913), 5–8; A.O. Sergiades, *Silver Cobalt Calcite Vein Deposits of Ontario*, Mineral Resources Circular No. 10, Ontario Division of Mines (Toronto 1968), 364; OBM, *Annual Report*, 18, (1909), 95, 128; ibid., 19 (1910), 21, 49, 116; ibid., 24 (1915), 60, 128; ibid., 30 (1921), 125; W.H. Collins, 'The Florence Lake and Montreal River Districts,' in GSC, *Summary Report for 1909* (1910) ,170

14 H.P. Davis, *The Davis Handbook of the Porcupine Gold District* (New

York 1911), 123; Collins, 'Geology of Gowganda,' 7; A.G. Burrows, 'The Gowganda and Miller Lakes Silver Area,' OBM, *Annual Report*, 18, pt 2 (1909), 1

15 W.H. Collins, 'Preliminary Report on the Gowganda Mining Division,' GSC, no. 1075 (1909), 7–10; OBM, *Annual Report*, 17, pt 1 (1908), 56; ibid., 18, pt 1 (1909), 95; N.R. Green, 'Gowganda Ho!' *Temiskaming Speaker*, 30 May 1957; G.M. Colvocoresses, 'Gowganda during 1911,' *Canadian Mining Journal* (15 April 1912), 259

16 TNOR, *Annual Report* (1907), 87; Davis, *Porcupine Gold District*, 123–4

17 PAC, National Map Collection, 'Map of the Gowganda, Elk City and Cobalt Silver District' (May 1909). The 'Gowganda Silver Area' map, the 'Gowganda, Miller and Elk Lake Area' map (1909), and (see below) the 'Sellwood-Gowganda Winter Road' (1909), in the collection of the Gowganda Museum also provide valuable information.

18 *Globe*, 17 January 1910; Davis, *Porcupine Gold District*, 123; *Gall's Guide and Directory of the Silver North* (1908), 105–7

19 *Rod and Gun*, 11 (June 1909), 75

20 Gowganda Museum, 'Sellwood-Gowganda Winter Road' (1909); and AO, RG52, I-A, no. 178, Burwash and Gowganda Winter Road Report, 1909. T.D. Regehr, *The Canadian Northern Railway: Pioneer Road of the Northern Prairies 1895–1918* (Toronto 1976), 257

21 W.H. Collins, 'Onaping Map Area,' GSC, Memoir no. 95 (Ottawa 1917), 246

22 Edward M. Burwash, 'Geology of the Nipissing-Algoma Line,' OBM, *Annual Report*, 6, pt 5 (1896), 167–83; A.P. Coleman, 'Iron Ranges of the Lower Huronian,' ibid., 10 (1901), 182; Collins, 'Geology Gowganda Mining,' 7, W.H. Collins, 'Montreal River District,' GSC, *Summary Report for 1910* (Ottawa 1911), 197–201, and his 'Geology of Onaping Sheet,' GSC, *Summary Report for 1911* (Ottawa 1912), 251; R.B. Stewart, 'West Shining Tree Silver Area,' OBM, *Annual Report*, 22 (1913), 190–3; and George B. Langford, 'Shining Tree Silver Area,' ibid., pt 2 (1927), 95

23 W.H. Collins, 'Onaping Map Area,' 109; R.B. Stewart, 'The West Shining Tree Gold District,' OBM, *Annual Report*, 21 (1912), 271–7. Deloro and Ogden townships were withdrawn from the Temagami reserve by *An Act to Amend the Forest Reserves Act*, 2 Geo v (1912) cap. 6.

24 Collins, ibid., 197; R.B. Stewart, 'West Shining Tree Gold Area,' OBM, *Annual Report*, 22 (1913), 233; W.R. Hodge, 'West Shining Tree Gold District,' *Engineering and Mining Journal*, 94, no. 8 (24 August 1912), 343; R.E. Hore, 'The Wasapika Gold Area,' *Canadian Mining Journal*, 40 (9 July 1919), 498, and his 'Gold Deposits,' ibid., 39, (15 August 1918)

25 Ontario, *Report on Road Construction under 2 George V, Chap. 2, 1912* (Toronto 1913), 31–2

26 L.H. Goodwin, 'West Shining Tree Gold District, Ontario,' *Engineering and Mining Journal*, 108, no. 7 (16 August 1919), 261. Also note: Collins, 'Onaping Map Area,' 109, 114, 246; R.B. Stewart, 'The Shining Tree Silver

Area,' OBM, *Annual Report*, 19, pt 2 (1913); 'West Shining Tree Gold District,' ibid., 21, pt 1 (1912), 272, 277, and 'West Shining Tree Gold Area,' ibid., 22 (1913), 235–6; W.R. Hodge, 'West Shining Tree Gold District,' 343–5; W.H. Weed, 'West Shining Tree Gold Prospects,' *Engineering and Mining Journal Press*, 116 (14 July 1923), 69; and R.E. Hore, 'Gold Deposits in MacMurchy and Churchill Townships,' *Canadian Mining Journal*, 39 (15 August 1918), 276.

27 Albert Tucker, *Steam into Wilderness: Ontario Northland Railway, 1902–1962* (Toronto 1978), 60–1. Latchford Museum, Corribeau to Lafleur, 9 March 1914; *Canadian Annual Review*, 1914, 360

28 AO Barnet Papers, Box 25, files 8 and 9; A.E. Barlow, 'The Temagami District, GSC *Summary Reports, 1902–3*, 15 (1903), 124–5; A.P. Coleman, 'Copper and Iron Regions of Ontario,' OBM, *Annual Report* (1900), 172–4, and W. Miller, 'Iron Ores of the Nipissing District,' ibid., 10 (1901), 160–80

29 Barlow, 'The Temagami District,' 125; OBM, *Annual Report*, 14 (1905), 31; ibid., 12 (1903), 20; 'Iron Waited Many Years for Development to Come,' *North Bay Nugget*, 5 September 1968, 102

30 E.L. Jamieson, *Caldwells of Lanark* (1973), 9; AO, Caldwell Diaries, 'Trip to Temagami,' 31 July – 19 August 1903

31 OBM, *Annual Report*, 14, (1905), 31; T.W. Gibson, *The Mining Laws of Ontario*, (Toronto: Department of Mines, 1933); OBM, *Annual Report*, 15 (1906), 26, 27, 87; B.H. Boyum and R.C. Hartviksen, 'General Geology and Ore-Grade Control at the Sherman Mine, Temagami, Ontario,' *Canadian Institute of Mines Transactions*, 73 (1970), 1061. Also note E. Lendeman and L.L. Bolton, 'Iron Ore Occurrences in Canada,' Mines Branch, Canada, Department of Mines, pub. no. 217, 2 (Ottawa 1917), 106, 107. Duncan McDowall, in *Steel at the Sault: Francis H. Clergue, Sir James Dunn, and the Algoma Steel Corporation 1901–1956* (Toronto 1984), provides an extensive survey of the difficulties faced by Canadian iron producers. See 18–22, 23–49, 75–6.

32 OBM, *Annual Report*, pt 1 (1907), 74; and P.E. Hopkins, 'Ontario Gold Deposits,' ibid., pt 2 (1921), 20; ibid. (1905), 73–4; ibid. (1906), 88; ibid., 17 (1908), 82; and ibid., pt 1 (1909), 132–3; D.F. Hewitt, 'Pyrite Deposits of Ontario,' Ontario, Department of Mines, Mineral Resources Circular No. 5 (Toronto 1967), 40

33 W.G. Miller, 'Iron Ores of Nipissing District,' 180; W.W. Moorhouse, 'Northeastern Portion of the Temagami Lake Area,' ODM, *Annual Report*, 51, pt 6 (1942), 25, 26; T.H. Janes, 'Sulphur and Pyrites in Canada,' Canada, Department of Mines Branch, Memorandum Series No. 118 (Ottawa 1952), 70; and Roman Shklanka, 'Copper, Nickel, Lead and Zinc Deposits of Ontario,' Mineral Resources Circular No. 12, ODM, *Annual Report*, (1969), 204

34 Miller, 'Iron Ores of the Nipissing District,' 175–80; Ontario, Commission of Crown Lands, *Report of the Survey and Exploration of Northern Ontario*,

1900, (Toronto 1901), 88–91; Coleman, 'Iron Ranges of the Lower Huronian,' 201–2

35 AO, RG3, OC58/80, 21 January 1907, OC58/561, 12 June 1907, and OC65/71, 27 September 1910; and AO, *Woods and Forests Report Book III*, 298–300; interview by Bruce M. Hodgins with Bill Eckersley, Hindson's assistant, successor, and son-in-law, and with Patrick Eckersley, Bill Eckersley's son, 1 March 1978

36 Ontario, Crown Lands, *Annual Report* (1902), viii; ibid. (1903), xi–xii; ibid. (1904), viii; and ibid. (1905), 7–8; LFM, *Annual Report* (1906), ix; ibid. (1907), vii–viii; ibid. (1908), xii–xiii, and App. 46, A. White, 'The Forest Resources of Ontario,' 134; and ibid. (1909), x–xi (x has the quotation)

37 LFM, *Annual Report* (1915), x; *Ontario Burnt Timber Books* (hereafter *BTB*), 1914 and 1915

38 LFM, *Annual Report* (1910), xi; ibid. (1912), xi–xii; ibid. (1914), ix; ibid. (1915), ix–x; J.M. Bentley, 'Three Weeks in Temagami,' *Rod and Gun*, 8, no. 8 (January 1907), 627–31; PAC, E.M. Coleman Papers, MG30, C83, John Harman Patterson diary, 'Sketches and Journal, Temagami 1901–10'; 'Down the Sturgeon River,' *Rod and Gun*, 6 (March 1905), 550

39 AO, 'Memorandum Regarding Reduction in Price to Be Paid for Timber in Block B in Temagami Forest Reserve,' 23 March 1914, Woods and Forests Report Book IV, 413–15; Collins, 'Preliminary Report on Gowganda,' 10

40 Richard S. Lambert with Paul Pross, *Renewing Nature's Wealth* (Toronto 1967), 260. See also AO, Memorandum, LFM to Lt Gov., 11 June 1906, *Woods and Forests Report Book III*, 230; Nelles, *Politics of Development*, 116–17.

41 'General Conditions with Respect to Pulpwood Areas Offered for Lease by Tender 18 May 1906,' pamphlet in LFM, *BTB*, vol. 2, 87; Memorandum, Deputy Minister to Minister, LFM, *BTB*, vol. 2, 87; DLF, *History of Swastika Forest District* (Toronto 1964), 24. See App. II, map 5, for boundary changes of forest districts and map 4 for location of pulp cuttings. Memorandum, Deputy Minister to Minister, LFM, *BTB*, vol. 2, 87

42 DLF, *Order-in-Council Books*, 3 December 1912; 'Ontario Pulp & Paper Company Limited Agreement,' 29 June 1912, Timber Commission, Exhibit 393, Box 18; Imperial Paper Mills *v.* Quebec Bank, *Dominion Law Reports*, 6 (1912), 475

43 George Carruthers, *Paper in the Making* (Toronto 1947), 687

44 Lambert and Pross, *Renewing Nature's Wealth*, 251–2; A.P. Pross, 'The Development of a Forest Policy: A Study of the Ontario Department of Lands and Forests' PHD diss., University of Toronto (1967), 151

45 Timber Commission, *Proceedings*, 8419

46 The Timber License Purchase Act, 2 Geo V (1912) cap. 7, Ontario; Thomas Southworth, 'Ontario's Progress towards a Rational Forestry System,' *Canadian Forestry Journal*, 3, no. 4 (December 1907), 160; Clyde Leavitt, *Fire Protection in Canada, 1913–1914* (Toronto 1915), 92–3; Clyde Leavitt, *Forest Protection in Canada, 1912* (Ottawa: Commission of

Conservation, 1913), 145–6 (quotation on 146); Commission of Conservation, *Annual Report* (1914), 205–7

47 Lambert and Pross, *Renewing Nature's Wealth*, 186–8; Bernard Fernow, 'Forest Resources and Forestry,' in vol. 18 of Adam Shortt and A.G. Doughty, eds, *Canada and Its Provinces*, 23 vols (Toronto 1913–17), 596–9. Nelles, *Politics of Development*, 210–11, presents Clark as an 'aggressive,' 'crusading,' 'mercurial,' and 'arrogant' professional whom Premier Whitney understandably mistrusted at a time when he was struggling to control pressures for public power.

48 Lambert and Pross, *Renewing Nature's Wealth*, 193–4, 314; AO, Pamphlet Collection, 1913, no. 23, *Northern Ontario: Its Progress and Development under the Whitney Government* (Toronto 1913), 9; P. Gillis and T. Roach, 'Early European and North American Forestry in Canada: The Ontario Example, 1890–1940,' in H.R. Steen, ed. *History of Sustained Yield Forestry: A Symposium* (Santa Cruz 1984)

6 This Is Ontario's Heritage

The title of this chapter is taken from an article by Matthew Parkinson, 'Lake Temagami, a Northern Ontario Playground,' *Canadian Magazine* (June 1914), 172. Material in this chapter has previously been published in Jamie Benidickson, 'Temagami and the Northern Ontario Tourist Frontier,' *Laurentian University Review*, 11, no. 2 (February 1979), 43–70, and 'Northern Ontario's Tourist Frontier,' in Geoffrey Wall and John S. Marsh, eds, *Recreational Land Use: Perspectives on Its Evolution in Canada* (Ottawa 1982), 155–74.

1 TNOR, *Annual Report* (1903), 35, *Annual Report* (1905), 13–14

2 George Altmeyer, 'Three Ideas of Nature in Canada, 1893–1914,' *Journal of Canadian Studies*, 11 (August 1976), 21–36. See also: Roderick Nash, *Wilderness and the American Mind* (New Haven, Conn., 1976), 141–60; Yi-Fu Tuan, *Topophilia, A Study of Environmental Perception, Attitudes and Values* (Englewood Cliffs, NJ, 1974), 92–128; Matthew Parkinson, 'Lake Temagami,' 167, and Frank Yeigh, 'Touring in Temagami Land,' *Rod and Gun*, 8, no. 5 (October 1906), 325

3 L.O. Armstrong, 'Visiting the Temagami Region,' *Rod and Gun*, 8, no. 4 (September 1905)

4 Harold C. Lowrey, 'The Unspoiled Country: Canada has a Great Asset in Temagami,' *Maclean's* (August 1919), 57; *North Bay Times*, 26 July 1906

5 CPR, *Timagaming: A Glimpse of the Algonquin Paradise*, 5th ed. (Montreal, April 1904), 3

6 Armstrong, 'Visiting the Temagami Region,' 419; CPR, *Timagaming; Smiley's Canadian Summer Resort Guide* (1906), 59

7 Fraser Raney, 'Canoe Trips in Temagami,' *Rod and Gun*, 12, no. 2 (July 1910), 186–93

8 'Away up North,' *Forest and Stream*, 28 April 1894; 'Condensed Canoe Trips,' *Forest and Stream*, 19 July 1913, 94–5; W.R. Wadsworth, 'With Rifle and Rod in the Moose Lands of Northern Ontario,' *Canadian Magazine*, 13 (1899), 52; James Edmund Jones, *Camping and Canoeing: What to Take, How to Travel, How to Cook, Where to Go* (Toronto 1903), 121–33; *Nizheshin Kabashwin (Good Camping Places in the Temagami Forest)* (Cleveland 1904)

9 J.M. Bentley, 'Three Weeks in Temagami,' *Rod and Gun*, 8, no. 8 (January 1907), 628; Gordon L. Cockburn, 'A Three Days' Fishing Trip at Mattawabika Falls,' *Rod and Gun*, 11, no. 8 (January 1910), 687; T.J.T., 'Two Weeks in Temagami,' *Outdoor Canada*, 6, no. 1 (February 1910), 20

10 Janet Foster, *Working for Wildlife* (Toronto 1978), 9–10; Richard S. Lambert with Paul Pross, *Renewing Nature's Wealth* (Toronto 1967), 449–51

11 Ontario, *Forest Reserves Act*, 61 Vict. (1898) cap. 10, sec. 3, and as amended 63 Vict. (1900), cap. 12, sec. 1, which was re-enacted without change by 10 Edw. VII (1910) cap. 8, sec. 3; AO, RG3, OC56/70 of 27 June 1906, OC59/187 of 23 August 1907, and OC67/210 of 10 October 1911; White's memorandum to the minister is in AO, *Woods and Forests Report Book IV*, 143–4.

12 O.E. Fisher, 'Canoe Cruises in Canadian Reserves,' *Forest and Stream* (24 September 1910), 506. See also: H.R. Hyndman, 'One Hundred and Fifty Miles by Canoe through Temagami,' *Rod and Gun*, 7, no. 7 (December 1905), 734–40; Karl Baedeker, *The Dominion of Canada* (Leipzig 1907), 239.

13 The material on Camp Keewaydin in the preceding paragraphs is drawn from a variety of primary and secondary sources: Camp Keewaydin Archives, 'Keewaydin 1903,' brochure, 13, 15; 'Keewaydin, 1908,' brochure, 42–3; 'A.S. Gregg Clarke to the Stockholders of the Keewaydin Camps Co.,' 29 December 1914; Fred A. Talbot, 'Back to the Woods,' *World's Work*, 18 (September 1911), 443; E.W. Thomson, 'The Boys of Temagami; American and Canadian Summer Camps,' *Boston Transcript* (12 August 1905); Abbott T. Fenn, *The Story of Keewaydin's 50 Years at Dunmore, 1910–1959* (Keewaydin Camps Inc. 1959); and Brian Back, *The Keewaydin Way: A Portrait 1893–1983* (Temagami 1983).

14 Ann Hall, 'Arthur Lewis Cochrane: A Biographical sketch' (BED diss., Queen's University 1964); PAC, Sir George Parkin Papers, Parkin to the Headmaster, Harrow-on-the-Hill, 13 February 1914; Trent University Archives, Ontario Camping Association Papers, 'Camp Temagami 1905,' brochure. For information on Parkin, see Carl Berger *The Sense of Power: Studies in the Ideas of Imperialism 1867–1914* (Toronto 1970) 33–41.

15 Talbot, 'Back to the Woods,' 443; *The Inter-Ocean* (Chicago), 22 September 1907

16 An extensive review of youth camping philosophy is found in Hedley S.

Dimock and Charles E. Hendry, *Camping and Character* (New York 1929). See John Henry Wadland, *Ernest Thompson Seton: Man in Nature and the Progressive Era, 1880–1915* (New York 1978), 298–306, for an insightful and provocative introduction to the evolution of youth camping and organization in the early twentieth century.

17 The reference to a camp for girls is from AO, RG3, OC58/56, 16 January1907.

18 'Canada and the Tourist,' *Canadian Magazine*, 15, no. 1 (May 1900), 4. Ontario Commissioner of Crown Lands, *Our Northern Districts* (Toronto 1894), 56. *Smiley's Canadian Summer Resort Guide*, 11th ed. (1904), 64

19 MNR, Survey Records Office, 'Instructions to OLS T.B. Speight to Survey Lake Temagami and the Islands Therein,' 2 March 1904, in *Instructions to Land Surveyors*, vol. 16. T.B. Speight, *Report, Description and Field Notes of Islands in Lake Temagami*

20 MNR, Survey Records Office, 'Instructions to Ontario Land Surveyor Alexander Niven to Complete the Survey of Lake Temagami and Islands Therein,' 30 May 1904, in *Instructions to Land Surveyors*, vol. 16. J.L. Haynes, *Report and Field Notes of the Survey of the Islands of Lake Temagami*

21 *Globe* (Toronto), 19 February, 19 March 1904

22 'What Should Be Done with the Islands and Other Uncultivatable Land of Ontario,' *Rod and Gun*, 7, no. 1 (June 1905), 12. Summer resort lands not subject to park or forest reserve regulations were administered under a series of orders-in-council beginning in 1896. The application of these orders was limited and localized until 1922 when uniform administrative procedures were introduced in response to pressure from a rapidly expanding tourist community. AO, RG3, OC120/163, 20 May 1922

23 AO, RG3, OC53/156, 12 August 1905, Enclosure, Frank Cochrane, 7 July 1905; MNR, Survey Records Office, Notebook 2198, 'Report and Field Notes of the Survey of the Islands of Lake Temagami, by J.L. Haynes'; AO, RG53, Provincial Secretary's Papers, *Temagami Island Lease Books*

24 Correspondence concerning Island 99, including Aubrey White to J.M. Gibson, 15 September 1909, confirming the issuance of a patent, was made available to the authors by Mr James Kerr Gibson.

25 AO, RG53, Provincial Secretary's Papers, *Temagami Island Lease Books*

26 AO, RG3, OC120/163, 29 May 1922

27 E.T. Guppy, 'Many Boat Lines Have Served Temagami Lake,' in J.C. Elliott, ed., *Temagami Centennial Booklet* (Temagami 1967); TNOR, *Annual Report* (1905), 14; *Rod and Gun*, 7, no. 3 (August 1908), 263; Cobalt *Daily Nugget*, 5 July 1912

28 *Smiley's Canadian Summer Resort Guide, 1906*, 63–4; 'The Keewaydin Club's Canoe Tours,' *Rod and Gun*, 6, no. 11 (April 1905), 622

29 A.A. Gard, *North Bay; the Gateway to Silverland* (Toronto 1909), 72; Cobalt *Daily Nugget*, 19 August 1912; *Canadian Annual Review*, 1914, 355; AO, Pamphlet Collection, *A Week in Wonderland. Teachers' Third*

Trip to Northern Ontario, 1922; *Temagami Experience*, 1, no. 1 (1976), 11

30 HBC Archives, A.12/L. Misc./ 'Bear Island 1914'; Grand Trunk Railway Passenger Traffic Department, *Playgrounds: A Booklet of Information Regarding the Tourist, Fishing and Hunting Resorts Reached by the Grand Trunk Railway System* (1918), 16

31 'Peerless Temagami: An Ideal Holiday in the New North,' *Globe*, 8 April 1905. 'In Temagami's Tangled Wild,' *Rod and Gun*, 7, no. 1 (June 1906), 36. T.J.T., 'Two Weeks in Temagami,' 18–20; GTR Passenger Traffic Department, *Playgrounds*, 16; HBC Archives, PAM A.12./FT Misc./291 A.12/L. Misc./6. For details on the economic position of the HBC's Temagami Post to 1920 see HBC Archives, PAM A74/9–A74/28.

32 Temagami Lakes Association (TLA) Archives, Youth Camps, File, 'Wabi-Kon.' Interview, Isabel LeDuc, 28 June 1978

33 Cobalt *Daily Nugget*, 2 May 1912, 22 July 1912

34 Cobalt *Daily Nugget*, 20 May 1912, 31 May 1912

35 'Tourists in Ontario,' *Rod and Gun*, 7, no. 4 (September 1905), 414

36 'Down the Sturgeon River,' *Rod and Gun*, 6 (March 1905), 550; Bentley, 'Three Weeks in Temagami,' 631

37 G.W. Creelman, 'From Timigami to Wanapitei,' *Rod and Gun*, 6 (March 1905), 548; 'Mississagua, French River and Timagami,' *Rod and Gun*, 6, no. 12 (May 1905), 681

38 PAC, Bronson Papers, F.P. Bronson to E.H. Bronson, 5 April 1900

39 PAC, Robert Bell Papers, 'Report Re Lake Temagaming and Cross Lake, 24 Feb. 1900,' copy

40 AO, Timber Commission, *Proceedings*, 8645. *Statutes of Ontario, An Act to Provide for the Removal of Obstructions in Rivers and Streams in Certain Cases*,' 1902, ch. 20, may have been a result of Latchford's experience with the Temagami dam.

41 'Concerning Lady Evelyn Lake,' *Rod and Gun*, 13, no. 8 (January 1912), 1000

42 PAC, Robert Bell Papers, 'Report Re Lake Temagaming and Cross Lake.' Ontario, *General Index to Journals and Sessional Papers 1901–1912*, 428

43 CPR, *Timagaming*, 17; James Dickson, 'A Glimpse of Ontario's Forest Reservations,' *Rod and Gun*, 7, no. 1 (June 1905), 37

44 Canadian Mining Institute, *Bulletin*, no. 17 (December 1911), 99; AO, RG8, 1-7-b-2 (1913), 107

45 *Rod and Gun*, 13, no. 6 (November 1911), 736, and 13, no. 8 (January 1912), 1000

46 Timber Commission. The political dimensions of the Timber Commission are thoroughly described in Peter Oliver, *G.Howard Ferguson: Ontario Tory* (Toronto 1977), 97–114

47 PAC, Latchford Papers, MG27, II, F7, vol. 24, file 91. Statement and Appendices from George H. Kohl, 31 May 1921 (copy)

48 Timber Commission, *Proceedings*, 8565–7
49 Ibid., 8568–81
50 Ibid., 8570, 8586–9
51 Ibid., Exhibit 389, Box 18, Rorke to Grigg, 9 August 1918, and *Proceedings*, 8616, 8630
52 Timber Commission, *Proceedings*, 8648
53 McIlwraith's letter to Ferguson is dated 17 October 1919. Timber Commission, *Proceedings*, 8665. Cochrane's evidence is at 8666 and following.
54 Timber Commission, *Proceedings*, 8594–7. TNOR, *Annual Report* (1918), 26
55 Memorandum, Rorke to Grigg for Timber Investigation, 8 February 1921, Timber Commissions, Exhibit 388, Box 18, and *Proceedings*, 8617, 8623, 8661, 8665, 8628
56 Timber Commission, *Report*, 26–7
57 'The "Bobs" on Temagami,' *Rod and Gun*, 7, no. 4 (September 1905), 424–5
58 O.E. Fisher, 'Canoe Cruises in Canadian Reserves,' 506
59 *Canadian Annual Review*, 1914, 355
60 *Rod and Gun*, 8, no. 9 (February 1912), 1112
61 Lowrey, 'The Unspoiled Country,' 15, 57
62 *Rod and Gun*, 28, no. 1 (June 1926), a special insert titled 'Ontario – North America's Premier Summer Playground,' iv
63 *Ontario: The Lake-Land Playground*, (Toronto 1923), 59

7 The Temagami Indians and the Forest Reserve

1 Indian Affairs, Temagami, 'Plan of Islands in Lake Temagami,' Lands and Forests map, 1905; McLean to White, 18 January 1906, referring to a blueprint map
2 Indian Affairs, Temagami, White to McLean, 25 January 1906; Petition, 23 February 1907; Cockburn to McLean, 12 March 1906, and McLean to Cockburn, 18 March 1907; McLean to White, 7 February 1910
3 Indian Affairs, Temagami, White to S. Stuart, Assistant Secretary, 20 January 1910
4 Indian Affairs, Temagami, Memorandum of Pedley, 6 November 1912; Bray to Pedley, 11 November 1912; White Bear to Cockburn, 28 January 1913; McLean to White, 7 February 1913; White to McLean, 22 February 1913; McLean to White, 25 February 1913; McLean to Cockburn, 25 February 1913; White to McLean, 3 March 1913; White to McLean, 13 March 1913; McLean to Cockburn, 17 March 1913; McLean to White, 18 March 1913; White Bear to Cockburn, 27 May 1913; McLean to Cockburn, telegram, 31 May 1913; McLean to White, 3 June 1913
5 Indian Affairs, Temagami, McLean to White, 14 June 1914; White Bear to Cockburn, 19 July 1913; same to same, 19 January 1914; Scott to Cockburn, 7 April 1914; Cockburn to Scott, 26 June 1914; Memorandum, D.C. Scott, 23 March 1915; Cockburn to McLean, 17 May 1915

6 Indian Affairs, Temagami, Alex Paul to George Cockburn, 3 July 1915; Alex Paul to Superintendent, 3 September 1917; Albert Grigg to McLean, 21 September 1917
7 Indian Affairs, Temagami, White Bear to Indian Affairs, 21 May 1910; White to McLean, 28 June 1911; Numerous letters and postcards with picture of dam, summer 1912, terminating with J. Bell, company secretary of British Canadian Power, to McLean of Indian Affairs; Paul to Pedley, autumn 1912; McLean to White, 4 October 1912
8 Indian Affairs, Temagami, White to McLean, 28 June 1911
9 AO, 'Re Forest Reserve at Lake Temagami,' 7 January 1901, *Woods and Forest Report Book II*, 445
10 Background material on the complex law of native hunting and fishing rights may be found in P.A. Cumming and N.H. Mickenberg, *Native Rights in Canada* (2nd ed., Toronto 1972), 207–26. See also Donna Lea Hawley, *The Indian Act Annotated* (Toronto 1986), 66–70, 90–5.
11 *Rod and Gun*, 11 (April 1910), 1080–2; 12, 1317–18; 13 (July 1911), 216
12 *Rod and Gun*, 10 (June 1908), 94; 10 (August 1909), 266; 'Dixmont,' 'Moose Hunting in Temagami,' *Forest and Stream*, 9 December 1911, 835–7
13 Richard S. Lambert with Paul Pross *Renewing Nature's Wealth* (Toronto 1967), 452
14 Ontario Game and Fish Commission, *Reports* (1909–11)
15 *Ontario Game and Fisheries Act*, 7 Edw. VII (1907) cap. 49, sec. 8; *Ontario Game Protection Act*, 63 Vict. (1900) cap. 49, sec. 32
16 The provision of the 1900 *Forest Reserves Act*, which prohibited hunting and fishing in reserves 'except under regulations' was re-enacted without change as 10 Edw. VII (1910) cap. 8, sec. 3. Firearms control during the closed season for moose, reindeer, and caribou apparently applied to the Temagami Forest Reserve, but no records of Indian complaints about enforcement have been located by the authors. See AO, RG3, OC56/70, 27 June 1906, and OC59/187, August 1907. So far as the authors have been able to determine no absolute prohibitions against recreational fishing were ever enforced; if they had been, commercial lodges could not have survived.
17 Indian Affairs, Temagami, White Bear to Department, 21 May 1910; White to McLean, 28 June 1911; AO, 'Memorandum for the Honourable the Minister of Lands, Forest and Mines,' 18 May 1911, *Woods and Forests Report Book IV*, 105–108. The order-in-council transferring authority to Lands and Forests was dated 23 May 1911. By 13 June 1911 the decision to rescind had been taken. The decision to allow hunting and fishing under general legislation was recommended by White to his minister on 28 September 1911 and implemented two weeks later. See *Woods and Forests Report Book IV*, 143–4, and AO, RG3, OC67/120, 10 October 1911.
18 American Philosophical Society, Philadelphia, Frank G. Speck Collection, unpublished paper, 3. Part of quote in Philadelphia *Public Ledger*, 23 November 1913. Quoted in TTP, Temagami Band Appellants' Factum, vol. 3, 76.

19 Frank G. Speck, *Family Hunting Territories and Social Life of Various Algonkian Bands of the Ottawa Valley*, Canada, Department of Mines, GSC, Memoir 70, no. 8, Anthropological Series (Ottawa 1915), 5–6. See also F.G. Speck, 'The Indians and Game Preservation,' *The Red Man*, 6, no. 1 (September 1913), 23–4. Quoted in TTP, Temagami Band Appellants' Factum, vol. 3, 72.

20 Speck, *Family Hunting Territories*, 13

21 HBC Archives, Fur Trade Annual Reports, A74/14 (1904–5), 24

22 HBC Archives, A.39/14/1, 'Legal Opinions and Correspondence re Seizure of Furs at Montizambert and Biscotasing.' The attorney-general's remarks were made in a letter of 6 June 1910 to H.S. Osler, one of several lawyers assisting the HBC with its defence. Osler outlined the company's legal argument in a letter to Foy dated 29 June 1910.

23 HBC Archives, A12/FT230/1, 'Game Acts 1892–1906,' Bacon to the Governor, 16 December 1916

24 HBC Archives, A12/FT230/1, London copy of a letter from the Fur Trade Commissioner to District Managers in Ontario, 7 December 1916

25 HBC Archives, Fur Trade Annual Reports, A74/23a (1914–15), 49; A74/24 (1915–16), 54–5; A74/25 (1916–17), 58. Temagami was at this time within the HBC's Lake Huron District.

26 Barbara M. Wilson, ed., *Ontario and the First World War 1914–1918*, Champlain Society (Toronto 1977), Editor's Introduction, cx

27 R.J. Fraser, 'The Effect of the War on the Indian Trapper of the North,' *Rod and Gun* (March 1915), 1001

28 Indian Affairs, Temagami, L.V. Rorke to A. Mackenzie, 12 July 1929, 'Plan of Subdivison of South End of Bear Island,' November 1916

29 The preceding paragraphs are based on correspondence in the HBC Archives, A.12/L. Misc./6, 'Bear Island 1914'

30 AO, RG53, Provincial Secretary's Papers, *Temagami Island Lease Books*.

31 HBC Archives, A.12/FT Misc./291. Material on Guppy is from Hal Pink, ed., *Bill Guppy: King of the Woodsmen* (London 1940), 209–14. The $140,000 claim appears high.

32 'The Sportsman Tourist,' *Forest and Stream*, 2 April 1904, 266

33 AO, 'Memorandum: Re Remunerations to Be Paid Guides in Temagami Forest Reserve,' *Woods and Forests Report Book III*, 248

34 Matthew Parkinson, 'Lake Temagami, a Northern Ontario Playground,' *Canadian Magazine* (June 1914), 170; Myrle Cameron, 'A Day's Journey in the Wilds,' *Rod and Gun*, 7, no. 8 (January 1911), 1020; Grey Owl, *Pilgrims of the Wild* (Toronto 1968), 12–13; 'In Temagami's Tangled Wild,' *Rod and Gun*, 8, no. 1 (June 1906), 42

35 Grand Trunk Railway Passenger Traffic Department, *Playgrounds: A Booklet of Information Regarding the Tourist, Fishing and Hunting Resorts Reached by the Grand Trunk Railway System* (1918), 16; 'Ontario Guides Will Organize,' *Rod and Gun*, 22, no. 1 (June 1920), 15–17;

'Northern Ontario Outfitters and Guides Association,' *Rod and Gun*, 22, no. 4 (October 1920), 602, 604

8 Lumbering and Pulpwood Operations between the Wars

1 Licences held by the Marshay Lumber Co. for limits within the boundaries of the TFR were as follows: 1914–33, Marshay; 1916–26, Frechette (33 square miles); 1919–26, Sweeny (E$\frac{1}{2}$); 1923–33, Sweeny (W$\frac{1}{2}$); 1923–33, Moffatt and Beulah (42 square miles); and 1928–33, Garibaldi (S$\frac{1}{2}$). Outside the Temagami Forest but in the immediate area, Marshay also had the rights to the parts of Garvey and Hennessy twps to the east of the CNR. See Timber Commission, *Proceedings*, 9418, 9806, 9824, 10,079, 10,668, 11,134; and BTB, vol. 5, 14. See also Timber Commission, *Special Report on the Marshay Lumber Company, Limited*, 44–6.

2 Licences held by Manley Chew in TFR were as follows: 1914–23, Fraleck; 1916–30, Howey; 1917–28, Grigg; 1919, Telfer. Timber Commission, *Proceedings*, 5192, 5223, 5197

3 Licences in TFR in name of Arnold and Bell: 1914–29, Burwash and Welcome Lake (10$\frac{1}{4}$ square miles of Valin Twp); 1916–27, Cotton (27 square miles); 1916–29, Valin (30 square miles); 1916–40, Beresford. Timber Commission, *Proceedings*, 21–38, 118ff, 3890ff, 5173ff. See also Timber Commission, *Special Report on the Spanish River Lumber Company Limited, and Associated Companies*, 50–5.

4 DLF, *History of the Gogama Forest District* (Toronto 1964), 18. The Ontario *Saw Mill Licenciate Book* 1924–30 (in AO), listed Duncan Campbell as operating a sawmill with a capacity of 6–7,000 ft at Moffatt between 1924 and 1930.

5 *Inactive Mills* book, 1924–43 (in AO); Acme also owned a sawmill at Ruel Station on CNR just west of the Temagami Forest (cutting 30 Mfbm in 1931–2 and 35 Mfbm in 1934–5), as well as a small tie mill in Creelman, which cut 400 ties in the 1931–2 season.

6 DLF, *History of Sudbury Forest District* (Toronto 1964), 25

7 See AO, Ferguson Papers, Box 95, 'Lumber Licences,' J.B. Gillies to Ferguson, 2 July 1926: 'At the 1918 sale on the Sturgeon we bought two townships but the market since then has been such that we were not warranted in going ahead with the mill we had in mind as we have not seen our way clear on the markets prevailing since then, to get back the price we bid for this timber.' This statement would explain the fact that Charlotte Whitton does not mention Gillies' cuttings on these limits, though they are drawn on the map of limits owned by Gillies. Charlotte Whitton, *A Hundred Years A-Fellin'* (Ottawa 1943), 108, and inside cover map

8 'Sturgeon Falls Pulp Company Agreement, 6 October 1898,' paragraph 12, Ontario *Sessional Papers*, 1898–9, no. 74

9 Timber Commission, *Proceedings*, 8419, 8439

10 Timber Commission, *Proceedings*, testimony of Colonel Gibson (counsel

for Spanish Mills), 7612; letter G.R. Gray (director of Spanish Mills) to Ferguson, 30 March 1918, 8380; and same to same, 1 August 1918, 8392. For discussion of townships where permits applied for were refused, see ibid., 8484–9.

11 Timber Commission, *Proceedings*, testimony of G.R. Gray, 11,061–92

12 Memorandum, Grigg to Ferguson, October 22, 1918, Timber Commission, Exhibit 385, Box 18

13 Timber Commission, *Proceedings*, 8352, 8372, 8397. The 1919 sales are listed in the *BTB*, vol. 4, 278. Prices include Crown dues, the upset price, and the bid, calculated on a board-measure basis. Details on the tenders bid and accepted in the July 1919 sale are found in *Proceedings*, 8398, and in Exhibit 387, Box 18.

14 Whitton, *A Hundred Years A-Fellin'*, 72–85

15 Major Sidney H. Burwash, 'Goward and the Timagami Timber Co. Ltd., 1924 to 1967,' J.C. Elliott, ed., *Temagami Centennial Booklet* (Temagami 1967), 22–3; Timber Commission, *Proceedings*, 16, 616–17, 618.

Shareholders of the A.B. Gordon Co. were A.B. Gordon, George Gordon, and H.J. Bartlett of Michigan. The original officers of the Timagami Timber Co. were C.W. Wilkinson of Toronto, president, and A.B. Gordon, vice-president, while George Gordon and Duncan McLaren of Toronto were directors.

The *Saw Mill Licentiate Book* provides information on Timagami Timber's production.

Limits held in the name of Timagami Timber in the Temagami Forest are as follows: 1924–39, Cassels; 1925–7, E½ Law; 1927–41, Strathy; 1930–41, Best (12 square miles); 1935–41, SE¼ Chambers and part Briggs; and 1937-?, Strathcona (29 square miles). For detail on the 1923 Cassels fire and subsequent sale, see Ontario OC131/186, 31 August 1923, and OC132/143, 12 October 1923.

16 Limits held by Geo. Gordon in the southeast of the Temagami Forest were 1927–35, SE¼ Law. Limits held by Geo. Gordon and Co. in the southeast of the forest were: 1935–38, SW¼ Law, and 1936–41, 12 square miles in the north part of Olive.

17 J.F. Turnbull, A.B. Doran, and A.C. Thrupp, 'Logging Operations on Temagami Forest Reserve in Ontario,' *Canada Lumberman*, 41, no. 22 (15 November 1921), 42–3

18 Wes McNutt, 'William Milne & Sons Limited,' *Temagami Centennial Booklet*, 45–6. Licences owned by Milne in the Temagami Forest were as follows: 1921–5, Askin (N and NE TNOR); 1925–31, SW¼ Riddell; ?–1927, Law (east part); 1934–?, Milne (east part, spruce for Abitibi); 1935–40, Briggs (5 square miles); and 1937–?, Strathcona and Briggs (22 square miles).

19 Lumber companies operating around the northern periphery of the Temagami Forest in the 1920s and 1930s included the Boivin Tie and Timber Co., the Fesserton Timber Co., the Double Diamond Lumber Co., the Tri-

angle Lumber Co., the Hawk Lake Lumber Co., the Night Hawk Lumber Co., the Edgar Gagne Lumber Co., the Feldman Timber Co., S. McChesney and Sons Co., M.T. Poupore, and Blakey and Kennedy. See Timber Commission, *Proceedings*, 5959, Ontario DLF, *History of the Cochrane Forest District* (Toronto 1964); DLF, *History of the Gogama Forest District*, 14–20; *BTB* and *Timber Sales Books* (in AO).

20 DLF, *History of the Swastika Forest District* (Toronto 1964), 26, 58–60. The *Saw Mill Licentiate Book* and the *Inactive Mills* book list many small operators in the Elk Lake and Matachewan areas, including M.A. Wilson, E.A. Woods, J.B. Moyneur, Rahn Lake Mines, and Arbade Gold Mines.

21 See letter Deputy Minister to James Bay Lumber Co., *BTB*, vol. 2, 152–3; DLF, *History of the Swastika Forest District*, 26; *Inactive Mills* book. Details on the Milner and Leith sale are found in Ontario, OC149/396, 7 January 1926, and OC153/365, 25 August 1926.

22 Department of Public Works records re Montreal River at Latchford 1907–40 in the possession of the authors. The observations on Booth's drive were made by G.W. Schneider who supervised the Latchford dam and other nearby facilities for DPW.

23 *Saw Mill Licentiate Book*. The Auld and Klock sale is explained in Ontario, OC147/401, 30 September 1925.

24 DLF, *History of the Swastika Forest District*, 24. Larry E. Hodgins, 'Economic Geography of Timagami District' (BA diss., University of Toronto 1958), asserts that Murphy was operating in the Montreal watershed after 1912, cutting jack pine for his Latchford lumber mill and spruce for Brodie of Ottawa; after the 'gale' of 1940 he moved to the Willow Island Lake area (54). See also *Saw Mill Licentiate Book* and *Inactive Mills* book. A.B. Gordon paid D. McLennan's debt of $71,000 and took over his inactive mill and limits (5½ square miles) in the mid-1930s. Because the limit was cut over, A.B. Gordon was granted, without competition, two parcels in Dane Twp, by OC, 4 December 1935. For the 1936–7 season he acquired by sale two concessions in Barber Twp. Considering that the quantity of timber on these townships was less than 2 M ft, it was 'not adequate for the full run of the mill at Latchford'; hence A.B. Gordon Co. was again granted, without competition, a parcel 15 square miles in the southeast portion of Klock Twp. Note OC, 10 December 1936

25 Ontario, OC138/347, 12 August 1924

26 Askin (fire damage and maturity), OC113/285, 28 July 1921; Macbeth (fire hazard), OC114/315, 20 September 1921; Coleman and Kittson (fire damage and wind threat), OC128/205, 3 May 1923; Cassels and Strathy (fire damage), OC131/186, 31 August 1923, and OC132/143, 12 October 1923; Milner and Leith (fire damage), OC149/396, 7 January 1926; Fripp and Musgrove (fire damage), OC159/426B, 16 August 1927

27 Ontario, OC132/143, 12 October 1923

28 PAC, RG39, Royal Commission on Pulpwood, *Evidence*, vol. 9, 36, testi-

mony of William Milne; G.A. Mulloy, 'A Visit to the Forest in the Sudbury–North Bay Districts,' *Forestry Chronicle*, 1, no. 2 (December 1925)

Dr Judson Clark criticized the forest reserve program in DLF, *Annual Report* (1922), 282, where he argued: 'Several large areas of provincial forest lands have been set apart as Forest Reserves. The statute provides that timber may not be cut on those reserve areas except when mature or when killed by fire. I submit that this leaves them on a par with all other forest lands, except that such reserved lands may not be cut over for the purpose of opening up for agricultural settlement.' The pathological research, especially concerning white pine blister rust is noted in *Annual Report* (1920), 224–31.

29 W.N. Millar, 'Sustained Yield – Its Legislative Basis in Canada,' *Forestry Chronicle*, 2, no. 4 (December 1927 [*sic*, 1926])
30 Richard S. Lambert with Paul Pross, *Renewing Nature's Wealth* (Toronto 1967), 195–9 and 321–3
31 17 Geo. v (1927), cap. 12
32 DLF, *Annual Report* (1927)
33 From a file folder in the general research material of DLF, *History Committee Records*, 'Ontario Forestry Board'; Lambert and Pross, *Renewing Nature's Wealth*, 201
34 A.P. Pross, 'The Development of Professions in the Public Service: The Foresters in Ontario,' *Canadian Public Administration*, 10 (1967), 395; 19 Geo. v (1929), cap. 13; 19 Geo. v (1929), cap. 14
35 Ontario, DLF, *Annual Report* (1929), 8. The *Provincial Forests Act*, 1929, secs 6, 7
36 DLF, *Annual Report* (1926), Minister's Report, 11
37 This phrase attributed to J.A. Brodie is quoted in Lambert and Pross, *Renewing Nature's Wealth*, 201. Brodie was in charge of research in 1927 and was made chief of the Division of Research in 1941
38 Pross, 'The Development of Professions,' 393, 395; Lambert and Pross, *Renewing Nature's Wealth*, 323; DLF, *Annual Report* (1928), Minister's Report, 14; H.V. Nelles, 'Timber Regulations, 1900–1960,' DLF, *History Committee Records*, 69–72; Ontario, DLF, file folder: 'Ontario Forestry Board'
39 DLF, *Annual Report* (1928), 14
40 Lambert and Pross, *Renewing Nature's Wealth*, 234–9, contains background information on the air service. Temagami details were provided by Wilfred Eckersley, interview, 1 March 1978
41 DLF, *Annual Report* (1929), 8, 150
42 AO, Prime Minister's Papers, 'Ferguson Papers: 1926 General Correspondence Re Timber License,' J.S. Gillies to Ferguson, 2 July 1926; J.S. Gillies to Ferguson, 10 July 1926. Ontario, DLF, *Timber Sales Books*, licences 144, 155, 158, 159, and 163 for the season 1927–8
43 DLF, *Annual Report* (1928), 12–13

44 Ontario, DLF, *Timber Sales Books*, vol. 8, 126
45 DLF, *Annual Report* (1928), 15; Lambert and Pross, *Renewing Nature's Wealth*, 263
46 DLF, ibid. (1931); *Saw Mill Licentiate Book*
47 Peter Oliver, *G. Howard Ferguson: Ontario Tory* (Toronto 1977), 343
48 *BTB*, vol. 2, 87, Memorandum, Deputy Minister to Minister Lyons, 11 January 1926. In DLF, *History of the Swastika Forest District*, 24, the following explanation is provided for Booth's reduced activity: 'By 1924 forest fires had reduced the accessible pulpwood stands to the point where annual cuts became too small to justify the long river drive to Ottawa.' 'Montreal River Pulp Concession Agreement,' 12 January 1928, vol. 10, 40
49 George Carruthers, *Paper in the Making* (Toronto 1947), 687; H.V. Nelles, *The Politics of Development: Forests, Mines and Hydro-Electric Power in Ontario, 1849–1941* (Toronto 1974), 447; 'Agreement Defining the Boundaries of the Pulp Limit Known as the Sturgeon Falls Limit,' in *Timber Sales Books*, vol. 8, 25. Timber Commission, *Proceedings* 78–93
50 DFL, *Annual Report* (1930), 18; DLF, Statement of Operations, 'Statistical Returns on the Manufacture of Pulp and Paper, 1928–1941'
51 AO, Ferguson Papers, Ferguson to Strachan Johnson, 17 April 1926, also quoted in Nelles, *Politics of Development*, 384
52 Ontario, OC, 11 October 1933
53 Sturgeon Valley settlers were cutting pulpwood at the time, either from their own lots or on Crown lands, and were shipping it by rail to the Eddy Co. at Hull. This cutting probably did not extend far into the TFR boundaries, because of the distance from the Sturgeon River valley settlements. DLF, *History of the Gogama Forest District*, explains that the Abitibi Company held eight townships in the district, but that it had not operated them since 1927, except through third-party agreements. Third-party agreements may have had to be registered with the department, but they have not been found.

Files from 'The Statistical Returns on the Manufacture of Pulp and Paper, 1928–1941,' relating to the Sturgeon Falls mill in the thirties state that its annual capacity was originally 135 tons of newsprint, but, by the end of the period, capacity is stated as being only 70 tons per annum. The Abitibi Company finally reached an agreement with the provincial government in 1945. In 1946 the Sturgeon Falls mill reopened and the company authorized the spending of $2 million. René Guenette, 'Histoire de Sturgeon Falls (1878–1960)' (thèse de maîtrise en arts [histoire], University Laval 1965), 16
54 DLF, *Annual Report* (1927), 14
55 OC, 24 December 1931; OC, 19 November 1930; OC, 24 December 1931, and 28 October 1932; OC, 10 April 1934
56 The number of licensed timber berths declined from 71 in 1927–8, to 30 in 1930–1, and 15 in 1931–2, but increased to 80 in 1935–6. Numbers do

not, of course, indicate size, species, or real activity. See also DLF, *Annual Report* (1928), (1929), (1931), (1938), (1941). There were many licences for cedar posts and poles in the Temagami Forest in the late thirties.

57 Lambert and Pross, *Renewing Nature's Wealth*, 326–32; C.D. Howe, 'Twenty-five Years in Retrospect and Some Suggestions for the Prospect,' *Forestry Chronicle*, 10, no. 1 (February 1934), 6

58 From *To the Electors – A Statement by Mitchell F. Hepburn* (Toronto 1934), quoted in Nelles, *Politics of Development*, 455. OC, 11 September 1934

59 OC, 11 September 1934; OC, 20 May 1936; OC, 22 October 1936; OC, 23 March 1935. In its attempt to stabilize the labour situation in the industry, the Henry government had specified in notices to timber sales that companies should use 'as far as possible, local labour.' See, for example, the notice for part of Dane Twp, 2 October 1933, *Timber Sales Books*, vol. 10, 43. In suspending the pulpwood manufacturing in 1935, the Liberals specified that 'local labour must be used in connection with the work of cutting or preparing the pulpwood for export and the wages paid must be fair and reasonable and satisfactory to the Minister.' The order-in-council of 23 March 1935 is reproduced in DLF, *Annual Report* (1936), 16

60 Nelles, 'Timber Regulations,' 84–5. 24 Geo, v (1934), cap. 66

61 DLF, *Annual Report* (1939), Minister's Report, 21; W.C. Cain, 'Forest Management in Ontario,' *Forestry Chronicle*, 15, no. 1 (March 1939), 23

62 Cain, 'Forest Management in Ontario.' For information on the evolution of the shoreline reserve policy in Algonquin and Quetico, see Gerald Killan and George M. Warecki of the University of Western Ontario, 'Saving Quetico-Superior: The Ontario Perspective, 1927–1960,' (paper presented at the Forest History Society Conference, Vancouver, October 1986).

63 The disciplinary clause was included in the notice of sale for the southeast of Chambers Township north of Beaver Lake, sold by tender 3 October 1935 to Timagami Timber: *Timber Sales Books*, vol. 10, 104. Cain in 'Forest Management in Ontario' refers to both the 'Timagami district' and the 'Temagami Tourist area.'

64 Cain stated in 'Forest Management in Ontario' that for the Temagami tourist area 'a progressive planting program has commenced with the object of filling in where nature failed to restock.' The annual reports for the period do not, however, begin to mention the distribution of trees through ranger headquarters until 1938, perhaps because the number was too small. 'Ranger headquarters' existed mainly north of Parry Sound. DLF, *Annual Report* (1939), 110; ibid. (1940), 140

65 Cain, 'Forest Management in Ontario,' 22

66 Lambert and Pross, *Renewing Nature's Wealth*, 344–53, and *Journals of the Legislative Assembly of Ontario* (1941), App., Majority and Minority Reports; ibid. (1939–40), App., 87

67 Ontario, Royal Commission to Investigate and Report upon the Affairs of Abitibi Power Company, Limited, 1940, *Report* (March 1941), 11. In a

1937 report that appears in the inquiry proceedings, vol. 3, 416–22, Abitibi indicated the difficulties of operating the Espanola and Sturgeon Falls mills on an economical basis.

9 Recreation and the Temagami Wilderness

1 *North Bay Nugget*, 5 July 1927; J.H. Thompson and Allen Seager, *Canada 1922–1939: Decades of Discord* (Toronto 1985), 85–7
2 Stanley and Laura Belle Hodgins, the parents of one of the authors, witnessed a car consumed by low-lying bog on their first automobile trip to Temagami in 1927. Muskeg continued to consume vehicles when the Ferguson Highway was later extended to Cochrane: see Peter Oliver, *G. Howard Ferguson: Ontario Tory* (Toronto 1977), 340
3 Abbott T. Fenn, *The Story of Keewaydin's 50 Years at Dunmore, 1910–1959* (Keewaydin Camps Inc. 1959), 18
4 Brian Back, *The Keewaydin Way: A Portrait, 1893–1983* (Temagami 1983), 93
5 Ibid., 98–111, 115
6 Ibid., 93–6, 116–18, 124
7 Ibid., 115–28
8 Ibid., 134, 136. Also Pamela Glenn, 'Youth Camp Marks Fiftieth Summer,' *Temagami Times*, 12, no. 3 (Fall 1982); and interviews by Hodgins at Wabun's fiftieth anniversary banquet, August 1982. Hugh Funnell to Pamela Glenn, March 1985
9 Ann Hall, 'Arthur Lewis Cochrane: A Biographical Sketch' (BED diss., Queen's University 1964), 30. This paper and other items on Camp Temagami may be found in the archives of the Ontario Camping Association (OCA) at Trent University. Other papers relating to Camp Temagami exist in the Temagami Lakes Association (TLA) Archives and in the personal possession of A.L. Cochrane's granddaughter, Carol Cochrane (Bangay) of North Bay.
10 *Globe and Mail*, 29 April 1947, and *Telegram* (Toronto), 6 November 1954. Cochrane distributed Boy Scout literature to leaders of the early camping movement such as Taylor Statten. See C.A.M. Edwards, *Taylor Statten: A Biography* (Toronto 1960).
11 OCA, *Blue Lake and Rocky Shore: A History of Children's Camping in Ontario* (Toronto 1983), especially prefatory material and 1–9
12 TLA Archives, Grafton Papers, especially the Wigwasati folders for 1930, 1931, 1938, 1942, 1949, 1952, 1953, and 1962
13 Papers and records concerning Camp Wanapitei in the possession of Bruce W. Hodgins. See especially brochures and registration forms 1932, 1954, 1956, and 1968. Note also, David Henderson Carr, *Youth Goes North: Adventures in Temagami, 1933–1980* (London 1981), 11–14. Interviews by Hodgins with Ed Archibald, 1956–9 and Mrs Maki, 1981
14 Northwoods Papers, OCA Archives, Trent University

15 Jamie Benidickson, 'Idleness, Water and a Canoe: Canadian Recreational Paddling between the Wars,' in B.W. Hodgins and M. Hobbs, eds, *Nastawgan* (Toronto 1985), 163–82

16 Detailed notes of these four trips have survived in the possession of one of Hubert Brown's daughters, Mrs Joan Hillary of Lakefield, Ontario. Copies are in the Trent University Archives. See also Bruce W. Hodgins, 'The Lure of the Temagami-based Canoe Trip,' in Hodgins and Hobbs, eds, *Nastawgan*, 189–202.

17 Ruth E. Terborg, 'Temagami for Women,' *Appalachia* (June 1936), 2–9

18 Department of the Interior, *Canoeing in Canada* (Ottawa 1934), 61. For more details see Benidickson, 'Idleness, Water and a Canoe.'

19 HBC, Temagami Post Journal, B488 a/2, 16 August 1938. Hugh Mackay Ross, *The Apprentice's Tale* (Winnipeg 1986), 158; 2nd letter of Ross to J. Benidickson, 1 December 1986

20 *Temagami Experience*, 2 (Summer 1976); TNOR, *Come to Temagami: Spend Your 1929 Vacation in North America's Premier Summer Resort*, brochure 1929

21 TNOR, *Come to Temagami*; general information on Temagami Inn (Lodge) comes from interviews by Pamela Glenn with Abe Posluns, Alex Solway, Irwin Haladner, Bill Metcalfe, Leny Potts, Gordon Turner, and Frank Spitzig, January and July 1985. Also note Ross, *Apprentice's Tale*, 162.

22 *Temiskaming Speaker*, 24 March 1976 (on the occasion of Herbert Wilson's 100th birthday); TNOR, *Come to Temagami*; and *Temagami Experience*, 2 (Summer 1976)

23 Ron Johnstone, 'White Bear Resort: A Past Permeated with the Legends of Hollywood,' *Temagami Times*, 14 (Spring 1984)

24 TNOR, *Come to Temagami*; interview by Ruth Snider with William Gooderham, September 1976, and 'Bill Gooderham, Member of the Year,' *Temagami Times*, 4, no. 2 (Autumn 1974)

25 TNOR, *Come to Temagami*; interviews by Ruth Snider with Alf P. Cook during the summer of 1975 and 1976 and by Pamela Glenn with Dr John Keith, Dr William Keith, and Mrs Reg McConnell and Dave McConnell, January 1985. Allabough with L.W. Thomas wrote *North of Fifty-Three* (Omaha, Nebr., 1919), which contained tales involving the Guppy family.

26 Capt. E.T. Guppy, 'Many Boat Lines Have Served Temagami Lake,' in J.C. Elliott, ed., *Temagami Centennial Booklet* (Temagami 1967), 7–9, and Niki Plumstead, 'Boats and Boat Lines of Lake Temagami,' *Temagami Experience*, 1 (1976), including reprint of 1929 timetable of Perron and Marsh

27 AO, RG53, *Temagami Island Lease Books*

28 Roy I. Wolfe, 'Summer Cottagers in Ontario,' *Economic Geography*, 27 (1951), 24, uses 'clannishness' to describe the pattern of Pennsylvania cottaging he identified.

29 E. Voorhis, 'Temagami,' *Beaver* (September 1929), 262; HBC, Temagami Post Journal, 'Temagami 1938–39,' B488a/2, entry for 31 January 1939

30 *Captains of the Clouds* still occasionally reappears on television. When the film was being made, Hugh Ross, the HBC manager on Bear Island rented his dog team for a brief cameo appearance. See Ross, *The Apprentice's Tale*, 183–4.
31 TLA Archives, Temagami Association Constitution, 1932; R.B. Newcomb to K.L. Wismer, 1 July 1932; Report of the Temagami Association, 1 July 1932; Notice of 1933 Association Day meeting. In 1935 the Temagami Association's founding president, R.B. Newcomb, killed his wife and then took his own life in a fit of depression related to his own deteriorating economic situation. In the late 1930s, a plaque in Newcomb's honour was affixed to a rock near the HBC post on Bear Island, where it remains.
32 See DLF, *Annual Report* (1933), 103, for an official version of the boat-building episode. Hepburn's charges against Finlayson are noted in Richard S. Lambert with Paul Pross, *Renewing Nature's Wealth* (Toronto 1967), 325.
33 HBC, Temagami Post Journal, entries for 20 August, 23 and 24 September, and 1 October 1932. Dignitaries frequently stayed on Island 1007 as guests of Mrs Christine Denton, widow of the Ohio industrialist Isaac Henry Denton, who originally leased the property in 1916 after visiting Robert Newcomb.
34 Premier Frost, accompanied by several cabinet colleagues and other members of the Legislature, stopped to visit Lake Temagami in September 1952 during the course of a trip to Moosonee on the Ontario Northland. *Globe and Mail*, 12, 13, and 14 September 1952, and A.O.C. Cole, interviewed by Bruce Hodgins, January 1985
35 Back, *Keewaydin Way*, 107, 128–36, 141–2, and 170–3. Heb Evans published accounts of his northern Canadian canoeing expeditions in *Canoeing Wilderness Waters* (New York 1975) and *The Rupert that Was* (Cobalt 1978).
36 Glenn, 'Youth Camp Marks Fiftieth Summer'
37 *Globe and Mail*, 24 August 1952; Hall, 'Arthur Lewis Cochrane,' 33–6; Jack Passmore, 'Among Ourselves,' *Canadian Camping*, 8 (February 1956), 17–19; Garrett Williamson, 'At 80, Originator of Boys' Camp Still Does Monte Cristo Dive,' *Saturday Night*, 5 July 1949; *Telegram*, 6 November 1954; OCA Archives, Trent University, Camp Temagami Papers
38 Wanapitei Papers in the possession of Bruce W. Hodgins, especially 1956 and 1968 brochures and registration forms
39 OCA, *Blue Lake and Rocky Shore*, passim, and interviews of Irwin Haladner by Pamela Glenn, summer 1984. AO, *Temagami Island Lease Books*
40 Johnstone, 'White Bear Resort'
41 Interviews with the late Henry Woodman and Margaret Woodman by Bruce Hodgins. Interviews of J.E. 'Ev' Choat by Pamela Glenn, summer 1984, 1985
42 C.E.S. Franks, *The Canoe and White Water*, (Toronto and Buffalo 1977), 60–5; B.W. Hodgins, 'The Written Word on Canoeing and Canoe Tripping before 1960,' in Hodgins and Hobbs, eds, *Nastawgan*, 141–62

43 Hodgins, 'The Lure of the Temagami-based Canoe Trip'

44 Joseph Schull, *Ontario since 1867* (Toronto 1978), 323. K.J. Rea, *The Prosperous Years: The Economic History of Ontario 1939–75* (Toronto 1985), 60

45 Ontario Post-War Tourist Planning Conference, *Report of Proceedings* (Toronto 1944), 11, 32, 38–9; James Addison Taylor, 'The Natural and Cultural Relationships of Tourist Outfitters' Camps in Northern Ontario' (PHD diss., University of Illinois 1962), 1–15. The *Travel and Publicity Act*, 1949, marked the creation of the new department: see AO, RG5.

46 Dominion-Provincial Tourist Conference, *Report of Proceedings* (Ottawa 1947), 5–9; see also Second Annual Ontario Tourist Conference, *Summary of Proceedings* (Toronto 1950)

47 Albert Tucker, *Steam into Wilderness: Ontario Northland Railway, 1902–1962* (Toronto 1978), 186; AO, Frost Papers, 'ONTC: Temagami File'; Larry E. Hodgins, 'Economic Geography of the Lake Timagami District' (BA diss., University of Toronto 1958), 87–90. The colourful history of the *Naiad* is told in Richard Tatley, *The Steamboat Era in the Muskokas*, vol. 1, *To the Golden Years* (Erin 1983), 238–9, and vol. 2, *The Golden Years to the Present* (Erin 1984), 194, 209, 228.

48 Hodgins, 'Economic Geography of the Lake Timagami District,' 87–90

49 Schull, *Ontario since 1867*, 292, 329; Jonathan Manthorpe, *The Power and the Tories: Ontario Politics 1943 to the Present* (Toronto 1974), 37–8

50 OA, Frost Papers, 'ONTC: Temagami File,' Archibald Freeman to R.D. Michener, 6 January 1947, C.E. Reynolds to Michener, 14 December 1946, Michener to D.C. Romain, 14 April 1947

51 Hodgins, 'Economic Geography of the Lake Timagami District'

52 Interviews with Abe Posluns, Irwin Haladner, Alex Solway, and Bill Metcalfe, by Pamela Glenn, January 1985. See also Ian A. Hunter 'The Origin, Development and Interpretation of Human Rights Legislation,' in R. St John Macdonald and John P. Humphrey, eds, *The Practice of Freedom: Canadian Essays on Human Rights and Fundamental Freedoms* (Toronto 1979), 79–80.

53 Johnstone, 'White Bear Resort'

54 William Gooderham interviewed by Ruth Snider, September 1976

55 Hodgins, 'Economic Geography of the Lake Timagami District,' 35, 49; and Jack Stevens, Fran Shannon, and Locke Goddard, interviewed by Pamela Glenn, January 1985

56 Roy I. Wolfe, 'Recreational Land Use in Ontario' (PHD diss., University of Toronto 1956), 72, 74

57 John and Marjorie Mackenzie, *Ontario in Your Car* (Toronto 1950), 110

58 Hodgins, 'Economic Geography of the Lake Timagami District,' 46–8; John Rumney, 'Lands and Forests,' in *Temagami Centennial Booklet*, 41

59 Hodgins, 'Economic Geography of the Lake Timagami District,' 93, 95–7

60 Ibid., 49; Mrs Ernest Chretien, 'This is "Ravenscroft,"' *Temagami Centennial Booklet*, 61. Brenda Purdie and Kathy Chretien of Ravenscroft, interviewed by Pam Glenn, January 1985

61 TLA Archives, Rodgers to D.P. Douglass, Deputy Minister, Mines, 14 June 1961; Sullivan to Douglass, 15 June 1961. On the early promise of the Temagami Mine, see 'Five Test Holes All in One in Temagami District,' *Financial Post* 48, no. 31 (4 September 1954).

62 The development of the road is described in Faubert and Watts *v.* Temagami Mining Co. Ltd [1960], *Supreme Court Reports*, 235.

63 TLA Archives, boatline schedules, 1962–7

64 Richard Twain, interviewed by Bruce Hodgins (who experienced these hunts himself), 15 November 1977. See also Ross, *Apprentice's Tale*, 173–4.

65 Hodgins, 'Economic Geography of the Lake Timagami District,' 51. R.W. Butler, 'The Development of Snowmobiles,' in G. Wall and J.S. Marsh, eds, *Recreational Land Use: Perspectives on Its Evolution in Canada* (Ottawa 1982), 365–90

66 TLA Archives, Rodgers to W.J.K. Harkness, 11 April 1959; Commercial Camp Owners of Lake Temagami to Minister of Lands and Forests, 25 August 1959; TLA Fish Committee Report for 1959; TLA President's Report, 25 January 1968

67 Order-in-council re Temagami Islands, 18 March 1942. The provincial background to the decision is discussed in Lambert and Pross, *Renewing Nature's Wealth*, 425–7. Interest in resort lands grew during the late 1930s, while as the Second World War ended the total of summer resort sales and patents rose from 225 in 1942 to about 830 in 1945. See DLF, *Annual Report* (1935), 9, and *ibid.* (1946), 66.

68 Hodgins, 'Economic Geography of the Lake Timagami District,' 42; MNR, *Lake Temagami Plan for Land Use and Recreation Development* (Toronto 1973), 24–6

69 Hodgins, 'Economic Geography of the Lake Timagami District,' 39–45, and chart following 58; MNR, *Lake Temagami Plan*, 24–6

70 MNR, Temagami, 'Mining Patents, Crown Land Sales, License of Occupation, Crown Leases, Vesting Orders, Easements, Order in Council and Land Use Permit,' App. 1, 1982, and Ontario, OC902/58, 27 March 1958

71 *An Act to Amend the Crown Timber Act*, 1964, cap. 16, sec. 11

10 The Temagami Indians, 1929–1970

1 Indian Affairs, Temagami, MacKenzie to Cain, 10 July 1929, with enclosures of Cain to Mathias, William Pishabo, Alex Mathias, John Catt [*sic.* Katt], 15 June 1929. Note also 'Plan of Subdivision of South End of Bear Island,' November 1916, with pencilled notes regarding Indian homes, made about 1929. Most of the information that follows on the matter of the land claims first appeared in Bruce W. Hodgins, 'The Temagami Indians

and Canadian Federalism, 1867–1943,' *Laurentian University Review*, 11, no. 2 (February 1979), 71–95.

2 Indian Affairs, Temagami, Rorke to MacKenzie, 12 July 1929

3 Indian Affairs, Temagami, McLean to Cockburn, 19 July 1929; Cockburn to McLean, 19 July 1929; MacKenzie to Rorke, 2 August 1929; Cockburn to Indian Dept., 10 June 1930, enclosing Pishabo to Cockburn, nd; Rorke to MacKenzie, 17 June 1930

4 Indian Affairs, Temagami, Pishabo to Cockburn, 25 January 1932; Thomas McGookin to IA Secretary, 14 July 1933

5 Indian Affairs, Temagami, Dept. Sup't-Gen. to Cain, 1 September 1933, with enclosures

6 Indian Affairs, Temagami, Petition from Chiefs and Members of the Temagami Band, 1 October 1935; Cain to MacKenzie, 18 November 1936; MacKenzie to Antonio Lévesque, 25 November 1936; McGill to Cain, 9 December 1936, and Cain to McGill, 4 January 1937; McGill to Cain, 14 January 1937; 'A. Paul' is probably the Métis Joseph Paul, because Aleck Paul was at Austin Bay, not Bear Island, and was not yet that old.

7 Indian Affairs, Temagami, Cain to McGill, 29 April 1938; McGill to Cain, 23 May 1938

8 Indian Affairs, Temagami, Cain to McGill, 29 June 1938; Marleau to MacInnes, 15 August 1938; Marleau to MacInnes, 23 August 1938; Caldwell to Acting Director of Indian Affairs, 28 August 1938

9 Indian Affairs, Temagami, McGookin to McGill, 13 September 1938; D.J. Allen, Sup't, Reserves and Trusts to Marleau, 13 October 1938 and Marleau to Allen, 16 November 1938

10 Indian Affairs, Temagami, J.C.G. Herwig (Canadian Legion) to McGill, 20 January 1939; McGill to Herwig, 23 January 1939; Tom Saville, in Ottawa *Citizen*, 20 January 1939; Little to McGill, 25 March 1939; McGill to Little, 1 April 1939; Little to McGill, 13 April 1939; Chief Mathias to Little, 13 April 1939; Marleau to D.J. Allen, 27 May 1939, enclosing *Nugget* clipping, and Marleau to Allen, 24 June 1939

11 Indian Affairs, Temagami, Cain to Allen, 20 October 1939; Allen to Director, 23 October 1939, and Marleau report to Dept., October 1939

12 Indian Affairs, Temagami, White to F.H. Peters, Surveyor-General, Dept. of Mines and Resources, 24 November 1939; McGill to Cain, 6 December 1939; Fullarton to McGill, 1 April 1940; MacInnes to Fullarton, 23 April 1940, and Fullarton to McGill, 29 April 1940

13 Indian Affairs, Temagami, Chief John Twain to Little, 8 July 1940; Little to McGill, 16 September 1940; McGill to Little, 21 September 1940; Twain to McGill, 16 June 1941; McGill to Fullarton, 7 January 1941; Twain to Little, 28 May 1941; McGill to Little, 10 June 1941

14 Indian Affairs, Temagami, H.W. Crosbie, Chief, Div. of Land, DLF, to Director of IA [McGill], 28 September 1942; [Charles Campsell], Deputy Minister of Mines and Resources, to MacDougall, Deputy Minister of Lands and Forests, 6 October 1942

15 Indian Affairs, Temagami, Crosbie to Campsell, 4 February 1943; C.N. Jackson, Acting DM of M and R, to MacDougall, 20 February 1943; Crosbie to Jackson, 3 March 1943; Ontario order-in-council, 18 May 1943, second draft; McGill to [Campsell] DM, 25 May 1943; F.J. Sullivan, DLF, to D.J. Allen, Sup't, IA, 30 June 1943; Sullivan to Allen, 2 October 1943. See also Bear Island Trial Decision, 455.

16 Indian Affairs, Temagami, Twain to Little from Parry Sound, 14 February and 8 March 1943, quotation from second letter; Twain to Little, 26 June 1943 and Director IA [McGill] to Little, 10 July 1943; R.D. Cummings to IA, 1 July 1943; Allen to Cummings, 18 September 1943.

17 Indian Affairs, Temagami, John Turner to J.P. Marchildon, 5 July 1943; J.P. Lavoie to DLF, North Bay, 6 July 1943; Mrs E. Groves to Marchildon, 6 July 1943; Crosbie to Allen, 26 July 1943; Allen to Crosbie, 28 July 1943

18 PAC, RG10, vol. 8863, file 1/18–11–8, vol. 1, Hugh Conn to Chief Twain, 30 March 1954, and Chief Twain to Conn, 5 April 1954. See also Bear Island Trial Decision, 455.

19 Indian Affairs, Temagami, Marleau to the Department, 28 December 1943, with enclosure; Shannon to Director Harold McGill, 17 December 1943

20 John Webster Grant, *Moon of Wintertime: Missionaries and the Indians of Canada in Encounter since 1534* (Toronto 1984)

21 Interview by Pamela Glenn with Second Chief Rita O'Sullivan, October 1984

22 Interviews by Pamela Glenn with Rod and Linda Major (Bear Island teachers), Mary Lanoie and Rita O'Sullivan, October 1984; Larry E. Hodgins, 'Economic Geography of the Lake Timagami District' (BA diss., University of Toronto 1958), 96

23 E. Voorhis, 'Temagami,' *Beaver* (September 1929), 263

24 Material for these paragraphs on the *Silent Enemy* comes from the following sources: *How the Silent Enemy Was Made*, souvenir edition; Donald B. Smith, *Long Lance: The True Story of an Imposter* (Toronto 1982), esp. ch. 15, 'The *Silent Enemy*,' 164–78; Hal Pink, ed., *Bill Guppy: King of the Woodsmen* (London 1940), 248–55; James M. Skinner, 'The Silent Enemy,' in his *The War, the West and the Wilderness* (New York 1979), 545–60; Eileen Creelman, 'Picture Map and Players: "The Silent Enemy," Story of Ojibway Indians, Opening Monday at Criterion,' *New York Sun*, 16 May 1930; a clipping entitled 'W. Douglas Burden Films Hardships of Indians in Canada,' 18 May 1930, from an unidentified New York paper; and Grey Owl, *Men of the Last Frontier* [1931] (Toronto 1973)

25 Colleen Parkes and Milan Novak, 'Fur Bearer Management in Ontario,' *Ontario Fish and Wildlife Review* 18, no. 3 (Fall 1979), 24–8

26 HBC, Temagami Post Journal, 24 and 25 March 1939

27 AO, RG3, Frost Papers, General Correspondence, Box 189, Twain to Frost, 30 March 1954, and Gemmell to Twain, 18 May 1954

28 Parkes and Novak, 'Fur Bearer Management.' Also Milan Novak, *The Beaver in Ontario* (Toronto, MNR, 1972); Ralph Bice, *Fur: the Trade that*

Put Upper Canada on the Map (Toronto, MNR, 1983); and J.E. Cameron, 'Don't Take Chances with Talaremia,' *Forest and Outdoors*, 47, no. 13 (March 1951). Grey Owl especially made his claims in *Pilgrims of the Wild* (Toronto 1935), 47–8. Details on beaver prices and federal programs come from the *Canada Year Books*, vols for 1920 to 1957; the quotation concerning 'aboriginal conservationist practices' is from the 1943–4 vol., 267.

29 HBC, Temagami Post Journal, 22 June 1940, 31 December 1940; and Hugh Mackay Ross, *The Apprentice's Tale* (Winnipeg 1986), 166

30 Interviews by Pamela Glenn with Stan Flemming (MNR Temagami) and with former Chief William Twain, October 1984; Bice, *Fur*, 32–40; also Parkes and Novak, 'Fur Bearer Management,' and Novak, *The Beaver*. Ontario, *Report of the Select Committee on Indian Affairs* (Toronto 1954), 10. See as well Leonard Butler, 'Canada's Wild Fur Crop,' *Beaver*, Outfit 281 (December 1950), 26–31; Leonard Butler, 'Nature of Cycle in Populations of Canadian Mammals,' *Canadian Journal of Zoology*, 31 (1953), 242–62; W. Macmillan, 'Beaver Bounces Back,' *Outdoors*, 9, no. 25 (December 1951); and C.F. Bodsworth, *Maclean's*, 15 July 1950

31 Bice, *Fur*, 63–70, 91–4

32 Hodgins, 'Economic Geography of the Lake Timagami District,' 84–5

33 Parkes and Novak, 'Fur Bearer Management,' 27–8; Novak, *The Beaver*, 15–20; and Canada, *Report on the Status of Canadian Wildlife Used by the Fur Industry* (Ottawa 1978), 3. MNR, *Lake Temagami Plan for Land Use and Recreation Development* (Toronto 1973), 32

34 Department of Travel and Publicity, press release, 28 July 1958. The HBC sold its Bear Island Post in the winter of 1971–2 to Bill Zufelt, who operated independently for several seasons.

35 Interview by Bruce Hodgins with Bill Eckersley, 1 March 1978

36 H.B. Hawthorn, ed., *A Survey of the Contemporary Indians of Canada: A Report on Economic, Political, Educational Needs and Policies* (Ottawa 1966), 360, and ch. 15

37 Ontario, *Report of the Select Committee on Indian Affairs*

38 Peter A. Cumming and Neil H. Mickenberg, *Native Rights in Canada* (Toronto 1972), 263–4, 279–80

11 Forest Operations and Resource Development in Temagami, 1940–1970

1 C. Parnell, 'Timber Cruising at Temagami,' *Beaver* (June 1943), 8–11

2 Richard S. Lambert with Paul Pross, *Renewing Nature's Wealth* (Toronto 1967), ch. 17

3 Ibid., 355, 397–404, 586

4 AO, Ontario, Royal Commission on Forestry, 1946–7, Box 4, *Proceedings*, 930–42; Box 5, Exhibit 59, 'On Timber Accounts,' 1

5 Ontario, MNR (and DLF predecessors), Temagami, Cutting Ledgers; Ontario, Royal Commission on Forestry, Box 19, file, 'Field Reports, North

Bay District'; Ruth Snider, 'General Return of Operations of Wm. Milne and Sons Ltd., 1921–1964' (undergraduate research paper, Trent University 1976)

6 Sidney Burwash, 'Goward and the Temagami Timber Co. Ltd.,' J.C Elliott, ed., *Temagami Centennial Booklet* (Temagami 1967), 22–3; Ontario, Royal Commission on Forestry, Box 19, file, 'Field Reports, North Bay District'

7 Ontario, Royal Commission on Forestry, Box 19, file, 'Field Reports, North Bay District'

8 Ibid.

9 Ibid., 'Re: Timber Allocation – Latchford Mills – A.J. Murphy Lumber Co. Ltd.'

10 Ibid. Note especially A.J. Murphy to Department of Lands and Forests, 8 September 1943; A.J. Murphy to Department of Lands and Forests, 18 October 1943; J.F. Sharpe to F.A. MacDougall, memo, 22 October 1943; J.F. Sharpe to A.J. Murphy, 22 October 1943; A.J.Murphy to J.F. Sharpe, 3 November 1943; AO, RG1E3, Ontario, DLF, *License Journal*, 34 (1938–43)

11 Ontario, Royal Commission on Forestry, Box 19, file, 'Field Reports, North Bay District,' and MNR, Temagami, Cutting Ledgers, 1960–1 and 1965–6

12 Royal Commission on Forestry, Box 19, file, 'Field Reports, North Bay District'; also note Charlotte Whitton, *A Hundred Years A-Fellin'* (2nd ed., Ottawa 1974), 78, 108. Whitton notes 1927 as the year the limit was obtained, but the *License Journal* appears to have no entry until 1942–3.

13 Royal Commission on Forestry, Box 17, file, 'Field Reports, Cochrane District'; DLF, 'Timber Dues – Accounts,' Binder vols 58 (1940–1), 63 (1945–6), 68 (1950–1), 73 (1955–6)

14 Ontario, DLF, *A History of Gogama Forest District* (Toronto 1964), 11, 18–19; Royal Commission on Forestry, Box 20, file, 'Field Reports, Sudbury District'; note also, D.H. Burton, 'The Gogama Fire of 1941,' DLF, Division of Research, 1949. Royal Commission on Forestry, Box 19, file, 'Field Reports, North Bay District'; DLF, 'Timber Dues – Accounts,' Binder vols 58 (1940–1), 63 (1945–6), 68 (1950–1), 73 (1955–6).

15 Royal Commission on Forestry, Box 17, file, 'Field Reports, Cochrane District'; Box 19, file, 'Field Reports, North Bay District'; Box 20, file, 'Field Reports, Sudbury District'

16 Royal Commission on Forestry, Box 13, file, 'Impressions of Areas Visited.' Note in particular, 'Impressions of North Bay, Temagami Areas' and 'Notes re Meeting of Operators, May 23, 1946 at Temagami, Ontario.'

17 Lambert and Pross, *Renewing Nature's Wealth*, 397–402

18 Ibid., 408, and *Statutes of Ontario, An Act to Provide for Forest Management*, 1947, cap. 38

19 Lambert and Pross, *Renewing Nature's Wealth*, 407

20 *Statutes of Ontario, An Act to Amend the Provincial Forests Act*, 1947, cap. 81; K. Morrison, 'The Evolution of the Ontario Provincial Park

System,' in G. Wall and J.S. Marsh, eds, *Recreational Land Use: Perspectives on Its Evolution in Canada* (Ottawa 1982), 102–21, quotation at 108

21 *Statutes of Ontario, Crown Timber Act*, 1952, cap. 15, sec. 44

22 *Statutes of Ontario, An Act to Amend the Crown Timber Act*, 1952, 1956, cap. 14, sec. 9

23 *Statutes of Ontario, An Act to Amend the Crown Timber Act*, 1964, cap. 16, sec. 11

24 Lambert and Pross, *Renewing Nature's Wealth*, 234–49; J.C. Dillon, *Early Days: A Record of the Early Days of the Provincial Air Service of Ontario* (Toronto, DLF, 1961); Bruce West, *The Firebirds* (Toronto 1974), 215–23. Lou Riopel, 'Early Flying Days at Timagami,' *Temagami Experience* (July 1978), 18. *Time*, 12 February 1951; Larry E. Hodgins, 'The Economic Geography of the Lake Timagami District' (BA diss., University of Toronto 1958), 90–1; Fran Shannon, interviewed by Pamela Glenn, January 1985

25 AO, RG3, ONTC, Box 7, 'Report on Temagami Situation'

26 Ibid., and Memorandum 're Temagami Townsite,' 14 April 1948, W.A. Orr to Honourable Geo. H. Dunbar

27 Ibid., 'Report on Temagami Situation'

28 Morrison, 'Evolution of the Ontario Provincial Park System,' 110

29 *Statutes of Ontario, Provincial Parks Act*, cap. 75, sec. 2

30 Lambert and Pross, *Renewing Nature's Wealth*, ch. 22

31 Morrison, 'Evolution of the Ontario Provincial Park System,' 110–17

32 AO, *Gillies Brothers Lumber Company Records*, Shanty Diaries and Journals 1954–63, annual journal entry for 31 December 1955

33 Ontario, DLF, 'Timber Dues – Accounts,' vol. 73 (1955–6); MNR, Temagami, Cutting Ledger, 1960–1 and 1965–6; Lorne Anderson interview, 29 March 1983; Brian Moulder interview, 3 March 1983

34 Royal Commission on Forestry, Box 19, file, 'Field Reports, North Bay District'; Ontario, MNR, Temagami, Cutting Ledger, 1947–66

35 Ontario, DLF, 'Timber Dues – Accounts,' Binder vols 68 (1950–1), 73 (1955–6); MNR, Temagami, Cutting Ledger, 1960–1

36 Ontario, DLF, 'Timber Dues – Accounts,' Binder vols 68 (1950–1), 73 (1955–6); MNR, Temagami, Cutting Ledger, 1960–1, 1965–6; DLF, *History of Gogama Forest District*, 11, 18–19

37 Ontario, DLF, *A History of Sudbury Forest District* (Toronto 1967), 27; Ontario, Royal Commission on Forestry, Box 26, 'Abitibi Power and Paper Ltd., Sturgeon Falls Concession,' 29 March 1946; Ontario, DLF, 'Timber Dues – Accounts,' vol. 73 (1955–6)

38 MNR, Temagami, Cutting Ledger, 1965–6, indicates that Johns-Manville was then cutting in Best, Cassels, Banting, Strathy, Chambers, and Aston townships. Brian Moulder interview, 29 March 1983

39 *Statutes of Ontario, Crown Timber Act*, 1961–2, cap. 27. See also Peter A. Love, 'Renewing Our Renewable Forest Resource: The Legislative

Framework,' *Dalhousie Law Journal*, 7, no. 3 (October 1983), 298

40 Roy T. Bowles and Mary-Ann Haney, 'The Changing Occupational Structure of the Canadian Timber Industry,' in K.L.P. Lundy and B.C.Warime, *Work in the Canadian Context: Continuity Despite Change* (Toronto 1981). Ian Radforth, 'Woodworkers and the Mechanization of the Pulpwood Logging Industry in Northern Ontario, 1950–1970,' Canadian Historical Association, *Historical Papers*, 1982 (Ottawa 1983), 71–102. See also Ian Radforth *Bush Workers and Bosses: Logging in Northern Ontario* (Toronto 1987).

41 Radforth, 'Woodworkers and Mechanization,' 73

42 Radforth, 'Woodworkers and Mechanization,' 95, notes that the forest industry's work-force overall in Ontario fell from 25,000 seasonal to 7,000 full-time jobs between 1950 and 1970.

43 W.W. Moorhouse, 'The Northeastern Portion of the Timagami Lake Area,' OBM, *Annual Report*, 51, pt 6 (1942), 22–3; MNR, *Lake Temagami Plan for Land Use and Recreation Development* (Toronto 1973), 19–21; MNR, Northeastern Ontario Strategic Land Use Planning Process, *Background Information and Approach to Policy* (Toronto 1978), 125

44 MNR, *Lake Temagami Plan*, 16

12 Crises, Confrontation, and the Lake Temagami Plan

1 *An Act to Establish the Ministry of Natural Resources* was given first reading on 17 March 1972: Ontario Legislature, *Debates*, 17 March 1972, 542. Stephen Lewis and R.G. Hodgson spoke on second reading: *Debates*, 28 March 1972 at 677 and 684, respectively. *Globe and Mail*, 3 February 1972

2 K. Morrison, 'The Evolution of the Ontario Provincial Park System,' in G. Wall and J.S. Marsh, eds, *Recreational Land Use: Perspectives on Its Evolution in Canada* (Ottawa 1982), 102–21. A.K. McDougall, *John P. Robarts: His Life and Government* (Toronto 1986), 133–41

3 MNR, *Lake Temagami Plan for Land Use and Recreation Development* (Toronto 1973), 22

4 *Temagami Times*, 1, no. 1 (Fall 1971); TLA Archives; Minutes of the TLA AGM, 4 August 1971, 4 August 1972, 3 August 1973; Minutes of the TLA Board, various meetings, 9 August 1971 to 29 June 1974

5 *North Bay Nugget*, 17, 22, 24 November 1973

6 John R. Hunt, 'Development Plan for Lake Temagami Revealed,' *North Bay Nugget*, 21 February 1972; MNR, *Lake Temagami Plan*, 47–8, 55–8

7 MNR, ibid., 51

8 Ibid., 23

9 Ibid., 23–4

10 Ibid., 15

11 Ibid., 58–61

12 The Ministry of Industry and Tourism was created in April 1972 by amalgamation of the Department of Tourism and Information with the Department of Trade and Development.
13 'Study Site for 'N. Ontario Place,' *North Bay Nugget*, 18 October 1972; Legislature of Ontario, *Debates*, 7 December 1972, 5282–3; 'Tourist Facility Fight,' *Daily Press* (Timmins), 11 December 1972; 'Maple Mountain Out in Open,' *North Bay Nugget*, 28 May 1973; Hon. Claude F. Bennett to Hugh Stewart, 23 October 1973, letter in the possession of the authors; Pete Emmorey, 'Maple Mountain: Giant Complex or Eerie Wilderness?' *Toronto Star*, 15 December 1973. No reports on the Maple Mountain area or skiing in this section of the province are listed in the basic inventory of government tourism studies before 1972. See Ontario Department of Tourism and Information, *A Compilation of Abstracts of Research Reports, 1964 to 1969*, vol. 1, and Ministry of Industry and Tourism, *A Compilation of Abstracts: Tourism Research Reports, 1970–72*, vol. 2
14 TLA Archives, Minutes of 17 July 1973; Press Release, 1973
15 Save Maple Mountain Committee (SMMC), Press Release, 2 October 1973. TLA Archives, Board Minutes, 6 October 1973, 7 August 1974. The authors of this book were among the co-organizers of the SMMC.
16 *Temagami Times* (Spring 1974), 1
17 *Toronto Star*, 30 March 1974; *Globe and Mail*, 8 April 1974
18 Bear Island Trial Decision, 358–9
19 *North Bay Nugget*, 9 February 1974
20 *Globe and Mail*, 16 May 1975
21 TLA Archives, Board Minutes, 13 August 1971
22 John E. Carroll, *Environmental Diplomacy: An Examination and a Perspective of Canadian-U.S. Transboundary Environmental Relations* (Ann Arbor, Mich., 1983), 255–60; Canada, House of Commons, *Still Waters: Report of the Sub-committee on Acid Rain of the Standing Committee on Fisheries and Forestry* (Ottawa 1981)
23 AO, 'Regulations Respecting Forest Reserves,' 11 December 1902, *Woods and Forests Report Book III*, 22–5
24 TLA Archives, Board Minutes, 25 August 1971, 16 July 1972, 19 August 1972, 17 July 1973, 6 October 1973. *Temagami Times* for 1972 and 1973
25 Note especially the lengthy article, 'Report on Acid Rain,' in the *Temagami Times* (Spring 1980). Specific dead and endangered lakes in Timiskaming are also identified in *Going, Going: Temiskaming Lakes Acid Rain Report*, produced in 1981 by the Temiskaming Environmental Action Committee. See also Michael Keating, *Globe and Mail*, 28 August 1981.
26 *Temagami Times*, 4, no. 1 (Spring 1974), reprinted 7, no. 1 (Winter 1977); TLA Archives, AGM Minutes, 3 August 1974
27 Eric W. Morse, *Fur Trade Canoe Routes of Canada Then and Now* (Ottawa 1968), Foreword by Pierre E. Trudeau, vii
28 Ontario, MNR, *Temagami: Canoe Routes* (Toronto 1977)

29 C.E.S. Franks, 'White Water Canoeing: An Aspect of Canadian Socio-Economic History,' *Queen's Quarterly*, 82, no. 2 (Summer 1975), 175–88
30 Lovat Dickson, *Wilderness Man: The Strange Story of Grey Owl* (Toronto 1973)
31 Brian Back, *The Keewaydin Way: A Portrait, 1893–1983* (Temagami 1983)
32 Craig Macdonald, 'The Nastawgan: Traditional Routes of Travel in the Temagami District,' in Bruce W. Hodgins and Margaret Hobbs, eds, *Nastawgan: The Canadian North by Canoe and Snowshoe* (Toronto 1985), 183–7
33 *Temagami Times* 5, no. 1 (Spring 1975); MNR, *Lake Temagami Plan*, 30
34 The Chimo property was subsequently acquired by Joe Shaw who intended to subdivide the site for cottage development. There have been numerous other recent changes in the ownership of commercial recreational properties in the Temagami area: Jack Janssen purchased White Gables, refurbished the facilities and reopened as Janssen House in 1986; the Fehrmans and Metcalfes sold Manito and Temagami Lodge respectively; David Knudsen of Langskib opened Camp Northwaters on the former Lorien (Cayuga) site; the Bernardos acquired Wabikon, and the Cleveland YMCA made plans to return to Lake Temagami.
35 *North Bay Nugget*, 5, 8 April 1974; 26 August 1974; 8 September 1975; 4 December 1975; 13 May 1976; 13 August 1977
36 *Temagami Experience* (July 1978, July 1979)
37 Craig Hubbard, 'Urban Helicopters,' *Corporate and Commercial Aviation* (December 1985), 20–2
38 See *North Bay Nugget*, 24 May 1977; and MNR, Strategic Land Use Planning Process, *Background Information: Temagami District* (Toronto 1980), 78–80
39 Ontario, MNR, Northeastern Ontario Strategic Land Use Planning Process, *Background Information and Approach to Policy* (Toronto 1978), 148
40 Bear Island Trial Decision, 353. See especially TTP, the Appellant Factum, vol. 3, 'History of the Teme-augama Anishnabay,' in the collection of materials prepared for the legal proceeding. (For a few years, the spelling of the tribal name went through several modifications.)
41 *Temagami Times* (Spring 1981, Fall 1981)
42 Office of the Executive Council of the Teme-augama Anishnabai, Bear Island, various newsletters, notices, and minutes
43 Bear Island Trial Decision, 353

13 Aboriginal Rights, Resource Management, and the Northern Ontario Wilderness

1 Indian Commission, Status Report, Temagami Indian Land Claim, 13, no. 1 (September 1981)

2 Newsletter, no. 5, Teme-augama Anishnabai. Certified Waiver, 22 October 1982
3 For details on the expert witnesses whose testimony forms much of the Temagami Trial Proceedings (TTP), see chapter 1, including especially notes 6 and 13
4 See chapter 1, nn53–9
5 Bear Island Trial Decision, 453–90. Particularly controversial is Justice Steele's conclusion that the Temagami Indians at the time of the Robinson-Huron treaty in 1850 were a 'very insignificant group' who were presumably to share in a small reserve on Lake Wanapitei granted to another group of Indians concentrated on the western shore of that lake. See ch. 2, nn16 and 18. Justice Steele's finding on this aspect of the case is likely to be vigorously challenged in the appeal proceedings. Ironically, as Justice Steele was preparing his decision in the Temagami case, the Supreme Court of Canada released its judgment in Guerin *v.* The Queen [1984] 2 Supreme Court Reports 335 (1984), 13 Dominion Law Reports (4th) 321. The Guerin decision acknowledges the significance of aboriginal land title as a legal right originating in the native peoples' historic occupation of their ancestral homelands.
6 Ibid.
7 CBC Radio, *Sunday Morning*, 16 December 1984. The Bear Island trial decision has inspired debate on the relationship of historical evidence to legal proceedings. See Donald Bourgeois, 'The Roles of the Historian in the Litigation Process,' *Canadian Historical Review*, 67, no. 2 (June 1986), 195–205, and Bruce A. Clark, *Indian Title in Canada* (Toronto 1987)
8 *Indian Self-Government in Canada: Report of the Special Committee* (Second Report, Ottawa 1983). Note Bruce W. Hodgins, 'A Third Order of Government: The Land Claims of the Temagami Indians in the Context of the Current Canadian Debate over Aboriginal Rights,' in *Cultural Dimensions of Canada's Geography*, Trent University Geography Department, Occasional Paper No. 10 (Peterborough 1984).
9 CBC, *Sunday Morning*, 16 December 1984
10 Pamela Glenn, 'Temagami Indians Ready for Another Session in Court,' *Temagami Times*, 15, no. 4 (Fall 1985); Pamela Glenn, 'Temagami Band to Proceed with Appeal,' *Temagami Times*, 16, no. 1 (Winter 1986)
11 Pamela Glenn, 'Temagami Band Offered 30 Million,' *North Bay Nugget*, 1 October 1986; Ian Scott to Chief Gary Potts, 30 September 1986; Office of the Ontario Minister Responsible for Native Affairs, 'Ontario Makes Offer to Teme-Augama Anishnabai on Temagami Land Claim,' 30 September 1986
12 Ian Scott to Chief Gary Potts, 30 September 1986
13 For example, Richard F. Grant (Chairman, Temagami Planning Board) to Ian Scott, 29 October 1986, and Ian Scott to Grant, 28 November 1986
14 *North Bay Nugget*, 15 October 1986, 13 January 1987, and 14 February 1987; and *Globe and Mail*, 16 October 1986

15 Canada, Department of Indian and Northern Affairs, *Living Treaties: Lasting Agreements: Report of the Task Force to Review Comprehensive Claims Policy* (Ottawa, December 1985), and *Globe and Mail*, 19 December 1986
16 Rudy Platiel, 'Ontario Memo Urges Tough Line on Treaties at Native-Rights Talks,' *Globe and Mail*, 4 March 1987. See also *Temagami Times*, 17 October 1987
17 *North Bay Nugget*, 10 April 1973; *Temagami Times*, 3, no. 2 (Spring 1973) and 10, no. 1 (June 1980); and MNR, *Lake Temagami Plan for Land Use and Recreation Development* (Toronto 1973), 43
18 *Temagami Times*, 5, no. 1 (Spring 1975)
19 TLA Archives, Board Minutes, 10 January 1976; TLA Archives, AGM Minutes, 31 July 1976; *Temagami Times*, 8, no. 1 (Winter 1978)
20 *Temagami Times*, 8, no. 2 (Spring 1978); Hough-Stansbury and Michalski, *Summary: Environmental Assessment of Lake Temagami*, for the Temagami Region Studies Institute (TRSI) (January 1980), 51
21 TLA Archives, James Auld to Tim Gooderham, 6 June 1980. TLA Archives, Presidential Report, 2 August 1980
22 TLA Archives, AGM Minutes, 2 August 1980; *Temagami Times*, 11, no. 1 (Spring 1981)
23 MNR, Northeastern Ontario Strategic Land Use Planning Process, *Background Information and Approach to Policy* (Toronto 1978). Conservation Council of Ontario, 'Brief to MNR ... (on the above),' 27 December 1978
24 MNR, Strategic Land Use Planning Process, *Background Information: Temagami District* (Toronto 1980), 15–18
25 Ibid., 34–40
26 MNR, *Temagami District Land Use Plan: Proposed Policy and Planning Options* (Toronto 1981)
27 Ian S. Fraser, 'A Staff Paper Prepared for the Royal Commission on the Northern Environment,' App. 14, in Ontario, Royal Commission on the Northern Environment, *Final Report and Recommendations* (June 1985)
28 MNR, *Background Information: Temagami District*, 69–70, 85
29 Alliance for the Lady Evelyn Wilderness, 1981
30 Ibid.
31 *Temagami Times* (Spring 1981)
32 G.B. Priddle 'Parks and Land Use Planning in Northern Ontario,' unpublished paper, delivered at the Ontario Parks Conference, University of Waterloo, 12 May 1981
33 MNR, Data Checklist for Candidate Waterways Parks, 'Makobe–Grays River,' and for Wilderness Parks, 'Lady Evelyn–Smoothwater'
34 *Temagami Times* (Fall 1981). The TLA AGM at Wanapitei in August 1981 was chaired by Bruce Hodgins, then TLA president.
35 Arlin Hackman, 'New Parks for Ontario,' *Seasons*, 23, no. 3 (Federation of Ontario Naturalists, Autumn 1983), 14–15. Note also MNR's brief,

Lady Evelyn–Smoothwater Provincial Park: Interim Management Statement (Toronto, 17 August 1984). See also MNR, *Temagami District Land Use Guidelines* (Toronto 1983), 57–8

36 MNR, *Temagami District Land Use Guidelines,* 17–18, 37–8, 47–9. MNR's *Temagami District Land Use Plan* had contained a most extensive presentation of detailed options. Note also *Temagami Times,* 13, no. 3 (Fall 1983), 10–11.

37 MNR, *Temagami District Land Use Guidelines,* 23–5

38 Information on the proposed Red Squirrel / Liskeard Road comes from many contemporary sources. Note especially: MNR, *An Environmental Assessment for Primary Access Roads in the Latchford Crown Forest Management Unit: Red Squirrel Road Extension / Pinetorch Corridor,* Draft Environmental Assessment (September 1986); MNR, Fact Sheet, 'Update on Environmental Assessment,' Temagami, 12 May 1986, and Fact Sheet, 'Environmental Assessment Summary: Red Squirrel Extension / Pinetorch Corridor,' Temagami, 26 September 1986; AYCTL 'Submission to Red Squirrel / Pinetorch Roads, Environmental Assessment,' June 1986; OCA, 'Brief to DelCan by OCA Environmental Concerns Committee,' 24 June 1986; Pamela Glenn, 'Road Extension Necessary to Mills – DelCan,' *North Bay Nugget,* 27 June 1986; 'Council Stand on Road Sticks,' *North Bay Nugget,* 24 July 1986; 'MNR says Ramsay Off Base in Red Squirrel Road Issue,' *North Bay Nugget,* 15 September 1986; *North Bay Nugget,* 30 September 1986; Laura E. Young, 'Tourist Operators Seek Alternatives to Red Squirrel,' *Temiskaming Speaker,* 16 July 1986, and 'Red Squirrel Debate Resumes in Temagami,' *Temiskaming peaker,* 28 July 1986; Brian Back, 'The Red Squirrel Road Case,' *Nastawgan* (Wilderness Canoe Association, Autumn 1986); and Mary Gooderham, 'Nature Lovers, Loggers Await Verdict on Wilderness Road,' *Globe and Mail,* 23 September 1986; and articles in the *Temagami Times,* 16, no. 2 (July 1986).

39 Robert B. McGee to Bruce Hodgins, 3 December 1984

40 MNR, *Environmental Assessment for Primary Access Roads in the Latchford Crown Forest*

41 Ibid.

42 David Israelson, 'Wilderness and Road Plan Attacked by Lodges, Camps,' *Toronto Star,* 25 November 1986; James Hamill to Walter P. Hinchman, President AYCTL, 25 November 1986, and Hinchman to AYCTL members, 29 November 1986

43 Michael Keating, 'Parks in Ontario, Quebec Listed Among Endangered,' *Globe and Mail,* 28 November 1986; David Israelson, 'Wilderness Area Put on World List as Threatened Site,' *Toronto Star,* 27 November 1986, and Drake McHigh Feature Stories, International Union for the Conservation of Nature and Natural Resources, Gland, Switzerland, 14 November 1986

44 *North Bay Nugget,* 5 August, 3–8 and 22 September 1987; *Toronto Star,* 22, 26 August and 5, 22 September 1987; *Globe and Mail,* 23 July, 6, 7, 24

August 1987. Margaret Atwood paddled through the Lady Evelyn Park in the summer of 1987. See Larry Scanlan, 'The Fight for the Lady Evelyn,' *Whig-Standard Magazine* (Kingston), 15 August 1987

45 *Globe and Mail*, 29, 30 January, 1 February 1988. Note also various articles in the *Temagami Times*, 18, no. 3 (February 1988).

46 John Daniel, Report to MNR (March 1980), based on inquiry by Temagami Area Working Group; *Globe and Mail*, 8 March and 18 May 1988

47 Rudy Platiel, 'Ontario Native Band Blocks Planned Road into Disputed Region,' *Globe and Mail*, 2 June 1988; Christie McLaren, 'Native Land Protest Scheduled for Summit,' *Globe and Mail*, 17 June 1988; Temagami Wilderness Society, 'Temagami Lawsuit,' memorandum 28 July 1988

48 Documents and minutes of the nine meetings of the steering committee, Temagami, 1981–3, including Claude Bennett to Ron Prefasi, 24 October 1983; *Temagami Times*, 13, no. 2 (Spring 1983), 1, and 13, no. 4 (Winter 1983), 1

49 Minutes of the first nineteen meetings of the Temagami Planning Board, 25 October 1983 to 27 November 1984; *Temagami Times* 14, no. 3 (Fall 1984), 3. The advisers were Robert Lehman Planning Consultants Limited of Barrie, Ontario.

50 'Draft Background Study: Temagami Joint Planning Area Official Plan,' 1984, 1–12. Bird and Hale Ltd, 'Water-Related Development and Lake Capacity: Lake Temagami' (October 1984), 1–11

51 George Moore Associates, 'Visual Resource Management Guidelines: Temagami Joint Planning Board' (November 1984), 1–17

52 Northland Engineering Limited to Township of Temagami, 'Re: Proposed Subdivision Cassels Lake,' 12 February 1987

53 Pamela Glenn, 'Survey Indicates Lake Temagami Becoming More Acid Rain Sensitive,' *Temagami Times*, 16, no. 2 (July 1986), 24

Epilogue

1 Bear Island Trial Decision, 463

2 C.A. Benson, *Forest Management in N'Daki Menan of the Teme-Augama Anishnabai* (May 1982), and his testimony during the Temagami Trial Proceedings (TTP), 6254–360. Henry A. Wright and Arthur W. Bailey, 'Red and White Pine,' ch. 13 in their *Fire Ecology: United States and Southern Canada* (New York 1982), 328–48

3 Bear Island Trial Decision, 461

4 For discussion of issues related to sustainable forest development see H.A. Regier and G.L. Baskerville, 'Sustainable Redevelopment of Regional Ecosystems Degraded by Exploitive Development,' in William C. Clark and R.E. Munn, eds, *Sustainable Development of the Biosphere* (Cambridge: Cambridge University Press for the International Institute for Applied Systems Analysis [headquarters in Austria] 1987), 75–100

5 MNR, *Temagami District Land Use Guidelines* (Toronto 1983), 23–5

6 Benson, *Forest Management in N'Daki Menan*

7 Ibid., 105–10

8 Gordon L. Baskerville, *An Audit of Management of the Crown Forests of Ontario*, Report to the Ontario Minister of Natural Resources (Toronto, 1 August 1986)

9 Baskerville, *Audit*, 84

10 For recent discussion of the limitations of multiple-use forest management with particular reference to wildlife and mature woodlands, see I.D. Thompson, 'The Myth of Integrated Wildlife/Forestry Management,' *Queen's Quarterly*, 94, no. 3 (Autumn 1987), 609–21. For a non-technical introduction to forest-management issues in general, see G. Baskerville, 'Understanding Forest Management,' App. to Baskerville, *Audit*.

11 On the general evolution of appreciative uses in the North American context see Samuel P. Hays, 'From Conservation to Environment: Environmental Politics in the United States since World War Two,' *Environmental Review*, 6 (Fall 1982), 14–41.

12 See for example, 'Temagami Loggerheads,' lead editorial, *Globe and Mail*, 8 February 1988; Don Dutton, '50 Arrested in Temagami Protest,' *Toronto Star*, 3 September 1988; and Mary Gooderham, 'Cite Job Loss, Loggers Vow to Block Road,' *Globe and Mail*, 1 September 1988.

13 *Globe and Mail*, 5, 30 November, 3, 7, 9, 20 December 1988; *Star*, 11, 30 November, 4 December 1988; and *North Bay Nugget*, 12, 14, 24, 30 November, 2, 3, 6, 9, 10 December 1988. *Insiders Dispatch* (Temagami Wilderness Society) November 1988 and TLA, 'Executive Report' No. 80, 11 December 1988

14 World Commission on Environment and Development, *Our Common Future* (Oxford 1987)

15 Chief Gary Potts to Premier David Peterson, 19 May 1987, and enclosures. Potts recently represented the Assembly of First Nations at the rally of Australian Aborigines in Sydney Australia. See *Globe and Mail*, 27 January 1988.

Index

Picture Credits

Jack L. Goodman, Sr The Temagami forest; **Frank Panabaker** *Logging, Temagami*, 30″ × 40″; **Canadian Souvenir Postcards** Preparing a shore dinner, Lady Evelyn Hotel 1908; **Archives of Ontario** Mulock and O'Connor at Temagami Lodge S6602, Winter supplies for Gowganda Acc 14776-34, Indian guide and family Acc 13889-41, Mrs Petrant, Granny Turner, and Mrs Newcomb S15144, Milne Lumber Company 16-6-184, Temagami waterfront 1950s S6607; **Public Archives of Canada** Cochrane's Camp Temagami C38384, Hudson's Bay Company post at Bear Island C44124, Ronnoco Hotel 1930 C42797; **National Museums of Canada** Chief Frank White Bear 023989, Second Chief Aleck Paul 023983; **Maclean Photo** Regatta day on Bear Island; **Ontario Ministry of Travel and Publicity** Shore supper Camp Chimo; ***North Bay Nugget***, September 1986 Gary Potts, Rita O'Sullivan, and Ian Scott; **Jeff Uyede** Red Squirrel Road blockade 1988; **Canapress** Temagami stand-off 1988